CANADIAN PUBLIC FINANCE

CANADIAN PUBLIC FINANCE
FOURTH EDITION

J.C. Strick
University of Windsor

Holt, Rinehart and Winston of Canada, Limited
Toronto Montreal Ft. Worth London Sydney Tokyo

Canadian Cataloguing in Publication Data
Strick J.C., 1937–
Canadian public finance

4th ed.
Includes bibliographical references and index.
ISBN 0–03–922794–4
1. Finance, Public — Canada. I. Title.
HJ793.S87 1991 336.71 C91–093372–3

Editorial Director: *Scott Duncan*
Developmental Editor: *Sarah Duncan*
Director of Publishing Services: *Steve Lau*
Editorial Manager: *Liz Radojkovic*
Editorial Co-ordinator: *Sandra L. Meadow*
Production Manager: *Sue-Ann Becker*
Production Assistant: *Denise Wake*
Copy Editor: *Lenore d'Anjou*
Cover and Interior Design: *Dave Peters*
Typesetting and Assembly: *Louisa Schulz*
Printing and Binding: *John Deyell Company*

This book was printed in Canada on acid-free paper.

1 2 3 4 5 96 95 94 93 92

ABOUT THE AUTHOR

J.C. Strick is a professor of economics at the University of Windsor. A graduate of the University of Alberta, he is the author of the books *The Economics of Government Regulation: Theory and Canadian Practice*, and *Policy, Politics and the Treasury Board in Canadian Government.* He has published articles in the area of public finance in such journals as the *Canadian Tax Journal* and *Canadian Public Administration*, contributed articles about federal/provincial relations to *The Canadian Economy*, and has written several reports for the federal government on communications economics and regulation.

In the Department of Economics, University of Windsor, Professor Strick teaches courses in public finance theory, Canadian public finance, and the economics of regulation and communications. He was the chairman of the Department of Economics from 1979 to 1987. He is a member of the Canadian Economics Association, the American Economic Association, the Canadian Tax Foundation, the National Tax Association — Tax Institute of America, the Institute of Public Administration of Canada, the American Society for Public Administration, and the American Association for Budget and Program Analysis.

PREFACE

A number of excellent textbooks cover the standard body of theory in public finance, but most of them are not Canadian and do not draw upon the Canadian experience for their application of the theory or for their description and analysis of government financial institutions, practices, problems, and policies. To obtain such information, the Canadian student of public finance must consult a wide variety of other sources. This book is designed to be a companion to the standard public finance theory textbook by providing up-to-date information on the most commonly studied aspects of Canadian public finance. It brings together this information in a single, concise volume for the convenience of both instructor and student and provides extensive bibliographic material on Canadian government finance.

The book may also serve as a textbook for courses in Canadian government taxation, expenditure, and economic policies in which theory is not emphasized or for which students have little background in economic theory.

The fourth edition of *Canadian Public Finance* incorporates extensive revisions to enhance its usefulness as a supplement or a text. The primary revisions for this edition consisted of updating policy material and data; expanding certain sections, reducing the significance of others, and adding some new ones; and strengthening some of the analytical and theoretical content. Tabulated material has been revised and updated, and some new tables and graphs have been added.

Chapter 1 has been expanded to include more material on income distribution, and an appendix has been added providing theoretical analysis of external economies and diseconomies and of pure public goods. Chapter 2 has been reorganized and expanded to include a section describing the major government expenditure programs. The section on Crown corporations, formerly in Chapter 3, has been moved to an appendix to Chapter 2 and expanded to include the privatization movement. A new Chapter 4 presents various aspects of taxation theory, including tax shifting and economic effects, along with a discussion of user charges. Chapter 5 has been completely rewritten to cover the recent changes in income taxes, and a detailed section on the goods and services tax has been added. Information and analysis regarding the various issues covered in Chapter 8 on federal/provincial relations have been updated, and new points, such as the controversial Meech Lake Accord and the legality of unilateral federal cuts in transfer payments to the provinces, have been added.

The chapter on fiscal policy goals has been revised to include a more comprehensive analysis of the budget as an instrument of fiscal policy.

The previous edition's chapter on federal and provincial fiscal policies has been restructured to form two chapters: Chapter 10, dealing with federal policy, with a new section on the deficit problem faced by Ottawa in the last decade; and Chapter 11, focussing on provincial fiscal issues and budget positions in the 1980s. The analysis of fiscal policy focusses on the primary structural budget balance as the main macroeconomic indicator of discretionary policy; some microeconomic analysis of fiscal measures is provided as a supplement.

The problem of large deficits in a growing and relatively prosperous economy has plagued both the federal and provincial governments in recent years and has been of major concern to governments, the business community, and the public. Thus, Chapter 12, which covers borrowing and the rapidly growing public debt, has been expanded to provide greater detail on various features of borrowing and debt; new sections cover the rapid growth of debt and debt management.

Appendix A, updated and enlarged from the previous edition, provides suggestions for further reading. Appendix B, which is new, is a list of sources of government financial statistics; it should prove useful to students for this course and others.

In preparing the fourth edition, I have benefited from suggestions by my colleagues in the Department of Economics at the University of Windsor and from suggestions and thoughtful criticisms from users of the book and from reviewers. The publisher and I thank those instructors who took the time to make suggestions for the improvement of this book. They are: Donald Brean, University of Toronto; George Carter, Ryerson Polytechnical Institute; E.J. Doak, St. Mary's University; William Furlong, University of Guelph; Wade Locke, Memorial University of Newfoundland; Jack Rink, Red River Community College; and Joseph Schaafsma, University of Victoria.

J.C. Strick
University of Windsor

Publisher's Note To Students and Instructors

This textbook is an important part of your course. For both the student and instructor, this book will greatly contribute to present and future studies. As the instructor, you chose this text out of many as the best one for you and your students. The author and publishers appreciate this acknowledgement of the considerable time and money we have invested to ensure its high quality.

If you are a student, we hope you will find this text an invaluable companion in meeting the objectives of your course. As well, it will become an excellent addition to your personal library.

Please remember that this is a copyrighted work, and as such, any photocopying of it means that the authors lose royalties that are rightfully theirs. This loss will discourage them from writing another edition of this text or other books. If this happens, we all eventually lose — authors, publishers, instructors, and students.

We are very interested in your reactions to the book, so be sure to send us the stamped reply card at the end of the text. Your input helps us continue to publish high quality books.

CONTENTS

CHAPTER 1

INTRODUCTION: THE PUBLIC SECTOR IN CANADA

Significance of Government in the Economy

The importance of government in the modern economy is enormous though difficult to measure. It is a producer, owner, regulator, subsidizer, and income redistributor, as well as a protector of the consumer and society. There is perhaps no line of economic activity that is not to some degree influenced by government, for it has permeated practically every aspect of economic life.

As an owner and producer, government is involved in the provision of goods and services that are not provided by private interests or are deemed to be provided in insufficient quantity. As a regulator and supervisor of private entrepreneurship, government issues licences, permits, and patents and has passed legislation governing such aspects of production as quality, content, packaging, advertising, safety standards, competitive practices, and occasionally pricing policies. Certain production activities are prohibited, others are limited, and still others are assisted through subsidies, tariffs, and marketing services.

Government is also concerned with the way in which goods and services — the proceeds of production — are distributed among members of society. Considerable government activity is directed toward redistributing income from wealthier groups to poorer groups through taxes and expenditures. In this process, the government has assumed an obligation to ensure that the less-privileged members of society, people of lesser means and the disabled and elderly, are provided with at least a minimum standard of living. Benefits to low-income groups may take the form of direct money payments or the provision of goods and services. Some redistribution programs involve direct transfers, such as old age pensions, family allowances, unemployment insurance, disabled persons' allowances, workers' compensation, and welfare payments to families with little or no income. Other programs have redistributional effects through their impact on real income; they include subsidized housing, and medical and hospitalization programs. These various expenditure programs are financed primarily through the tax system, which, to the degree that it is progressive, tends to impose a relatively greater burden on higher income groups and consequently also has a redistributive effect.

Finally, government is responsible for the protection of people and property through the administration of justice and national defence.

In meeting its obligations, the government acts as an employer, as a producer of goods and services, as a purchaser of materials, and as a redistributor of income, thus assuming considerable direct significance in various aspects of the economy. The most comprehensive and widely employed measure of government influence in the economy in general is the ratio of total government expenditure to gross domestic product (GDP), which is the value of all goods and services produced in a country in a given year. This ratio tends to overestimate the importance of government as a producer of goods and services because its spending includes transfer payments as well as direct expenditures on goods and services. The measure does, however, indicate the proportion of the total expenditure stream in the economy that is affected directly by government through its spending on goods and services and its transfer payments to individuals and to business and social organizations. These expenditures by all levels of government combined — federal, provincial, and local (the last are called "municipal" in this text) — were approximately 44 percent of GDP in 1989.

The composition and growth of government expenditure are analysed in detail in Chapter 2.

Social Goals and Government Activities

Every society faces the basic economic problem of allocating its available resources among competing uses and of distributing the proceeds of production among its members. Given the scarcity of resources, it is not possible to meet all of the demands for goods and services. If the goal of society is to achieve some optimal level of social services, resources must be used to provide those goods and services that society desires most, and they must be used as efficiently as possible in the process. Furthermore, optimal social welfare implies that the returns from production — income — which give an individual command over goods and services, should be distributed in an equitable manner.

In a market economy, prices determine the use of resources and the distribution of income. If the system is perfectly competitive, the prices of goods and services and of the factors of production are determined by supply and demand. Resources are allocated to the production of those goods and services that consumers want and for which they are prepared to pay. The income of consumers — their ability to pay for goods and services — is in turn determined by the prices they can command for their productive services in the factor market. This system, characterized by consumer and producer sovereignty and referred to as the free enterprise system, will theoretically, under certain conditions, assure an efficient use of resources to provide all goods and services most desired by society. In practice, however, the price system suffers serious limitations in performing this function. Not even Adam Smith would unqualifyingly advocate an undisturbed market mechanism as the complete solution to the problem of resource allocation and income distribution, and few economists today would propose that what is determined in the marketplace will necessarily be optimal for the welfare of society.

Government participates in the economy to assist the market mechanism to achieve the objectives of society. In fact, government activities are usually divided into three main categories reflecting those objectives: (1) activities designed to promote the efficient allocation of resources; (2) activities designed to redistribute income and wealth in accordance with standards of equity determined by national consensus; and (3) activities designed to maintain a stable rate of economic activity and promote economic growth.[1] The focuses of these objectives are the effective and efficient use of resources and the fair distribution of the proceeds from resource use. Although government and society may have other goals — the preservation of individual freedoms, national unity, and cultural aspirations are examples in Canada — the study of public finance has traditionally centred on the three basic socioeconomic objectives of government.

Resource Allocation

In economic theory, an optimum allocation of resources — a Pareto optimum — is described as a situation in which, given the availability of resources, the state of technology, and the distribution of income, one individual cannot be made better off without making another individual worse off. A Pareto optimum,[2] in simple terms, is a situation in which prices equal the marginal costs of production, factors such as labour are paid the value of their contributions to production, there are no excess profits, and all factors are employed.

For the market mechanism to achieve a Pareto optimum requires certain conditions in the market. First, the market must have perfect competition, characterized by perfect knowledge, homogeneous products, large numbers of buyers and sellers, and perfect mobility of resources. Second, there must be no external economies or diseconomies in production and consumption. Finally, all the goods and services for which there is an effective demand must possess the properties of excludability and rivalry in consumption.

In the perfectly competitive market model, prices and output are determined by the interactions of supply and demand, and each firm in the market takes the price as given. There are a sufficiently large number of buyers and sellers, so one cannot influence the price of a particular product or service. Perfect competition also assumes that each individual consumer has a complete knowledge of products and services available and of their attributes; that each producer is familiar with and aware of the availability of the factors of production; and these factors can be readily shifted from one use to another. In equilibrium in perfect competition, each firm will produce so that its price just equals its marginal cost and its minimum average cost. The firm will enjoy normal profits. (Normal profit is the opportunity cost of the entrepreneur who owns the firm; it is a return just sufficient to keep the entrepreneur in business and is included in the average cost curve in the model of the firm.)

The absence of externalities in consumption and production implies that all benefits of consumption accrue directly to the buyer and that all costs are included in the firm's costs of production. In other words, the price of a commodity as determined by supply and demand will reflect the benefits of supplying an additional unit of the commodity and will cover all costs involved in its production.

Goods and services must be exclusive and rival in consumption if they are to be bought and sold in the marketplace. Goods and services that are exclusive can be withheld from consumers who are not prepared to pay for them. Goods are rival when consumption by one individual reduces the amount available to others. Goods and services that possess these features are known as private goods. In contrast, other goods and services are consumed collectively and consumption by one person does not reduce their availability to others. These are known as public goods, and no market for them can exist.

The conditions for Pareto optimality are not completely fulfilled in the economies of today's world. Few, if any, products and services are bought and sold in a perfectly competitive market; rather, the markets for most have a variety of imperfections that distort the allocation of resources away from Pareto optimality. Most lines of consumption and production produce varying degrees of external benefits and costs. And certain goods and services are public in nature and will not be provided by the marketplace despite society's desire for them. Such situations, discussed in greater detail throughout this chapter, are cited as providing justification for government involvement or interference in the economy to improve efficiency in the use of resources in order to move it closer to Pareto optimality.

Imperfections in Competition

Government has accepted a responsibility to reduce imperfections in the economy or to mitigate their consequences. Among these imperfections are lack of knowledge on the part of the consumer and on the part of factors of production, factor immobility, and monopoly control. Government attempts to correct these problems through a variety of activities and services.

Consumer Services. If consumers are to obtain the greatest satisfaction from their limited resources, they must be familiar with the goods and services available to them. But in an economy characterized by variability and multiplicity of products that are technologically sophisticated and promoted by large-scale advertising and a host of other sales techniques, the consumer is open to exploitation. The government attempts to establish safeguards and regulations to protect consumers and to improve their knowledge of goods and services.

At the federal level in Canada, this function is undertaken primarily by Consumer and Corporate Affairs Canada; laws and regulations protecting the consumer are also administered by numerous other departments and agencies. The provinces have counterpart bureaus, such as Ontario's Ministry of Consumer and Commercial Relations.

Consumer and Corporate Affairs Canada attempts to protect consumers against fraud, deception, and unsafe products. Regulations have been established governing the accuracy of weights and measures and the character of advertising; labelling requirements stipulate the information that must be shown on packages and containers. Factory-inspection spot checks are made on certain goods before they are sold. Standards are established for the construction of buildings, automobiles, and a host of consumer durables. The department is also a focal point for consumer complaints and inquiries. It assists consumers with their problems and distributes information on a wide range of consumer subjects.

Consumer and Corporate Affairs Canada also works in close liaison with other agencies administering consumer-protection legislation. Among these is the Department of Transport, which regulates the safety of air and rail facilities. Another is the Food and Drug Directorate of Health and Welfare Canada, which is charged with supervising the manufacture and distribution of food and drug products. New drugs are tested and must be approved before they can be marketed; food-processing plants are inspected, and foods are tested for their nutritional value.

Factor Services. Unemployed workers may be unaware of available jobs or lack the skills necessary for the work available. Government attempts to correct these imperfections in the labour market. Employment and Immigration Canada trys to bring together employers and prospective employees through regional offices called employment centres. These centres provide information to employers concerning the labour market and information to workers about job opportunities. In addition, they offer counselling to workers and serve as contacts for workers for government training programs.

Unemployed workers are also assisted through various government-established or -supported labour training and mobility programs, including occupational training for the unskilled, retraining for changing job qualifications, and relocation grants covering some costs of moving from one area to another in search of employment. Under the Adult Occupational Training Act, the federal government finances occupational training programs in industrial establishments and educational institutions and provides allowances and wage support to workers enrolled in them. Programs are offered in, for example, critical-trades skills training, industrial training, nontraditional trades for women, and native opportunities.

Government is also engaged in ensuring that workers are not subjected to undue hazards in the performance of their work. Provincial workers' compensation boards, for example, conduct continual investigations into safety conditions in factories, mines, and other places of employment. And federal and provincial governments combined to establish, in 1988, a system of providing workers and employers uniform information about hazardous materials present in the workplace.

Monopoly Regulation. The most significant type of imperfection in the real world market economy is unquestionably the existence of monopoly or elements of it. Indeed, practically every line of production and distribution is characterized by some degree of monopoly, ranging from the extreme of pure monopoly through oligopoly to monopolistic competition.

Theoretically, the monopoly element results in inefficiency in the use of resources by making output smaller and prices higher than they would be under competitive conditions. Competition, except in cases of natural monopoly,[3] leads to the largest possible output at the lowest price, directs resources to their most productive channels, and encourages technological change and high productivity as producers attempt to gain an advantage over competitors. Government has accepted a responsibility to prevent the creation of monopolies in many situations, as well as to reduce the degree of monopoly and restore prices and output to more competitive levels.

The Canadian government has attempted to regulate monopoly through legislation since 1889, when it passed An Act for the Prevention and Suppression of Combinations in Restraint of Trade. This law and its successors, most of which were called the Combines Investigation Act, proved difficult to enforce and were thus often ineffective. In recent years, the government has attempted to strengthen its competition policy through the new Competition Act, passed in two stages (1976 and 1986). Under it, restrictive agreements such as price fixing and restricting the entrance of competitors are unlawful, as are practices such as misleading advertising and unfair forms of promotional games and contests. Mergers and other business practices are examined by the Bureau of Competition Policy to determine whether they are in the public interest or whether they promote or impede economic efficiency. Many kinds of charges are heard by the Competition Tribunal, which can order the dissolution of mergers and cartels, terminate patents and copyrights, and impose heavy penalties. Even for the few matters treated under the criminal law, individuals have the right to initiate civil suits to recover damages incurred as a result of violations of the legislation.

Natural monopolies, such as public utilities and some forms of transportation and communication, present different problems. Government regulation may be required to ensure that the firm does not use its monopoly position to exploit consumers, manipulate prices, and earn large excess profits. Government generally uses commissions and boards to regulate and control prices and services in such industries. To change prices, rate structures, or services provided, the monopoly is required to obtain the permission of the regulatory agency.

Canada has such agencies at the federal, provincial, and municipal levels, primarily to regulate public utilities. For example, the telephone industry has been viewed as a natural monopoly, and telephone services under federal jurisdiction are regulated by the Canadian Radio-television and Telecommunications Commission (CRTC). The commission protects the monopoly position of Bell Canada in the provinces of Quebec and Ontario, but the firm must obtain CRTC approval for any changes in the rates of the various services it offers.

Another way in which government is involved in supply management is by restricting competition in order to benefit certain groups. The establishment of farm marketing boards is an example. These boards restrict production and prevent the interprovincial movement of goods in an attempt to maintain price levels and prevent cyclical fluctuations in farm prices and farm incomes. Although the policies of monopolistic institutions such as marketing boards may interfere with the market mechanism and move the economy away from optimum resource allocation, government justifies them on the grounds of improving income redistribution and stability for the groups affected. Critics of regulation say, however, that governments have tended to resort to excessive regulation, resulting in inefficiencies and high costs of production. The argument is that producers who do not face competition but have assured profit levels or rates of return have few incentives to maintain maximum efficiency.[4]

An alternative to government regulation of production and prices is public ownership of industries that tend to be natural monopolies. Provincial and municipal governments own and operate many utilities.

Monopoly regulation also extends to the factor market. Unions tend to be monopoly sellers of labour services. Both federal and provincial laws give workers the legal authority to bargain collectively on wages and working conditions. Legislation governs bargaining procedures as well as procedures to be followed in the event of an impasse. Unions have the right to strike by temporarily withdrawing labour services, but government has the power to intervene and force the continuation of labour services that are deemed necessary for the public interest.

External Economies and Diseconomies

The existence of externalities in consumption and production accounts for a considerable proportion of government activity in the economy. It has generally been accepted that where external economies and diseconomies exist, government participation is justified to alter the use or allocation of resources in the interest of social welfare and efficiency.[5] Government may channel more resources into areas of production and consumption that experience external economies; where there are external diseconomies, it may initiate actions to reduce them or discourage resource use there.[6] A diagrammatic analysis of externalities is presented in the appendix to this chapter.

External Economies. Benefits that accrue to society in addition to those received directly by the individual engaged in the production or consumption of a commodity or service are called external economies. Education is frequently viewed as a service with external economies in consumption. When an individual obtains an education, he or she benefits personally, but society as a whole also benefits in terms of increased productive potential. Under the price system, individuals buy education in accordance with the benefits they expect to receive personally and with their financial means; in making their purchase decisions, they do not consider the additional benefits that may accrue to society. Government, on the other hand, is concerned with social benefits and endeavours to provide education facilities in excess of what the market would provide, either by subsidizing private educational institutions or by assuming direct responsibility for education.

A similar rationale can be applied to government provision of health care and other services. The funding of health services is a major government activity, justified partially on the grounds of the social benefits they yield. Similarly, research activities to improve technology and productivity and develop new products and services have the potential of yielding benefits to society and so are financially supported by government.

In Canada, education is a provincial responsibility, and hospital insurance and medical programs are administered by the provinces. Many of these services are, however, given partial financing by the federal government. Both the federal and provincial governments support a variety of research programs in agriculture, forestry, and other natural-resource industries, in numerous manufacturing and service industries, and in educational and research institutions.

External Diseconomies. Costs that accrue to society from consumption and production in addition to the direct costs to the individual consumer and producer are called external diseconomies. Recently, considerable attention has been focussed on such diseconomies, particularly pollution. Pollution of the environment is not generally included in the private costs of production — and is thus not reflected in the market price of goods and services — yet its costs to society are high. Harm to health resulting from water and air pollution, contamination of fish and waterfowl from the dumping of production waste into lakes and streams, and similar destruction of some resources in the use of others are common in modern industrialized economies. Examples abound in Canada. Fishing has been banned in a number of lakes and streams because of mercury contamination, resulting in the loss of food for some native peoples, of sport fishing, and of occupation for commercial fishers. The Great Lakes are being threatened by pollution discharged into the air from surrounding industry and returned in the form of acid rain. Many logging firms make only minor attempts at reforestation after stripping an area, and firms engaged in open-pit mining may leave unsightly landscapes.

Diseconomies in consumption are also common. Excessive consumption of alcohol is likely to lead to increased rates of traffic accidents, crime, and absenteeism from work — costs to society over and above the costs to consumer. The consumption of tobacco and drugs produces social costs in their hazards to general health and work effectiveness.

In cases of external diseconomies in both consumption and production, the government has assumed an obligation to intervene with varying degrees of supervision and control. With respect to consumption, the federal government has passed legislation prohibiting the use of drugs, such as heroin and marijuana, that society deems to have high social costs. Attempts are made to curtail the consumption of alcohol and tobacco. High excise taxes on these products are designed to increase their prices and discourage their purchase. Smoking is banned in many public buildings and facilities. Cigarette and hard-liquor advertisements are banned on television, and producers are forced to stipulate on cigarette and tobacco packages that the product may be detrimental to health.

Government policies to combat external diseconomies in production may include the establishment of standards, payment of subsidies, imposition of taxes, charges for effluents, or some combination of these. For example, government may set pollution-emission standards, backed by penalties, that force the industry to curb pollution through the use of antipollution devices or changes in the production process.[7] Subsidies can be applied to help industry defray the costs of pollution-control devices. Government can also impose taxes on commodities whose production causes pollution; such taxes have the effect of raising prices, reducing consumption and production, and, therefore, lowering the amount of pollution generated. Effluent charges that vary with the type and quantity of pollution can cause polluting firms to try to curb emissions through pollution-control devices or changes in production methods. Both the federal and provincial governments have legislated pollution controls, with penalties ranging from fines to prison sentences. In addition, tax concessions have been granted to encourage firms to introduce pollution-control measures. Environmental legislation has often not been rigorously enforced, however, perhaps partly because of public apathy, partly because of pressure from vested interest groups, and partly because of the technological complexity of the problem.

Much has been said and written about external diseconomies, such as pollution, and the role of government in controlling them. Theoretically, government action to control external diseconomies in production does not contradict the operation of the market mechanism. Indeed, government action is intended as a corrective for market failure. The basic problem is that the market pricing mechanism fails to include the total costs of production. For example, the emission of sulfer dioxide in the production of copper and nickel is a basic source of acid rain, yet the damage or cost resulting from those emissions has not been included in the costs of production by the nickel and copper industry. Instead, the cost has been reflected in pollution and thus borne by all society, both present and future generations. In a sense, production with external costs has been subsidized in the past, the subsidy being the deterioration of the environment, so that goods could be produced at a reasonable price to consumers.

Legislation forcing manufacturers to introduce pollution-control devices results in additional costs to the manufacturer and higher prices of manufactured goods. But these costs should have been included and passed on to the consumer in the form of higher commodity prices to begin with. By forcing firms to internalize the external costs, government regulations can be viewed as assisting the market mechanism to perform its function. Those benefiting from the use of a commodity when they purchase it will cover the entire cost, instead of passing part of it on to the rest of society. Higher costs and prices may lead to reduced sales or termination of production, but, it is argued, this is the law of the marketplace, which leads to the production of those goods and services that people desire and are prepared to pay for.

Others argue, however, that this solution is oversimplified, that certain realities of the economy must be taken into consideration. If industry is forced to reduce output or possibly even close because of excessively high costs of pollution-control equipment, the result is a loss of jobs, representing a cost to society. If industry is forced to raise prices to cover increased costs, it runs the danger of losing its competitive position in foreign trade (assuming other countries do not follow similar antipollution policies). The result will be costs to society in terms of reduced employment in the domestic market.

It appears, therefore, that there is a tradeoff between a clean environment and other economic goals, such as employment and economic expansion. Society may have to decide how much unemployment and how great an increase in prices it is prepared to accept in order to reduce pollution. The government cannot ignore the realities of this tradeoff and should attempt some compromise to minimize the external diseconomies subject to the constraints of other goals. One policy that could be followed would be to use subsidies, grants, and tax concessions to help industries cover the initial costs of large investments in antipollution equipment, thereby distributing some of the initial cost to society, rather than expecting the producers and consumers involved to carry the full burden.

Public concern over external diseconomies in production has been increasing in recent years. To a large extent, the past disregard stemmed from public emphasis on maximizing material wealth and status without due regard to the quality of life. A gradual awakening to the tremendous costs that result from the neglect of external diseconomies has focussed increasing attention on these costs. Ensuing public pressure has produced more government supervision of the production process, which is reflected in the strengthening of environmental protection legislation. For example, in 1987 the Ontario government enacted its new Environmental Protection Act with much more stringent pollution regulations and much more severe penalties on polluters. The maximum fine for a polluting firm was increased from $25 000 to $50 000 per day and to as much as $250 000 per day if the offence involves a hazardous waste; prison terms were also introduced for individuals and company officials found guilty of pollution. Other provinces in Canada have also recently taken steps to put more teeth into their environmental protection laws. In 1989, the New Brunswick government passed the Clean Water Act, which sets maximum daily fines for any industrial, corporate, or municipal polluter at $1 million, and the government of British Columbia proposed legislation calling for the province's pulp and paper operators to reduce toxic discharges by at least 70 percent over a five-year period. At the same time, the federal and Quebec governments announced a joint program to force about 50 of the worst industrial polluters of the St. Lawrence River to reduce their discharges by 90 percent by 1993. At the international level, the governments of Canada and the United States have signed joint agreements to control pollution, such as acid rain, in the Great Lakes area.

Public Goods and Services

Government has assumed responsibility for providing a number of important goods and services that are public in nature. As already noted, unlike private goods, public goods are nonexcludable and nonrival in consumption.[8] When a good or service is nonexcludable, people cannot be kept from enjoying its benefits even if they do not pay for it. When a good is nonrival, one person's consumption does not reduce or affect another person's consumption of it. The marginal cost of an additional person's consumption is zero, so it is not desirable to exclude anyone or to ration the good. Goods and services that possess these features are called pure public goods. Since they are consumed collectively, the market will not provide them. Examples include national defence and a pest-control program. In both cases, benefits accrue to all individuals residing in an area regardless of whether they pay for the service, and there is no additional cost if additional individuals benefit from it. Society may desire pure public goods and services, but resources will be channelled to their provision only if government undertakes to do so because it is neither feasible nor economical for the private sector to provide them.

In addition to pure public goods, there are goods and services that can be viewed as impure or quasi-public. These are goods to which exclusion can be applied, although they may be nonrival to a degree. Provision by the private sector would be inefficient and impractical, necessitating large administrative costs to collect fees or charges from consumers. It is, for example, more efficient for government than for the market to provide highways, bridges, streets, sidewalks, parks and recreational facilities, sewage facilities, and protection or security services. Government provides such services free of direct charge, finances them from taxation revenues, and avoids the high costs of administering user fees.

Government may also provide goods and services that are not public or even quasi-public but could be provided by private enterprise once markets are established. This situation frequently occurs when private interests are reluctant to enter a specific field because risks are so high and initial outlays so heavy that returns are very uncertain and cannot be expected for several years. Government may, therefore, take the initiative in the provision of the good or service. For example, transcontinental air services were begun in 1937 when the federal government established Trans-Canada Air-Lines (now Air Canada); Polymer Corporation was created during the Second World War to produce synthetic rubber; Atomic Energy of Canada Limited was established to research and develop nuclear energy. Private interests later entered some of these areas, but governments, in many cases, continued their operations in direct competition with private enterprise. Government investments are, of course, subject to market risks similar to those of private investments and may not always be successful (although government enterprises may have recourse to public funds through government loans and parliamentary appropriations should they encounter financial difficulties).

Fundamental to the market system is the principle of consumer sovereignty, which means that consumers are free to choose how they will spend their incomes given the goods and services available to them. In addition to instances in which government interferes with consumer sovereignty because of externalities, there are situations in which it compels individuals to consume a private good or service or to consume a greater quantity than they desire. This interference with consumer preferences applies in the case of merit goods, which are particular commodities that the government deems to bestow a greater amount of benefit to individual consumers than do the individuals themselves.[9] In other words, in the paternalistic view of government, the commodity is sufficiently meritorious that it should be consumed, or more should be consumed than the amount purchased in the marketplace. Examples include elementary education and automobile seat belts, which are made mandatory by government. Other examples include the performing arts, since government financial support makes theatre, concerts, and so on more readily available to consumers than they would be without subsidies.

The provision of public, quasi-public, and merit goods and services does not necessarily involve direct government employment of resources. Government can choose to make such goods available in two ways: (1) by directly employing labour and using materials to produce them; or (2) by permitting private firms to produce them for the government through contract. In both cases, resources are channelled from private use to public use, but only in the first method does government directly employ factors of production.

Redistribution of Income

One of the goals generally attributed to society is a fair distribution of income and wealth among its members. Opinions vary on what is fair, but it is generally agreed that severe inequalities in income levels are not acceptable. History has shown that the market system usually produces a distribution of severe inequality. An equitable distribution of incomes is, however, difficult to define and involves value judgements on the part of society and those elected to govern.

The distribution of income in a country, including the degree of equality, is influenced by many factors including individuals' capabilities, educational opportunities, property holdings and laws of inheritance, the scarcity or abundance of specific resources, and the homogeneity of resources. Factors are not homogeneous, and certain factors will always be scarce. Some individuals are more capable and ambitious than others, have a greater entrepreneurial spirit to initiate a successful enterprise, or can command factors in scarce supply. Indeed, one of the foundations of the free enterprise system is individualism — the freedom to pioneer and take risks for motives of higher income, more power, or prestige.

Some people may have lower incomes because of ill health, lack of skills, old age, or social barriers that make it difficult for them to develop their potential. Some occupations are seasonal and comparatively low paying, such as farming and fishing. Certain regions of a country may lack an economic base conducive to high incomes and lag in economic development and growth. The incidence of low incomes bordering on poverty is generally concentrated in rural areas and among the elderly and undereducated.

Government takes measures to counter some of these situations by redistributing income. It is worth noting, however, that it is often difficult to establish a clear distinction between government income-redistribution programs and government resource-reallocation programs. Some programs serve both objectives. Medicare, for example, yields external benefits to society, but at the same time, if it benefits the poor relatively more than the wealthy, it reduces the income gap between the two groups.

Canadian governments have recognized their obligation to redistribute income and wealth to attain a greater degree of equality and to reduce the incidence of poverty. The means to this end at the federal and provincial levels are a number of welfare and income-maintenance programs, including Old Age Security payments, family allowances, payments under the Canada Assistance Plan (which incorporates a number of welfare programs, such as widows' allowances and pensions for the blind and disabled), and subsidies and quotas in agriculture to maintain and stabilize farm incomes — as well as programs to increase and improve education, provide technical training and labour retraining, and assist labour mobility. In addition, there are unemployment insurance and workers' compensation plus minimum wage regulations and rent controls. Another government approach is transfer programs that provide real goods and services, such as subsidized housing, medical care, hospitalization, and education. Since these programs usually benefit the poor relatively more than the wealthy, some income redistribution is realized. The various redistribution programs are financed by a tax system that attempts to use progressive income tax rates and various exemptions in consumption-based taxes to place a greater burden on higher-income groups than on low-income groups.

The Canadian government has also made a commitment to try to reduce regional economic disparities. Differences between provinces in terms of resource endowment, population, proximity to markets, investment opportunities, and so on lead to different degrees of economic development, industrialization and industry structure, employment, and income levels. In the Atlantic provinces, average per capita income is only half of that in more prosperous regions, such as Ontario and Alberta. To reduce this inequality, the federal government has introduced a variety of policies, including the payment of subsidies and tax concessions to encourage industry to develop in these areas, worker retraining and mobility programs, equalization grants to the governments of the poorer provinces to enable them to provide their residents with public services comparable to those of other provinces, and the establishment of special programs and funds to develop opportunities for employment at an adequate wage.

Does this array of programs achieve a fair distribution of income and wealth? Statistics on Canadian income distribution reveal considerable inequality. Table 1–1 illustrates the point by dividing the country's families into five income groups with each group containing the same number of families (quintiles). In 1987, the lowest quintile earned only 2.8 percent of total income, while the highest group earned 42.7 percent. After transfers are taken into account, the share of the lowest quintile rises while that of the highest quintile falls. After federal and provincial income taxes are taken into consideration, the gap between the two groups is further reduced. (It is generally accepted that there is a tendency toward equality when the gap between the lowest and highest quintiles decreases.) Also shown in the table is the Gini coefficient, a summary measure of income inequality. In 1987, it fell by 0.071 after transfers were paid and fell again by 0.034 when income taxes were paid. These results suggest that although

TABLE 1–1
Income Distribution in Canada
with Effect of Transfers and Taxes, 1987

Families	Income before transfers	Total money income[a]	Income after tax[b]
Lowest quintile	2.8%	6.5%	7.6%
Second quintile	11.1	12.4	13.4
Middle quintile	18.0	17.8	18.2
Fourth quintile	25.3	24.0	23.6
Highest quintile	42.7	39.4	37.2
Total[c]	100.0%	100.0%	100.0%
Gini Coefficient[d]	0.401	0.330	0.296
Average Income	$31 924	$35 965	$29 361

[a] Total money income received from all sources including government transfers.
[b] Total money income minus federal and provincial income taxes paid.
[c] Because of rounding, some totals are not exactly 100 percent.
[d] A Gini coefficient of zero means uniform income for all groups (perfect income equality), while a coefficient of one means one unit receives all of the income (perfect inequality). A decrease in the Gini coefficient is interpreted as a decrease in inequality.

Source: Statistics Canada, *Income after Tax, Distributions by Size in Canada, 1987*, cat. 13–21.

both government cash transfers to families and the income tax system are income equalizers, the impact of transfers is greater than that of income taxes. Indeed, in 1987 for all families with total money income less than $17 500, transfers represented more than one-half of their income.

The redistribution policies of the government have, at best, prevented the degree of income inequality from deteriorating. It would appear that the traditional objective of redistributing income to reduce the gap between the rich and the poor has been replaced by the concern of the government to bring the level of the lowest income group up to an "acceptable" subsistence level. This concern is reflected in policies and programs such as those designed to benefit the aged, the infirm, the handicapped, the unemployed, single parents, and the working poor.

One of the difficulties with an objective of achieving greater equity in income distribution is the existence of factors that tend to limit redistribution. Attempts to divide total income more evenly among members of society may reduce the amount to be divided. Excessive taxation of the upper-income groups and business in order to finance transfers and goods and services benefiting lower-income groups may stifle incentives to work, to invest, to maintain maximum efficiency in production and distribution, and to engage in risky business ventures. The result would be a waste of resources; economic growth, capital accumulation, and consequently future production and employment would be lower than they otherwise might have been, decreasing the total income available for distribution among society's members. Government may, therefore, have to strike a compromise between the objective of a more equitable distribution of income and the objective of efficiency in the use of resources and economic growth.

Economic Stability and Growth

Over the last half-century or so, the Canadian government, like most modern governments, has accepted an obligation for economic stabilization and the attainment of the general goals of high levels of employment, reasonably stable prices, and an adequate rate of economic growth. This function of government is a relatively new one, dating from the Depression of the 1930s.

History has shown that the market economy is characterized by fluctuations in economic activity, with periods of rapid expansion and rising prices, periods of economic decline and unemployment, and periods of stagnation characterized by slow economic growth, rising unemployment, and inflation. Classical economics viewed these fluctuations as temporary maladjustments that the forces of the market would remedy. It became apparent with the Depression, however, that prolonged periods of economic stagnation and high levels of unemployment could occur, with the market system unable to prevent them or to remedy them speedily once they set in. It was in this depressed economic climate that J.M. Keynes wrote his *General Theory of Employment, Interest and Money* in which he built the foundation for macroeconomics and discretionary fiscal policy. Refining Keynesian theory, economists in the United States, such as Alvin Hansen, argued for increased government participation in the economy to influence the rate of economic activity and prevent fluctuations. With Keynes, they said that the stable operation of the market economy required government action.

Keynesian fiscal policy became traditional policy. It consists of discretionary adjustments to government tax and expenditure policies to influence aggregate demand. During a period of economic decline, government increases expenditure and reduces taxes. The resulting deficit in the budget indicates that government is putting more purchasing power into the economy than it is taking out, producing a net increase in aggregate demand and providing a stimulus for increased output of goods and services and, therefore, increased employment.

Periods of excessive economic expansion generally produce rapidly rising prices or inflation and require just the opposite policy. Inflation may be caused by excessive demand or rapidly rising costs of production. Government can temper aggregate demand by reducing its own demand through a decrease in its expenditure. Similarly, increased taxes may reduce private demand by reducing purchasing power in the hands of the public and leaving people with fewer funds to spend on consumption and investment.

Governments employ monetary policy in conjunction with discretionary fiscal policy in attempts to stabilize the economy and promote economic growth. Indeed, in recent years, with budget flexibility hampered by continuous large annual deficits, monetary policy has become the primary stabilization instrument. Monetary policy includes varying the money supply and regulating interest rates. High interest rates and a reduction in the growth rate of the money supply may be used for contractionary effects to combat inflation, with just the opposite policy in periods of economic decline.

Alternative or in addition to fiscal and monetary policy during a period of inflation, government may use more direct controls, such as wage and price regulation. The governments of most democracies have been reluctant to interfere in economic activity to this extent and have tended to rely on the more indirect means of tax and expenditure policy. In the past, Canada, the United States, and the countries of Western Europe have resorted to rigid, direct controls only in periods of emergency, such as crises in national security. More recently, however, a number of countries, including Canada, have experimented with temporary wage and price regulations in the face of serious inflation.

The Canadian government's first use of discretionary fiscal policy occurred during the latter stages of the Depression. It was not until 1945, however, that it officially and openly declared an obligation for fiscal policy. Since that time the country has experienced periods of decline and prosperity, and the government's fiscal policy has varied in both its intensity and its degree of success. (Canadian fiscal policy is discussed in detail in Chapter 10.)

Other Objectives

Governments may use their spending, taxing, and regulatory powers to promote various social and cultural goals. In Canada, the federal government has historically used these powers to bring the country's various regions together to establish, maintain, and enhance an integrated economy and a national identity. This has been particularly true of federal transportation and communications policies. The National Policy of 1879 included the construction of a transcontinental railway to bring the regions together and a tariff wall to promote the development of Canadian industry. The creation of the Canadian Broadcasting Corporation (CBC) was followed by various regulations, including specification of broadcast content, to foster Canadian programming and culture.

The government has also used regulation and direct participation to attempt to increase Canadian ownership and control of the country's industry. These efforts have included the pursuit of a national energy policy involving the co-operation and participation of government and the private sector in developing the country's energy resources in the interests of Canada. One such enterprise is Petro-Canada, established by the federal government in 1976 as a Crown corporation to participate in the exploration for oil and gas and the refining and marketing of petroleum products.

Government involvement in the provision of goods and services that are essentially private in nature may stem from a desire to maintain or develop certain industries to diversify the economy's industrial base and to create employment opportunities. This activity may involve the establishment of government enterprise (such as Air Canada) or the takeover — nationalization — of existing private enterprise. The objective of nationalizing an industry may be to redirect its operation in the public interest. On the other hand, government may nationalize failing private enterprises to prevent the industry from terminating operations and laying off workers. Examples of the latter goal include the federal government's purchase of Canadair Ltd. and de Havilland Aircraft of Canada Ltd. during the mid-1970s. Assisted by large federal grants, these two corporations operated as Crown corporations until their sale to private interests during the privatization movement of the latter 1980s. (The operation and administration of Crown corporations is further examined in the appendix to Chapter 2.)

The Canadian government's efforts in nation-building include its policy of promoting the use of both English and French throughout Canada. Other nation-building measures are demonstrated in relations with the provinces. Jurisdictional disputes over areas of authority are not uncommon; generally they arise when the federal government's view of a policy in the national interest conflicts with the narrower regional interests of the provinces. Some recent disputes have centred around energy, telecommunications, offshore mineral rights, and constitutional reform.

It has not been uncommon for special regional social and cultural objectives and for political philosophies to guide the expenditure and tax policies of provincial governments. For example, the CCF (Co-operative Commonwealth Federation, which was the forerunner of the New Democratic Party) came to power in Saskatchewan in 1944 promoting a form of socialism. Its policies included the improvement of social security measures and greater government involvement in economic planning and in the production and distribution sectors of the economy through the establishment of Crown corporations and co-operative ventures with private interests. Many of these ventures were later terminated and some government-owned corporations sold when there came to power right-wing governments that placed greater emphasis on the marketplace for directing activities in the economy.

The government of Quebec has traditionally sought to protect and promote its French language, culture, and identity on the Anglo-dominated North American continent. This objective has been pursued through a variety of measures, including some of the province's economic, social, and educational policies. For example, in 1988 the Quebec government, fearing that a declining birth rate in the province would make Québécois a smaller and smaller minority in the Canadian community, sought to encourage couples to have more children by introducing bonus payments for newborns: $500 for the first child, $1000 for the second child, and $6000 for each subsequent child.

SUMMARY

In summary, most government activity in the economy can be classified under one or more of the three major objectives of government: to secure adjustments in resource allocation, to achieve equity in income distribution, and to promote economic stability and growth. The market system, which operates under its own constraints and limitations, is unable to achieve these goals to the satisfaction of society. Canadian governments at all levels are heavily involved in assisting the economy to achieve these objectives. Their activities include promoting competition, combatting external diseconomies such as pollution, providing public services, redistributing income through taxes, transfers, and a variety of income-maintenance programs, and applying fiscal and monetary policies to combat unemployment and inflation and to promote economic growth.

The various government objectives frequently conflict, together with problems regarding the most effective methods of achieving them. Economic analysis can contribute to establishing compromises and solutions to these issues, but they must be resolved within the political and administrative decision-making structure and processes. In essence, the study of public finance must include elements of politics and public administration as well as economics.

ENDNOTES

1. This classification of government activities, found in a number of textbooks in public finance, was first presented in the classic, R.A. Musgrave, *The Theory of Public Finance* (New York: McGraw-Hill, 1959).

2. The term "Pareto optimum" is named after the economist Vilfredo Pareto (1848–1923), who first put forward the conditions or criteria for economic efficiency in the economy. These efficiency conditions, defined for consumption and production, are explained in most intermediate textbooks in microeconomics, as well as in various public finance textbooks. See, for example, Robin W. Boadway, and David E. Wildasin, *Public Sector Economics*, 2nd ed. (Toronto: Little, Brown, 1984), ch. 2.

3. A natural monopoly is a situation in which economies of scale enable one large firm to produce at lower costs than a larger number of small, competing firms. Ensuring that the monopoly does not engage in price manipulation to gain excess profits may

require government regulation, although the threat of competition can induce a monopoly to behave competitively.

4. For an examination of regulation in Canada — including regulatory agencies, processes, objectives, and effects — see John C. Strick, *The Economics of Government Regulation: Theory and Canadian Practice*, (Toronto: Thompson Educational Publishing, 1990).

5. It has been argued that externalities are caused by the lack of property rights and can be corrected by the marketplace through the assignments of such rights. Water, for example, is a resource viewed as "common property." No one has exclusive property rights over such resources, so there is a tendency to abuse and waste these resources. Firms can dump industrial wastes into streams and lakes without paying to do so. The assignment to one firm of property rights to the stream or lake would exclude other firms from using it unless they paid for its use, including the right to pollute it. Payment for the right to pollute would result in the internalization of the external diseconomy since the cost of pollution would be included in the price of the goods and services sold by the polluting firms. Such payments, however, would cause the offending firm to consider carefully whether pollution is worthwhile in comparison to steps that could be taken to avoid pollution. The issue of property rights and externalities, which is discussed in a number of textbooks in public sector economies, was first presented in R. Coase, "The Problem of Social Cost," *Journal of Law and Economics*, 3, 1960.

6. For a more detailed presentation of externalities and the desirability of government action, see Richard A. Musgrave, Peggy Musgrave, and Richard M. Bird, *Public Finance in Theory and Practice*, Cdn. ed. (Toronto: McGraw-Hill Ryerson, 1987), ch. 4; and Joseph E. Stiglitz, *Economics of the Public Sector*, 2nd ed. (New York, Norton, 1988), ch. 8.

7. See Strick, *The Economics of Government Regulation*, ch. 12.

8. See, for example, Stiglitz, *Economics of the Public Sector*; and Boadway and Wildasin, *Public Sector Economics*, pp. 57–60.

9. A discussion of merit goods is presented in Musgrave, Musgrave, and Bird, *Public Finance in Theory and Practice*, pp. 72–73.

APPENDIX TO CHAPTER 1

EXTERNALITIES AND PUBLIC GOODS: A DIAGRAMMATIC ANALYSIS

In the market model of supply and demand, the supply (*S*) and demand (*D*) curves show the relationship between price and quantity. The demand curve illustrates the amount of a commodity that will be taken off the market at various prices by consumers. The price a consumer is willing to pay for a unit of the commodity measures the additional benefit or utility that he or she receives from its consumption. The demand curve, therefore, can be viewed as the marginal private benefit (MPB) curve in consumption. The supply curve reflects the costs of producing the commodity; it is derived from the firm's marginal private cost (MPC) curve and represents the cost associated with the production of an additional unit of the commodity. The equilibrium market price (*OQ*) and quantity (*OP*) are determined where *S* = *D* or MPC = MPB, which is point *E* in Figure A1–1.

External Economies

External economies are benefits accruing to third parties, those other than the consumers and producers of a commodity. In Figure A1–1, the marginal external benefit (MEB) is the additional benefit received by third parties as a result of the production and consumption of additional units of the commodity. The marginal society benefit (MSB) is sum of the marginal private and external benefits: MSB = MPB + MEB. Assume that no external diseconomies exist so that MPC is equal to marginal social cost (MSC).

In the absence of externalities, the market equilibrium price (*OP*) and quantity (*OQ*) will be the efficient levels in perfect competition. With the existence of external economies, however, market equilibrium is no longer efficient. At output *OQ*, marginal social benefit exceeds marginal social cost by *EF*. Net benefit to society can be increased by increasing output from *OQ* to *OR*, where MSC = MSB at *G*. The total net gain to society from this increase in output is represented by the area *EFG*. The condition for private equilibrium is MPC = MPB, but the condition for social equilibrium is MSC = MSB.

Thus, Figure A1–1 illustrates that in presence of external economies, the market will not produce enough output to maximize benefits to society. A private firm will not expand output to *OR*, the efficient amount for society, because to sell that amount, it would have to reduce price to *OB* and incur a loss equal to *GH* per unit, or a total loss equal to *AGHB*.

To ensure that the social optimum amount of the commodity is produced, the government can pay a subsidy to the firm to cover its loss or, alternatively, assume direct responsibility for production. If it follows the latter policy, the government may

FIGURE A1-1
External Economies

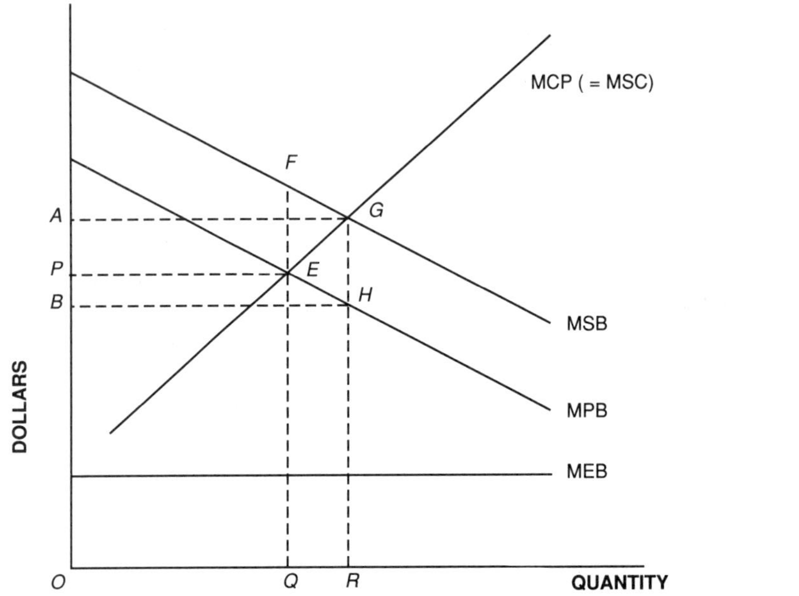

provide *OR* of the commodity free of charge and finance the total cost (*OAGR*) from tax revenues, or it may charge a nominal fee equal to *OB* and finance the remainder of the cost from tax revenues.

External Diseconomies

External diseconomies are costs accruing to third parties, those other than the consumers and producers of a commodity. The marginal external cost (MEC) illustrated in Figure A1–2 is the additional cost to third parties as a result of the consumption or production of additional units of the commodity. Assume that the external cost is pollution that results from production and that the amount of pollution associated with each additional unit of production is constant, as shown by MEC. The marginal social cost (MSC) is the sum of the private and external costs: MSC = MPC + MEC. Assume that there are no external benefits so that MPB = MSB.

In the absence of externalities, the market price (*OP*) and quantity (*OQ*) will be the optimal levels in perfect competition. When an external diseconomy exists, however, the marginal social cost exceeds the marginal social benefit by *EF*. This cost is not priced in the marketplace and is not included in the manufacturer's cost of production, but it is a cost to society and represents a net loss of welfare or benefits. Net benefit to society can be increased by reducing output from *OQ* to *OT*, where MSC = MSB at *G*. The total net gain to society is equal to *EFG*, which is the difference between the total cost of producing *TQ* (= *TGFQ*) minus the total benefit received from *TQ* (= *TGEQ*).

FIGURE A1-2
External Diseconomies

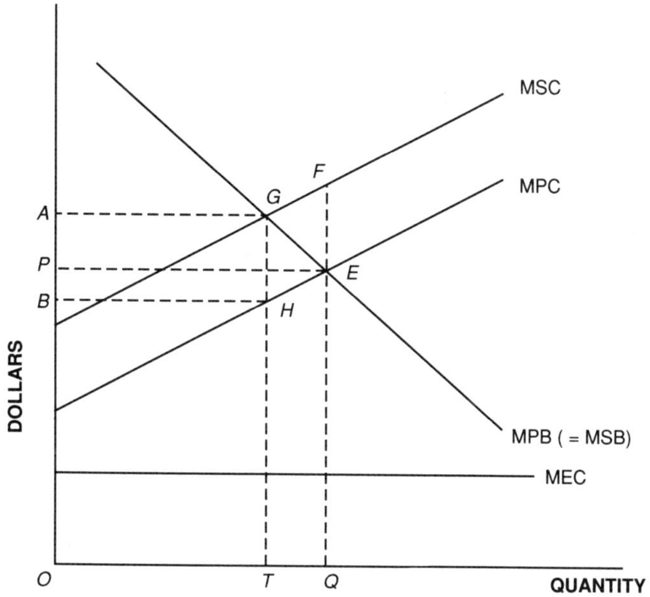

To achieve the socially optimal level of output (*OT*), the government can impose a tax on the commodity equal to *FE* per unit at output *OQ*. The tax becomes a cost to the firm, raising the costs of production from MPC to MSC and resulting in a loss to the firm equal to *FE* per unit of output. The firm will, therefore, scale back output to point *G*, where the price per unit is just sufficient to cover the cost of the unit produced. At output *OT*, the tax will be *GH* per unit, with total taxes paid equal to *AGHB*. The tax succeeds in reducing output and consequently the amount of pollution but does not eliminate this diseconomy entirely. The cost of the pollution remaining is represented by *AGHB*.

Alternatively, the government can legislate antipollution laws, forcing the firm to purchase pollution-control equipment or alter its methods of production. The resulting increased costs to the firm will be reflected in a leftward shift of the MPC curve and a decrease in production. To the extent that pollution is reduced by the firm's action of incurring costs to prevent pollution, it is said that the firm has internalized the external diseconomy.

Pure Public Goods

Pure public goods and services are characterized by the properties of nonexcludability and nonrivalry in consumption. They are consumed collectively, and the consumption of one person does not reduce the amounts available to others.

The difference between private goods and public goods is illustrated by the nature of the demand curves for the goods. The market demand curve for a private good consists of the horizontal summation of all of the individual demand curves for the good. In Part A of Figure A1–3, D_A, D_B, and D_C are the respective demand curves for individuals *A*, *B*, and *C*. For example, D_A shows the amount individual *A* is prepared to purchase at various prices. Given price *OP*, *A* desires quantity *OA*, *B* quantity *OB*, and *C* quantity *OB*. The three consumers together are prepared to purchase an amount $OM = OA + OB + OC$ at price *OP*. The market demand curve for the private good is the sum of the quantities demanded at given prices or $D_M = \Sigma Q_D$.

In the case of a private good, each individual consumes different quantities at any given price. In the case of a pure public good, on the other hand, each individual pays a different price for a given quantity. A pure public good is nonexclusive, which means that all individuals consume the same amount. It is also nonrival, which means that consumption by one individual does not impede consumption by others. Part B of Figure A1–3 illustrates the situation, D_A, D_B, and D_C are the marginal benefit curves or demand curves of individuals *A*, *B*, and *C* respectively. D_A, for example, shows the amount of additional benefit *A* receives from consuming a unit of the good at the margin and, therefore, the amount that person is prepared to pay for each unit given the total amount produced. If production of the public good is *OQ* — for example, the level of police protection represented by OQ number of police personnel — the total amount is available to each individual. Because the good is nonrival, the amount consumed by *A* does not reduce the amounts available to *B* and *C*. Because it is nonexcludable, *B* and *C* cannot be excluded from consuming *OQ*. Thus, the amount *OQ* is there to be consumed in equal amounts by all consumers. At output *OQ*, the marginal benefit to *A* equals *OA*; to *B*, it is *OB*; and to *C*, it is *OC*. These marginal values reflect the amount each individual is prepared to pay for the public good, so collectively they will pay an amount *OM* per unit for *OQ* output. The demand curve for a pure public good is the vertical summation of the individual marginal benefits at each level of output. For output *OQ*, $OM = OA + OB + OC$, and $D_M = \Sigma MB$.

FIGURE A1-3
Derivation of Demand Curves for Private and Public Goods

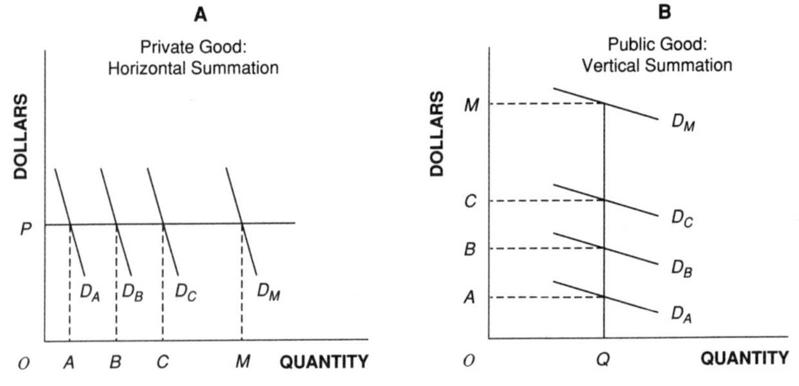

CHAPTER 2

GROWTH AND COMPOSITION OF PUBLIC SECTOR EXPENDITURES

A general trend in most countries has been for the public sector to grow more rapidly than the private sector and to absorb an increasingly larger relative share of total resources. Various factors have contributed to this trend;[1] the most significant for Canada are outlined in this chapter, which also describes some theories of public sector growth and provides Canadian data.

FACTORS INFLUENCING PUBLIC SECTOR GROWTH

Wars and Military Expenditures

Government expenditures usually rise dramatically during a country's involvement in war. Canada experienced this sort of growth during the two world wars, although it is questionable whether they had a displacement effect on the long-run trend of government expenditures. The cold war with communism following the Second World War and the limited war in Korea from 1950 to 1953 served to keep defence expenditure at a high level, but it has been on a declining trend since then. Today, defence expenditure in Canada accounts for only about 8 percent of federal government spending. The comparable figure is 25 percent in the United States, whose high military expenditures coincide with its assumed leadership obligations in the noncommunist world.

Social Conscience

As noted in Chapter 1, in Canada there has been a gradual awakening of what may be termed the social conscience. Society has come to accept increasing obligations to assist the underprivileged and those who are unable to provide for themselves. In general, a large percentage of the increase in government expenditure in Canada during the last three decades has been for programs designed to redistribute income more equitably. Spending for this purpose has often been on direct transfers to individuals or on goods and services in programs designed to benefit the lower-income groups relatively more than the higher-income groups. The most prominent expenditures have been for social service and health-care programs, including family allowances, Old Age Security (OAS), unemployment insurance, and medicare.

Technological Change

Rapidly changing technology has produced highly sophisticated, capital-intensive means of production requiring an educated and skilled labour force, which, in turn, has contributed to technological development and increased productivity. Society has recognized that technological change and education are important to the development of a country and its standard of living and that education and labour training yield considerable benefits to all of society. It was primarily because of such recognition that government assumed responsibility for education and vocational training, which account for a significant proportion of government spending.

Changing technology also has provided modern society with an increased supply of sophisticated private goods, which has brought about a corresponding increase in demand for public goods. For example, the increased production and use of automobiles has required more and better roads and highways; the development of larger and faster airplanes has meant larger and more modern air terminals. Thus, the private and public sectors of the economy are interdependent and complementary in the provision of goods and services.

Population Growth and Urbanization

The demand for public goods and services generally grows with the population. Moreover, population growth in this century has been accompanied by an urbanization movement that has brought large increases in the demand for social goods and services, which are most appropriately provided by government. These items include transportation facilities, sanitation, water supply, police and fire protection, and housing, which in Canada primarily fall to the responsibility of the provincial and municipal governments. Not only has the demand for the quantity of these goods and services increased; as people become more affluent in terms of improvements in the quality of private goods, they also expect an improvement in the quality of public goods.

Keynesian Theory

The Keynesian revolution in economic thought fostered increased government involvement in directing and influencing economic activity, which has required increased government spending. Since the Depression of the 1930s, governments in many Western countries, including Canada, have made efforts to fine tune the economy to prevent or reduce the severity of cycles in economic activity and to promote economic growth. Increased government spending for public works, public investment projects, and assistance to industry are examples of governments' efforts to provide employment and to stimulate the economy.

More recently in Canada, government has been attempting to shape and influence industrial development. Nowhere is this more evident than in the energy and natural resources industries, where billions of dollars have been expended on nuclear energy development and on joint investment ventures with the private sector in petroleum exploration, extraction, and distribution. During the period of economic decline and inflation of the early 1980s, the Canadian government became active in assisting companies in financial difficulty (for example, Chrysler Corp., Dome Petroleum) through loan guarantees. Grants to industries that locate in designated areas of chronic high unemployment have also been initiated.

Productivity and Costs

The rising relative cost of public goods and services also may have contributed to the increasing relative size of the public sector. Between 1947 and 1988, the gross domestic product implicit price index rose from 18.8 to 134.3 (1981 = 100), while the price index for government's current expenditures on goods and services (a component of GDP) increased from 10.5 to 142.8.

Some contend that lower efficiency and productivity in the public sector have contributed to this differential. If wages and salaries rise by the same amount in both sectors but productivity in the public sector lags, then unit costs and consequently prices of public goods and services rise relative to unit costs and prices in the private sector. It is argued, though not conclusively, that the lower rate of productivity change in the public sector is partly because of the nature of the services provided and partly because of differences in the behaviour of private suppliers and government bureaus.[2]

It is certain, however, that much government activity involves the provision of services and that productivity in service industries generally lags behind productivity in goods-producing industries. Furthermore, services, particularly public services such as health care and education, are highly labour-intensive, and periodically public service wages and salaries have tended to rise more rapidly than wages and salaries in the private sector, thus contributing to the relative rise of unit costs in the public sector.

Government Political Philosophy

The growth of government can also be influenced by the philosophy of the particular political party in power over the longer term. The party elected to power reflects the mood and values of the electorate at the time. In Great Britain following the Second World War, for example, the growth of government relative to the economy increased during the tenure of the Labour Party, which emphasized social programs and the increased participation of government in the economy through the nationalization of various industries. During the 1980s, under the tenure of the Conservative government led by Margaret Thatcher, restraint on social spending and the privatization of a number of government-owned corporations contributed to a decline in the size of government relative to GDP.

In Canada, as mentioned in the previous chapter, the election of socialist-leaning governments — the Co-operative Commonwealth Federation (CCF) and the New Democratic Party (NDP) — in Saskatchewan, Manitoba, and British Columbia brought increased provincial involvement in economic activity and the establishment of new government enterprises or Crown corporations. These governments initiated public health programs, government-run automobile insurance, and other socioeconomic activities that were the forerunners of similar programs adopted by the federal government and other provinces. In turn, the election to power of more conservative governments usually produced announcements of retrenchment in government involvement in economic activities. Recently, privatization of Crown corporations at the federal and provincial levels helped ease the subsidy burden on government budgets.[3]

The Political Process and Bureaucratic Considerations

The increasing size of the public sector can be considered a reflection of the operations of the political process (a point implicit in some of the previous discussion of this chapter). Some recent attempts to explain government expenditure growth focus on the nature of collective decision-making — choice — and on bureaucratic behaviour. A number of public-choice theories and models in the literature on public finance concentrate on the supply side of government spending — the motivations and actions of the suppliers of government goods and services.[4] Theories developed in this area focus on the self-interest behaviour of political parties, elected representatives, and bureaucrats.

Anthony Downs, for example, theorizes that political parties will present to the electorate a budget based on a mix of programs that they believe will maximize their votes and thus their chances of reelection. Whether it will produce an efficient supply of government services cannot be assured however, for, according to Downs, the social function of political parties is a byproduct of their self-interest motive. The mix could lead to an oversupply or an undersupply of government services.

The vote-trading or "log-rolling" model features elected legislators' exchange of votes to obtain support for projects for their constituencies that otherwise might not receive the support necessary for passage by the legislature. In other words, member *A* of the legislature agrees to support a project for the constituency of member *B* if *B* agrees to support *A*'s project. If the benefits from each project are local but are financed by all taxpayers, expenditures can be carried to the point at which the benefits from the marginal expenditure are far less than the costs to society in the form of taxes. The result is an oversupply of government services and an inefficient use of resources.

William Niskanen focusses on the behaviour of bureaucrats, arguing that they are motivated by the desire to accumulate power and the prestige that derives from administering a major government department or section of a department. Bureaucrats may thus be motivated to expand the size of the budget and the output of their administrative units, which can lead to the expansion and growth of government beyond the optimum level.

No matter which, if any, of these models is correct, it is clear that political parties believe they can be elected more readily by offering to do more for society, and keeping election promises usually entails considerable increases in government expenditure. While this may be interpreted as reflecting social demands for government services, these demands perhaps would not be as high if greater attention were drawn to the costs of proposed services and the relationship between taxes and government-provided goods and services. Unfortunately, election promises generally concentrate on what the government will offer the public, with little said about the method of financing or who will bear the burden. Voters consequently believe the fiscal illusion that they will benefit from activities and other individuals will bear the burden of financing them.

Even when electioneering (or elected) governments present estimates on costs, they are often underestimated. Examples of federal programs that proved over time to be significantly more costly than forecast include medicare, the revised unemployment insurance program, and the National Energy Program.

Government Expenditure Growth Theories

A number of attempts have been made to develop a theory of public sector growth in a mixed economy.[5] In particular, these attempts have focussed on the growth trends and the time patterns of changes in government spending. A general theory of public sector growth would not only serve to explain past behaviour but would also permit predictions to be made about the future growth and size of government.

One of the earliest such attempts was Wagner's Law, developed by German economist Adolph Wagner (1890), who found a functional relationship between a growing economy and government spending. According to Wagner's Law, the relationship is elastic in that a change in GDP produces a more than proportionate change in government spending. He attributed this elasticity of government spending to the income elasticity of demand for social goods and services. As income in the economy increases, demands for government-provided goods, services, and law and order increases in a greater proportion.

Most studies of government expenditure growth in industrialized countries during this century substantiate the existence of a functional relationship as described by Wagner's Law. The relationship has indeed been elastic: as GDP increased, government expenditures increased in a greater proportion. It has been difficult to determine, however, what factors have contributed most significantly to this relationship. For example, R.A. Musgrave theorizes about the possible effects of economic and sociocultural factors and concludes that the combined contribution of these factors to the relationship between government expenditure and GDP over the course of a country's growth was theoretically indeterminate.[6]

Although Wagner's Law has been shown to hold for many industrialized countries, evidence of its application to developing and underdeveloped economies is inconclusive. Some analysts hypothesize that the relationship of government expenditure to per capita income may in fact be inelastic in the early stages of a country's development, reflecting the provision of society's basic needs by the private sector rather than government; elastic during the industrialized stage, reflecting the need for government-provided capital, infrastructure, and complementary services; and inelastic again in the postindustrialized stage, reflecting government's sufficient provision of social goods and services and society's preference for a greater proportion of consumer goods and services.[7]

Other theories have focussed on the time pattern of expenditure growth—the shape of the trend path of government spending relative to GDP over a long period of time. In the early 1960s, Peacock and Wiseman put forward their theory of displacement, inspection, and concentration. Their observations of the historical growth of government spending in the United Kingdom showed the growth to be steplike, each step indicating a surge in the government expenditure to GDP ratio. They contended that these surges resulted from major social or economic disturbances, such as wars and economic depressions. Each disturbance caused the existing growth path of government expenditure to be replaced by a new, higher-level growth path to reflect the higher expenditure/GDP ratio. After the disturbance ended the higher level of expenditure was maintained by government involvement in new activities and by a higher tax tolerance level (established when taxes were increased to finance the increased government spending during the disturbance). According to this theory, therefore, disturbances cause a displacement of resources from the private sector to the public sector. This displacement becomes permanent because the disturbance forces the attention of society and government to economic and social problems previously neglected; government consequently acquires new obligations that require increased expenditures.

Attempts have been made to apply the Peacock-Wiseman theory to Canada to determine the effect of major disturbances, such as wars. The general conclusion is that wars have not had a permanent displacement effect on the long-run growth trend of Canadian government expenditure.[8] For example, at the end of the Second World War, the government expenditure/GDP ratio in Canada was approximately 50 percent. By 1950, it had been reduced to less than 25 percent, practically equal to the ratio that had existed just prior to the war.

None of the theories developed to explain government sector growth has been accepted as a general theory. They have tended to be applicable to particular periods and to particular countries but have not been universally applicable. They have contributed, however, to the understanding and analysis of the factors that influence and affect government expenditure growth.

Thus, although analysis reveals that Canadian government expenditure as a percentage of GDP increased from 15 percent in the 1920s to almost 45 percent in the 1980s, it is difficult to determine if this rising trend will continue into the future.

A controversial related issue is whether there is a critical limit to the size of government in relation to the economy. There has been speculation that a limit does exist, and once it is surpassed, forces may be set in motion to reduce the size of government.[9] The limitations to government expenditure growth, according to this hypothesis, are related to taxation. In their theory, Peacock and Wiseman referred to a tax-tolerance level that constrained government spending during periods between economic and social disturbances. Taxes are never popular, and governments must maintain an awareness of the potential effects of major tax increases. Opposition to high taxes may be reflected in greater efforts at tax avoidance;[10] in taxpayers' "voting with their feet" and moving to jurisdictions where taxes are lower; in the flight from the country of wealth; in governments' being voted out of office; in adverse effects on incentives to work, invest, take risks, and so on, which would stifle economic growth; or in the organization of groups of taxpayers and consumers to voice opposition to new taxes, as occurred when the federal government proposed its new goods and services tax (GST) in 1989. Taxes deemed to be unfair or fear of higher tax rates may even prompt "tax revolts." In September 1990, the governing council of the village of Elstow, Saskatchewan, fully supported by residents, declared that as a municipal government, it would neither collect nor pay the unpopular federal GST when it came into effect in

January 1991.[11] It was contended that the proposed tax was unfair and inflationary and that its rates would likely spiral in the future. During the late 1970s and 1980s, tax revolts were triggered by the unpopularity of high property taxes in several US states.[12] Irate taxpayers in jurisdictions that permit voter-initiated referendums were able to force enactment of a number of tax-limitation statutes. The electorate was not deterred by arguments that tax-limitations would lead to a reduction in government services.

An indication of how Canadian and US governments have perceived public tax-tolerance levels in recent years is the fact that the federal governments in both countries have been reluctant to raise taxes by the necessary amount to balance their budgets. During the 1980s, they continued to incur large annual budgetary deficits, attempting to reduce them by emphasizing expenditure reduction and control rather than tax increases. (The Canadian government's efforts to reduce its deficit are described in Chapter 10.)

Government Expenditure Trends and Patterns[13]

Total government expenditure in Canada has increased considerably over the past six decades as illustrated in Table 2–1. Disregarding the massive increase during the Second World War, the trend was a persistent increase in government expenditure as a percentage of GDP until, in 1980, it stood at 40.3 percent. A major increase in total government spending, combined with a small increase in GDP, caused this figure to jump to 46.3 percent by 1982. It remained near this level until 1988, when it fell to 44.0 percent. A similar trend can be found in many other Western countries.[14] Table 2–2 shows the trend in government expenditure as a percentage of GDP for a number of such countries. When the size of government is measured in this way, government in Canada is larger than in the United Sates and Japan but smaller than in a number of other industrialized countries including France and Italy.

Tables 2–3 and 2–4 illustrate trends in the share of activities by different levels of government in terms of expenditures before and after intergovernment transfer payments. In Table 2–3, which shows expenditures before transfers, transfers paid to other levels of government are attributed to the government that makes them. For example, the federal government finances part of the medicare program by making transfer payments to the provinces, which administer the program. The transfer payment represents a cost to the federal government in support of medical services. Thus, the table reports the percentage — share — of total government activities *financed* by each level of government. Viewing expenditures in this manner, one can observe in Table 2–3 that prior to 1940 government activities were relatively decentralized, with the federal government financing approximately 40 percent of the total. There were massive increases in spending during the Second World War; afterward, the trend was again to a gradual decentralization of expenditures, with the federal share falling and the provincial/municipal share increasing. This trend reflected large expenditure increases in such costly provincial functions as health care, welfare, and education, together with changes in cost-sharing arrangements for these functions. With respect to the latter, for example, part of the federal assistance to the provinces for

Table 2–1
Government Expenditures as Percentage of Gross Domestic Product for Selected Years 1926–1989

	Expenditures (*percentage of* GDP[a])
1926	15.7
1929	16.1
1933	27.4
1939	21.4
1944	50.5
1947	24.3
1950	21.3
1955	25.6
1960	28.8
1965	28.7
1970	34.9
1975	39.9
1980	40.3
1982	46.3
1984	46.5
1986	46.1
1988	44.0
1989	44.0

[a] Expressed as a percentage of gross national product up to the year 1947.

Source: Statistics Canada, *National Income and Expenditure Accounts,* 1926 to 1974, cat. 13–001, and Canada, Department of Finance, *Quarterly Economic Review: Annual Reference Tables,* June 1990 (Ottawa).

education was changed in 1967 from specific-purpose cash transfers to tax transfers, a move that had the effect of reducing the federal share of total government expenditure and increasing the provincial share. The decline in the federal share of expenditures continued until it reached approximately 50 percent in the mid-1970s; since then, it has remained fairly stable at about that share.

In Table 2–4, transfers are subtracted from the expenditures of the paying governments and added to the expenditures of the recipient governments. Thus, the figures report the percentage — share — of total government spending *administered* by each level of government. A comparison of federal and provincial/municipal shares again shows a trend toward decentralization from the early 1950s to 1970. During the 1970s, federal and provincial relative shares were fairly stable, and they continued so in the 1980s with the federal share fluctuating between 42 and 44 percent and the provincial share remaining close to 33 percent. The municipal government share fell from almost 26 percent in 1970 to nearly 17 percent in 1988.

TABLE 2–2
International Comparison of Total Government Expenditures as Percentage of Gross Domestic Product or Gross National Product for Selected Years 1970–1989

	Percentage of GDP or GNP			
	1970–74[a]	1975–81[a]	1985	1989
Canada	35.9	39.9	46.8	44.0
France	38.5	45.0	52.1	49.8
Germany	41.2	48.2	47.2	44.9
Italy	36.1	42.0	51.0	52.0
Japan	21.9	30.3	32.6	33.0
United Kingdom	38.3	43.0	44.1	36.9
United States	32.2	33.9	37.8	36.9

[a] Average.

Source: Canada, Department of Finance, *Quarterly Economic Review: Annual Reference Tables*, June 1990 (Ottawa), p. 143.

Table 2–5 illustrates the share of expenditure functions among the federal and provincial/municipal governments for the fiscal year 1987/88. Intergovernment transfers are included only in expenditures of the receiving government, so the data reflects the cost of the services administered by each level of government. The table shows that the provincial/municipal level did more than 58 percent of government spending in 1987/8. The functions in which the federal government spends considerably more than the provincial/municipal governments are protection of persons and property, social services, foreign affairs, and debt charges. Provincial/municipal governments account for most of the spending in health care, education, the environment, and recreation and culture.

Table 2–6 presents an economic classification of total government expenditure for selected years from 1926 to 1989. It can be observed that there have been some changes in the composition of expenditures, particularly during the Second World War. Currently, approximately 48 percent of government expenditure is devoted to goods and services and capital formation, with the remainder going to transfer payments in the form of payments to persons and to business (including subsidies and capital assistance) and interest payments. Transfers to persons and to business have increased in importance in recent years, rising from about 25 percent of total government spending in 1970 to more than 30 percent by 1988.

Table 2–7 shows trends in the relative significance of the various expenditure functions at the federal level over the last four decades. Among the more notable features have been the decline in the relative importance of spending on protection of persons and property (primarily defence) from 35 percent of gross expenditure in 1954 to less than 10 percent in the 1980s, and the increase in social services from about

TABLE 2–3
Expenditures by Level of Government before Intergovernment Transfers[a] for Selected Years 1926–1988
(National Accounts Basis[b])

	Federal[c]		Provincial[d]		Municipal		Hospitals[e]		Total
	Amount ($ million)	Share of total (%)	Amount ($ million)	Share of total (%)	Amount ($ million)	Share of total (%)	Amount ($ million)	Share of total (%)	Amount ($ million)
1926	321	39.6	166	20.5	323	39.9			810
1929	362	36.5	240	24.2	389	39.3			991
1933	380	39.7	240	25.1	336	35.1			956
1939	483	40.1	382	31.7	340	28.2			1 205
1944	5 320	89.0	310	5.2	350	5.8			5 980
1950	2 370	58.1	969	23.8	741	18.1			4 080
1954	4 654	65.6	1 164	16.4	1 273	18.0			7 091
1962	7 486	56.7	3 372	25.6	2 277	17.3	62	0.5	13 197
1970	15 262	49.0	10 777	34.6	4 908	15.8	67	0.2	31 148
1975	36 070	52.8	24 224	35.5	7 871	11.5	123	0.2	68 228
1980	63 019	50.7	47 375	38.1	13 581	10.9	365	0.3	124 340
1982	89 369	51.5	67 171	38.7	16 819	9.7	156	0.09	173 515
1984	110 691	53.5	76 463	37.0	19 233	9.3	343	0.2	206 730
1986	120 792	51.7	91 308	39.1	21 490	9.2	52	0.02	233 642
1988	138 854	52.4	101 673	38.4	24 280	9.2	272	0.1	265 079

[a] Transfers paid to other levels of government are included as expenditures of the transferring government, but excluded from expenditures of the recipient government.
[b] Current expenditures plus gross capital formation.
[c] Includes expenditures from the Canada Pension Plan beginning 1970.
[d] Includes expenditures from the Quebec Pension Plan beginning 1970.
[e] Statistics Canada series report hospital expenditure separately only beginning in the 1960s.

Sources: Statistics Canada, *National Income and Expenditure Accounts*, 1926–1974, cat. 13–531; 1968–1982, cat. 13–201, and *Fourth Quarter*, 1988, cat. 13–001.

TABLE 2–4
Expenditures by Level of Government after Intergovernment Transfers[a] for Selected Years 1926–1988
(National Accounts Basis[b])

	Federal[c]		Provincial[d]		Municipal		Hospitals[e]		Total
	Amount ($ million)	Share of total (%)	Amount ($ million)	Share of total (%)	Amount ($ million)	Share of total (%)	Amount ($ million)	Share of total (%)	Amount ($ million)
1926	306	43.1	164	20.2	340	42.0			810
1929	345	34.8	234	23.6	412	41.6			991
1933	324	33.9	286	29.9	346	36.2			956
1939	404	33.5	436	36.2	365	30.3			1 205
1944	5 165	86.4	414	6.9	401	6.7			5 980
1950	2 119	51.9	1 059	26.0	902	22.1			4 080
1954	4 224	59.6	1 348	19.0	1 519	21.4			7 091
1962	6 352	48.1	2 632	19.9	3 356	25.4	857	6.5	13 197
1970	11 865	38.1	8 718	28.0	8 036	25.8	2 395	7.7	31 148
1975	28 400	41.6	20 461	30.3	14 504	21.2	4 923	7.2	68 288
1980	50 188	40.4	40 733	32.8	24 877	20.0	8 542	6.9	124 340
1982	73 525	42.4	56 237	32.4	32 047	18.5	11 706	6.7	173 515
1984	90 786	43.9	66 545	32.2	35 518	17.2	13 881	6.7	206 730
1986	99 703	42.7	78 532	33.6	39 899	17.1	15 508	6.6	233 642
1988	114 148	43.1	88 443	33.4	44 892	16.9	17 596	6.6	265 079

a Transfers paid to other levels of government are excluded from the expenditures of the transferring government but included in the expenditures of the recipient government.
b Current expenditures plus gross capital formation.
c Includes expenditures from the Canada Pension Plan.
d Includes expenditures from the Quebec Pension Plan.
e Statistics Canada series report hospital expenditure separately only beginning in the 1960s.

See Table 2–3.

TABLE 2–5
Consolidated Government Expenditure Functions, 1987/8
(financial management statistics basis)

Expenditure function	Total	Share spent by Federal government	Share spent by Provincial and municipal governments
	($ million)	(percentage of total)	
General services	15 646	39.9	60.1
Protection of persons and property	21 388	61.9	38.1
Transportation and communications	13 088	26.7	73.3
Health	35 378	3.4	96.6
Social services	64 209	64.6	35.4
Education	32 749	2.8	97.2
Environment	5 425	7.9	92.1
Foreign affairs and international assistance	3 357	100.0	0.0
Recreation and culture	5 359	17.4	82.6
Resource conservation and industrial development	13 015	40.9	59.1
Debt charges	43 926	58.4	41.6
Other	12 618	58.3	41.7
Total	266 158	41.2	58.8

Note: Intergovernment transactions are eliminated. Transfers from one level of government to another are excluded from the expenditure of the paying government, but are included in the expenditure of the receiving government. The shares therefore reflect those transactions occurring between level of government and the general public.

Source: Statistics Canada, CANSIM matrix 3160, July 19, 1990.

22 percent to approximately 30 percent. The two most costly programs in social services are the Old Age Security program, with expenditures of approximately $16 billion in 1990, and unemployment insurance, with expenditures of about $12 billion. These two items accounted for about 20 percent of total budgetary expenditures. Transfer payments to the provinces (specific- plus general-purpose transfers) accounted for 15 percent of the total. If social services were disaggregated into the various social programs, the largest single expenditure item in the federal budget would be the interest on the public debt, whose share increased from about 8 percent in the late 1970s to more than 26 percent by 1990.

The most significant trend at the provincial level has been the increase in health care, social services, and education costs as a proportion of gross provincial expenditures (see Table 2–8). The major increases took place in the late 1950s and early 1960s, when the provinces placed priority on these functions. In 1990, these three functions

TABLE 2–6
Shares of Government Expenditure by Economic Classification for Selected Years 1926–1989

	Goods and services	Transfers to persons	Transfers to business	Gross capital formation	Interest on public debt	Other
			(percentage of total)			
1926	48.1	9.1	0.2	13.1	28.5	0.9
1929	47.3	9.3	0.5	18.5	23.7	0.7
1933	41.0	18.8	0.8	9.0	29.6	0.7
1939	47.0	18.8	1.4	12.3	22.8	0.6
1944	82.4	4.3	4.5	1.6	7.1	0.1
1950	47.3	25.1	1.8	12.2	13.3	0.4
1954	53.9	22.9	1.4	12.2	9.2	0.4
1962	49.7	22.2	3.3	14.4	10.0	0.5
1970	52.9	22.5	3.2	10.2	10.5	0.8
1975	48.6	24.9	6.9	9.2	9.6	0.9
1980	47.4	24.4	7.5	6.6	13.4	0.7
1982	45.3	25.1	7.2	6.1	15.6	0.7
1984	43.1	25.9	7.9	5.5	16.8	0.9
1986	43.0	26.4	6.1	5.4	18.1	1.0
1988	42.7	26.8	5.3	5.2	19.1	0.9
1989	42.3	26.5	4.9	5.3	20.1	0.9

Source: Statistics Canada, *National Income and Expenditure Accounts*, 1926–1974, cat. 13–531; and Department of Finance, *Quarterly Economic Review: Annual Reference Tables*, June 1990 (Ottawa), p. 89.

accounted for 62 percent of gross provincial expenditure. At the same time, expenditure on communications and transportation declined significantly, from almost 25 percent in 1954 to just over 5 percent in 1990. Another development has been the increase in the share of debt charges, from not quite 7 percent in the late 1970s to more than 12 percent in 1990.

At the municipal level, education expenditures have been most prominent; although their significance tended to decline in the 1970s, they still accounted for close to 40 percent of gross expenditure in the late 1980s (see Table 2–9). Communications and transportation functions have gradually declined in relative importance, as have expenditures for the protection of persons and property. At the same time, expenditures for recreation and culture and for environmental improvements have taken increasing shares of municipal budgets.

In summary, total government expenditure as a percentage of GDP has continued to increase. A trend to decentralization of expenditures appears to have been reversed in the early 1980s. During the last two decades, the most costly government functions at each level of government have been related to social services, particularly health care, welfare, and education, reflecting growing public demands for extended and improved services in these areas.

Demographic changes have played a major role in the trends in government spending. The baby boom of the 1940s and 1950s created a need for more educational facilities in the 1960s and 1970s. In recent decades, the ageing of the population and the gain in life expectancy have produced a high growth rate for the elderly — the proportion of Canadians age 65 years and over increased from 7.6 percent in 1961 to 10.6 percent by 1986. This demographic trend has already had a significant impact on the demand for health and social services and is expected to continue into the next century.

Changes in work and the work force have also influenced government spending. The increasing number of working couples and single-parent families has increased the need for daycare facilities. During the last few decades, rapidly changing technology has brought with it the need for a highly skilled and trained labour force and has thus increased demand for technical training facilities.

Major Government Expenditure Programs

As already noted, the public service programs that have mushroomed and proved the most costly since the Second World War have been in the areas of health care, social services, and education.[15] Expenditures on national defence, although falling in relative size, still take a significant proportion of the budget. Growing areas of concern, such as the environment, are beginning to absorb larger portions of government budgets, but their share is still relatively small.

The basic features of some of these costly areas are outlined in the following subsections.

Health-Care Services

Health care in Canada is provided under a system of public, universal medical insurance — medicare — that covers both hospital care and physicians' services. Health care comes primarily under the jurisdiction of the provincial governments, but the federal government provides financial assistance.

The medicare system evolved over a number of years. In 1957, the federal government, following the lead of Saskatchewan and British Columbia, passed the Hospital Insurance and Diagnostic Services Act, by which Ottawa agreed to contribute approximately 50 percent of hospital costs to provinces that introduced and administered a program by which hospital facilities and services would be provided free of charge to Canadians. In 1966, the Medical Care Act extended Ottawa's contribution to include these programs covering physicians' services and established conditions regarding the comprehensiveness, coverage, accessibility, portability, and administration of health-care services. Today, although health-care programs vary from province to province, all must adhere to the guidelines to qualify for the federal contribution.

The provincial governments grant hospitals annual budgets to provide their various services, including surgery, nursing care, therapeutic and rehabilitation services, and the training of health-care personnel. Most such personnel are salaried, although some, such as physicians, are paid on a fee-for-service basis. (The fees are negotiated between

TABLE 2–7
Shares of Federal Government Gross Expenditure[a] by Function for Selected Fiscal Years ending March 31 (financial management basis[b])

Expenditure function	1954[c]	1966	1978	1988	1990[d]
			(percentage of total)		
General services	4.4	3.9	5.6	4.4	4.8
Protection of persons and property	35.3	19.0	10.4	9.5	9.4
Transportation and communications	3.2	6.8	6.4	2.7	2.3
Health	1.1	5.6	6.8	5.5	5.2
Social services	21.8	22.1	34.0	33.1	28.8
Education	0.4	2.9	4.2	3.1	2.8
Resource conservation and industrial development	3.9	6.1	7.7	6.3	4.2
General-purpose transfers to other levels of government	7.4	4.9	7.6	5.9	6.7
Debt charges	10.6	12.7	7.7	20.0	26.3
Other	11.9	16.0	9.6	9.5	9.5
Total[e]	100.0	100.0	100.0	100.0	100.0
			($ million)		
Total amount	4 663	8 756	45 965	136 264	149 320

[a] Includes conditional transfers to other levels of government.
[b] Based on financial management statistics such as the public accounts, and therefore not comparable with the national accounts data in Tables 2–3 and 2–4.
[c] The figures for 1954 have been partially adjusted to the classifications of the revised series beginning 1966; although they are not strictly comparable with the revised series, the deviations are minor.
[d] Preliminary.
[e] Because of rounding, some totals are not exactly 100 percent.

Sources: Statistics Canada, *Financial Statistics of the Federal Governnment of Canada,* 1953 and 1954, Statistics Canada, *Federal Government Finance,* 1969 cat. 68–211; and CANSIM matrix 2778, July 19, 1990.

provincial health ministries or commissions and the appropriate professional associations or organizations.)

In addition to hospital care and physicians' services, the provinces provide a wide variety of public and community health programs. These include maternal and child health care, health programs in schools and homes, family planning, nutrition services, mental health services, alcohol and drug education and rehabilitation services, community sanitation, and health inspections.

TABLE 2–8
Provincial Government[a] Gross Expenditures[b] by Function for Selected Fiscal Years ending March 3l (financial management basis[c])

Expenditure function	1954[d]	1966	1978	1988	1990[e]
			(percentage of total)		
General services	3.6%	3.3%	6.6%	5.2%	5.3%
Protection of persons and property	5.5	3.6	3.5	3.2	3.4
Transportation and communications	24.9	17.5	7.7	4.9	5.1
Health	17.5	23.4	24.3	25.4	26.0
Social services	8.6	10.0	14.6	17.0	17.6
Education	16.2	25.6	23.6	19.3	18.8
Resource conservation and industrial development	7.0	5.2	5.1	5.6	5.1
General transfers to local governments	2.0	3.1	2.6	1.6	1.2
Debt charges	11.4	4.4	6.5	12.3	12.3
Other	3.2	2.5	5.6	5.5	5.2
Total	100.0	100.0	100.0	100.0	100.0
			($ million)		
Total amount	1 485	6 343	43 585	122 076	138 652

[a] Including governments of the Yukon and Northwest Territories.
[b] Includes all conditional transfers received from, and paid to, other levels of government.
[c] Based on financial management statistics, such as the public accounts, and therefore not comparable with the national accounts data in Table 2–3 and 2–4.
[d] The figures for 1954 have been partially adjusted to the classifications of the revised series beginning 1966; although they are not strictly comparable with the revised series, the deviations are minor.
[e] Preliminary.
[f] Because of rounding, some totals are not exactly 100 percent.

Source: Statistics Canada, *Financial Statistics of Provincial Governments*, 1953, cat. 68–207; Statistics Canada, *Provincial Government Finance, Revenue and Expenditure*, cat. 68–207; and CANSIM matrix 2751, July 19, 1990.

Approximately one-quarter of provincial budgets are allocated to health-care services. Of this amount, about 62 percent is directed to hospital care, 30 percent to medical care, 4 percent to preventive care, and 4 percent to other health-care services. Only two provinces, Alberta and British Columbia, levy premiums to help finance their share of the costs of medicare. The remaining provinces finance their programs from general revenues.

TABLE 2–9
Municipal Government Gross Expenditure[a] by Function for Selected Calander Years 1953–1989 (financial management basis[b])

Expenditure function	1953	1965	1978	1989
	(percentage of total)			
General services	6.5	5.9	4.6	5.3
Protection of persons and property	10.6	9.9	7.5	8.4
Transportation and communications	17.8	17.2	11.6	10.6
Health and social services	8.0	5.1	7.9	9.7
Education	34.8	35.3	42.1	39.9
Recreation and culture	3.2	4.5	5.9	6.3
Environment	5.8	5.7	8.6	8.7
Debt charges	6.0	7.6	7.2	6.5
Other	6.8	8.8	4.6	4.6
Total[c]	100.0	100.0	100.0	100.0
	($ million)			
Total amount	1 091	3 943	23 125	53 756

a Includes all transfers received from other levels of government.

b Based on financial management statistics and therefore not comparable with the national accounts data in Tables 2–3 and 2–4. The 1953 and 1965 figures are part of a different time series from that of the 1978 and 1989 figures and are therefore not strictly comparable with the latter; however, the two series do indicate the general trends over the 1953–90 period.

c Because of rounding, some totals are not exactly 100 percent.

Sources: Statistics Canada, *Historical Review of Financial Statistics of Governments in Canada, 1952–1962*, cat. 68–503; *Municipal Government Finance*, 1966, cat. 68–204; and CANSIM matrix 2764, July 19, 1990.

Social Services

The provision of various social or welfare services is shared by the three levels of government. Major programs include the Canada Assistance Plan (CAP), Old Age Security (OAS), unemployment insurance, and family allowances.

Canada Assistance Plan. The CAP is a comprehensive program developed by the federal and provincial governments in 1966 for the purpose of co-ordinating Ottawa's financial contributions to the provinces for a variety of provincially administered welfare programs. Today the programs cover aid to needy mothers and dependent children; provisions of child-care agencies, nursing homes, and care for the elderly; assistance to native people; young offenders programs; and assistance to the aged and the handicapped. The federal government's contribution covers 50 percent of the cost of whatever services a province provides under the plan. The growth of federal expenditure is, therefore, a direct consequence of the increase in eligible provincial spending, and spending has risen with the enhancement of social assistance support and the increase in the number of recipients. For the fiscal year 1990/1, Ottawa's CAP contributions totalled almost $6 billion.

Old Age Security. Government in Canada first paid old age pensions in 1927, under a program administered by the provinces with financial contributions from the federal government. In 1951, the federal government passed the Old Age Security Act, which provided for pensions to people over 70 years of age, paid and administered by the federal government. Subsequent amendments to the act lowered the age eligibility to 65 years and introduced an inflation-adjustment factor. By 1990, the basic OAS pension for a 65-year-old was more than $340 per month.

In 1967, the federal government also introduced a supplement to the OAS payment to assist pensioners in need; this guaranteed income supplement (GIS) was later augmented by a spouse's allowance. The GIS payment is inflation-adjusted and geared to income. In 1990, it was approximately $400 for a single pensioner and more than $250 for a married person whose spouse also received OAS. The supplement was eliminated when a married couple's income exceeded $12 000.

The ageing of the population and the full indexation of benefits to inflation have made OAS the largest and fastest-growing component of federal government spending. Benefits are increased four times a year to reflect changes in the consumer price index. About 3 million elderly persons — approximately 8 percent of the population — received OAS benefits in 1990/1.

The OAS pension itself is universal and independent of the level of income. In 1989, however, the government began to phase into its income tax structure a social benefits repayment program to recapture all OAS payments from recipients whose total net income exceeds $50 000. This "clawback" should reduce the cost of the program, which was estimated to total $17.6 billion in 1990/1.

Unemployment Insurance. Unemployment insurance provides government-paid benefits to workers during periods when they are unemployed. The program was first introduced in 1941, prompted by the experience of high unemployment during the Depression and following a constitutional amendment that gave the federal government jurisdiction over unemployment insurance.

The basic features of the unemployment insurance program consist of financing based on premiums paid by employers and employees, benefits based on insurable earnings, and eligibility based on length of period employed and regional unemployment rates. For 1990, the premiums amounted to 2.25 percent of insurable earnings (up to a ceiling) for employees and 3.15 percent for employers. Effective July 1, 1991 the premiums were scheduled to increase to 2.80 percent and 3.92 percent on employees and employers respectively. These contributions were expected to yield more than $12 billion in 1990/1 or approximately 10 percent of total federal budgetary revenues. The payment of benefits accounted for more than one-third of direct payments to individuals.

To receive benefits, a worker must have ten to fourteen weeks of insurable employment, with the exact amount depending on the region's unemployment rate. For every week of insurable employment, a claimant receives one week of benefit, to a maximum of twenty-five weeks. Extended and regional-based benefits beyond twenty-five weeks consist of one week of benefit for every two weeks of insurable employment. The weekly benefits are 60 percent of insurable earnings with a ceiling on the amount that can be received in one week. Claimants are required to wait two weeks before receiving benefits and may receive benefits for a maximum of fifty weeks. Penalties in the form of longer waiting periods and lower benefits are imposed on workers who quit their jobs without just cause.

Spending on unemployment insurance benefits has continued to grow over the years, reflecting increases in average benefits indexed to the growth in average wages.

Family Allowances. In 1945, the federal government introduced the family allowance program, providing a monthly payment to families for every child under age 16 who was attending school. In 1974 the age limit was increased to 18 years. In 1990, the family allowance was $33.33 per child per month, except in Quebec and Alberta, which have arranged to vary payments with the age of the child.

Expenditures for the family allowance program were estimated at $2.7 billion for 1990/1. Almost 4 million households received payments.

The family allowance program was introduced as an income-maintenance program for families with children, although it was made universal, to be paid to families irrespective of income level. Recent changes in the personal income tax, however, have resulted in a recapture through taxing payments made to middle- and upper-income families.

Education

The provinces are constitutionally vested with jurisdiction over education. Elementary and secondary education is administered by local school boards, which are financed by property taxes and provincial grants (except in Prince Edward Island, New Brunswick and Quebec, where all financing is from provincial revenues). Private schools, many of them under religious auspices, are provided with tax support or grants by provincial governments, each province having devised its own method of assistance to these schools.

Postsecondary education (and vocational training) are financed through a combination of tuition fees, provincial grants, and federal contributions. The federal contributions are part of the federal/provincial fiscal arrangements and consist of tax transfer points and cash payments. Each postsecondary educational institution operates as an autonomous entity with its own administration.

In 1988/9, the provinces spent more than $40 billion on education, 63 percent of which was for elementary and secondary education. Of the total amount spent on education, 17 percent came from local taxes, 10 percent from the federal government, and 8 percent from private sources.

National Defence

National defence, which is a federal responsibility, involves the protection of Canadian sovereignty, continental defence in co-operation with the United States (the North Atlantic Alliance), commitments to defend Europe through the North Atlantic Treaty Organization, and various international peacekeeping activities.

Defence expenditures for the fiscal year 1990/1 were estimated at approximately $12 billion or less than 10 percent of total budgetary expenditure. About one-quarter of defence spending is allocated to capital acquisitions; the remainder is primarily for personnel costs, supplies, and the operation of defence bases.

During the 1980s, the government set out to refurbish Canada's defence capabilities. In a 1987 white paper, it announced a major modernization program including a fleet of nuclear submarines, a new fleet of antisubmarine patrol planes, additional fighter-interceptor aircraft, new all-terrain vehicles and battle tanks for the land forces, and modernization of the armed forces' communications systems. The continued high annual budgetary deficit, however, forced scaling back of these plans. In 1989 and 1990, a number of announced programs were cancelled for an estimated savings of $3.4 billion over a five-year period, and the government announced that the growth in defence spending would be limited to 5 percent a year.[16]

Environmental and Conservation Programs

Public concern about the environment in recent years has prompted governments to adopt stronger measures to protect it, primarily by regulating pollution and waste disposal. The federal government, for example, has established national standards regarding the use of toxic chemicals and their transport and passed legislation governing pollution emissions, the use of leaded fuel, and the use of ozone-depleting substances. The Department of the Environment in 1990 budgeted almost $0.5 billion for its environmental and conservation programs. In the same year, provincial and municipal environmental budgets totalled more than $6 billion, an increase from about $1.5 billion in 1975, to cover regulatory activities as well as municipal sewage treatment, waste disposal, and water purification.

Growing public concern regarding waste disposal and other environmental hazards will likely result in an increase in the proportion of budgetary expenditures allocated to environmental protection in the future.

ENDNOTES

1. Some of these factors are discussed in R.A. Musgrave, *Fiscal Systems* (New Haven, Conn.: Yale University Press, 1969) ch. 3; and in Thomas E. Borcherding, ed., *Budgets and Bureaucrats: The Source of Government Growth,* (Durham, NC: Duke University Press, 1977). A discussion of factors influencing government expenditure growth in Canada is presented in Richard M. Bird, *The Growth of Government Spending in Canada,* Tax Paper no. 51 (Toronto: Canadian Tax Foundation, 1970); and in Donald J. Savoie, *The Politics of Public Spending in Canada* (Toronto: University of Toronto Press, 1990).

2. A number of studies compare the efficiency and productivity of the public and private sectors for areas in which enterprises operate in both sectors and so offer opportunity for a meaningful comparison. For example, in the case of two Australian airlines, similar in every respect, the private one was found to be twice as efficient as the public one in terms of freight and mail, 22 percent more efficient in terms of passengers, and 13 percent more efficient in terms of revenue per employee. For more information on this study and others comparing the public and private sectors, see Borcherding, ed., *Budgets and Bureaucrats*, ch. 4 and 6.

3. In 1987/8, federal budgetary funding for Crown corporations totalled more than $5 billion, including a $536 million subsidy to VIA Rail. In addition, the federal government had almost $24 billion outstanding in accumulated loans to and investments in Crown corporations.

4. For example, see Borcherding, ed., *Budgets and Bureaucrats*; and W.N. Niskanen, *Bureaucracy and Representative Government* (Chicago: Aldine-Atherton Press, 1971). A survey of some collective choice and self-interest theories can be found in D.G. Hartle, *A Theory of the Expenditure Budgetary Process* (Toronto: University of Toronto Press, 1977), ch. 1 and 2.

5. See Bernard P. Herber, *Modern Public Finance*, 5th ed. (Homewood, Ill.: Richard D. Irwin, 1983), ch. 16; and Borcherding, ed., *Budgets and Bureaucrats.*

6. Musgrave, *Fiscal Systems*, ch. 4.

7. See Musgrave; Ibid.; Bird, *The Growth of Government Spending in Canada*; and Herber, *Modern Public Finance.*

8. See Bird, *The Growth of Government Spending in Canada*, pp. 107–17.

9. C. Clark, "Public Finance and Changes in the Value of Money," *Economic Journal*, December 1945. Clark argued that once the critical limit was exceeded, the high taxes would result in disincentives to save, work and invest and lead to inflation. The reduction in supply of goods and services and the inflation would put pressure on governments to reduce their spending and scale back taxes. Clark's theory produced considerable controversy and criticism.

10. See M. Hochstein, "Tax Ethics: Social Values and Noncompliance," *Public Opinion*, February/March 1985.

11. The local authorities declared Elstow a "GST-free zone" and announced the municipal government would not charge the 7 percent tax on sewers, water, garbage collection, or licences and permits or the tax on equipment and other purchases. *Globe and Mail*, September 21, 1990.

12. For an analysis of tax and expenditure limitations in the United States, see H. Ladd and T. Tideman, eds., *Tax and Expenditure Limitations*, (Washington, DC,: The Urban Institute Press, 1981); and J. Rose, ed., *Tax and Expenditure Limitations: How to Implement and Live within Them* (New Jersey, Rutgers University: Center for Urban Research Policy, 1982).

13. A detailed study of government expenditure in Canada before 1967 is contained in Bird, *The Growth of Government Spending in Canada*; R.M., Bird, *Financing Canadian Government: A Quantitive Overview* (Toronto: Canadian Tax Foundation, 1979);

and J. Harvey Perry, *A Fiscal History of Canada — The Postwar Years*, Tax Paper no. 85 (Toronto: Canadian Tax Foundation, 1989).

14. An outline of earlier trends in government expenditure growth in the United States and other countries of the Organization for Economic Co-operation and Development is contained in G. Warren Nutter, *Growth of Governments in the West* (Washington, DC: American Enterprise Institute, 1978).

15. Details on various federal, provincial, and municipal expenditure programs, including the amounts spent on them, are presented in Canadian Tax Foundation, *The National Finances* (Toronto: CTF, various years); and *Provincial and Municipal Finances*, (Toronto: CTF, various years).

16. Canada, Department of Finance, *Budget*, February 20, 1990 (Ottawa), p. 27.

APPENDIX TO CHAPTER 2

CROWN CORPORATIONS

Crown corporations are important in the infrastructure of the Canadian economy. Many exert a significant influence in the sector in which they operate. The activities of Crown corporations range from regulatory duties performed by a small commission or board to large-scale commercial and financial operations under an elaborate corporate structure. They either compete with similar operations in the private sector or monopolize activities that might otherwise be carried out in the private sector.

The Range and Extent of Crown Corporations

In 1982, the Auditor General of Canada identified 306 corporations in which the federal government was whole or part owner.[1] These Crown corporations had assets of approximately $67 billion, spent more than $30 billion annually, and employed more than 263 000 people.

At the federal level alone, Statistics Canada lists more than 40 government enterprises engaged primarily in commercial or industrial activities.[2] In 1986, they recorded assets valued at about $6.10 billion. (During the 1980s, the total assets of federal enterprises had fallen as a number of them, including Air Canada, were privatized.) Expenditures totalled $26.9 billion and revenues $26.5 billion; more than $21 billion of revenue represented sales of goods and services and $1.6 billion consisted of federal government subsidies.

At the provincial level, Statistics Canada identifies approximately 130 government-owned enterprises engaged in commercial or industrial activities. In 1986, these enterprises had assets of $146 billion of which $85 billion was in electric power, $42 billion in finance and real estate, and $9 billion in transportation and communications. Total income was $36.7 billion and total expenses were $33.7 billion, with a recorded profit of $3 billion. Employment in provincial and territorial enterprises totalled more than 152 000 workers.[3]

Most Crown corporations are wholly owned by the government; shares issued are owned by the Crown and the directors of the corporation are appointed by the Governor in Council. Some Crown corporations are, however, owned jointly by the government and private interests. An example is Telesat Canada, a corporation responsible for providing satellite communications services; it is owned half by the federal government and half by the country's major telephone companies.

Many Crown corporations were established for the purpose of achieving government policy objectives. Air Canada (formerly Trans-Canada Air-Lines) and Canadian National Railway were used to provide transcontinental transportation services to help unify the country. The Canadian Broadcasting Corporation (CBC) has a mandate to express and promote the Canadian identity. The Canada Mortgage and Housing Corporation administers loans, grants, and subsidies to help improve housing for

Canadians. Atomic Energy of Canada Ltd. was created in 1952 to develop domestic uses of atomic energy. In 1976, Petro-Canada Ltd. was established as a major instrument of the federal government's National Energy Program with a mandate of actively engaging in oil and gas exploration, development, and marketing to ensure Canadians an adequate and continuous supply of oil and gas.[4]

At the provincial level, Crown corporations are found in a large number of economic sectors including banking and finance, forest development and manufacturing, automobile insurance, hotels and tourism, housing, industrial development, liquor control and marketing, lotteries, power utilities, transportation, communications, and oil and gas production and distribution.

In addition to the Crown corporations that provide goods and services directly to the public, a number provide regulatory services and exert a major impact on markets in the private sector. These include the federal-level marketing and price stabilization boards, such as the Canadian Wheat Board, the Canadian Dairy Commission, and the Agricultural Stabilization Board, and similar agencies at the provincial level.

Crown corporations of a commercial or industrial nature are expected to operate like firms in the private sector. Those that produce and sell goods and services, such as Canadian National Railways and Canada Post Corporation at the federal level and the public utility corporations at the provincial and municipal level, are expected to be self-financing and even generate profits. Profitable Crown corporations may be required to return some of their income to the government as a shareholder. Deficits, on the other hand, may be financed by a parliamentary appropriation. Many corporations rely heavily on government funding, in the form of appropriations or of loans, investments, and advances. In the late 1980s, VIA Rail received annual government funding of more than $500 million, while the CBC received annual appropriations of almost $1 billion.

The reasons for providing certain services and conducting specific operations through a Crown corporation, rather than through a regular ministerial department, are varied and vague. It is argued that the corporation is the most appropriate organizational form for undertaking government activities of a commercial nature because it allegedly combines public accountability with business efficiency. The rationale for conferring corporate status on administrative or regulatory agencies, however, has never been clearly enunciated, and any advantages derived from incorporation are not readily apparent.

Control over Crown Corporations

All Crown corporations in Canada are subject to some form of executive control and influence, as well as a degree of legislative control. Each corporation is responsible to a minister to whom it reports and who represents it in the legislature.

Partly because of the varied nature of the functions they perform, Canadian Crown corporations have acquired a considerable degree of diversity in form and structure. The federal Financial Administration Act, which controls most Crown corporations, groups them into three classes — department, agency, and proprietary corporations — primarily on the extent of financial autonomy and the nature of the function performed.

Departmental corporations are Crown corporations responsible for administrative, supervisory, or regulatory services of a governmental nature. They are generally treated similarly to a government department, and their financial transactions are accounted for as budgetary revenues and expenditures. Examples are the Agricultural Stabilization Board, the National Gallery of Canada, and the Atomic Energy Control Board.

Agency corporations are generally responsible for the management of trading and service operations and procurement and construction activities. Their budgets are separate from the general government budget but must be approved by the appropriate minister, the President of the Treasury Board, and Parliament. The methods of financing include parliamentary appropriations, statutory grants, and operational income. Included in this group of corporations are the Canadian Mint, Telefilm Canada, and Defence Construction Ltd.

Proprietary corporations enjoy the most autonomy of the three kinds of Crown corporations. They are not closely associated with government departments, nor do they act as agents for them, and they have boards of directors chosen from the business community. They manage financial, commercial, or industrial activities, generally operate in a competitive environment, and are normally expected to finance themselves from the operating revenues. Proprietary corporations are required to submit their capital budgets to the government for approval and to provide summaries of corporate plans and capital budgets to Parliament, along with their annual reports. Examples are the CBC, Canadian National, and the Central Mortgage and Housing Corporation.

Several Crown corporations, such as the Bank of Canada, the Canadian Wheat Board, and the Canada Council, do not belong to any of these three categories. They are exempt from the provisions of the Financial Administration Act and operate under their own statutes. They are, in general, treated like the proprietary corporations.

All Crown corporations are required to submit annual reports to the minister to whom they are responsible, who in turn is required to present it to Parliament. The corporations are also subject to a post-audit, either by the auditor general or an outside auditor.

Capital required by Crown corporations may be provided by loans and advances from the government, by parliamentary appropriations from general revenue, or by borrowing on the capital market. Since Crown corporations are ultimately the responsibility of the government, all must submit their capital budgets to the cabinet for approval, regardless of the method used to finance them. This process provides the government an opportunity to review and influence their operations and decisions.

In his 1982 report, however, Auditor General Kenneth Dye expressed serious concern about how well the government monitors and controls Crown corporations. Dye pointed out that, with their extensive and variable operations, these corporations have a major impact on the public and the economy: "A sub-government has been created to fulfill some of the social and economic aims of Government," but without adequate accountability to Parliament.[5] The Auditor General recommended legislation for improved parliamentary accountability and control of government expenditures and activities through the corporate form. In response, the federal government amended the Financial Administration Act in 1984 to bring Crown corporations under more effective executive and legislative control.[6] A major change was the introduction of the requirement that all Crown corporations submit multiyear corporate plans annually for cabinet approval. These plans provide government with the basis for reviewing and approving corporate objectives and strategies and a benchmark for assessing subsequent performance.

Privatization

During the 1980s, the Canadian government began to transfer ownership and control of some federal Crown corporations to the private sector in a program known as privatization. This divesture trend was also evident in the provinces and in Western Europe and Great Britain. The main justification put forward was the desire to increase efficiency, competitiveness, and productivity. Many government-owned corporations that engaged in commercial and industrial activities were either monopolies or operated in direct competition with companies in the private sector. Some had been established as instruments of government policy, designed to achieve specific objectives, and were deemed no longer required. Furthermore, certain corporations remained unprofitable, and government subsidization was a drain on government finances, contributing to the large deficits that were being incurred during the 1980s.

Privatization at the federal level became a major element in the new Conservative government's agenda for economic renewal announced in 1985. In the words of the government:

> Selling corporate interests will have a number of benefits. It will reduce the size of government in the economy and make room for private sector initiatives; it will improve market efficiency and the allocation of resources; it will improve firm efficiency through market discipline and by reducing political and bureaucratic impediments[7]

The government announced plans to review its Crown corporations and their operations and to privatize those for which there was no convincing public policy reason for retaining in the public sector.

In 1986, the Office of Privatization and Regulatory Affairs was established to oversee the privatization process (along with a program of reforming and streamlining government regulatory activities). By 1989, the government had sold all or part of sixteen Crown corporations including Air Canada (1989), Canadair Ltd. (1986), de Havilland Aircraft of Canada Ltd. (1986), Canada Development Corporation (1987), Canadian Arsenals Ltd. (1986), Teleglobe Canada (1987), and Northern Transportation Ltd. (1985). In 1990, in a continuation of its privatization program, the government announced plans to sell the government-owned portion of Telesat Canada and to privatize Petro-Canada.

The provincial governments followed suit. During the 1980s, they privatized some thirty major government-owned companies, including relatively large commercial and industrial entities such as Québécair, Saskatchewan Oil and Gas, Pacific Western Airlines (Alberta), and various divisions of BC Hydro. The corporations sold, like those at the federal level, were primarily those engaged in activities in competition with the private sector.

In addition to sales, both the federal and provincial governments dissolved a number of Crown corporations that no longer provided important services and amalgamated others whose services overlapped.

The privatization process generally took two forms: the sale of shares in the Crown corporation to the public or the direct sale of the corporation to a private company. An example of the former was the privatization of Air Canada; shares were sold to the public with proceeds totalling more than $700 million. Using the latter process, Canadair was sold to Bombardier Inc., de Havilland to Boeing Commercial Airplane Co., and Teleglobe Canada to Memotec Data Inc. Most of the Crown corporations privatized by the provincial governments were sold directly to existing companies in the private sector.

It is too early to determine the success of privatization in terms of the objectives of increased efficiency and productivity of the corporations. Air Canada continued its restructuring and cost-cutting process as well as the establishment of a feeder-line network begun earlier in competition with its rival, Canadian International Airlines; it recorded profits of more than $1 per share in both 1989 and 1990. De Havilland, a deficit-ridden operation under the federal government, was expected to benefit from the marketing skills of Boeing, one of the world's largest aircraft manufacturers, and find new markets for its newly developed Dash-8 aircraft. Recently, however, Boeing has indicated an intention of selling de Havilland. Canadair, into which the federal government had pumped more than $2 billion to help to erase its debt and provide it with operating capital, embarked on a venturesome program to construct the world's first small commercial jet airliner.

In Europe, where privatization began earlier than in Canada, it is also difficult to assess the impact of privatization on the economic efficiency of the corporations involved.[8] As in Canada, it was argued that, freed of ponderous bureaucracy, former government-owned companies could be expected to engage in more dynamic and aggressive cost-cutting and marketing operations and would be able to take advantage of more flexibility in reorganizing and streamlining operations. The changes were expected to produce increased productivity, lower costs, increased competitiveness, and expansion into new markets.

ENDNOTES

1. Canada, *Report of the Auditor General of Canada to the House of Commons, Fiscal Year Ended 31 March 1982* (Ottawa: Supply and Services Canada, 1982), p. 52.

2. Statistics Canada defines government enterprise as "organizations created or acquired and owned by government to sell goods or services on the open market and whose principal revenues derive from such sales." Statistics Canada, *Federal Government Enterprise Finance, 1986*, cat. 61–203.

   For a summary of the financial statements of the federal government enterprises, see Canada, *Public Accounts of Canada*, vol. 2, *Annual Report to Parliament on Crown Corporations and Other Corporate Interests of Canada, 1989*, (Ottawa: Supply and Services Canada, 1989).

3. Statistics Canada, *Provincial Government Enterprises Finance, 1986*, cat. 61–204.

4. Statistics Canada, *Federal Government Enterprise Finance, 1986*, cat. 61–203.

5. Canada, *Report of the Auditor General. . . 1982*, p. 9.

6. The essence of the 1984 changes in the Financial Administration Act dealing with Crown corporations is analyzed in Canada, *Report of the Auditor General of Canada to the House of Commons for the Fiscal Year Ended 31 March 1989*, (Ottawa: Supply and Services Canada, 1989), ch. 5.

7. Canada, Department of Finance, *Budget Papers*, May 23, 1985 (Ottawa), p. 27.

8. See R. Hemming and A. Mansoor, *Privatization and Public Enterprises* (Washington, DC: International Monetary Fund, 1988).

CHAPTER 3

BUDGETING AND FINANCIAL MANAGEMENT

Decision-making in government can be represented as a pyramid or hierarchy of responsibility. The higher the position of the decision-maker in this pyramid, the more general but more basic are the decisions made. At the upper levels, decisions must be made about the functions and policies of government, while the lower levels of administration usually implement policies.

In the Canadian government, the cabinet is responsible for establishing priorities among the major economic and social functions of government and for determining policy in these areas. The cabinet collectively establishes priorities in principle, defines broad objectives, and sets down the basic policies. It is the function of the individual ministries or departments to develop the objectives in detail, to determine alternative means by which the objectives may be achieved, to choose the most efficient or effective course of action, and to implement and administer the resulting programs. Decisions are therefore required at various stages of implementation and levels of administration. This decision-making process is a lengthy and complex one in which the dividing line between politics and administration may be rather vague. The elected representatives or politicians are at the pinnacle of the decision-making pyramid and bear the ultimate responsibility for government policy and action, but their policies may be initiated or greatly influenced by lower-level administrators through the advice and information they provide.

Apart from major policy decisions, many decisions on government activity are made during the formulation of the government budget. The budget document is a reflection of decisions made and, in this sense, the decision-making process and the budgetary process are synonymous.

The budget, simply defined, is a detailed statement of the government's expected revenues and planned expenditures. More specifically, it is the plan of operations prepared by the cabinet for approval by the House of Commons, showing the government's objectives, programs and activities, and purchases for the coming fiscal year. The budget serves the executive as a plan of action; it serves the legislature as a means of control over the executive and it serves administrators in the internal management of their respective departments.

The Financial Structure of the Canadian Government

The financial structure of the federal government of Canada rests on a constitutional and statutory framework dating back to the Constitution Act, 1867 (formerly titled the British North America Act, 1867). This act gave constitutional foundation to the principles of public financing basic to responsible government; subsequent legislation established necessary financial administrative machinery and procedures. Many of the financial practices that were adopted had been developed in the pre-Confederation provinces and were simply carried forward in the new federal structure. Frequent revisions were required in both the financial structure and procedures over time to keep pace with changing conditions and the ever-increasing scale of government operations. Today, the basic statutory financial structure is governed by the Financial Administration Act, the Auditor General Act, and the Government Reorganization Act and is supplemented by arrangements established through cabinet decisions. This structure is illustrated in Figure 3–1.

Parliament is supreme in the financial structure of the government, and ultimate control of the public purse rests with that body. It is responsible for examining and approving government expenditures and tax changes and for holding the executive to account for the use of public funds. All tax revenues must be placed in a central fund, the Consolidated Revenue Fund, and no money can be expended from this fund unless its appropriation is authorized by Parliament.

The cabinet is responsible for preparing the budget and presenting it to Parliament. Much of this work is performed through a system of cabinet committees, including the Priorities and Planning Committee, the Expenditure Review Committee, the Treasury Board, and policy committees.

The Priorities and Planning Committee (P & P) comprises the Prime Minister as chairperson, the Minister of Finance, the President of the Treasury Board, and several other ministers for a total of approximately twenty members. Supported by the Treasury Board secretariat, this committee has the important function of determining the government's overall agenda and major policies. It develops broad policy objectives, assigns priority rankings to these objectives, and determines the resources to be directed toward each. All of the cabinet committees, with the exception of Treasury Board, report to the P & P Committee. It is the only group other than the Treasury Board mandated to authorize expenditures.

The Expenditure Review Committee (ERC) consists of eight members, including the Minister of Finance and the President of the Treasury Board, and is chaired by the Prime Minister. A relatively new committee (established in early 1989), it reviews all government expenditures to ensure that they are directed to the priorities established by the P & P Committee and are kept within the limits set. The ERC was established during a period of continued high government budgetary deficits and mandated to exercise expenditure control to contribute to deficit reduction. Ministers are required to appear before the committee to justify the expenditure requests of their departments, and it can decree that programs and departmental personnel positions be reduced or eliminated. The ERC secretariat is staffed largely from the Department of Finance.

The Operations Committee reviews the government's weekly agenda to ensure co-ordination in responding to issues and developing new policies. It is basically an executive management committee that examines issues and policy questions, steers them to the P & P committee, and co-ordinates the various cabinet policy committees; in essence, it guards access to the P & P Committee. Chaired by the Deputy Prime Minister on behalf of the Prime Minister, it is composed of the Minister of Finance, the President of the Treasury Board, and seven other senior cabinet ministers.

FIGURE 3–1
Financial Structure of the Federal Government

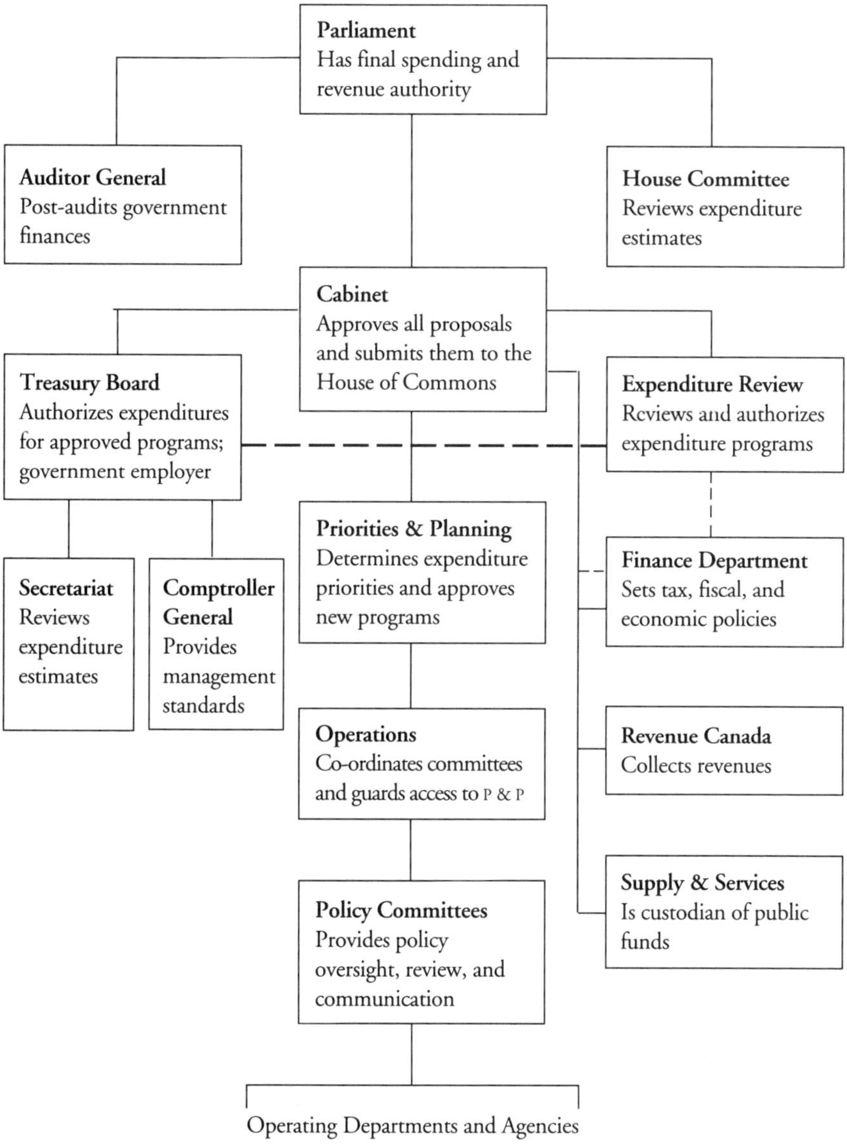

Source: Canada, Treasury Board; and Office of the Prime Minister, *Release*, January 30, 1989.

Several policy committees within the cabinet committee system affect finance in that they are responsible for reviewing and co-ordinating policies in their respective areas of jurisdiction, although they have no power to authorize expenditure. They include the Economic Policy Committee, which focusses on policies to help industry become more competitive; the Human Resources, Income Support and Health Committee, which works on the development of policies and programs to ensure adequate support for less fortunate Canadians and safeguards for the health of citizens; the Communications Committee; the Environment Committee; and the Foreign and Defence Policy Committee. These policy committees have eight to twelve members each.

The Treasury Board is a statutory committee of the Privy Council. Composed of the President of the Treasury Board, the Minister of Finance, and four other cabinet ministers, it has legal responsibility for the authorization of expenditures and is generally responsible for allocating resources for approved policies and programs. More specifically, it is responsible for detailed review and analysis of departmental expenditure estimates prior to their submission to Parliament. The board also assists the P & P Committee and the ERC by providing information on the resource implications of policy and program proposals. In addition, the board is responsible for personnel policy, for collective bargaining in the public service, and for promoting efficiency in government administration. Through the Office of Comptroller General, the board seeks to develop and maintain administrative and management systems and techniques to facilitate planning, financial control, and program evaluation.

The Minister of Finance and the Finance Department play a crucial role in the budgetary process. The minister is an active participant in the cabinet committee system and is responsible for presenting the government's budget to the House of Commons. The department provides information and advice on economic affairs and on the financial implications of alternative policies, forecasts economic conditions and anticipated revenues, and is responsible for determining tax policy and tax changes and the effects of these changes on revenues and on economic activity.

Two other departments involved in the budgetary process are Supply and Services Canada and National Revenue Canada. As the Receiver General for Canada, in charge of the Consolidated Revenue Fund, the Minister of Supply and Services is the custodian of public funds. The department is responsible for the release of funds to operating departments, following appropriation by Parliament, and for the compilation and maintenance of the public accounts of Canada. Administration and interpretation of tax legislation is the responsibility of National Revenue Canada, which also collects all tax proceeds for the government and deposits them in the Consolidated Revenue Fund.

An agency with a major function in the budgetary process is the Office of the Auditor General. The Auditor General is an agent of the House of Commons, responsible directly to the House and charged with auditing government expenditures and revenue collections. This agent's traditional role as the financial watchdog of Parliament has been to ensure that public funds are fully accounted for and expended in accordance with the wishes of the legislature. In 1977, the Auditor General Act extended the auditor's function to making observations on the economy, efficiency, and effectiveness of government expenditures. (In regard to effectiveness, however, the Auditor General is restricted to assessing procedures established within departments to measure and report on the effectiveness of programs. This restriction prevents the auditor from evaluating policy or determining whether a particular policy or program is justified, thereby retaining the traditional political neutrality of the office and protecting it from becoming involved in partisan political debate.)

The Budgetary Process

The federal budgetary process combines traditional elements basic to the parliamentary system of government with historical practices and elements of theoretical budgetary systems. Changes over time have frequently consisted of incorporating into the process new developments in budget theory in attempts to promote efficiency in decision-making and financial management. The 1960s witnessed the introduction of the Planning-Programming-Budgeting System (PPBS), which emphasized planning and performance evaluation in government budgeting. In 1979, the introduction of the Policy and Expenditure Management System (PEMS) and the concept of "expenditure envelopes" attempted to address some of the practical problems encountered in the expenditure-planning phase of PPBS. Developments in the 1980s led to replacement of the envelope feature with a new cabinet committee structure designed for more centralized authority over government expenditures. (Features of these various budgetary and management systems and their interrelation are discussed in the appendix to this chapter.)

The most significant changes in the budgetary process came with the introduction of PPBS, whose theory emphasizes long-term planning in government and the identification of objectives and outputs, the examination of alternative means of achieving objectives, the presentation of expenditures in the form of clearly defined programs and activities, the continuous review of ongoing programs, and quantitative techniques for evaluating programs and measuring performance. Many of these features remain the basis of the current budget system, as is evident in the following description.[1]

The Budget Cycle

The Canadian government's fiscal—budget—year covers the period April 1 to March 31. The budget, however, is a rolling, multiyear expenditure plan, and the fiscal year is just one period in it. Budgeting in government, a series of annually repeated stages, involves establishment and annual updating of a long-term fiscal plan; determination of expenditure directions and priorities and of expenditure and revenue levels by the cabinet and cabinet committees; multiyear planning by departments of their expenditure programs; review and approval of these programs by the Expenditure Review Committee and the Treasury Board; preparation of detailed expenditure estimates for the fiscal year by departments and review by the Treasury Board; authorization and appropriation of expenditures by Parliament; determination of revenues, tax proposals, and their implications by the Finance Department; administration of spending and revenue collection; and finally an independent audit for the House of Commons by the Auditor General. Table 3–1 details the cycle, beginning with the establishment of the fiscal plan each January.

TABLE 3–1
The Budgeting Cycle for the Fiscal Year
April 1, 1989 to March 31, 1990

1988	
January	Fiscal plan P&P sets priorities
February–March	Departments prepare strategic overviews and operational plans
April	Treasury Board reviews department overviews and operational plans
May	Strategic overviews examined by Policy Committee
June	Treasury Board approves operational plans, with directions to departments
July	Possible changes in the fiscal plan by P&P
August–September	Departments prepare main estimates within context of the fiscal plan, overviews and operational plans
October–November	Treasury Board reviews main estimates
December	ERC and P&P review and approve budgetary expenditures
1989	
February	Main estimates tabled in house and referred to standing committees House votes interim supply
February	Budget Speech
April–June	Main estimates voted by Parliament (appropritation acts)
October–December	Preparation, review, and approval of supplemenatry estimates
1990	
January–March	Submission of approval of final supplementary estimates
April–October	Auditor General audits 1989–90 expenditures and prepares Auditor General's Report
November–December	Public Accounts Committee examines public accounts and Auditor General's Report

Source: Canada, Treasury Board, Ottawa.

Budget Preparation

The preparation of the budget begins with establishing a long-term fiscal plan, followed by the department's drawing up of strategic overviews and multiyear operational plans and making their main expenditure estimates for the coming fiscal year.

The Fiscal Plan. The fiscal plan is a principal planning document in which the government identifies and plans its expenditures over a multiyear period, reviews its projections on the state of the economy, and examines revenue projections and the forecast budget balance. The responsibility for developing the fiscal plan rests with the cabinet's Priorities and Planning Committee. In planning expenditure, P & P determines overall priorities among government functions or policy sectors; these priorities then serve as the basis for weighing new policy proposals. If a function — transportation, for example — is identified as having priority, it will be eligible for increased funding.

The fiscal plan includes projections of anticipated revenues and of expenditures for specific functions for a five-year period, starting with the current fiscal year. Updated and extended by twelve months each year, the fiscal plan in essence becomes a rolling five-year plan. Highlights of the plan are tabled in the House of Commons when the Minister of Finance presents the budget; however, it is not subject to formal approval by Parliament nor does it become part of the spending authority granted by that body.

The responsibility for authorizing spending on new programs in the priority areas designated by P & P rests with the Expenditure Review Committee (ERC), which reviews proposed departmental expenditures in detail and directs spending to the priority areas. Policy areas or departments targeted for expenditure restraint or reduction are carefully examined, and spending on specific programs may be limited, reduced, or cancelled. Departmental ministers are required to appear before the ERC to justify their expenditure requests. (Previously, the scrutiny of new expenditure proposals was conducted by the Treasury Board. The establishment of the ERC relieved the board of this function to some degree, so it has been able to focus better on the more routine work of expenditure review (described later).

The work of the P & P Committee and the ERC were evident in the expenditure controls and allocations announced by Finance Minister Michael Wilson in his February 1990 budget speech. As part of the government's continued efforts to reduce its large annual deficits, the minister introduced an expenditure control plan to the fiscal plan. This initiative identified five categories of programs in terms of the degrees of expenditure control to which they are to be subjected: (1) programs exempt from reductions (major transfer payments to persons); (2) programs constrained to a 5 percent annual growth for two years; (3) programs frozen for two years; (4) programs reduced; and (5) programs and projects eliminated. The minister estimated that the controls imposed through this plan would yield savings totalling almost $20 billion over a five-year period.[2]

Strategic Overviews and Operational Plans. On the basis of the expenditure framework established by the fiscal plan, each department prepares annually a multiyear strategic overview and a multiyear operational plan. The overview is a summary statement of the department's objectives, alternative strategies for pursuing them, proposed changes to existing programs, and a summary of program evaluations. Each overview is submitted to the appropriate cabinet policy committee, which examines and co-ordinates policy proposals and strategies within its area of jurisdiction. These committees possess no spending authority and cannot approve new spending proposals.

The details of a department's strategic overview appear in its multiyear operational plan. This plan provides information on the department's operations: how each program and activity contribute to its objectives; the benefits (quantified where possible) and costs of each program and activity for each year; the methods used to evaluate efficiency and effectiveness of operations; and historical and projected trends of the level of program costs and benefits. Each department's plan, updated annually and extended by one year, shows expenditure estimates for the current year, the new year, and two additional years. Following review and approval of the operational plan by the Treasury Board, the department uses the portion on the upcoming year as the basis for preparing its expenditure plan for the coming fiscal year; the expenditure plans accompany the department's main estimate submissions in October.

Estimates. When the estimates from the various departments and agencies are collated, they communicate to Parliament the nature and level of the government's expenditure plans for the upcoming fiscal year. They are designed to meet the information needs of members of Parliament, who have the responsibility of approving spending and authorizing appropriations of public funds. They also play a crucial role in enabling the House of Commons to hold the government accountable for its actions.

The estimates are divided into three parts, each providing successively more information on government expenditure plans.[3] Part I, titled *The Government Expenditure Plan*, provides an overview of federal spending. Part II, which gives the main estimates, provides the basis for parliamentary appropriations. Details of expenditure proposals are arranged by department and agency in alphabetical order; for each department, information is presented by program, activity, objects of expenditure, person-years, and appropriation vote number. Part III presents the expenditure plans in considerably more detail than Part II, providing information on the objectives and results of individual programs and on capital projects; a separate volume for each department and agency is tabled in Parliament.

Form of the Estimates. The form in which the main estimates of government spending are presented reflects the various purposes they serve. The classification of expenditures for the Department of Health and Welfare is shown as an example of this form in Table 3–2.

For the estimates, a "program" is defined as a major departmental operation designed to achieve specific objectives. The "program overview" provides a brief outline of a program's various aspects, including recent performance, future plans, and effectiveness. An "activity" is a breakdown of a program and indicates the kind of work done to achieve its objectives; activities may be divided into subactivities and capital projects so as to identify work, operations, and processes more precisely. A narrative on each program and its activities describes the operations.

Where appropriate, the expenditures of each program are divided into three categories: operating expenditures, capital expenditures, and grants and contributions. Each category for each program is assigned an appropriation vote number, which forms the basis of parliamentary authority — that is, the approval of expenditures and appropriation of funds. (Certain other expenditures that are authorized by legislation do not require annual parliamentary approval and appropriation. They are identified as statutory or "S." Changes to these expenditures require a statutory amendment.)

The expenditures in each vote category are further classified by standard objects of expenditure, of which there are thirteen. These standard objects, or inputs, identify

TABLE 3–2
Expenditure Estimates Form:
Programs, Activities, Authority, Supplementary
Department of Health and Welfare

Programs
Health
Social
Departmental administration

Program overview: Health program
Recent performance
Background
Future planning
Program effectiveness

Analysis by activity: Health program
Food safety
Drug safety
Environmental quality
Health insurance
Health services and promotion
Indian and Northern health services
Fitness and amateur sport

Authority: Health program vote no.
5 Operating expenditure
10 Capital expenditure
15 Grants and contributions
S Payment for insured health services
S Contribution to employee benefit plans

Supplementary information: Profile of program resources, health program
Financial requirements by objects of expenditure (i.e., personnel, rentals, repair and maintenance, materials and supplies, etc.)
Personnel requirements
Capital expenditures
Transfer payments
Revenues

Other information

Source: Canadian Supply and Services, *Estimates for the Fiscal Year Ending March 31, 1991,* cat. BT 31–29, (Ottawa, 1990). Reproduced with the permission of the Minister of Supply and Services, 1991.

expenditures in terms of goods and services purchased and include such things as personnel, materials, equipment.

The program-activities classification, with its emphasis on objectives and methods of achieving the objectives, is oriented toward what departments expect to achieve — the outputs. The standard objects identify inputs and what administrators must purchase to perform their tasks. Appropriation vote numbers serve parliamentary controls — once the expenditure is authorized and the appropriation made, funds cannot be transferred from operations under one vote number to operations under another without the approval of Parliament.

Treasury Board Review

The Treasury Board secretariat conducts comprehensive examinations of the departments' proposed expenditures, as contained in the operational plans and the main estimates. This review concentrates on whether programs and activities are consistent with previously approved strategies and policies; whether expenditures for programs are within approved resource levels; and whether cost estimates are realistic and reflect the most efficient use of resources. During this review process, the performance and efficiency of operations within departments are also examined. If the secretariat judges that estimates are inflated or inadequate justification has been provided, it is likely to reduce estimated expenditures.

Following a review of the secretariat's recommendations, the Treasury Board submits the approved estimates to the P & P Committee for ratification. The ratified estimates are forwarded to the departments and agencies, which adjust their operational plans for any changes made during the review process.

After final approval by the cabinet, the expenditure estimates are presented to and tabled in Parliament some time in February.

Review and Appropriation by Parliament

Parliament is constitutionally vested with the ultimate responsibility for the control of public funds; section 53 of the Constitution Act provides that all financial bills, revenue, and appropriation, must originate in the House of Commons. This requirement is further clarified in the Financial Administration Act, which stipulates that no payments may be made out of the Consolidated Revenue Fund without the authority of Parliament. Yet only the executive collectively can introduce money bills into the House; in this respect, it is cabinet that is responsible for the direction and use of government funds.

Consideration by Committees and Parliament. The three parts of the expenditure estimates are tabled by the President of the Treasury Board in the House of Commons, which immediately refers them to standing committees for a detailed examination. Various House standing committees, each generally consisting of twenty elected members from all parties, specialize in particular major functions of government. Thus, the Standing Committee on Agriculture reviews the estimates of Agriculture Canada, and the Standing Committee on Transport and Communications examines the estimates of the Department of Transport. The work of scrutinizing the government's estimates is done in these committees, which are empowered to call the minister and the officials of the department concerned to give evidence on its plans, operations, and expenditures. They can recommend changes in the estimates but do not have the power to effect changes.

The standing committees are given three months (March, April, and May) to complete their examination of the estimates. Then they must report to the House, which conducts a general debate on government policy and departmental operations. (That debate occurs during the twenty-five days allotted to "business of supply," which are allocated as follows: thirteen days before the end of June, five days in the fall, and seven days before the end of the fiscal year. The days need not be consecutive.) The minister of each department is responsible for explaining departmental policies and objectives and answering questions. Collectively, the cabinet is responsible for the general budget of expenditure, but individually each minister is responsible for the administration of his or her department and the implementation of its programs.

The approval of the expenditures is followed by the introduction of the appropriations bill, which is subject to three short, formal readings in the House and passed. After being considered by the Senate, it is signed by the Governor General and becomes an act of Parliament.

The three-part expenditure estimates document contains the major estimates of government expenditure, but they are by no means the only ones submitted to Parliament. Several sets of supplementary estimates are usually presented during the course of the fiscal year. Since each department must prepare its estimate of expenditure for the following year at the beginning of the current fiscal year, the main estimates are frequently incomplete. Departments discover that original estimates did not provide for some needed items and requests on other items were insufficient. (This is certain to be the case if a change in government policy calls for increased activity and services and consequently increased expenditure.) The supplementary estimates must be submitted to the Treasury Board, along with corresponding changes in the budget year and multiyear operational plans, and follow the review routine discussed earlier. It is through supplementary estimates that a certain degree of flexibility is maintained in the expenditure side of the budget.

Since the main estimates are not approved by Parliament until some time after the beginning of the fiscal year on April 1 and since appropriations for the preceding fiscal year lapse on March 31, provision must be made to carry on the functions of government until the main appropriations bill is enacted. This is accomplished by interim bills, which grant a fraction of each of the tabled estimates to meet expenses in the new fiscal year until the main bill is passed. An interim supply act is complete in itself and remains operative even though Parliament refuses to appropriate the main estimates of one or more of the departments concerned.

As already noted, the constitution requires that any expenditure of public money from the Consolidated Revenue Fund be made only on the authority of Parliament. The federal government adheres to this provision with one exception: the use of Governor General's warrants for meeting unforeseen and emergency expenditures. The Consolidated Revenue and Audit Act, 1878 authorized the use of Governor General's warrants, and this provision was reenacted in the Financial Administration Act. The government has this authority only when Parliament is not in session or is adjourned *sine die*, and such warrants must be presented to the House of Commons within fifteen days after the commencement of the next session. The Financial Administration Act stipulates that amounts granted by warrants must be included in, not additional to, the next appropriation act. Expenditures covered by warrants are, therefore, subjected to a *post facto* approval by Parliament.

Indirect Control The parliamentary control of government expenditures takes an indirect form. It is exercised by forcing departments to defend and justify their policies and operations through question period and debate on the floor of the House, through examinations of the estimates and scrutiny of general policy in standing committees, and through the post-audit by the Auditor General and subsequent review by the Public Accounts Committee.

The examination of estimates by the House standing committees is primarily to obtain information, rather than to exercise control, as they have no authority to reduce or change the estimates. They can, however, conduct a more objective and thorough examination of departmental programs than can the House sitting as a committee of the whole in that they can devote more time to the estimates and may call the minister and officials to give evidence. Departments, knowing that they may be called on to give detailed explanations and justifications of their operations, are likely to plan their expenditures carefully to avoid adverse publicity and possible embarrassment. Moreover, the continuity of the standing committees and their establishment along functional lines allows their members to develop expertise and specialization, thereby increasing their potential for effective expenditure scrutiny. The function of parliamentary committees when examining estimates is to put the spotlight on what departments are doing, to focus debate on government operations, to criticize, and to do all this on an informed basis.

Administration of Spending

Following the appropriation of funds by Parliament, each department is required to submit to the Treasury Board a division of each appropriation into allotments, generally based on the activity classification detailed in Part II of the estimates. The release of funds from the Consolidated Revenue Fund and the consequent spending is made in accordance with this allotment division. Only on Treasury Board approval may funds be transferred from one allotment to another; doing so is generally a routine board operation. Under no circumstances, however, may funds be transferred between appropriations without parliamentary approval.

The Minister of Supply and Services is designated as the Receiver General for Canada, responsible for the Consolidated Revenue Fund and for releasing funds to departments on request. The funds are released following a pre-audit by the deputy minister of each department, certifying that the amounts requested are in accordance with the appropriations and allotments authorized

Another responsibility of Supply and Services Canada is the preparation of the Public Accounts of Canada. Prepared at the end of the fiscal year, they include a report on the financial transactions of the fiscal year, statements of revenue and expenditures, and statements of the government's assets and liabilities, together with financial reports of Crown corporations.

Revenue Determination and the Budget Speech

The determination of expected government revenues is closely related to forecasts of economic conditions. Responsibility for these forecasts rests with the Department of Finance, working in close liaison with other government departments and agencies such as Statistics Canada and the Bank of Canada. From the information obtained, the Taxation Division of the Finance Department estimates the yield of various revenue sources in the coming fiscal year and determines the effects upon revenues of possible tax changes. These estimates are included in the fiscal plan.

The budget speech, presented by the Minister of Finance to the House of Commons, brings together estimated expenditures and revenues and introduces proposals for changes in taxation. There is no set date for the budget speech. In recent years, attempts have been made to establish an early calendar-year date; it has not been uncommon, however, for the minister to present two budgets within a fiscal year as changing economic conditions force changes in economic and taxation policies.

Most budget speeches follow a standard pattern in form and presentation. They begin with a general review of the country's economic and financial conditions and government economic policy during the previous year. An outline of proposed government policies follows. Finally comes an outline of the government's fiscal position, including proposals for tax changes and the effect they are expected to have on the budget and the economy. Estimates of revenues are compared with the expenditure estimates, and the size of the surplus or deficit is predicted.

Following the presentation of the budget speech, the House holds a debate, which is limited to six days (not necessarily consecutive). It provides an opportunity for the members to discuss government policy in financial and economic matters, such as unemployment, economic growth, and taxation.

The budget speech document is frequently accompanied by supplementary budget papers. There are generally a paper explaining budget proposals in greater detail and a notice of ways and means motion containing the proposed amendments to existing tax legislation. Major government policy initiatives may also be presented as papers accompanying the budget speech.

Traditionally, proposals for tax changes are made only during the presentation of the budget speech. There have been notable exceptions, however, with tax changes introduced by the Minister of Finance, not in a budget, but in an economic statement to the House. No matter how introduced, proposed tax changes are presented to the House as tax bills, which are required to go through the usual three readings before passage. Tax changes consisting of amendments to existing legislation can, however, be made effective immediately upon the introduction of the resolutions in Parliament during the budget speech if the government so desires.

Responsibility for the administration of tax legislation — that is, control and management of all internal taxes and levies — rests with the Department of National Revenue. The department has two components — taxation, and customs and excise

— each of which is administered as an independent department. All revenue collected is deposited in the central Consolidated Revenue Fund.

Budget Secrecy

Traditionally, the budget speech has been prepared under a cloak of secrecy, and any leaks prior to its presentation were viewed as extremely serious, leading to demands for the resignation of the Finance Minister. For example, Minister of Finance Marc Lalonde was severely criticized by the opposition parties in the House of Commons when part of a page of his April 1983 budget was photographed during a prebudget meeting with the news media.

This concept of secrecy originated at a time when the main concern of the budget was taxes and tariffs; the government wanted to keep changes secret until they were announced in order to prevent anyone from financially profiting from advance knowledge. By the 1980s, however, the budget had become a complex document dealing with a large variety of economic and social issues on which consultation between government and elements of the private and public sectors is considered desirable. The need for a more open approach was officially addressed in a 1982 green paper, *The Budget Process — A Paper on Budget Secrecy and Proposals for Broader Consultation* by Minister of Finance Allan MacEachen. The paper contained recommendations for more openness and consultation, including the establishment of task forces to analyze proposed budget measures and the presentation of prebudget position papers for public discussion.

In his February 1984 budget, Minister of Finance Lalonde reported that most of the green paper proposals had been implemented and that his budget had been "characterized by a dramatic increase in the use of task forces, advisory committees, discussion papers, draft legislation, and technical explanatory notes"[4] to provide better understanding and debate over budget proposals. Lalonde reported that consultations on a variety of tax and economic issues had been held before and after his previous budget and had continued through the preparation of the budget at hand; organizations representing labour, business, farm groups, and others had participated, and, he reported, such meetings were accepted as an integral part of the budget process. The minister emphasized, however, that precautions would continue to be taken to ensure that no one could profit from advance knowledge of proposed tax and tariff measures.

This position on budget secrecy was repeated by Finance Minister Michael Wilson in 1985 in a white paper entitled *The Canadian Budgetary Process: Proposals for Improvement.* It stated:

> The government believes that the fundamental rationale for budget secrecy now, as always, is to prevent the possibility of profit from advance knowledge about matters to be announced in a budget ... [but] ... this commitment to budget secrecy should not be incompatible with government intentions to involve the public more meaningfully in the budgetary process.[5]

Consultations with outside parties were continued, with efforts to obtain public input without compromising the principle of secrecy that traditionalists and successive governments continued to emphasize.

Nevertheless, the government suffered a major embarrassment in 1989 when the 1989/90 budget came into the hands of the news media one day prior to its planned presentation in the House of Commons. The incident could serve as the plot for an espionage movie. On the eve of the budget day, the Global Television office in Toronto received an anonymous call from someone who claimed to have a copy of the budget and wished to make it available to the network at no charge. A rendezvous between the caller and Doug Small, Global's Ottawa bureau chief, was arranged. Two cars met momentarily in the parking lot of a west-end Ottawa gasoline station, a parcel was exchanged, and the mysterious messenger drove off. Inside the parcel was a copy of the summary "budget in brief." Small read the document on the network's 7:00 PM news telecast. A panicky and highly embarrassed government decided that it must present the budget immediately. Since the House of Commons had adjourned for the day, Finance Minister Wilson called a late-evening press conference; at it, he presented the highlights of his budget, although by this time the entire country was already aware of the contents. In the days following, the opposition parties clamoured for Wilson's resignation over the budget leak. The Finance Minister refused, arguing that the leak was a breach of trust. Prime Minister Brian Mulroney went further, declaring over national television that the document had been stolen and a crime committed. The Royal Canadian Mounted Police immediately launched an investigation and then, amid allegations from some of its own members of political interference, charged Small and two other people with possession of stolen goods. After weeks of court hearings, the judge dismissed the case, calling the prosecution an abuse of the judicial process. No theft had occurred. The document in question was one of a pile of misprinted copies that had been dumped into a trash container at the government printing plant and had been retrieved by a recycling-firm worker. It remained for Small to put the whole bizarre episode into perspective: asked if he would leak a federal budget again, he replied, "Darn tootin."[6]

This incident clearly demonstrated the difficulties of maintaining budgetary secrecy, given the many opportunities for leaks as the budget is prepared, printed, distributed, and finally presented. It also further undermined a practice that many have argued is outdated and unnecessary.

An examination of the federal budgets for the last several years shows very few measures that could have produced significant financial gains from advance knowledge. There was general agreement, for example, that the 1989/90 budget contained not a single item from which anyone could have profited as a result of advance knowledge. But traditions die hard, and there appears to be a reticence to change long-standing practices.

Decision-makers should weigh the benefits and costs of complete budget secrecy. On the positive side is the prevention of possible gain from advance knowledge. Yet in the United States, all budgetary measures are fully debated before taking effect, and knowledge of changes prior to their implementation is not a concern. Thus, concern about advance knowledge does not appear to justify the exaggerated secrecy currently surrounding Canadian budgets on every matter, however minor or inconsequential.

Potential protections from secrecy appear to be far outweighed by negative factors. One is the need for provisional implementation of budget measures. Even more important is the impediment to the consultation process and, therefore, to the introduction of measures potentially more effective in achieving set objectives. In the past, the government has often been embarrassed when tax changes contained in the budget have had to be revised — even withdrawn completely — because careful scrutiny by outside experts and interested parties showed they were unworkable or would have undesirable effects. Furthermore, the lack of open consultation produces the possibility that potentially beneficial changes may be ignored because government is unable to give them rigorous scrutiny. In other words, the range of options may be narrowed. Every year the government receives a large number of suggestions from individuals, business, and organizations such as chambers of commerce. An open environment would provide opportunities to examine the various options in terms of objectives and economic effects.

The Post-Audit

The final stage of the budgetary cycle is the audit of financial transactions. Following the collection and disbursement of public funds, the Auditor General conducts a post-audit of the financial transactions and reports the findings to the House of Commons. Although appointed by the Governor General, the Auditor General is independent of the executive and answers only to the House. The Auditor General Act requires that the Auditor General examine government accounts and report instances of misuse or mismanagement of public funds, fraud, overexpenditure of appropriations, expenditures not authorized by Parliament, and other irregularities; make observations on the economy and efficiency of departmental operations; and assess procedures within departments for measuring the effectiveness of their expenditure programs. Through this post-audit, the House receives a full accounting for the manner in which approved budgetary plans are administered.

The Auditor General's annual report is normally tabled in the House of Commons simultaneously with the public accounts to which it relates. These two documents are then referred to the Public Accounts Committee for review. In examining the accounts, that committee may call the Auditor General to give evidence and public officials to explain and justify the operations of their departments and account for inefficiencies or mismanagement.[7]

Budget and Financial Management Review Agencies

Two agencies within the budget system deserve special attention because of the significance of their roles. They are the Treasury Board and the Office of the Auditor General.

The Treasury Board

The Treasury Board occupies a unique position in the budgetary system of Canada.[8] Created in 1867 by an order-in-council as a committee of the Queen's Privy Council of Canada, it was given a statutory basis by the Department of Finance Act, 1869, which empowered it to act "on all matters relating to Finance, Revenue, Expenditure or Public Accounts, which may be referred to it by Council."[9] At that time, it consisted of the Minister of Finance as chairman and three other members of the Privy Council and was served by a staff organization or secretariat within the Department of Finance.

An 1885 amendment to the Department of Finance Act increased board membership from four to six. In 1967, a new cabinet portfolio of President of the Treasury Board was created, and the secretariat was transferred out of the Finance Department to form a separate department. The board currently consists of the president, the Minister of Finance as an *ex officio* member, and four other cabinet ministers.

The Treasury Board has been described as "an inner Cabinet on financial and administrative policy."[10] Its role did not develop in a planned or systematic fashion, however, but evolved slowly, moulded by the exigencies of the times, until the board emerged as the central financial control agency in the government's administrative structure and the managerial arm of the executive. Its traditional function has centred on allocating among competing uses the limited resources at the government's disposal and on using them efficiently. In essence, the Board performs a function in government similar to that of the price mechanism found in the market economy, and this function stems from its key position and role in the budget system. The creation of the Cabinet Expenditure Review Committee has now relieved the Treasury Board of the basic function of reviewing and approving new expenditure proposals. It continues, however, to allocate resources for approved policies and programs. In addition, the Treasury Board is responsible for establishing the government's personnel policy and representing the government in collective bargaining.

Resource Allocation. The allocation function is the focus of the Treasury Board and places it — including its secretariat — in a position in which it can wield considerable influence on the activities of government. As the traditional expenditure reviewer, it is an influential budget control agency in the government and assists the P & P Committee and the ERC in their policy and expenditure reviews by providing cost analyses of programs and program changes, by identifying expenditure implications of program changes, and by isolating programs considered to require closer scrutiny of efficiency and effectiveness. The board studies departmental multiyear operational plans and makes recommendations on the level of resources required for programs in each of the five years. In addition, it conducts a thorough analysis of the main estimates submissions, the objectives being to ensure that proposed programs and activities reflect established government objectives and are consistent with the policies and programs approved by the policy committees, that cost estimates are reasonable and reflect the most efficient use of resources to achieve program objectives, and that expenditure proposals are consistent with the prescribed estimates format.

The Treasury Board has been greatly assisted in its role of resource allocation by the creation of the cabinet committee system for determining spending priorities and establishing spending levels for the various policy sectors. Both the P & P Committee and the ERC have relieved the board's secretariat of some of the burden of analyzing policy and of promoting long-term planning and expenditure restraint by departments.

Personnel Policy. Wages and salaries for the public service are a significant element in total government expenditures; consequently, the Treasury Board has been made responsible for determining personnel and salary levels. An amendment to the Financial Administration Act in 1967 gave the board wide-ranging powers in the area of personnel management, including determining staff requirements and utilization, classifying positions, and determining and regulating remuneration, hours of work, and standards governing physical working conditions. (Previously, the Treasury Board and the Public Service Commission shared responsibility in many personnel matters, but under the current arrangements the commission concentrates primarily on meeting staff requirements by recruitment and promotion.)

Collective Bargaining. When collective bargaining was introduced to the public service in 1967, the Treasury Board was designated as the government representative in the bargaining process. Bargaining takes place between officials of the Personnel Policy Branch and certified bargaining agents or organizations representing employees. The board establishes guidelines for what the government is prepared to offer and, given this mandate, the secretariat proceeds with the negotiations.

In the event of an impasse, bargaining agents have a choice of two options: binding arbitration or conciliation offering in certain circumstances the right to strike. Binding arbitration requires that the dispute be referred to the Public Service Arbitration Tribunal, consisting of a permanent chairperson and two three-member panels appointed by the Treasury Board, one representing the employer and the other employees. For each dispute referred to arbitration, the tribunal consists of the chairperson and two other members, one selected from each panel.

Conciliation also offers recourse to a third party: a conciliation board composed of representatives of the two disputing parties and a chairperson selected by mutual consent. The function of this board is to attempt to reconcile differences between the opposing parties. If no settlement is reached, the employees may strike, provided they are not in the category of employees performing duties or services determined necessary for the safety or security of the public, to whom the right to strike is denied.

Financial Management and Control: The Comptroller General

The Treasury Board is concerned with efficiency in government administration as part of its function of financial supervision. In 1978, this function was strengthened with the creation of the Office of Comptroller General within the board secretariat. The Comptroller General, a deputy minister, was made responsible to the President of the Treasury Board for the promotion of improved financial management techniques and reporting systems in government, including adequate accounting procedures, improved cash management, and procedures for program evaluation.

More specifically, the Comptroller General's responsibility includes the development of government-wide policies on financial and operational administration, internal audit and related planning, and reporting control systems. Considerable emphasis has been placed on the need for program and activity evaluation within departments, and the Comptroller General provides guidelines for this purpose. The Comptroller General's office is also responsible for prescribing the form of the expenditure estimates and the public accounts and for responding to the findings and recommendations of the Auditor General's annual report.

Office of the Auditor General

The office of the Auditor General, created in 1877, is one of the oldest agencies in the federal government. Although the Auditor General is officially appointed by the Governor in Council, the office is an agency of the House of Commons and responsible directly to it.

Until 1977, the Office of the Auditor General operated under the provisions of the Financial Administration Act. The Auditor was responsible for examining the government accounts to ensure that they were properly kept, that all public money was fully accounted for, and that public funds were expended in accordance with parliamentary appropriations.

In 1977, the functions of the office were expanded with the passage of the Auditor General Act. Two significant changes were the extension of the role of the audit to include a value-for-money evaluation and the introduction of a cyclical approach to comprehensive auditing for Parliament.

The legislation sets value for money as the criterion for the Auditor General's examination of government expenditure accounts. This kind of audit focusses on the adequacy of financial management and control systems departments employ to gauge the economy, efficiency, and effectiveness of their programs and activities. The objective is an assessment of government progress in these three areas.

Economy refers to the terms and conditions under which personnel and material resources are acquired; an economical operation is one that acquires appropriate quality and quantity at minimum cost. Efficiency relates to inputs and outputs; an efficient operation is one that produces the maximum output for any set of resource inputs. Effectiveness concerns the extent to which a program achieves its stated objectives. In the value-for-money audit, however, the Auditor General does not question the appropriateness of departmental program and activity goals or the values underlying them; thus the auditor does not really measure effectiveness. Rather, the mandate is to determine if departments have established satisfactory procedures for measuring and reporting the effectiveness of programs. This restriction protects the Auditor General from political issues and partisian political debate.

The cyclical, comprehensive audit approach represents a considerable change from the traditional transactions audit, which focussed on improprieties in the management of public funds. Parliamentary review of such findings tended to be time-consuming and controversial and did not facilitate or contribute to members' understanding of the strengths and weaknesses of the financial administrative system or the management of public funds. The cyclical, comprehensive audit requires the Auditor General to do a detailed examination of each major department or agency at least once every four years. The objective is to provide Parliament with information that will facilitate members' understanding of the general effectiveness of departmental operations and financial control systems. (The four-year period was selected because it coincides with the average life of Parliament.)

These changes in the audit functions have, to a degree, made the office of the Auditor General an agency of change and improvement in government financial administration. In addition to disclosing deficiencies in the management of public funds, the Auditor General provides concrete, written recommendations for improvements in administration, achievement of economies, increased efficiency, and enhanced program results. Although the Auditor General cannot impose any suggestions for improvements on the government, the office can exert considerable influence by working closely with the Comptroller General and the Public Accounts Committee.

Features of Provincial and Municipal Budgeting

Provinces

Many of the budgetary and financial practices found at the provincial level of government parallel those existing in the federal government. Departments are required to prepare estimates of expenditures for each fiscal year and submit them to cabinet for approval, which in turn must present them to the legislature for authorization. A number of provinces have established cabinet planning and priorities committees and treasury boards or central financial screening agencies, similar to the federal Treasury Board. Provincial offices of auditor general or comptroller general exist to perform pre-audits and post-audits. In general, public accounts are prepared and tabled in the provincial legislatures, which have established public accounts committees to review the accounts, together with audit reports.

Provincial governments have experimented with a variety of budgeting systems: planning-programming-budgeting, management by objectives, management by results, and program-based management information. As at the federal level, these systems have been used in attempts to introduce more formal procedures in budgeting and to stress the provision of information for decision-makers in provincial governments.[11]

Municipal Governments and Other Local Jurisdictions

The administrative jurisdictions established by provinces for purposes of governing generally consist of cities, towns, townships, villages, and municipalities. (The term "municipality" frequently refers to a rural jurisdiction.) All of these various jurisdictions are grouped under the term "municipal government," although they range from small villages to huge cities.

Municipal governments are the creations of the provincial government and have only those powers granted them by it. With hundreds of such governments, the province must impose control to maintain a degree of uniformity and order in financial management. Consequently, provincial governments prescribe some basic municipal budget features and procedures.

Budgeting at this level varies depending on the organization of the municipal government. It generally consists of an elected council, committees of the council, a treasurer, and various departments and boards. Each year the departments and boards submit expenditure estimates to the treasurer or commissioner of finance, who submits them to council. These estimates are reviewed by the council or its finance committee and are revised as the council sees fit, although its authority to alter the estimates of some boards is limited. Where there is a board of control or a city manager, the estimates are first reviewed by these offices before submission to council. As in the case of their higher counterparts, municipal governments are required to have their accounts audited at the end of the fiscal year.

In general, municipal governments distinguish between current and capital budgets for the purpose of finance. Long-term borrowing is mainly restricted for capital budgets and is also subject to provincial approval. Municipal governments may also engage in short-term borrowing to finance current expenditures, but as a rule it is reserved to provide financing pending receipt of taxes, which are generally paid at the end of the year; borrowing for this purpose is frequently done by promissory note.

The current budgets of municipal governments generally follow the widely accepted format of classification of expenditures by function or department and agency, by program and activity, and by items of expenditure. Like their higher-level counterparts, municipal governments have attempted various versions of budget systems: program and performance budgeting, zero-base budgeting, and management by objectives. In essence, however, most municipal governments follow incremental budgeting for current operations. Expenditures are presented for the current fiscal year along with estimates for the new year and the corresponding changes from one year to the next.

Capital budgets are usually prepared over a multiyear (often five-year) period and are updated annually, representing a long-term plan for capital works. Capital projects are given priorities. Also outlined are methods of finance, which may take the form of provincial government grants and loans, revenues from current taxes and reserves, or proceeds from debentures sold in the capital market. The provincial governments exercise control over the capital budgets of municipal governments, their borrowing, and the debts incurred. Requirements and methods vary among the provinces, but the objectives are similar. In Ontario, for example, control is exercised by the Ontario Municipal Board. Its approval is required for any municipal government expenditure to be financed by borrowing. Limitations are placed on the terms of repayment for debentures and on the total debt outstanding. As a general rule, the debt outstanding is not permitted to exceed 25 percent of taxable assessment.

Most provinces have, in addition to municipal governments, other governing jurisdictions, such as elected school boards responsible for administering education. School boards strike their own budgets and a separate tax rate is levied for the financing of these budgets. Other agencies in the municipality may have jurisdiction over special services, such as public utilities, public housing, and public health, and may depend in varying degrees on the local budget for finances.[12]

The structure of municipal government has been subject to considerable discussion in recent years. In many provinces there has been a trend toward larger geographical jurisdictions with the establishment of regional districts and regional governments. Legislation in the provinces provides for development planning at municipal and regional levels, with planning carried out, for example, by municipal boards, committees of municipal councils, or regional commissions. Plans may include zoning bylaws, housing subdivision development, land use, and multiyear capital works programs. In most provinces, these development plans require the approval of the provincial government.

ENDNOTES

1. Information on various aspects of the budgetary process of the federal government can be found in Canada, Treasury Board, *Policy and Expenditure Management System Manual*, including updates (Ottawa); Treasury Board, *Role of the Treasury Board Secretariat and the Office of the Comptroller General*, TBS 1317 (Ottawa); Library of Parliament, *Cabinet Committees: Restructuring the System* (Ottawa, 1989); Office of the Prime Minister, *Release*, January 30, 1989, and *Release*, May 10, 1990; D.J. Savoie, *The Politics of Public Spending in Canada*, (Toronto: University of Toronto Press, 1990); and K.A. Graham, ed., *How Ottawa Spends*, (Ottawa: Carleton University Press, 1989), ch. 1.
2. Canada, Department of Finance, *Budget*, February 20, 1990, (Ottawa), pp. 75–84.
3. See Canada, Treasury Board, *1990–1991 Estimates* Part I, *The Government Expenditure Plan*; Part II, *Estimates for the Fiscal Year Ending March 31, 1991*; and Part III, *Program Expenditure Plans*; and Treasury Board, *Guide to the Preparation of the Estimates* (updates).
4. Canada, Department of Finance, *Budget Papers*, February 15, 1984 (Ottawa), p. 33.
5. Canada, Department of Finance, *The Canadian Budgetary Process: Proposals for Improvement* (Ottawa, May 1985), p. 27.
6. *Ottawa Citizen*, July 17, 1990, p. 1.
7. See Canada, *Report of the Auditor General of Canada to the House of Commons, Fiscal Year Ended 31 March 1989*, (Ottawa); and Canada, *Public Accounts of Canada 1988–89)*, vol. 1, *Summary Report and Financial Statements*; vol. 2, *Details of Expenditures and Revenues*; vol. 3 *Financial Statements of Crown Corporations* (Ottawa).
8. For a detailed analysis of the development of the role of the Treasury Board, see J.C. Strick and W.L. White, *Policy, Politics and the Treasury Board in Canadian Government* (Toronto: Science Research Associates, 1970).
9. Statutes of Canada 1869, ch. 4.
10. Norman Ward, *The Public Purse* (Toronto: University of Toronto Press, 1964), p. 212.
11. For an overview of public administration in provincial government, see M. Chandler and W. Chandler, "Public Administration in the Provinces," *Canadian Public Administration* 25, no. 4: (Winter 1982) 580–602.
12. T.J. Plunkett and K.A. Graham, "Whither Municipal Government?" *Canadian Public Administration* 25, no. 4, (Winter 1982): 603–18.

APPENDIX TO CHAPTER 3

FINANCIAL MANAGEMENT SYSTEMS IN GOVERNMENT

As noted throughout Chapter 3, a number of management systems have been developed over the years to promote efficiency in resource allocation, to improve operational performance, and to improve other aspects of financial management in government. Different systems have been in vogue at different times as earlier ones fell from favour and were replaced with new concepts or as old concepts were rediscovered and new labels attached to them. Basically, these systems are not mutually exclusive but in varying degrees are complementary. They differ primarily in their orientation and the emphasis each places on a particular aspect of the financial management process. For example, program budgeting emphasizes planning in government and the identification of program outputs; performance budgeting focusses on the measurement of performance or efficiency in government operations; management by objectives stresses the organizing of work to achieve specified objectives in a defined period of time; systems analysis consists of a variety of techniques for analyzing alternative uses of resources; zero-base budgeting emphasizes the review of programs and the establishment of priorities among program expenditure levels (packages); and the planning-programming-budgeting system (PPBS) emphasizes planning, the establishment of clearly defined objectives, the presentation of expenditures on the basis of programs and activities, the relation of resource inputs to outputs, and quantitative techniques for evaluating programs and alternatives and for measuring performance.

The Canadian government formally adopted PPBS in 1966. Attempts to improve some of its practical limitations led to further changes, including the introduction of the concept of expenditure envelopes in 1980. With these changes, the system became known as the Policy and Expenditure Management System (PEMS), which continued until the introduction of a new cabinet committee system in 1989. This appendix provides a chronology of the changes in financial administration practices in the federal government and the objectives they were designed to achieve.

Background

Until after the middle of this century, the estimates of Canadian government spending were prepared annually on the basis of the objects of expenditure. The major limitations of this process were the almost complete lack of formalized planning within departments, the absence of clearly enunciated objectives to which expenditures could be related, and the deficiency in quantitative justification of expenditure proposals. As a result, expenditure review and control functions, such as those exercised by the Treasury Board, proved to be extremely difficult. Attention was focussed on inputs, rather than on outputs. Furthermore, there was a tendency to concentrate on the proposed increments to continuing programs, rather than on periodic examinations of entire programs. Without quantitative information and criteria, the expenditure review and priority-determining procedures developed into exercises in judgement with considerable arbitrariness in expenditure changes and reductions. The budgetary process produced a budget document that was a poor reflection of decisions made and did not permit the House of Commons to conduct a meaningful scrutiny of proposed policy and consequent operational activity, resulting in a weakening of that body's traditional function as guardian of the public purse. Parliament did not focus on the real issues or objectives but concentrated on the incremental changes in expenditure items, which were trivial relative to total government spending.

Recognizing the need to modernize and improve its financial management system, the federal government undertook an extensive review of the system through the Royal Commission on Government Organization (the Glassco Commission).[1] In its 1962 report, the commission proposed sweeping changes in the budgetary process. Among its recommendations were planning departmental operations and identifying objectives; developing and applying objective criteria for evaluating alternates and reviewing performance; changing the form of the estimates and the allotment control system; and delegating increased authority to departments in the management of their financial operations.

Although the majority of the commission's financial recommendations were approved in principle by the government, its report was not taken as a rigid blueprint for change. Its importance stemmed from its philosophy; it served as a catalyst for change and the modernization of government financial administration. In the developments that followed, new techniques and possibilities were explored and adopted for improved effectiveness in budgeting, and these developments led to the formal acceptance and introduction of PPBS in 1966.[2]

Strengths and Shortcomings of PPBS

Some of the features of the PPBS approach in Canada included long-range planning and program submission, the classification of expenditures in the form of programs and activities, and the identification and explanation of program objectives. In addition, emphasis was placed on the development of quantitative techniques of analysis. These features of PPBS were of primary concern to the Treasury Board and senior department managers to supplement judgement in decision-making and permit a more objective evaluation of programs and operational performance.

Generally, the direction and intent of PPBS was to facilitate decision-making and efficiency in management at all levels of government. It was designed to provide department administrators, individual ministers, the Treasury Board, cabinet, and the House of Commons with a more orderly array of information as well as with more meaningful information. The manner in which information is presented by administrators may have a significant influence on the decisions made. Ideas for policy and advice on ministerial proposals come from the administrators, and both groups benefit from a more orderly system. Collectively and individually, ministers can more effectively discharge their decision-making responsibilities on objectives and priorities if they possess relevant facts. The system also had the potential to assist Parliament in its traditional function of financial control, the effectiveness of which had occasionally been openly debated.

Although PPBS was widely acclaimed in theory, difficulties were encountered in its practical operation. The problems stemmed largely from the inappropriateness of an analysis-based system in a political, decision-making environment characterized by pressure groups, compromises, and political expediency. Other difficulties also reduced the effectiveness of the system. Successive reports of the Auditor General in the 1970s[3] pointed to a number of shortcomings in the operation of the federal government's PPBS and financial management in general: poor quality of data in the expenditure proposals; the Treasury Board's lack of intensive evaluation of continuing department programs; the departments' and board's lack of program analysts trained to apply analytical techniques; and deficient financial control within departments. One of the Auditor General's recommendations to improve financial management and control was the creation of the Office of Comptroller General.

The federal government's immediate response to the Auditor General's recommendations was to appoint the Royal Commission of Enquiry on the Financial Organization and Accountability in the Government of Canada (the Lambert Commission) in November 1976 to examine the structure, systems, and procedures whereby financial management and control were exercised and administrators held accountable for their administration.

The 1979 Lambert Commission report[4] concluded that financial planning and control in the federal government were clearly inadequate. Many of the commission's recommendations for improvement were accepted by the government and formed the basis of a reformed system, which was outlined in the December 1979 budget in a white paper entitled *The New Expenditure Management System.*[5] Most notable among the features of this system were the "envelope" or resource-sector concept, long-term forecasting of both revenues and expenditures, and comprehensive auditing.

The Policy and Expenditure Management System (PEMS)

The policy and expenditure management system was introduced in 1979/80 with the envelope concept, cabinet policy committees, the establishment of expenditure limits for envelopes, and value-for-money assessments. Many other features of PEMS were carryovers from the earlier PPBS, including long-term planning, the program-activity format of budget estimates, the identification of program objectives, the development and use of analytical techniques for evaluating programs and performance, and an emphasis on program outputs.

The envelope concept was a primary feature of PEMS, designed to facilitate planning and control of cabinet policy and expenditure. Within the federal government, ten policy sectors and corresponding resource envelopes were identified. The policy sectors consisted of major functions of government and groups of closely related functions identified by departments, agencies, or programs. The envelopes defined the resources allocated to each policy sector and contained the estimated cost of existing and projected programs. It was the responsibility of cabinet's Priorities and Planning Committee to determine an overall expenditure limit and government priorities among envelopes. If P & P identified an envelope as having priority, it would be allocated additional funds or "new policy" reserves. Once the expenditure limits were placed on the envelopes, it was the responsibility of the cabinet policy committees to determine priorities within their respective envelopes and how any new policy reserves would be used.

Envelope priorities were established before detailed expenditure programs were developed, so proposed programs had to be in accordance with these priorities and within the fiscal constraints. Having expenditure limits on envelopes implied that choices had to be made among new program initiatives and among new and existing programs. The system was to provide opportunities to reduce or eliminate existing programs in order to free resources for new programs. Furthermore, expenditure limits over a multiyear period required that future costs of proposed and ongoing programs be considered in current decisions.

The grouping of related functions and programs into envelopes was intended to provide the cabinet committee members with an opportunity to view the relationships among programs and program objectives and to facilitate comparison of the costs of programs and trends in these costs. The requirement that funds for new initiatives be generated from savings in existing programs was expected to provide each policy committee with an incentive to devote attention to systematic review and evaluation of programs within its envelope.

The PEMS decentralized budgetary decision-making. Before the system was put in place, the P & P Committee would issue guidelines on expenditure priorities, which would be conveyed to the departments through the Treasury Board. The responsibility for interpreting the guidelines and ensuring that departments followed them, for effecting cost reductions, and for exercising general expenditure restraint fell on the Treasury Board, particularly on its secretariat. In contrast, the PEMS committee system assigned greater responsibility for these duties to the cabinet policy committees and a much larger number of cabinet ministers.

In part, PEMS had been introduced to correct some practical shortcomings in the PPB system, particularly in the expenditure planning and control phases of the budgetary process. There appears to be little evidence that PEMS achieved its objectives, however. Its introduction coincided with large increases in federal spending and heralded the beginning of the era of high government deficits. This should not, however, be attributed to the system per se. A budgeting system operates in a political environment and is subject to the whims of its users. Expenditure and deficit reduction in government, in the final analysis, can be achieved only if there is the political will to do so.

It could be argued that the decentralized system of decision-making featured in PEMS involved too many cabinet ministers and was, therefore, subjected to excessive pressures. Each policy committee member in essence wore two hats: one as a member of a committee directed to examine and control new policy and program proposals, and another as a member of an operating department who desired to obtain funding for expanding operations or new programs. The two were frequently in conflict.

Centralized Systems

The cabinet committee system introduced in 1989 centralized expenditure control in a newly created Expenditure Review Committee and in the Priorities and Planning Committee. It has been contended that the creation of the centralized system was driven primarily by financial crisis — the inability of the government to control the deficit. The system is geared to expenditure control in which the ERC targets certain departments and programs for varying degrees of constraint or reduction. In effect, a department's spending authority is reduced, and it is then left to the department to determine the programs and personnel that have to be axed. All cabinet committees — with the exception of Treasury Board, which is a statutory committee of the Privy Council and fulfills statutory duties — have been placed under the cabinet P & P Committee. The policy committees that were responsible for policy and spending priorities in their respective areas have been stripped of financial responsibilities. Cash reserves, previously directed to policy sectors and allocated among priorities within the sectors as determined by these committees, have been placed under the exclusive control of the ERC. In addition, all issues directed to P & P are first screened by the Operations Committee. The objective is to ensure that no new policy or expenditure proposal is submitted to P & P unless it has first been examined and approved by the ERC. Thus, control is at the top with the Prime Minister, as chairperson of P & P and of the ERC, and the Deputy Prime Minister, as the chairperson of the Operations Committee. The effectiveness of this system in controlling expenditures, like that of the previous systems, depends, however, on political will and remains subject to the particular whims of the Prime Minister and a select group of cabinet ministers.

Program Evaluation and Performance Measurement

Program evaluation has become an increasingly important element of government management systems. The nature of the federal government's program review and evaluation process has evolved from a focus primarily on inputs to an analysis of how resources are used, the objectives of programs, and the effectiveness of programs in achieving these objectives. There is an ever-increasing emphasis on outputs and the need for expanding and improving the information base on which budgetary decisions are made.

Program evaluation as it is currently interpreted by the Treasury Board is "the formal assessment of programs and their results … and … involves the systematic gathering of both verifiable information on a program and demonstrable evidence on its results and cost effectiveness."[6] The focus is on such basic elements as program rationale, impacts and effects, objectives achievement, and alternatives. Consideration of program rationale raises questions about the relevance of the objectives of the program and whether the program makes sense. The examination of impacts and effects and the analysis of objectives achievements concentrate on the results of the program and on whether the program achieved what was expected. In addition, analysts and policy-makers examine alternatives to consider whether there are better, more cost-effective ways to achieving the results.

Benefit-cost analysis, one method of evaluating programs and projects, involves identifying, quantifying, and comparing benefits and costs in money terms. On the basis of criteria such as benefit-cost ratios or net benefits, priorities can be established among programs and uneconomical programs can be identified. Benefit-cost analysis has numerous limitations as a decision-making aid, however, and its practical usefulness is restricted primarily to "lumpy" capital projects for which benefits and costs can be realistically quantified. It is of little value in determining priorities between two functions of government or between two activities with large-scale but intangible benefits and costs. In such cases, judgements are made by the decision-maker responsible, with the political process as the ultimate judge of the value of the program.

Once the decision is made to implement a program and it becomes operational, there is a need for performance measurement to provide its administrators with information to monitor how well it is operating. These administrators do not possess indicators found in the business world, such as profits and returns on investment, and must develop other indicators. Government operations compile many kinds of information about performance, such as information on the economy with which resources are acquired, the efficiency with which they are transformed into goods and services, the quality and volume of outputs, productive and idle time, client demand for services, and the effectiveness of government operations in terms of their contributions to achieving the objectives of programs.

Economy and efficiency indicators are generally concerned with information relating resource inputs to outputs or results achieved, while effectiveness indicators relate results achieved to results planned. The former indicators often express the results-to-resources relationship in terms of outputs per unit of labour input and costs per output. Efficiency generally concerns the minimization of costs while maintaining an adequate level and quality of service. Effectiveness indicators depend on the nature of the program. Consider, for example, an occupational training program designed to increase the employability of unemployed and low-income workers. The training itself is the resources-related output, and the efficiency indicator would be the cost per worker trained. The effectiveness of the program, however, would be measured by the percentage of retrained workers who find training-related employment. The Treasury Board has cited a variety of examples of efficiency indicators that could be applied in specific programs. In veterans' services, an efficiency indicator could be the average processing time of applications for benefits. In airport customs inspection, it could be the percentage of flights cleared in less than 30 minutes. Effectiveness indicators suggested by the Treasury Board include the number of aircraft accidents per 10 000 flight hours, the number of recalls of contaminated food products, and the rate of settlement of disputes without work disruption — applied respectively by the Civil Aeronautics Regulator Services, the Health Protection Branch, and the Federal Mediation and Conciliation Service.[7]

Performance indicators like these are widely applied in federal departments and agencies, yet it is unlikely that anyone in the public service believes that all relevant factors and variables can be quantified or all activities evaluated in apolitical terms. There are few areas of decision-making, however, that would not benefit, in varying degrees, from the attempt to introduce improved methods of analysis — whether they take the form of a more orderly array of data on resource requirements, physical outputs, or objectives, or whether they emphasize comparative measurements of costs and benefits of competing programs or of alternative methods of achieving a stated objective.[8]

ENDNOTES

1. The Royal Commission on Government Organization was appointed in September 1960, under the chairmanship of J. Grant Glassco, to "inquire into and report upon the organization and methods of operation of the departments and agencies of the Government of Canada and to recommend changes therein which they [the Commissioners] consider would best promote efficiency, economy, and improved service in the dispatch of public business." Canada, *The Royal Commission on Government Organization* (Ottawa: Queen's Printers, 1962), vol. 1.

2. For a brief description of the development of PPBS in the federal government, see J.C. Strick, "Recent Developments in Canadian Financial Administration," *Public Administration*, no. 48 (Spring 1970).

3. Canada, *Supplement to the Annual Report of the Auditor General to the House of Commons for the Fiscal Year Ended March 31, 1975* (Ottawa, 1975); and *Report of the Auditor General to the House of Commons for the Fiscal Year Ended March 31, 1976* (Ottawa, 1976).

4. Canada, *Royal Commission on Financial Management and Accountability, Final Report* (Ottawa March 1979).

5. Canada, Department of Finance, *The New Expenditure Management System* (Ottawa: 1979).

6. Canada, Treasury Board, *Guide on the Program Evaluation Function* (Ottawa, 1981), p. 3.

7. Canada, Treasury Board, *Program Performance Measurement* (Ottawa, 1979).

8. For some of the more recent initiatives of the Office of Comptroller General to improve management and analysis in government, see Canada, Treasury Board, *Cash Management in the Government of Canada* (Ottawa, 1988); *Enterprising Management* (Ottawa, 1989); and *Management Update* (monthly).

CHAPTER 4

GOVERNMENT REVENUE SOURCES AND ISSUES

The primary source of government revenue is taxation. It is usually supplemented with revenues from user charges, fees and permits, and borrowing. This chapter presents an overview of types of taxes, principles of taxation, the possible effects of some taxes on the economy, and the application of user charges.[1] It also outlines the development of taxation in Canada. Borrowing is discussed in detail in Chapter 12.

TAX BASES

The kinds of taxes found in a typical tax structure include taxes based on income, on consumption, on wealth and transfers of wealth, and on business activity.

Income-Based Taxes

Two important revenue sources for Canada are taxes on income; the personal income tax and the corporation income tax. In addition, wages earned and paid are often subject to payroll taxes.

Personal Income Tax. An income tax requires a definition of the tax base. For the personal income tax, the most widely accepted theoretical definition of income is often called the Haig-Simons definition, so named after the two economists who developed it. Income is defined as the value of an individual's increase in wealth plus his or her consumption in a specified period of time, normally one year. This measure is a comprehensive one that includes both money income and income received in the form of goods and services. (As noted in the next chapter, the Canadian Income Tax Act uses a variation of the Haig-Simons concept in its definition of income.)

Total or gross personal income is not, however, usually considered a measure of capacity to *pay* taxes. An individual may incur unavoidable personal expenses, such as medical costs. He or she may also have costs associated with earning income, including interest paid on funds borrowed for investment purposes. In addition, a certain minimum amount of income is required for purchase of the food, clothing, and shelter necessary for subsistence. Consequently, specified amounts of income are normally exempt from taxation, and deductions are permitted for nondiscretionary expenditures. Taxable income then consists of gross income minus these exemptions and deductions.

An alternative method for taking into account nondiscretionary costs and permitting a minimum allowance to reflect lack of taxpaying capacity is to provide tax credits for these items. Total tax is first calculated on gross income and then amounts are subtracted from the total tax to arrive at the tax payable.

Corporation Income Tax. A corporation is taxed on net income, which is defined as the total income it has earned less all expenses incurred in earning that income. There are two alternative treatments of corporate income for tax purposes. The most common method treats the corporation as a separate tax-paying entity and grants shareholders a tax credit on their dividends for the amount of tax paid by the corporation. The second method taxes corporation income through its shareholders. Net income is allocated to shareholders in proportion to the number of shares held, and this income is then subjected to the personal income tax. Both methods permit the integration of personal income and income earned by shareholders through the corporation. This approach avoids double taxation of corporation income — that is, once by a corporation income tax and again by the personal income tax on dividends received.

Payroll Taxes. Payroll taxes are levies on wages and salaries. Separate from income taxes, they may be payable by workers on wages earned and/or by the employer on wages paid. Revenues are usually earmarked for specific purposes, such as the Old Age Security program and the unemployment insurance fund.

Consumption-Based Taxes

Taxes based on consumer spending include the spending tax, general sales taxes, and specific taxes called excises.

The Spending Tax. A direct approach to the taxation of consumption is the spending tax. It is applied to the amount of an individual's total income spent on consumption, which can be calculated, in effect, as gross income minus savings for a given period — say, one year. Deductions and exemptions may be permitted and various rates applied, as for a personal income tax. This type of tax rewards savings because an individual can reduce the tax burden by increasing the proportion of total income saved.

Sales Taxes. A general sales tax may be applied to transactions at various stages of the production and distribution process. It may be a multistage or a single-stage levy. Taxes of the former type include the turnover tax and the value-added tax: those of the latter type include the manufacturers' sales tax, the wholesale tax, and the retail sales tax.

A general sales tax is a widely used consumption-based tax that is an important source of government revenue in many countries. It is a broadly based tax, applied as a percentage of the sale price of all goods and services except those specifically exempted. For the most part, a sales levy taxes consumption indirectly. The tax is usually imposed on the seller, who collects and remits the amount but is expected to pass the tax forward to consumers through an increase in the selling price.

A turnover tax is imposed at a constant rate on sale value at every transaction in the production and distribution process. For instance, the tax is imposed on raw materials, on semifinished goods, and on the finished product. A widely used variation is the value-added tax, which is applied in almost 50 countries. Like the turnover tax, a value-added tax is imposed on transactions at all the various stages of production, but it is levied only on the value that has been added at each stage. In the administration of a value-added tax, credits are usually given sellers for the tax they have paid on purchases or inputs; this approach avoids tax pyramiding (tax paid on tax) and multiple taxation (taxation of the same product more than once). Given the tax rate, the total amount remitted to the government by the vendors at all the different stages of taxation equals the amount of tax paid by the consumer on the selling price of the finished product. The goods and services tax (GST) introduced by the Canadian government in January 1991 (described in the next chapter) is essentially a value-added tax.

A manufacturers' sales tax is imposed on producers, often of final and near-final goods. The base prices to which the tax is applied are those charged for finished goods and services. Double taxation can be avoided by exempting inputs, such as raw materials and semifinished products, or by giving a credit for any tax paid by one manufacturer to another on the purchases of inputs. A tax on the manufacturer's selling price is called a hidden tax. It becomes built into the prices of goods purchased by consumers, who frequently are unaware of the tax or the amount they are paying. A manufacturers' sales tax was part of the Canadian tax structure from 1921 to 1990 but was replaced by the GST in January 1991.

A wholesale sales tax is basically similar to the manufacturers' sales tax, except that it is levied on the prices the wholesaler charges the retailer and is remitted by the wholesaler.

Retail sales taxes are imposed at the retail level on goods and services sold to the consumer. The retailer collects the tax and remits it to the government. This is the nature of the general sales tax levied by all provinces in Canada except Alberta, which does not impose a sales tax.

An excise is a tax on specified goods or services or a selected group of them. The tax may be expressed as a percentage of the selling price (an *ad valorem* tax) or as dollars or cents on weight, volume, or number (a unit tax). Traditionally, excise taxes have been imposed on two groups of goods. One group consists of goods deemed to generate external diseconomies in consumption, such as alcohol and tobacco products. To the extent that the excise tax is reflected in higher selling prices of the goods, the tax is viewed as a means of curtailing their consumption and thereby reducing external costs. These excises are known as sumptuary taxes, designed to limit purchases of the goods taxed. The second group of goods taxed are considered luxury items. They include such consumer goods as cosmetics, jewellery, wine, and tobacco. (As applied in Canada, the luxury tax at one time also included radios and television sets, automobiles, and clocks and watches.) In addition to these two groups of goods, excise taxes are also imposed on items such as motor fuel, air conditioners in automobiles, and air travel.

Taxes on Wealth and Transfers of Wealth

In contrast to personal and corporation income taxes, which are based on income flows, wealth taxes are based on stocks of personal and real property. Wealth taxes include the net wealth tax and real property taxes. Taxes on transfers of wealth include death and gift taxes.

Net Wealth Tax. A tax on net wealth consists of an annual levy on the value of all a person's assets (land, vehicles, stocks and bonds, savings, jewellery, and so on) minus any claims against these assets.

Property Tax. A real property tax is a levy on land and accompanying buildings. The property tax is much used in Canada, where it is imposed, primarily by municipalities (as discussed in Chapter 6).

This tax is levied on the property and is not related to the income or ability to pay of the owner or to the equity he or she may have in it. The usual justification for this tax is that local governments use revenues from the tax to service the property and thus tend to increase its value. Services such as law enforcement protect property, while streets and sidewalks make the property accessible.

Death Taxes. A death tax is one imposed on wealth at the time of death. When it is applied to the wealth of the deceased before it is distributed to heirs, it is known as an estate tax. When it is levied on the heirs of the estate in proportion to the amounts each receives, it is called an inheritance tax or succession duty. Before 1972 the Canadian federal government imposed an estate tax. The provinces, on the other hand, applied succession duties. All the provinces have now discontinued this tax, but inheritance taxes are still levied by many state governments in the United States.

Death taxes are controversial. The reason for their imposition can generally be traced to objectives of income redistribution. There may be a desire to limit intergeneration accumulations of wealth. It may also be argued that death taxes tap income that may have escaped the personal income tax. On the other hand, to the extent that the accumulated wealth had earlier been taxed as income under the personal income tax, death taxes may be viewed as double taxation.

Gift Taxes. It is common for a death tax to be accompanied by a gift tax, which is a levy imposed on the donor of a gift. The purpose is to prevent avoidance of estate taxes. Without a gift tax, all death taxes could be avoided by transferring wealth before death.

Business Taxes

In addition to the corporation income tax, a wide variety of levies may be applied to business establishments and business activities. They include commercial concentration taxes, which are based on square metres of floor space; taxes on storage capacity; taxes on an establishment's rental value; and taxes on paid-up capital of a company. These taxes usually contribute only a very small proportion of total government revenues and are mostly imposed by the lower levels of government.

PRINCIPLES OF TAXATION

Some of the early literature on taxation focussed on attempts to develop principles on which a tax or tax system could be structured. Such criteria were viewed as desirable to avoid or reduce arbitrariness in taxation. Over time, most people have come to accept three principles as embodying the primary features that a tax or a tax system should possess: (1) equity in the distribution of the burden of taxation; (2) economic efficiency; and (3) administrative feasibility.[2] These principles sometimes conflict; in such cases, unless a government places priority on a particular principle, compromises are required.

Equity

The principle of tax equity is related to society's goal of an equitable distribution of income. In fact, taxes, combined with transfers are employed for purposes of income redistribution. Accordingly, the distribution of the burden of a tax should adhere to the standards of equity or fairness adopted by society for income distribution. The generally accepted rule of equity in taxation is equal treatment of equals. Horizontal equity requires those in similar circumstances to pay equal taxes. Vertical equity requires those who are better off to pay more taxes.

The benefit approach to taxation uses the benefits from government expenditures as the base for taxation. According to the equal treatment of equals rule, people should pay taxes in proportion to benefits received. Difficulties arise, however, in applying this approach. First, there is the difficulty of measuring and allocating benefits from government activities. Second, the distribution of the tax burden in proportion to benefits received could result in a situation in which — to take an extreme example — a millionaire and a pauper, each receiving the same benefits, would be required to pay the same amount in tax dollars. This distribution is unlikely to conform to the standards of equity established by society for income distribution, since it is generally accepted that extremes in income disparities should be avoided.

In contrast is the ability-to-pay approach in the application of the equal treatment of equals rule. Individuals who have equal ability to pay taxes should pay equal taxes, while those with greater ability pay more taxes. The most widely adopted measure of ability is income, but a combination of income and wealth is used in some cases. Horizontal equity is attained by requiring two individuals to pay equal amounts of tax if they have the same amount of income after adjustments for factors that may affect their well-being, such as number of dependants and medical expenses. Vertical equity requires individuals with larger incomes to pay more taxes. An issue that arises here is the determination of how much more higher-income groups should be required to pay.

Taxes may be progressive, proportional, or regressive with respect to income. These concepts are generally defined in terms of the average tax rate — that is, the proportion of income that is paid in taxes as income increases. In a proportional tax, the average tax rate is constant; in a progressive tax, it rises as income increases; and in a regressive tax, it falls as incomes rise.

The same concepts can be used to describe marginal tax rates, which are the tax rates that are applied to increments of income as income rises. Marginal tax rates should not be confused with average tax rates. Marginal tax rates are progressive when the rates on additional amounts of income increase as income rises. An example of a progressive marginal tax rate structure is: a 10 percent rate on the first $1000 of taxable income, a 15 percent rate on the next $1000, and a 20 percent rate on the third $1000. Marginal tax rates are regressive when they fall as income rises. Given efficient tax collection, progressive marginal tax rates produce progression in the average tax rate.

It has been extensively argued that vertical equity in taxation requires progressive taxation. Of the numerous theoretical attempts to justify progression, most are based on the assumption of the diminishing marginal utility of income. In this concept, as income increases, the utility or welfare gain from additional dollars of income falls.

Therefore, taxing away additional dollars results in a smaller sacrifice or loss of welfare to a high-income individual than to a low-income person. These theories remain controversial, however, and the case for progressive taxation, including the degree of progression, is inconclusive.[3] Nevertheless, governments commonly apply progressive marginal tax rates in the personal income tax.

Many other taxes in a country's system may not have progressive rates, however. Sales taxes, for example, are considered regressive with respect to income; although the statutory tax rate may be a constant percentage of price, the dollar value of the tax paid on an item constitutes a higher percentage of the income of a low-income purchaser than of to a high-income purchaser.[4] The degree of regressiveness of the sales tax can be reduced by exempting from it items that usually make up a large proportion of the budgets of low-income families (that is, food and clothing) or by a system of sales tax credits that produce tax refunds to low-income families as compensation for sales tax paid. Similar tax refunds can be applied to property taxes to help ease their burden on low-income families.

Economic Efficiency

In raising revenues, taxes transfer control over real resources from the private sector to the public sector. According to the tax principle of economic efficiency, a tax should raise the revenues required in a way that does not distort the efficient allocation of resources. In other words, in an economy characterized by an efficient allocation of resources shaped by market forces, a tax should be neutral in its effect on this allocation. A tax is considered economically neutral and efficient if it does not alter choices or decisions in production, consumption, savings, and investment. To the extent that market imperfections and externalities contribute to an inefficient allocation of resources, however, taxes may be applied in a nonneutral manner to help the economy achieve an optimal allocation of resources. Tax incentives may be used to achieve certain economic goals, and tax penalties to discourage particular courses of action.

Raising or lowering the personal income tax affects the level of disposable income that people have available for consumption and can thus affect total consumption and production. But in the process, the tax is unlikely to cause changes in the *relative* prices of consumer goods or, therefore, in consumption patterns. The personal income tax is consequently considered to be neutral in consumption. It may, however, affect the supply of labour by altering workers' labour/leisure decisions. Similarly, a general sales tax, although it is passed on to consumers and causes an increase in prices, is unlikely to change relative prices and encourage consumers to make substitutions in consumption. But since such a tax penalizes current consumption, it may alter savings/consumption decisions. Excise taxes on selected goods may produce direct nonneutral effects. Assume two commodities, X and Y, that are substitutes in consumption. A tax on X but not on Y may cause the price of X to rise relative to that of Y and bring about substitution of Y for X. Excise taxes may, however, be imposed precisely for their nonneutral effects. As already noted, goods whose consumption is deemed to generate external costs, such as alcohol and tobacco, may be taxed to curtail consumption and reduce the amount of externalities produced. Similarly, a tax on the commodities produced by a firm that pollutes the environment may serve to increase prices and reduce production and associated pollution. In such cases, taxes have a positive nonneutral impact on the allocation of resources, serving to move the economy to a more efficient allocation.

A large body of literature in public sector economics has been devoted to analyzing the effects taxes may have on incentives, labour/leisure decisions, savings/consumption decisions, investment decisions, and decisions in production. These possible effects are influenced by the degree of shifting and the incidence of various taxes, issues that are discussed later in this chapter.

Administrative Feasibility

A tax should not be so complex that it cannot be understood by the taxpayer, yet it should be sufficiently comprehensive so that the potential for tax avoidance is minimized. Simplicity is required for ease of administration. Also, a tax should be inexpensive to administer relative to the revenues it generates, and sufficiently flexible to be changed easily in response to changing economic conditions.

Tax legislation should clearly define the tax base and specify exemptions and deductions if tax avoidance is to be minimized. The equity concept of equal treatment of equals is undermined if, given two individuals with equal taxable income, one finds loopholes in the legislation that enable reduction of his or her tax burden. A major difficulty facing government, however, is how to devise tax rules comprehensive enough to block all possible loopholes while keeping the legislation readily understandable and the tax forms simple. Furthermore, taxpayers should be able to comprehend the rules and understand the tax implications of any course of action they may take.

Tax administration involves both the government bureaucracy and the taxpayer. Individuals, as well as businesses, large and small, are required to keep income and expense records for tax purposes. If the tax is complex, record-keeping can be time-consuming and expensive. Tax complexity may even force ordinary individual taxpayers to seek professional assistance to interpret tax rules and to complete their tax returns.

Fiscal policy requires, in part, tax flexibility to meet changing economic conditions that may bring inflation, recession, or unemployment. A long delay in implementing tax policy changes to combat, for example, the beginning of an economic slowdown could reduce the effectiveness of such policy.

Tax Incidence, Tax Shifting, and Economic Effects

Tax incidence refers to the distribution of the burden of a tax; in essence, it is the final resting place of the tax burden. A tax may be imposed on and remitted by one entity, but if the burden of the tax can be shifted — passed on — to another entity, then the tax incidence is on the latter. Taxes may be shifted forward to consumers in the form of increased prices or backward to factors of production. The incidence of taxes and the degree of shifting are significant for analyzing the economic effects of taxes.

Personal Income Tax. It is generally acknowledged that the personal income tax is not a tax conducive to direct shifting of the burden. For income that consists of wages and salaries, the person on whom the tax is levied will pay it and bear the burden.

As noted earlier, the personal income tax is considered neutral in its effects on consumer choices and consumer patterns of spending. It may, however, affect both choices between work and leisure and investment decisions. The labour/leisure decision may be subject to an income and a substitution effect from the income tax. The income effect is positive, causing people to work more in an attempt to maintain their pre-tax incomes and standards of living. At the same time, the tax reduces the cost of leisure, prompting individuals to substitute leisure for work. Theoretically, the net result of the positive income and negative substitution effects is indeterminate. Empirical studies are also inconclusive.[5] In various surveys of professional and nonprofessional groups in the labour force, some workers report income effects, others report substitution effects, and still others report no effects on work decisions. Most studies indicate the effects of the personal income tax to be negligible on the supply of labour in the economy.

The effect on investment decisions results from including investment income, such as interest, dividends, and capital gains, in the personal income tax base. Such taxation reduces the amount of funds available for investment. A reduction in private investment could, in the long run, reduce economic growth and production unless balanced by an increase in public investment. The tax may also adversely affect incentives to take risks and invest, although the disincentive effect on risk-taking may be offset by permitting the deduction of losses from income for tax purposes. As with work/leisure decisions, there is no conclusive evidence on the net effect of the income tax on investment decisions. Some investors may be inclined to take more risk and attempt to increase their potential yield to offset their taxes on investment returns, while others may opt for safer though lower-yielding investments.

Corporation Income Tax. The corporation income tax offers a number of potential economic effects, including effects on prices, output, and production efficiency. The results depend on the assumptions of tax shifting and incidence. According to the theory of the firm, profits are maximized at the output at which marginal cost equals marginal revenue. A tax on monopoly profits does not disturb the profit-maximizing conditions; therefore, the firm pays the tax with no adjustments in production or prices. In practice, however, corporations may be motivated by factors other than profit maximization, particularly in the short run, and the imposition of a tax on profits may cause adjustments in corporate behaviour.

Assuming that corporations do not shift the income tax, it reduces corporate profits and the funds the firm has available for investment and expansion of production capacity. The incentive to expand capacity and increase potential profits may also be reduced if a significant portion of those profits will be absorbed by tax. In addition, the firm's incentive to maintain efficiency in production to maximize profits may be lessened if those profits are subjected to tax.

Assume that a firm does not operate at a profit-maximizing position but desires instead to earn a certain satisfactory level of profit or rate of return on capital while pursuing other objectives, such as increasing its sales and market share. When the corporation income tax is imposed, the firm may adjust its output and raise its prices in order to increase profits by an amount sufficient to pay the tax and retain its acceptable level of profits.[6]

A firm may also attempt to shift the tax backward to factors of production. One way of doing so is to not pass to factors the full benefits of increased productivity. Instead, the firm may use part of the cost savings to increase its pre-tax profits, pay the tax, and hold after-tax profits at the original profit level.

Empirical studies show that, despite a major increase in corporation income tax rates over the past several decades, corporate after-tax rates of return on capital have, on the average, either increased or remained constant. Most studies conclude that in the long run corporations have managed to shift the corporation income tax fully. Evidence indicates that, over time, output from each unit of investment has generated larger profits before taxes, and it is out of the gains from this increased productivity that higher taxes appear to have been paid.[7]

Various features, other than the tax rate, are frequently built into the corporation income tax structure for the purpose of attaining certain economic effects or fiscal objectives. The expenses incurred by a firm on capital equipment are deducted from gross income over time by a schedule of depreciation rates or capital cost allowances. In attempts to encourage investment in capital equipment, governments have used a policy of accelerated depreciation, which permits more rapid writeoffs than normally allowed. Another device for stimulating business investment is the investment tax credit, which is a deduction from tax payable of a certain percentage of the amount of investment the firm made during a tax year. This policy serves to increase the amount of after-tax profits, leaving the firm more funds to invest.

Sales and Excise Taxes. In general, sales and excise taxes are imposed on the seller with the expectation that they will be shifted to the consumer in the form of higher prices. In certain cases, such as the retail sales tax in the Canadian provinces, the tax is imposed directly on the consumer at the time of purchase of the taxed items.

The degree of forward shifting and, consequently, the effect of sales taxes on the prices and output of the taxed commodities depend on their price elasticity of supply and demand. A unit sales tax on the seller is generally treated as a cost of production and causes the seller's supply curve to move to a higher position. In a competitive market, a new, higher price is established by the interaction of supply and demand. In general, the greater the price elasticity of demand, the smaller will be the increase in price and the larger will be the reduction in quantity. Given that the price elasticity is greater in a competitive market than in a monopolistic market, it follows that the degree of tax shifting will be lower in the former than in the latter. A sales tax that is not completely shifted forward will be absorbed in part by the seller through reduced profits or by factors of production out of productivity gains.

It was mentioned earlier that excise taxes are frequently imposed on goods with external diseconomies in order to curb their consumption and reduce the amount of diseconomies generated. The effectiveness of a tax for this purpose depends on the price elasticity of demand for the product. If the demand is highly inelastic, the tax will produce an increase in price by practically the full amount of the tax but will not be very successful in curbing consumption.

It is difficult to determine empirically the degree of shifting of the sales tax because other, difficult to isolate factors may also be contributing to the price changes observed for the taxed goods. Nevertheless, the general conclusion of empirical analysts has been that, in most cases, the prices of commodities rise by roughly the amount of a sales tax imposed on them and fall by the amount of tax when it is eliminated. In other words, there appears to be full shifting of the sales tax.[8]

USER CHARGES

Certain goods and services provided by government have the characteristics of private goods and services and may be priced and sold directly to the public for fees called user charges. These charges are applied to water supply, hydroelectric power that is provided by governments, public parks and recreational facilities, hunting and fishing privileges, lumber-cutting and pulping privileges on government-owned lands, highways and bridges. Charges may be applied to cover all or part of the costs of the services. Unlike taxation, which attempts to apply the principle of ability-to-pay in the financing of government services, user charges are based on the benefit principle. Consumers pay for the goods and services in proportion to the amounts they use, regardless of their levels of income and wealth.

One argument for user charges is that, in addition to financing goods and services, they promote a degree of discipline in government spending by bringing market-type forces to bear on both demand and supply. Goods and services are purchased in the same manner as private goods — that is, in accordance with consumers' desire and ability to pay for them. Assuming that the fees charged cover costs of production, user charges also focus attention on costs and tend to promote efficiency. The alternative to the discipline provided by user charges is political or bureaucratic judgement, with the resulting possibilities that too much or too little may be supplied relative to public preferences and that there is no indicator to gauge the efficiency of production.

Many people oppose user charges, however, on the grounds that their use of the benefit principle represents an inequitable form of financing government activities, conflicting with the objective of redistributing income from higher-income groups to lower-income groups. A user in each group pays the same price for a service, but the amount paid by the low-income user represents a higher proportion of income than the amount paid by the high-income user. The incidence of the finance burden is, therefore, regressive and contrary to the generally accepted principle of progression as applied in the personal income tax.

Despite the recognized regressiveness of user fees and difficulties of administering them in certain cases, some people argue that governments in need of additional revenues could resort to greater reliance on fees.[9] User charges, it is maintained, are no more regressive than sales and excise taxes. The regressiveness of such taxes is reduced through the exemption of essential goods and services and tax rebates for low-income families. Similar accommodations, it is maintained, could be made for user fees.

Areas frequently mentioned in which user fees could be imposed (or applied more extensively) include education, recreational facilities, garbage and refuse collection, waste discharge privileges (that is, permits for industrial discharges into lakes and rivers), transportation facilities, and health care. For example, in his 1990 budget, the Treasurer of Ontario introduced proposals for extending user fees in the long-term care of the elderly. Elderly people living in nursing homes or homes for the aged would be required to pay a greater share of the cost of room and board; those with low incomes would be exempt from the higher fees. Elderly people who remained in their own homes but required services such as housekeeping and meal preparation would be charged on a sliding scale according to income.[10] The additional fees, it was estimated, would yield $100 million by the middle of the decade.

In late 1989, the federal government approved a new policy for extending application of user charges as part of its deficit-reduction program and in the belief that "users and other beneficiaries of government services should pay their fair share, rather than have these services funded, in general, by all taxpayers."[11] As an incentive to encourage departmental managers to recover costs of services through charges, the government provided that part of the proceeds could be invested in improvements to the services generating the revenues. The government forecast that the extended application of user fees would bring an additional $120 million in revenue by 1992/3.

Historical Development of Taxation in Canada

The tax structure of a country is usually a product not of systematic creation but of evolution, shaped over time by variety of forces. This is certainly true of Canada, as is evident from Table 4–1. Taxes or levies of one form or another can be traced to early colonial days. The pre-Confederation provinces of Canada were administering a number of taxes and charges, and these formed the basic tax structure of the new Canadian nation and provided the framework for future development.

The development of taxation following Confederation was influenced by a number of factors.[12] The division of taxing powers contained in the Constitution Act, 1867, probably played the strongest role in shaping the future direction of taxation at the federal and provincial levels of government. The act limited the provinces to direct taxes while granting unlimited taxing powers to the federal government. In 1867, direct taxation was unpopular and uncommon, and most of the revenue of the former provinces of Canada was derived from two indirect taxes — excise taxes and customs duties — which were assumed by the federal government. The provinces were left with the property tax and a variety of direct charges, licences, fees, and fines.

A second influence on the development of taxation in Canada was the government's effort to promote economic development of the country. In 1879, the federal government introduced the National Policy, a program designed to stimulate industrial development, transportation facilities, and westward expansion and settlement. The policy featured high tariffs to encourage and protect infant industry and to produce, along with higher excises, larger revenues to finance the construction of a transcontinental railway and other facilities. Economic development was, therefore, the major force behind federal taxation in the late nineteenth century. It also influenced provincial taxation for, as the economy and population grew, increased demands were placed on the

TABLE 4–1
Major Tax Events in Canada

	Event
Before 1916	Federal taxes: customs duties, excise taxes; Provincial and Municipal taxes: real and personal taxes, property taxes, succession duties, taxes on corporations, personal income taxes
1916	Federal corporation income tax
1917	Federal personal income tax
1920	Federal manufacturers' sales tax
1921	Monopoly sale of liquor by provinces
1922	Gasoline tax by provinces
1936	Retail sales tax by provinces
1941	Rental by federal government of personal income tax, corporation income tax, and succession duty fields from the provincial government
1949	Major reconstruction of federal personal income tax; dividend tax credit introduced
1962	Return of rented tax fields to provinces; provision of tax abatements by federal government
1972	Reform of the federal personal and corporation income tax following some recommendations of the 1966 report of the Royal Commission on Taxation Capital gains tax introduced; tax base expanded; federal death and gift taxes repealed
1974	Federal indexation of tax brackets and personal exemptions
1988	Reform of the personal and corporation income taxes: personal marginal tax rates reduced to 3 rates of 17, 26, and 29 percent; exemptions and deductions replaced by tax credits; corporation income tax rates reduced from 36 to 28 percent
1989	Canada–US Free Trade Agreement providing for gradual elimination of customs duties on imported goods produced in Canada and the US
1991	Goods and services tax of 7 percent, replacing 13.5 percent manufacturers' sales tax

provinces for services and activities falling under their areas of jurisdiction. They responded by finding a number of new sources of revenue and extending existing sources.

Many of the tax sources that were tapped by both levels of government in their search for revenues were based on American precedents. For example, succession duties were in wide use by US state governments before being adopted by Ontario in 1892. Similarly, personal and corporation income taxes and various excises imposed by the federal government were in existence for a considerable period in the United States before being imposed in Canada.

The American influence on Canadian tax structure and rates has continued to the present. The Canadian and US economies have traditionally been closely related and became even more so following the Canada–US Free Trade Agreement that came into effect on January 1, 1989. Taxation can affect trade and investment between the two countries. For example, tax burdens on corporations and investment gains that are significantly higher in Canada than in the United States have the potential for adverse effects on the competitiveness of Canadian industry, on exports, and on foreign investment in this country. The same can be said of sharp differences in the taxation systems of any trade partners. With the increasing trend toward global trading patterns and multinational corporations, there is pressure for international tax harmonization. Introducing a tax reform package in 1987, Minister of Finance Michael Wilson emphasized that it is "important that our tax system not place Canadians at a competitive disadvantage in domestic or international markets" and that Canada must "recognize the competitive reality of tax systems in other countries."[13]

Finally, taxation in Canada, as in most countries, has been influenced by international events such as wars and major economic disturbances. Historical trends show significant increases in tax levels during the two world wars and the Korean war, with the imposition of new taxes and increases in the rates of existing ones during these periods. After these emergencies were over, taxes were usually lowered, but precedents for taxes in new fields and for higher rates had been established, and it was only a matter of time before they rose to their previous levels. The federal government entered the direct tax field for the first time during the First World War, imposing personal and corporation income taxes. Seeking additional revenue, it also extended its excise tax structure to include a variety of new goods and imposed a general sales tax at the manufacturers' level. Taxes were lowered during the 1920s, but they were again increased during the Depression as both the federal government and the provinces sought to bolster sagging revenues. During the Second World War, federal taxes reached new levels. They were reduced following the war, only to be increased later to finance the Korean War, defence commitments, and expanding government activities in new areas of social service.

By the 1960s, the Canadian tax structure was well entrenched, with a host of different levies at all levels of government. At the federal level, the personal and corporation income taxes were supplemented by the manufacturers' sales tax, excise taxes, excise duties, customs duties, estate and gift taxes, and revenues from contributory welfare programs. Provinces were also tapping personal and corporate incomes and imposed sales taxes, succession duties, and a variety of charges. The property tax remained the primary tax source at the municipal level of government.

The federal tax system has experienced two recent attempts at major restructuring — in 1972 and 1987 — as well as some other important developments. The changes that came into effect in 1972 implemented the most comprehensive tax reform in Canada since the income tax had been introduced in 1917. It was the climax to a tax reform movement begun ten years earlier with the appointment of a royal commission on taxation. There had been no major study of the Canadian tax system since the Rowell-Sirois Commission's investigation in the late 1930s. Many inequities existed in the tax system, and little was known of the effects of the tax structure on the economy.

The Royal Commission on Taxation did not propose patchwork changes in the existing tax system but instead offered an entirely new structure based on premises and principles established by the commission.[14] Numerous novel concepts and features were contained in the recommended system, which many termed a radical departure from the tax structure of the time. The focus of the commission's investigation and report was personal and corporation income taxation. Among the significant features of the proposed system were a comprehensive tax base, the taxation of capital gains, the concept of the family as the tax-paying unit, changes in personal and business deductions and exemptions, changes in tax rates that would shift more of the burden from lower-income to higher-income groups, integration of personal and corporate income, income averaging, elimination of the dual rate of corporation income tax and of special concessions to the extractive industries, and the closing of numerous tax loopholes.

Although the system proposed by the commission was not accepted in its entirety, legislation in 1972 did make some notable changes in income taxation.[15] The most significant in the personal income tax included increases in personal exemptions and exemptions for the elderly, an increase in deductions for pension plans and registered retirement savings plans, changes in the dividend tax credit, and the extension of income averaging. Also introduced were deductions for employment expenses, moving expenses, and child-care expenses. The tax base was broadened by bringing into it previously exempt income including capital gains, unemployment insurance benefits, training allowances, and research grants and fellowships. The introduction of the tax on capital gains resulted in the abolition of the estate and gift tax.

Nineteen seventy-four saw another significant development in federal taxation: the introduction of indexation, whereby the marginal tax brackets and certain exemptions were to be adjusted annually by an inflation factor. The 1970s also witnessed moves by both federal and provincial governments to tap more and more heavily the natural resource industries of oil and gas for revenue.

Major changes in features of personal, corporation, and sales taxation were again proposed by the federal government in June 1987.[16] The changes in personal and corporation taxes became effective in January 1, 1988, while replacement of the manufacturers' sales tax with a form of value-added tax was set for some unspecified future date. (The manufacturers' sales tax was eventually replaced by the more comprehensive goods and services tax (GST) effective January 1, 1991.)

Several objectives were specified in the tax reform of 1987. First and foremost was an attempt to make the tax system more equitable. Higher-income individuals and profitable businesses would be required to carry a larger share of the tax burden. This goal was to be achieved by expanding the tax base through the elimination (or reduction) of some of the selective preferences by the higher-income groups and profitable corporations, by increasing the sales tax credit for lower- and middle-income families, and by converting personal exemptions and some deductions into tax credits.

(Exemptions are subtracted from income; credits are subtracted from tax payable. Tax credits provide the same absolute dollar reduction in tax regardless of income level, whereas exemption and deductions provide greater benefit to taxpayers in the higher tax brackets.) More effective rules would reduce artificial tax avoidance to ensure that individuals in similar economic circumstances were taxed more equitably. In essence, the government was emphasizing taxation according to the familiar ability-to-pay principle and the concepts of horizontal and vertical equity.

The second objective of tax reform was to make the tax system more compatible with economic growth, job creation, and industry competitiveness. Marginal tax rates for both individuals and corporations were reduced as a means of encouraging investment, rewarding success, and increasing productivity. In 1987, the federal personal income tax had a total of ten tax brackets with marginal rates progressing from 6 percent on the first $1318 of taxable income to 34 percent on income in excess of $63 347. Tax reform reduced the number of tax brackets to three, with marginal rates of 17 percent on the first $27 500 of taxable income, 26 percent on the next $27 500, and 29 percent on the remainder. The corporation income tax rate for general business was reduced from 36 to 28 percent, and the small business rate from 15 to 12 percent.

A third objective was to simplify the tax system, making it easier for taxpayers to understand and comply with the system. It was expected that a simpler structure of tax rates and fewer special preferences would facilitate such understanding. One of the casualties of simplification was income averaging for tax purposes. A system of forward averaging had been in effect, permitting a taxpayer to spread across several years an unusually large amount of income received in any one tax year (such as a lump-sum payment) and consequently avoid the higher marginal tax rates that would normally have applied to the increased income. As a consequence of the lowering of tax rates and moving to only three tax brackets, the forwarding averaging system was eliminated after 1987.

The government also sought closer consistency and integration of the tax system with the objectives of other government programs. For example, numerous social programs and transfer payments had been designed to redistribute income and to assist the needy. Reducing the income tax burden on low-income groups by converting tax exemptions and deductions to tax credits was viewed as complementary to these other programs and their objective of income redistribution.

A final objective of the 1987 tax reform was to make the tax system a more reliable source of government revenue by removing special preferences and curbing opportunities for tax avoidance. Special preferences erode the tax base and create inequities among taxpayers. For example, in 1984, the many tax preferences in the system reduced taxable personal income to only 60 percent of assessed income. In that year, the Minister of Finance claimed, 52 percent of taxpayers with incomes in the $75 000 to $100 000 range paid an average federal tax rate of 20 to 25 percent, while 21 percent of the same group paid a rate of less than 15 percent, and 4 percent of taxpayers with incomes in excess of $100 000 paid no tax at all.[17] Similar inequities had developed in the corporate sector because of special allowances and credits and growing tax avoidance.

TABLE 4–2
Shares of Tax Revenue for All Canadian Governments, 1988/9

Source	Percentage of total collected by: Federal government	Percentage of total collected by: Provincial and municipal governments
Personal income tax	61.1	38.9
Corporation income tax	66.6	33.4
General sales tax	48.8	51.2
Other consumption taxes	33.3	66.7
Natural resources	2.9	97.1
Health and social insurance	65.1	34.9
Property and related taxes	0.0	100.0
Customs duties	100.0	0.0
Total taxes	51.9	48.1

Sources: Statistics Canada, CANSIM matrices 2777, 2751, and 2764, July 19, 1990.

In announcing the 1987 proposals, the government, as in previous cases of tax reform, attempted to assure Canadian taxpayers that it was not instituting tax increases in the guise of tax reform. Indeed, with reference to the reform of the personal income tax, the Minister of Finance estimated that the changes would reduce income taxes for more than 80 percent of taxpaying households and that about 850 000 individuals would no longer pay federal income tax,

Tax Revenue Features

Canadian tax and other revenue sources are shared by the federal and the provincial and municipal governments, as shown in Table 4–2.[18] The federal government is dominant in the income tax field and has sole jurisdiction over custom import duties. Consumption-based taxes (sales and excises) are shared almost equally by the federal and provincial governments.

Table 4–3 shows the proportion of gross domestic product absorbed by federal government revenues. During the last three decades the proportion has fluctuated between 16 and 18 percent, with the lowest figures occurring during the mid-1960s and the later 1970s. From 1979, however, there was a gradual increase from 15.7 percent of GDP to 18.2 percent by 1988.

The changing significance of each federal tax in terms of revenue yield is shown in Table 4–4. The most notable trends after the mid-1960s were the relative increase in the share of personal income tax and the decline in the corporation income tax and excise taxes and duties. The latter change reflected decreasing tax rates on corporations

TABLE 4–3
Total Federal Revenues as Percentage of Gross Domestic Product for Selected Years 1961–1989 (national accounts basis)

	% of GDP
1961	16.6
1965	15.8
1970	17.4
1975	18.5
1978	15.8
1979	15.7
1980	16.3
1982	17.7
1984	17.2
1986	18.1
1987	18.2
1988	18.2
1989	18.0

Source: Canada, Department of Finance, *Quarterly Economic Review: Annual Reference Tables*, June 1990 (Ottawa).

and on commodities and a reduction in the scope of excise taxes over the period shown. Revenue from the manufacturers' sales tax declined during the 1970s and then rose reflecting increased rates (from 10 percent in 1984 to 13.5 percent by 1989).

The personal income tax remained the most important source of revenue for the federal government, accounting for over 40 percent of total revenue for 1988/9. Revenues from this tax declined from 38.3 percent in 1976/7 to 34.8 percent in 1981/2, reflecting the transfer of personal income tax points to the provinces under the 1978 federal/provincial fiscal agreements. After 1982, personal income tax revenue increased in relative importance, reflecting the changes in the tax and the imposition of surtaxes.

Commodity- or consumption-based taxes, such as sales taxes, excises, and customs duties, were the second highest revenue-producers at 20 percent in 1989, a significant increase from their 16.5 percent level in 1982. Payroll taxes, such as unemployment insurance and Canada Pension Plan contributions, at 15 percent in 1989 also followed a rising trend. Levies on oil and gas, which consisted primarily of the oil export charge and the petroleum compensation fund levy, yielded large revenues in the early 1980s but were dropped later in the decade. In the nontax category, revenue from sales of goods and services showed a sharp decline when the post office became a Crown corporation in 1982.

TABLE 4–4
Historical Summary of the Federal Government's Revenues

Source	Revenues for fiscal year ending March 31			
	1967	1977	1982	1989
	(percentage of total revenue)			
Taxes				
Personal income	28.8	38.3	34.8	41.4
Corporation income	16.4	13.9	11.2	10.1
Manufacturers' sales	19.6	10.2	8.5	13.3
Excise taxes & duties	7.3	5.4	3.3	2.7
Customs import duties	7.2	5.1	4.7	3.8
Unemployment insurance contributions	3.2	6.4	6.6	9.7
Universal pension plan levies	5.5	4.3	4.4	5.3
Oil and gas		1.7	9.7	
Other	3.0	1.9	3.0	4.2
Total tax revenue	91.0	87.2	86.2	90.5
Nontax Revenue				
Return on Investments[a]	3.7	6.3	7.1	6.1
Sales of goods & services	3.9	4.6	5.0	2.3
Other	1.4	1.9	1.7	1.1
Total nontax revenue	9.0	12.8	13.8	9.5
Total	100.0	100.0	100.0	100.0
	($ billion)			
Total Amount	$10.6	$38.5	$72.5	$118.0

[a] Income derived from loans and advances to government enterprises and other governments and from investments in government enterprises.

Sources: Statistics Canada, *Federal Government Finance*, cat. 68–211; and CANSIM matrix 2777, July 19, 1990.

ENDNOTES

1. A detailed discussion and analysis of taxation, including kinds of taxes, principles, economic effects, and other theoretical and practical aspects, can be found in most standard textbooks on public sector economics. See, for example, R.A. Musgrave, P. Musgrave, and R.M. Bird, *Public Finance in Theory and Practice*, Cdn. ed. (Toronto: McGraw-Hill Ryerson 1987); H.S. Rosen, *Public Finance*, 2nd ed. (Homewood, Ill., Richard D. Irwin, 1988); and J.E. Stiglitz, *Economics of the Public Sector*, 2nd ed., (New York: W.W. Norton, 1988).

2. The three principles discussed in this chapter embody most of the desirable features of a tax that are frequently mentioned in public finance literature. See, for example, Stiglitz, *Economics of the Public Sector*, p. 390; and James Meade, *The Structure and Reform of Direct Taxation* (London: Allen and Unwin, 1978), ch. 2.

3. See W.J. Blum and H. Kalven, *The Uneasy Case for Progressive Taxation* (Chicago: University of Chicago Press, 1978).

4. Evidence of the regressive nature of provincial retail sales taxes in Canada is presented in François Vaillancourt and Marie-France Poulaert, "The Incidence of Provincial Sales Taxes in Canada, 1978, and 1982," *Canadian Tax Journal* 33(May/June 1985).

5. Canada, *Studies of the Royal Commission on Taxation*, no. 4, *The Effects of Income Taxation on Work Choices* (Ottawa: Queen's Printer, 1967).

6. This type of behaviour of the firm is described in the Baumol model of sales-maximization and is illustrated in many textbooks on public sector theory. See W. Baumol, *Economic Theory and Operational Analysis*, 3rd ed. (Englewood Cliffs, NJ: Prentice-Hall, 1973).

7. Canada, *Studies of the Royal Commission on Taxation*, no. 18 *The Shifting of the Corporation Income Tax in the Short Run*, (Ottawa: Queen's Printer, 1967).

8. O. Brownlee and G.L. Perry, "The Effects of the 1965 Federal Excise Tax Reductions on Prices", *National Tax Journal*, XX, no. 3, 1967.

9. See R.M. Bird and N.E. Slack, *Urban Public Finance in Canada* (Toronto: Butterworth, 1983), ch. 6. The application of user fees by Canadian municipalities is also discussed in M. Sproule-Jones and J. White, "The Scope and Application of User Charges in Municipal Governments," *Canadian Tax Journal* 37 (November/December 1989).

10. Treasurer of Ontario, *1990 Ontario Budget* (Toronto: Ministry of Treasury and Economics, 1990); and *The Globe and Mail*, April 25, 1990, p. A11.

11. Canada, Treasury Board, *Information: Federal Expenditure Reductions and Management Improvements* (Ottawa, December 15, 1989), p. 7.

12. For a detailed history of taxation in Canada, see such standard works as A.E. Buck, *Financing Canadian Government* (Chicago: Public Administration Service, 1949); J. Harvey Perry, *Taxes, Tariffs, and Subsidies* (Toronto: University of Toronto Press, 1955), vol. 1 and 2; J. Harvey Perry, *Taxation in Canada* (Toronto: University of Toronto Press, 1961); and A. Milton Moore, J. Harvey Perry, and Donald I. Beach, *The Financing of Canadian Federation* (Toronto: Canadian Tax Foundation, 1966), ch. 1.

13. Canada, Department of Finance, *The White Paper: Tax Reform 1987* (Ottawa, June 18, 1987), p. 4.

14. Canada, *Report of the Royal Commission on Taxation* (Ottawa: Queen's Printer, 1966).

15. Canada, *Summary of 1971 Tax Reform Legislation* (Ottawa: Queen's Printer, 1971).

16. Canada, Department of Finance, *The White Paper: Tax Reform 1987* (Ottawa, June 18, 1987); *Tax Reform 1987: Income Tax Reform* (Ottawa, June 18, 1987); and *Tax Reform 1987: Sales Tax Reform*, (Ottawa: June 18, 1987); Canada, *Goods and Services*

Tax: An Overview (Ottawa, August 1989); and Department of Finance, *Goods and Services Tax Technical Paper* (Ottawa, August 1989).

17. Canada, *The White Paper*, ibid., p. 8.

18. Data on various aspects of federal government revenue are presented annually in Statistics Canada, *Federal Government Finance Revenue and Expenditure, Assets and Liabilities*, cat. 68–211; (Ottawa); Statistics Canada, *National Income and Expenditure Accounts*, cat. 13–001 (Ottawa); Canada, Department of Finance, *Economic Review* (Ottawa); Revenue Canada, *Taxation Statistics* (Ottawa); and Canadian Tax Foundation, *The National Finances* (Toronto)

CHAPTER 5

THE FEDERAL TAX STRUCTURE

The Canadian federal tax system includes a variety of taxes, including the personal income tax, the corporation income tax, consumption-based taxes (the general sales tax, excise taxes, excise duties, and customs duties), and payroll taxes. This chapter presents a nontechnical examination of the basic features of these taxes and of tax expenditures.[1]

Personal Income Tax

The various items constituting income, deductions, exemptions, and credits in the federal personal income tax structure are outlined in Table 5–1. These items are explained, along with certain qualifications that may not be evident from the table, in the following pages.

Income

The Income Tax Act defines income for tax purposes as all gains from offices held, employment, business, property, and other sources. Income includes both money gains and certain real gains and therefore represents increases in wealth during a year on a source-by-source basis.

Money gains consist of wages, salaries, gratuities, rents, dividends, interest, unemployment insurance benefits, fellowships, bursaries and scholarships in excess of $500, research grants, training allowances, amounts contributed on an employee's behalf to a public medical care plan, pensions, capital gains, annuities, family allowances, alimony received, gifts from an employer, tuition fees paid on a taxpayer's behalf, living and expense allowances, and foreign income received. Real gains consist of income in kind — that is, in the form of goods and services rather than cash. Examples include the value of board and lodging freely provided and the use value of a company-supplied automobile. Similarly, if an employer sells assets to an employee at a bargain price, the difference between the price charged and the fair market value is a taxable gain to the employee. The same calculation must be applied to stock options whereby an employer purchases shares of the employer corporation at a price that is less than their market value. Real income in the form of imputed gains from consumer durables is , however, excluded from the measurement of income. Durables, such as owner-occupied homes, yield a stream of services valued as the rent that could have been received if the home had been rented out. The benefit received is imputed income and adds to the wealth of the individual, but because of practical difficulties of measuring such income, it is excluded from the concept of income for tax purposes. Income is viewed as economic gain in the form of *measurable* flows of wealth.

TABLE 5–1
Federal Personal Income Tax
Calculation of Taxable Income and Tax

Income		
Income from employment		
Pension income		
Old Age Security		
Canada Pension Plan		
Other pensions		
Income from other sources		
Family allowance		
Unemployment insurance benefits		
Taxable amount of dividends from Canadian corporations		
Interest and other investment income		
Rental income		
Taxable capital gains		
Alimony or separation allowances		
Registered retirement savings plan income		
Other income (specify)		
Self-Employment Income (net)		
Business income		
Professional income		
Commissions		
Farming and fishing income	Total income	1
Deductions from total income		
Annual union and professional dues		
Child-care expenses		
Alimony paid		
Moving expenses		
Registered pension plan contribution		
Registered retirement savings plan contributions		
Carrying charges		
Capital gains deduction		
Other deductions	Total deductions	2
	Taxable income(1 – 2)	3
	Federal income tax on taxable income	4
Non-refundable tax credits		
Basic personal amount		
Age amount		
Married amount		
Amounts for dependent children		
Canada or Quebec Pension Plan contributions		
Unemployment insurance premiums		
Pension income amount (maximum $1000)		
Disability amount		

Tuition fees (self)	
Education amount (self)	
Tuition fees and education amount transferred from child	
Amounts transferred from spouse	
Medical expenses less 3 percent of net income	
Total amount	5
17 percent of total amount	6
Charitable donations and gifts to Canada or a province	
17 percent of first $250	
29 percent of balance	
Total	7
Total Nonrefundable tax credits (line 6 + line 7)	8
Other tax credits	
Child tax credit (refundable)	
Federal sales tax credit (refundable)	
Federal political contribution tax credit	
Federal dividend tax credit	
Foreign tax credit	
Total other tax credits	9
Total tax credits (line 8 + line 9)	10
Net federal tax payable (line 4 – line 10)	11

The base to which the personal income tax applies consists of total income, as defined above, received during a calendar year. To arrive at net income, the taxpayer makes various subtractions from total income. These consist of business and personal expenses incurred in earning the income or nondiscretionary expenditures that reduce tax-paying ability. From net income, certain other deductions, such as the capital gains deduction and business and property losses, are made to arrive at taxable income. The tax is calculated on that amount. Then various tax credits are subtracted. They are adjustments for tax-paying ability, nondiscretionary expenditures, and taxes already paid on the taxable income.

Business Income and Deductions

A business is an activity involving the production, purchase, or sale of goods and/or services. It may consist of manufacturing, commercial trade, or the practice of a profession. In arriving at taxable income, the taxpayer must deduct expenses incurred in the process of obtaining income from the business, including wages and salaries paid, cost of materials, interest on borrowed money used in the business, contributions to an employee's pension fund, expenditures on scientific research, expenses in connection with attending conventions (limited to two per year), advertising costs, donations, automobile expenses, and foreign taxes paid. Deductions for capital expenditures are made by way of capital cost allowances (depreciation) as specified in the Income Tax Act.

There are two methods of accounting used in determining income from a business: the cash method and the accrual method. Farmers and fishermen may use the cash method, but most other businesses are required to use the accrual method. In the cash method, amounts are included in income in the year in which they are actually received and expenses are deducted in the year paid. Under the accrual method, amounts are included as income in the year they are earned, and expenses are deducted in the year incurred, whether or not they have been paid.

A business may choose a fiscal year other than the calendar year. If it does so, income and expenses are calculated for that fiscal period, and it is considered the taxation year.

Personal Deductions

In addition to any business expenses a taxpayer may have, there are other deductible outlays, justified on the grounds that they are nondiscretionary and reduce tax-paying ability or on economic grounds.

Retirement Plans. The Canadian government assists and encourages people to save for retirement by permitting deductions for contributions to a Retirement Pension Plan (RPP) and to a Registered Retirement Savings Plan (RRSP). Pension reform in 1990 provided generous deductions for such plans. Beginning in 1991, a taxpayer may contribute 18 percent of the previous year's earned income, up to a limit of $11 500. This limit is scheduled to rise by $1000 each year to $15 500 in 1995, after which the limit will increase by the amount of annual wage increases. If an individual belongs to a registered employer-sponsored pension plan, the annual RRSP contribution limit is reduced by a pension adjustment, a measure calculated by the employer based on the value of contributions to the employer-sponsored plan.

Employment-Related Expenses. Certain expenses incurred by an employee are deductible from income. A taxpayer may deduct expenses incurred while working away from home, such as board and lodging, provided the employer does not reimburse for them. (This applies only if employees must leave their ordinary residences and live and work at distant sites where they cannot reasonably be expected to establish a home for their families.) Similarly, moving expenses incurred by taxpayers who change jobs (whether for a change in employers or a transfer) are deductible provided that the new residence is at least 40 kilometres closer to a new job location. Students who have been in full-time attendance at a university or other postsecondary education institution in Canada can deduct expenses incurred in moving within Canada to take a job, including summer employment. A student who moves to attend a university or postsecondary institution full-time within Canada or outside of Canada may deduct moving expenses against scholarships, research grants, and other awards if the move results in a new residence at least 40 kilometres closer to the educational institution.

Annual membership dues in a trade union or in an association required to maintain professional status, such as those paid by a lawyer, engineer, or accountant, are deductible.

An employee who is required to travel as part of his employment and does not receive an allowance for travelling expenses may deduct travel expenses. Commission salespeople who pay their own expenses may deduct all expenses incurred in earning their commissions. Employees who maintain offices in their homes and meet certain requirements may deduct a proportion of the expense of operating and maintaining the home, such as those incurred for electricity, fuel, and minor repairs. Similarly, taxpayers who maintain an office in their place of residence for the purpose of conducting a business may deduct a portion of the household expenses if they meet specified conditions, but the amount deducted cannot exceed the income from the business.

Child-Care Expenses. If a family has both parents working or only one parent and he or she is working, deductions for child-care expenses, such as the costs of babysitting and nursery daycare are allowed up to $4000 per child for children less than seven years of age and up to $2000 per child for those between the ages of seven and fifteen. For a two-parent family, the deduction is available to the parent with the lower income and may not exceed two-thirds of that person's earned income. Expenses must be supported with receipts and must be incurred to enable the claimant to be employed or to conduct a business.

Investment-Related Deductions. Certain expenses related to the income earned from investments are deductible from total income. They include interest paid on funds borrowed to purchase bonds, stocks, and other investments; safety deposit box charges paid to banks or others for safe custody of investments; and investment counselling fees and portfolio management fees paid to a bank, a trust, or an investment dealer or counsellor.

Tax Credits

Tax credits are deductions from the tax payable. They are employed to reduce the tax burden on members of lower-income groups, to achieve equity, to achieve economic objectives and, in certain instances, to avoid or reduce double taxation.

Before the tax reform put in place in 1988, the primary tax credits found in the federal personal income tax structure were the dividend tax credit, child credits, and credits for the federal sales tax and foreign taxes paid. One of the main features of the reform was the conversion of the personal exemptions and certain other deductions into tax credits. The personal exemptions that were converted into credits were the basic personal exemption, the married exemption, and the exemptions for dependent children, the aged, and the disabled. The other deductions that were changed into credits involved pension income, tuition fees and other education expenditures, unemployment insurance premiums, medical expenses, disability allowances, contributions to the Canada (or Quebec) Pension Plan, and charitable donations.

The rationale behind the conversion of these exemptions and deductions into credits was in keeping with the central objective of tax reform: to make the personal income tax more equitable by eliminating loopholes and by shifting a greater proportion of the tax burden to higher-income groups. Deductions from taxable income benefit high-income earners more than low-income earners because the former are subject to higher marginal tax rates and therefore enjoy a greater tax reduction from a deduction. For example, under the previous system, each $1000 of exemption was worth $60 of federal tax saving to a taxpayer in the lowest tax bracket but $340 to a taxpayer in the highest tax bracket. Tax credits, however, provide the same dollar reduction of tax to all taxpayers, regardless of their level of income. Lower-income and middle-income families with large personal exemptions were expected to benefit significantly from the conversion.

Since the 1988 tax year, personal exemptions have been replaced by "personal amounts." Various other former deductions are now also referred to as "amounts." These amounts are added together and converted into tax credits by multiplying the aggregate by 17 percent, the lowest personal tax rate. (Special rates are applied to charitable donations and gifts to government, as illustrated in Table 5–1.) Under the reformed tax rate structure, that rate is applied to the first $27 500 of taxable income. Consequently, a 17 percent tax credit provides benefits equivalent to a deduction for taxpayers with taxable income of or less than $27 500 and limits the tax benefits for those at higher income levels and higher marginal tax rates.

Tax credits may be refundable or nonrefundable. If the total of refundable credits exceeds the total tax payable, the difference is refundable — returned to the taxpayer. With nonrefundable tax credits, however, if the credits are more than the federal income tax, the difference is not refunded. The two refundable federal tax credits are the child tax credit and the federal sales tax credit, both of which existed in the prereform tax system. All of the tax credits introduced by the reform of 1988 are nonrefundable.

Nonrefundable Tax Credits

This section describes the tax credits that are conversions of former exemption and deduction amounts and that came into effect with tax reform in January 1988. The credit is 17 percent of the amounts shown, unless otherwise specified.

Personal Credits. Invariably, a tax structure exempts from taxation a certain amount of income determined as essential for existence and, therefore, unrepresentative of tax-paying ability. The amount is usually arbitrarily determined but takes into consideration such factors as marital status, support of dependants, age, and physical or mental disability. The Canadian tax system provides these exemptions in the form of nonrefundable credits of 17 percent of personal "amounts." Each taxpayer is entitled to a basic personal amount. In addition, there are a married amount, amounts for dependent children, an age amount for taxpayers 65 years or over, and a disability amount for the taxpayer or dependants.

The basic personal amount for the 1990 taxation year was $6169, so the basic personal tax credit was 17 percent of this amount or $1049. Like other personal amounts, it is increased annually through tax indexation,[2] which, since 1986, has been limited to the annual increase in the consumer price index in excess of 3 percent.

The married amount for 1990 was $5141 if the taxpayer's spouse had a yearly net income of less than $514. If that income was more than $506 but less than $5655, then the taxpayer could claim a married amount of $5655 less the spouse's net income. If the spouse's net income exceeded $5655, the spouse was required to file a separate return.

The deduction for dependent children is affected by their age and income, whether they are physically or mentally infirm, and the number of children claimed. In the 1990 tax year, for children age eighteen or younger whose net income was less than $2750, the maximum amounts allowable were $399 for each of two children and $798 for each additional one. The applicable deduction was reduced by $1 for every $1 of net income a child had in excess of $2570. No amount was allowable for a child over eighteen years of age unless he or she was physically or mentally infirm. In such cases, the maximum amount allowable was $1512, reduced by $1 for every $1 of net income earned by the child in excess of $2570.

A special age amount, which was $3327 in 1990, may be claimed by taxpayers 65 years of age and over. This amount could also be claimed by taxpayers who suffered physical or mental disabilities such as the blind or the bedridden.

In each of these cases, the tax credit is 17 percent of the specified amount.

Private Pension Income Credit. A taxpayer may claim a tax credit of 17 percent of the first $1000 of certain types of pension income. This amount is restricted to income from private pension plans, annuity payments from registered retirement savings plans, and other annuity payments. Income from the Canada (or Quebec) Pension Plan, Old Age Security benefits, and lump-sum payments from registered retirement or savings plans are excluded. A taxpayer, however, can claim contributions to the Canada (or Quebec) Pension Plan; the maximum in 1990 was $574, which converted into a tax credit of $97.60.

Education Expense Credits. A student may claim, as a tax credit, 17 percent of tuition fees paid (but not amounts for books or other expenses) if the fees exceeded $100 and were paid to an educational institution in Canada or to a degree-granting institution outside Canada where the student attended a degree course full-time for at least thirteen consecutive weeks. Only the student may claim tuition fees, even if someone else paid them. Tuition must be claimed on a calendar-year basis; for example, only fees paid for courses taken from January 1 to December 31, 1990 could be claimed on the student's 1990 return.

In addition, there is an education claim of $60 for each month during the tax year that a student was in full-time attendance at a designated educational institution. Such institutions include universities and colleges in Canada, universities outside Canada if the student was enrolled in a degree course of at least thirteen consecutive weeks, and some schools that have job retraining or education courses.

If a student does not need to claim tuition fees and the education amount to reduce federal tax to zero, the unused part, to a maximum of $3529, may be transferred to his or her parent or grandparent (but not to more than one person). In other words, the amount transferable is $3529 less the amount used by the student.

The credit is 17 percent of the amount, transferred or not.

Medical Credits. A taxpayer may claim as an "amount" all medical expenses in excess of $1542 or 3 percent of net income, whichever is less. Expenses paid on a taxpayer's behalf by a government or private medical plan are not deductible. If a medical plan pays only a portion of the total medical expense and the taxpayer is required to pay the remainder, the difference may be claimed as a medical expense.

The term "medical expense" includes payments to a medical practitioner, a dentist, a hospital, or a nursing home and payments for eyeglasses, crutches, and the like and for prescription medicines and drugs, whether paid within or outside of Canada. Premiums a taxpayer pays to a private medical plan may be claimed, but not payments to a government plan. Premiums paid by a taxpayer's employer on his or her behalf under a government hospitalization or medical plan are reported as taxable benefits, but premiums paid by an employer under a private health services plan are not taxable benefits.

Once the medical amount is calculated (by subtracting $1542 or 3 percent of net income from the allowable expenses), the credit is figured at the rate of 17 percent.

Amounts Transferred From Spouse. If an individual has certain amounts available that need not be claimed to reduce his or her federal income tax to zero, they may be transferred to the spouse's return. The amounts that may be transferred are the age amount, the pension income amount, the disability amount, and the tuition fees and education amounts. The spouse's unused amounts are converted to tax credits at the rate of 17 percent.

Charitable Donations Credit. Claims are permitted for contributions to registered charitable institutions up to a maximum of 20 percent of net income. Institutions that qualify as registered charities include organizations such as the Canadian Red Cross, the Canadian Cancer Society, United Appeal, hospitals, churches, educational institutions (including specified foreign universities), and United Nations agencies. The donations may include cash or property. If the gift is property, the taxpayer is deemed to receive proceeds equal to its value, so he or she may be liable for tax if a capital gain is involved.

Any unused or unclaimed donations may be carried forward five years. Official receipts are required for all donations claimed. The amount of the tax credit for charitable donations depends on their total. If they add up to $250 or less, the tax credit is 17 percent of the donations. If the total is larger, the tax credit is 17 percent of the first $250 and 29 percent of the excess amount.

The rationale for permitting deductions for charitable donations appears to be that charities perform important social functions similar to those performed by government and supplement numerous government services.

Gifts to Canada and Provinces. The full amount of gifts to the government of Canada or a province is eligible for a tax credit. The credit is calculated as 17 percent of the first $250 of total gifts and 29 percent of the remainder. Unlike the claim for charitable contributions, which is limited to 20 percent of net income, the claim for donations to government is unlimited.

Federal Political Contribution Tax Credit. Credit may be claimed for contributions to a registered federal political party or to a candidate for election to Parliament. The allowable credit is 75.0 percent of the first $100 of the contribution, 50.0 percent of the next $450, and 33.3 percent of the amount in excess of $550. The maximum credit that may be claimed in a tax year is $500, which is reached when $1150 has been contributed. Any amount that is not required to reduce federal tax payable to zero cannot be carried forward.

Dividend Tax Credit. Dividends received by shareholders on equity shares have already been subject to corporation tax as income of corporations. The federal government permits a taxpayer to deduct from federal tax 13.3 percent of the taxable amount of dividends received from taxable Canadian corporations. The tax on dividends is computed by grossing-up the dividend received by 25 percent, calculating the tax payable at the taxpayer's marginal rate, and subtracting from that amount 13.3 percent of the grossed-up dividend. The method of computing the taxable dividend and the dividend tax credit is as follows:

Dividend received	$400
Gross-up: $400 x 25%	100
Taxable dividend	$500
Tax (assume 17% rate) $500 x 17%	85
Dividend tax credit: $500 x 13.3%	67
Tax payable	$18

Foreign Tax Credit. The federal government grants a tax credit for taxes paid to a foreign government on income from that country. The foreign tax credit deduction is, however, the lesser of the foreign taxes paid or the amount of the Canadian tax payable on the income received from the foreign country.

Refundable Tax Credits

The two refundable tax credits in Canada's federal personal income tax are the child tax credit and the sales tax credit. In both cases, if the credits reduce tax payable to an amount less than zero, the taxpayer is entitled to a refund from the government.

Child Tax Credit. For 1990, the basic tax credit was $575 for each eligible child, plus a supplementary credit of $203 for each child of less than seven years of age. The supplement was reduced by 25 percent of child-care expenses claimed. The aggregate credit was further reduced by 5 percent of the total net income of both spouses in excess of $24 769.

Federal Sales Tax Credit. The sales tax credit was introduced as a credit for the federal manufacturers' sales tax. When the manufacturers' sales tax was replaced by the goods and services tax (GST) in 1991, the credit was increased. The credit is independent of actual sales taxes paid by the taxpayer. It is available for all persons nineteen years of age or over.

For 1990, the credit for the manufacturers' sales tax amounted to $140 for the taxpayer, plus $140 for a spouse and $70 for each dependent child under the age of nineteen. It was reduced by 5 percent of the total net income of the two spouses in excess of $18 000. Beginning in 1991, the GST credit is $190 for each adult and $100 for each dependent child less 5 percent of family income in excess of $24 800. Unlike the previous sales tax credit, however, the GST credit is paid in advance every three months.

Taxation of Nonresidents

Persons not resident in Canada but receiving income from either employment or a business in the country are subject to income tax at regular rates on income from Canadian sources. Nonresidents are required to file a Canadian tax return, but certain restrictions apply to the deductions and credits that may be claimed. Following the "90 percent rule," if at least 90 percent of a nonresident's income for the year is included in the taxable income he or she earned in Canada, all the deductions and credits may be claimed. Nonresidents are taxed on capital gains from property held in Canada, but they are not eligible for the lifetime capital gains tax exemption that residents enjoy.

Investment income and certain types of other income earned by nonresidents is subject to a withholding tax at the source of the income. The general nonresident withholding tax rate is 25 percent of the gross amount, with no deductions permitted. The rate is reduced to 15 percent for residents of countries with which Canada has a tax agreement or treaty. The nonresident receiving the payment is not required to file a Canadian tax return as the tax is remitted to the Canadian government by the payor. Income earned by nonresidents that is subject to the withholding tax includes interest, dividends, certain pensions and retirement allowances, rents, royalties, estate or trust income, and alimony payments.

Tax Rates

The federal personal income tax uses a different rate for each of three tax brackets. For 1990, they were:

Taxable income	Tax
0 to $28 275	17%
$28 276 to $56 449	26%
$56 550 and over	29%

The rates are fixed but the tax brackets are indexed annually (that is, they are increased by the amount of increase in the consumer price index in excess of 3 percent, as described in the next subsection).

The Department of Finance estimated that in 1988 approximately 66 percent of taxpayers were in the 17 percent tax bracket, 29 percent were in the 26 percent tax bracket, and only about 5 percent were in the 29 percent tax bracket.

Provincial personal income tax rates, except in Quebec, are expressed as a percentage of federal basic tax and vary from province to province. In 1990, they ranged from 46.5 percent in Alberta to 62.0 percent in Newfoundland, averaging about 55 percent. Applying this average, the combined federal and provincial rate was approximately 26 percent on taxable income less than $28 275 and approximately 45 percent on income in excess of $56 550.

Rate Structure Changes. The rate structure of the federal personal income tax has been revised a number of times over the years. The trend has been toward fewer tax brackets and reduction in the progressiveness of the marginal tax rate structure.

Before the major tax reform introduced in 1972, there were thirteen brackets; marginal rates progressed from 12 percent on the first dollars of taxable income to 60 percent on taxable income of $400 000 and over. The combined federal and provincial rates ranged from 15 to 82 percent. The tax reform of 1972 gradually reduced the lowest federal tax rate to 6 percent and set the maximum rate at 47 percent on taxable income of $60 000. The maximum combined federal and provincial tax rate was 61 percent. Subsequent tax revisions, together with changes in federal/provincial fiscal arrangements, had, by 1987, reduced the number of tax brackets to ten, with a maximum federal rate of 34 percent on income in excess of $63 347.

Surtaxes. The tax rates for 1990 shown in the previous subsection do not include the federal surtax. A surtax is an additional tax expressed as a percentage of tax payable. The federal government has frequently used a surtax as a temporary tax increase, either to forward some fiscal policy or to obtain additional revenues to help cover budgetary deficits in particular years.

The federal surtax for 1990 was 5 percent of the basic federal tax plus 3 percent on the amount by which the basic federal tax exceeded $15 000. The surtax is calculated as a percentage of the basic federal tax, which is the tax payable before deductions of the foreign tax credit, the federal sales tax credit, the federal child tax credit, or the political contribution tax credit. Since most provincial taxes are calculated as a percentage of the basic federal tax, the federal surtax does not affect the provinces' personal income tax revenues.

Indexation

In 1974, the federal government introduced a system of indexing two of the elements of the personal income tax (personal exemptions and the tax brackets) by an inflation factor based on annual increases in the consumer price index. The rationale for indexing was to avoid letting inflationary gains in money income increase the tax/income ratio for taxpayers. In other words, if an individual's money income increased by 10 percent in any one year but the inflation rate was also 10 percent, that individual's real income in terms of purchasing power would remain constant. Therefore the tax/income ratio should remain constant. But since the income tax base is defined in nominal terms, any increase in money income is subject to the tax and may push the taxpayer into a higher marginal tax bracket. In that case, the person ends up paying a higher tax rate simply because of inflation. Such "bracket creep" is one significant way that inflation increases individual tax burdens and indexation is designed to reduce this bracket creep.

Between 1974 and 1982, the tax index — calculated as the full amount of the increase in the consumer price index for the twelve-month period ending September 30 of the previous year — ranged from a low of 6.6 percent to a high of 12.2 percent. For 1983 and 1984, as part of the government's inflation-control program, ceilings were placed on the income tax index at 6.0 and 5.0 percent respectively. In 1985, indexation based on the full consumer price index increase was resumed, only to be changed again in 1986. For 1986 and subsequent taxation years, the indexing factor has been limited to the annual increase in the consumer price index in excess of 3 percent. Between 1974 and 1987, the compound effect of indexing increased the dollar amount of tax brackets and personal exemptions by 163 percent.

Tax reform in 1988 introduced changes in tax brackets and the amounts of certain personal exemptions, and indexing is now based on these amounts. Currently, the items indexed are the tax brackets, the basic personal amount, the married amount, the age amount, the disability amount, the amounts for dependent children under eighteen years of age and for older children who are physically or mentally infirm, items found in the child tax credit, and the base amount for the recapture tax or social benefits repayment.

Social Benefits Repayment

Effective in the 1989 tax year, the government introduced a special recapture or "clawback" tax on Old Age Security (OAS) and family allowance payments, a tax technically called "social benefits repayment." It applies to recipients of OAS and family allowance benefits who have income in excess of a base amount. That amount was $50 000 for 1989, and it has been indexed in subsequent years by the amount that the consumer price index exceeds 3 percent.

The tax is calculated by subtracting the base amount of $50 000 from net income, multiplying the result by 15 percent, and adding the lesser of this amount or the OAS and/or family allowance payment to net federal tax. Assume, for example, that a taxpayer with one dependent child has net income of $60 000 with a family allowance payment of $400. The recapture tax is calculated as:

Net income before adjustments	$60 000	
Minus base amount	$50 000	
Total	$10 000	
Multiply by recapture tax rate: $10,000 x 15% =	$1 500	
Subtract family allowance benefit	400	(A)
Total	1 100	(B)
Social benefits repayment (the lesser of A or B)	$400	

The social benefits repayment is deducted from total income and added to net federal tax payable.

With a base amount of $50 000, a $400 family allowance benefit is recaptured in its entirety at an income level of $52 666, while an OAS payment of $4000 is completely recaptured at an income level of $76 666.

The social benefits repayment provision was introduced as a means of gearing family allowance and OAS payments to need. The federal government had earlier proposed ending the universality of these two programs and subjecting claimants to a means test. In other words, payments from these two programs would have been made dependent on income levels, and in effect they would no longer have been available to upper-income groups. Strong public opposition to terminating the principle of universality in social assistance programs, however, caused the government to retreat from its plans, and, as an alternative, it introduced the recapture tax.

When the recapture tax was instituted, it was phased in so that in 1989 only one-third of the calculated clawback was collected, with two-thirds collected in 1990, and the full amount beginning in 1991.

Capital Gains Tax

A capital gain is the income or profit realized when assets (such as stocks and bonds) are sold at higher prices than were originally paid.

Although capital gains taxation has long existed in many countries, Canada refrained from imposing such a tax before 1972. It was a deliberate economic policy to stimulate growth and development in the country. The Royal Commission on Taxation contended, however, that the lack of a capital gains tax produced gross inequities in taxation. It further argued that the evidence of adverse economic effects from such a tax was inconclusive. Given that equity was its overriding principle, the commission strongly recommended a capital gains tax as part of the new tax system it proposed.[3]

The government imposed a capital gains tax effective January 1, 1972. The general rule was that half of a capital gain was included in income for tax purposes, while half of capital losses was deducted from gains. Certain types of gains, such as those realized on the sale of principal residences and farms were given special treatment, and there was an exemption of $1000 on personal property and items such as works of art and jewellery.

In 1985, the basic structure of the capital gains tax was changed. A lifetime exemption of $500 000 in capital gains was introduced, to be phased in over a six-year period. Further changes in 1988 maintained the lifetime exemption for capital gains realized on the disposition of farm property and small business corporation shares but reduced it to $100 000 for other types of capital properties.

Technically, the exemption is stated in terms of a deduction of taxable capital gains, which in 1989 was two-thirds of total gains,[2] to a maximum of $66 667 (or two-thirds of $100 000); the figures were increased in 1990 to three-quarters of total gains to a maximum of $75 000. For example, if a taxpayer had claimed no capital gains before 1990 and during that year had a gain of $100 000, he or she had a deduction of taxable capital gain of $75 000 for 1990 and had reached the lifetime limit. If the same taxpayer had claimed capital gains in years following 1984, the lifetime limit on the taxable portion of capital gain of $75 000 was reduced by three-quarters of total gains in 1990 plus the cumulative taxable capital gains reported since 1984 plus one-eighth of amounts deducted in these earlier years. Many have criticized this method of calculating capital gains deductions as needlessly complex for the average taxpayer.

The deductible portion of capital losses was two-thirds of total capital losses in 1989 and three-quarters of losses in 1990. Capital losses are deductible only from realized capital gains. They may be carried back against capital gains of the three preceding years and carried forward indefinitely against future gains.

Current exemptions from the capital gains tax include gains realized on a principal residence, gains on the sale of personal-use property if the proceeds of disposition are less than $1000 and windfall gains such as lottery winnings for which chance is the determining factor.

The federal gift and estate tax was abolished effective January 1, 1972 with the institution of the capital gains tax, which covers gifts and estates. Gains on estates are subject to tax upon the death of a taxpayer. Bequests between husband and wife are exempt from the tax. A wife who inherits an asset from her husband, for example, is deemed to have acquired it at her husband's original cost, and the capital gains tax is payable when she sells the asset or transfers it by gift or bequest. A gift of an asset is considered a sale at fair market value, and the donor includes in income the difference between the cost and that value subject to the rules of the lifetime exemption.

The capital gains tax also applies to taxpayers entering or leaving Canada. A departing taxpayer is given two options: the tax can be paid on the accrued gains on assets upon departure, or the payment can be deferred until the assets are sold. In the latter case, security must, of course, be given at the time of departure to cover the tax on the accrued gain, and when the assets are sold, the taxpayer must file a tax return as a Canadian resident.

When a taxpayer enters Canada, any assets are valued at their fair market value as of the date of arrival. Tax must be paid only on gains realized while the taxpayer is in Canada. Gains that nonresidents realize on assets held in Canada are treated in the same manner as those of Canadian residents.

Special rules apply for calculating capital gains and losses on assets purchased before 1972 when the capital gains tax went into effect.

Alternative Minimum Tax (AMT)

Beginning in the 1986 tax year, the federal government implemented an alternative minimum tax (AMT), a tax directed to those high-income individuals who would otherwise pay little or no tax in a particular year because of tax shelters, loss carryovers, or the like. The tax is payable if it is greater than the tax that would be payable if calculated in the ordinary manner. In other words, an individual's income tax is calculated using the various standard deductions and tax credits applicable, together with any other deductions, such as loss carryovers and capital gains exemptions, that may apply. The AMT is then calculated, and it applies if it is found to be greater than the tax calculated in the normal manner.

The basic exemption for the AMT is $40 000 of adjusted taxable income. The rate is 17 percent of adjusted taxable income in excess of $40 000. The adjusted taxable income in this case equals gross income minus most normal deductions but not deductions for such items as contributions to registered retirement plans or deductions that are viewed as tax shelters. The latter include capital cost allowances on buildings and certified films and depletion and exploration allowances relating to resource investments; these can be deducted only from income generated by such investments and cannot be used to generate a loss. Furthermore, certain personal amount credits are not allowed. The combined federal and provincial rate for the AMT is approximately 26 percent averaged among the provinces.

Major variations in tax liability from one period to another may, of course, result from timing differences in the receipt of income, for which taxpayers should not be penalized. A tax shelter in one year may simply defer taxes if it produces taxable income in future years. It would be double taxation to impose income tax on income when it is placed in the tax shelter and then again when it is taken out. For this reason, the amount by which the AMT exceeds the tax liability calculated in the normal manner can be carried forward as a tax credit for up to seven years and can be deducted from ordinary tax payable in excess of AMT payable.

Administration

The personal income tax is paid on income received during the calendar year. A withholding system applies to wages and salaries, with the tax deducted at the source by the employer. Each taxpayer with income in excess of the basic personal exemptions (for a single or a married person, as appropriate) is required to file an income tax return by April 30 of the following year. The employer furnishes the taxpayer with two copies of a T–4 income statement showing total earnings and amounts withheld as tax and pension contributions.

If income tax is deducted from less than three-quarters of an individual's total income for the year (because of self-employment or other reasons), he or she is required to pay quarterly instalments of the estimated tax on the amount not subject to withholding. For most taxpayers, these instalment payments are due on or before March 15, June 15, September 15, and December 15. Farmers and fishermen are required to pay two-thirds of their estimated tax by December 31 and the balance by April 30 of the following year.

In completing the annual tax return, the taxpayer calculates his or her taxes and makes any adjustment required through additional payment or, in the event of an overpayment, a request for a refund. The completed tax return is sent to National Revenue Canada, where it is processed. Calculations are checked for accuracy, T–4 statements are compared, and the information is put into a computer. Each taxpayer then receives a notice of assessment indicating whether the return is in order or the department has made adjustments. The taxpayer has the right to appeal if he or she disagrees with the department's assessment. Even if the case is under appeal, however, unpaid taxes bear interest after April 30.

The penalty for late filing of a tax return is 5 percent of the unpaid balance of the tax plus 1 percent of the unpaid balance for each full month that the return was late. A taxpayer who files a return late more than once during a four-year period may be subject to larger penalties. Failure to file a return subjects a taxpayer to a fine of $1000 to $25 000 and as much as twelve months' imprisonment. A taxpayer who fails to make or is deficient in required instalment payments is charged interest on the amount owing; he or she is also liable for a penalty equal to 50 percent of the amount by which the instalment interest exceeds $1000. Penalties for deliberate evasion of tax or for false returns are fines of 50 to 200 percent of the tax sought to be avoided, and imprisonment for as much as five years.

Corporate Income Tax

The reform of the corporation income tax introduced in 1988 produced significant changes, which were phased in between 1988 and 1991. The changes were designed to reduce corporate tax rates in order to encourage industrial investment and expansion, to keep Canadian industry internationally competitive, to broaden the tax base by about 20 percent by reducing or eliminating certain tax preferences, and to curb artificial tax avoidance. It was estimated that these changes would increase federal corporate tax revenue by $5 billion dollars over five years.

The corporation income tax as it applied to the 1990 tax year is outlined in the following subsections, with some comments on the changes introduced by tax reform.

Corporate Income Tax Base

The corporation is treated as a separate tax-paying entity in Canada. The only integration between the corporation income tax and the personal income tax is the partial credit permitted individuals on their personal income tax for dividends received from a corporation.

The base for the corporation income tax consists of the firm's gross income from all sources, including three-quarters of capital gains, minus expenses incurred in earning the income. These expenses include wages and salaries paid; cost of materials, light, heat, and so on; interest on borrowed funds used in the business; and the cost of capital equipment. The cost of capital equipment is deducted over time in accordance with a system of set depreciation or capital cost allowances, reflecting the fact that such equipment is used in the production process over a number of years.

Depreciation (Capital Cost) Allowances

Depreciation represents the decline in value of an asset through usage or the passage of time. The federal government has established a schedule that corporations must follow in calculating depreciation costs for tax purposes. The schedule identifies 41 asset classes, each of which is assigned an annual depreciation charge, ranging from 4 percent on such durable property as roads and bridges to 100 percent on such quickly used-up assets as tools and dies. For most of the asset classes, the diminishing-balances method of depreciation is applied, by which a given percentage is deducted each year on the balance value of the asset. Ten classes employ the straight-line method whereby a given percentage of the cost of the asset is deducted each year.

The federal government has, on occasion, introduced policies of double or accelerated depreciation, temporarily increasing the allowance permitted on certain assets in an attempt to stimulate investment in plant and equipment or encourage industry to modernize. Similarly, policies of deferred depreciation have been employed in past periods of inflation to discourage excessive investment.

Tax reform reduced the capital cost allowance for a number of classes of assets, some by as much as 40 percent of the earlier rate. In addition, a special allowance for resource industries, known as the depletion allowance, was phased out.

Corporate Income Tax Rates

The federal government employs a basic rate on taxable corporate income with reduced rates for manufacturing businesses and for small, Canadian-controlled, private corporations (CCPCs). For 1990, the general corporation tax was 28 percent of corporate net income or profits. This rate was reduced to 24 percent for manufacturing corporations and to 12 percent for the first $200 000 of income of CCPCs, manufacturing or nonmanufacturing.

Since 1987, a surtax of 3 percent has been imposed on federal corporate income tax payable as a revenue-raising measure to help reduce the large federal deficit. It was followed by another tax increase on large corporations, called the large corporation tax, effective June 1989. The latter tax was made creditable against the 3 percent surtax so that a corporation was subject to the greater of the two. The large corporation tax applied to about 3600 of Canada's largest corporations and was expected to generate approximately $1 billion in its first full year of application.

The large corporation tax rate of 0.175 percent is applied to a capital base consisting of the shareholders' equity, surpluses, reserves, loans and advances to the corporation, and specified indebtedness represented by bonds, debentures, mortgages, and other securities of the corporation. The tax is levied only to that part of a corporation's capital employed in Canada, and nonresident corporations that have permanent establishments in this country compute capital employed here on the basis of their Canadian assets. All corporations are permitted a $10 million basic capital deduction from taxable capital employed in Canada. This deduction has the effect of limiting the tax to larger corporations. The tax is applied to both nonfinancial corporations and financial institutions, including insurance companies; for deposit-taking institutions, however, deposits and similar liabilities are not included in financial capital.

Over the years, the federal government has used special provisions and tax rates in the corporation income tax as part of its fiscal policy to stimulate investment, employment, and regional development. One such provision, as already noted, has been acceleration or deceleration of the capital cost allowance for particular assets or classes of assets.

Another such tool is the investment tax credit, which is the deduction from tax payable of a certain percentage of a specified investment. Before 1987, a general tax credit of 7 percent was provided for investment in new productive facilities. This tax credit was phased out, terminating in 1989. The current investment tax credits are primarily for selective investments of a regional or research-related nature. They include a 30 percent tax credit for special investment for manufacturing and processing in selected slower growth regions, a 15 percent general investment credit for the Atlantic region, rates ranging from 20 to 35 percent of the costs of research and development, and a credit of 25 percent of investment in qualified high-cost exploration for oil and gas.

Special provisions in the tax legislation apply to the extractive resource sector — that is, the oil, gas, and mining industries. Royalties are levied on oil and natural gas produced on federally owned lands in the North and in the offshore areas of the East and West coasts. Royalties escalating from 3 to 12 percent with the value of production are imposed on mineral production in the Yukon and the Northwest Territories.

Payment of Corporate Income Tax

Corporations are required to pay their income taxes in monthly instalments. Payments must be remitted by the last day of each month and are considered to have been on time only if actually received by the due date. To ensure prompt payment, late or deficient instalments are subject to interest charges. The charge for a calendar quarter is the average rate of interest on 90-day federal Treasury bills sold during the first month of the preceding quarter, plus two percentage points. The same interest rate applies to refunds to corporations for overpayments of tax.

CONSUMPTION-BASED TAXES

Before 1991, the federal government levied three consumption-based taxes: the manufacturers' sales tax, excise taxes, and excise duties. Effective January 1, 1991, the manufacturers' sales tax was replaced with the goods and services tax (GST). Since the GST is highly controversial, its imposition and workings are examined in particular detail in this section. Excise taxes and excise duties are also described.

Terminating the Manufacturers' Sales Tax

The replacement of the manufacturers' sales tax with the GST was a time-consuming process in a climate of considerable controversy and debate. The manufacturers' sales tax had been introduced by the federal government in 1920 and appeared adequate at the time, given the relatively uncomplicated nature of production and distribution and the fairly clear dividing lines between production and distribution. But as the economy became more complex, with increasing degrees of vertical integration among manufacturers, wholesalers, and retailers, the inadequacies of the manufacturers' sales tax became increasingly apparent. Numerous studies, such as those by the Royal Commission on Taxation in 1966 and the Federal Sales Tax Review Committee in 1983, detailed its faults and recommended major reform. Yet the tax continued as a major component in the federal government's revenue structure with nothing but piecemeal changes to attempt to correct its most glaring deficiencies.

The manufacturers' sales tax was a general sales tax levied at the manufacturers' level on all goods manufactured in or imported to Canada. Two groups of goods were exempt. In order to avoid double taxation, the first such group was various producer goods, including materials and partly finished goods used in further production, production machinery and equipment, and fuel and power used in the production process. (Building materials were, however, subject to the tax.) In an attempt to reduce the degree of regressiveness of the tax, the second group of exempt goods included certain consumer goods that constitute a significant portion of the purchases of lower-income families, including most foods, clothing and footwear, prescription drugs, and household fuel and power. Also the tax did not fall on most services.

The general tax rate fluctuated between 9 and 12 percent during most of the 1970s and 1980s; in 1989, it was increased to 13.5 percent. Certain items were subject to a different rate, such as construction materials and equipment, taxed most recently at 9 percent, and alcoholic beverages and tobacco products, at 19 percent. The tax was applied on the manufacturers' selling price exclusive of all other excise taxes but inclusive of excise duties and customs tariffs.

Problems with the Tax. The government pointed to numerous structural failings of the manufacturers' sales tax: notably, that it damaged competitiveness, favoured imports, was discriminatory, and was excessively complex and therefore subject to avoidance. The tax harmed the competitiveness of Canadian industry in that it included many goods used as inputs in the production process, which led to a degree of double taxation and to higher prices for the final products. It favoured imports over domestic goods because it was levied on the price of the former exclusive of the costs of marketing and distribution, whereas these costs were usually included in domestic manufacturers' selling prices. The importer consequently paid less tax and could price more competitively than a Canadian producer. It was estimated that the tax as a percentage of the retail price was about one-third higher on domestic goods than on competing imports.

The base of the tax was very narrow, applying to only about one-third of the goods and services Canadians purchased.[4] It therefore discriminated against certain sectors of the economy and the consumers of the goods subject to the tax.

Finally, the tax was viewed as excessively complex and costly for government to administer and caused major compliance difficulties. The distinction between taxed and nontaxed items was difficult to define and resulted in major disputes and court challenges. In an attempt to increase fairness and equity in the application of the tax, the government had provided more than 22 000 special provisions and administrative interpretations to the governing legislation. The Auditor General of Canada contended that administrative complexities and poor monitoring of the approximate 75 000 companies that paid the sales tax probably cost the government billions of dollars in unpaid tax.[5] This was in addition to an estimated $300 million of revenue lost by other measures that manufacturing companies took to avoid the tax, such as setting up separate marketing and distribution subsidiaries so as to exclude advertising and other marketing costs from the price on which the tax was applied.

Opposition to the Change. The Conservative government's views on the merits of replacing the manufacturers' sales tax with the GST were not shared by the political parties then in opposition, the provincial governments, various sectors of the economy, or many taxpayers. The provinces complained that the GST encroached on the retail sales tax field, a major source of revenue to them. Consumer groups and labour unions argued that the imposition of the GST would increase consumer prices and fuel a wage/price spiral and a new round of inflation. They refused to accept the government's contention that the new tax would add no more than 1.25 percentage points to the consumer price index in 1991 and have almost no impact in subsequent years. The residential construction industry and prospective homeowners argued that the GST would add substantial increases to the prices of new homes and make new housing unaffordable to many Canadian families. Many small businesses and the professional services sectors expressed opposition to the administrative burden being thrust upon them and irritation at becoming tax collectors for Revenue Canada.

It was further argued that the GST, like any general sales tax, was regressive and inequitable. It would impose a greater burden on the poor than on the wealthy in the sense that lower-income groups would pay relatively more of their income in tax than would higher-income groups. In addition, it was contended that the GST represented a major tax increase on all Canadians. In presenting the details of his proposal in August 1989, the Minister of Finance produced data showing that, at the then-proposed rate of 9 percent, the GST would generate $5.5 billion more in revenue in 1991 than the manufacturers' sales tax would have yielded, but this increase would be offset by higher sales tax credits and other tax reductions.[6]

The original GST legislation contained various provisions that addressed some of these concerns — there were, for example, tax-free and tax-exempt items, housing rebates, and tax credits for lower-income families. Other potential problems were dealt with by changes after the proposal was first tabled, and the proposed rate was reduced from 9 to 7 percent. Nevertheless, opposition to the tax remained widespread and strong, with some of the more vocal opposition groups calling for a tax revolt (that is, for taxpayers to refuse to pay federal taxes).

Few disputed the fact that the manufacturers' sales tax had major deficiencies and that past attempts to eliminate them had proved inadequate. The GST is viewed as technically superior because it is comprehensive in coverage and is imposed at the retail level, thereby avoiding the distortions caused by the manufacturers' sales tax. The GST is also very similar to the general sales taxes imposed by some 48 other countries. The emotional outrage expressed in various quarters of the country, as evident in public statements and the media, was characteristic of opposition to a major tax increase. People saw themselves paying tax on many more purchases, and collecting the tax — which would fall to many individuals and firms — was viewed as an inconvenience and a burden. Many also feared the GST as a potential major tax grab by the federal government. Ottawa attempted to assure the public that the government's overall fiscal position would be essentially unaffected by the impact of sales tax reform, with additional revenues applied to increasing the sales tax credit and to offsetting increases in the costs of indexed social programs. Critics, however, feared that the government would move quickly to exploit the large revenue-generating potential of the GST to reduce its huge annual budgetary deficits, with consequent increasing tax burdens on consumers.

The outpouring of opposition proved futile. The Conservative government mustered majorities in both houses of Parliament, and after much emotional debate there, the GST legislation became effective on January 1, 1991.

Goods and Services Tax (GST)

Unlike the manufacturers' sales tax, which is a single-stage levy on manufacturers' selling prices, the GST is characterized by a multistage collection process. It is a tax on all sales or supply of goods and services that are not specifically excluded. A system of input tax credits removes the tax from productive inputs and ensures that it falls on final consumption. The tax rate is 7 percent of selling prices, exclusive of any provincial retail sales taxes.

TABLE 5–2
Goods and Services Tax

	Sale by producer A to producer B	Sale by producer B to producer C	Sale by producer C to consumer
Sale value	$100.00	$300.00	$800.00
GST	7.00	21.00	56.00
GST credit		7.00	21.00
GST remitted	7.00	14.00	35.00

Total GST remitted = $56.00 = Amount paid by the consumer

In the GST system, a purchaser is required to pay the 7 percent tax to the seller of the good or service. The seller is required to remit to the government the difference between any tax paid on inputs (input tax credit) and the tax received on sales. Consider the following example as illustrated in Table 5–2. Assume that producer A sells an input to producer B for $100 on which A collects the GST of $7. Producer B uses the input to produce a semifinished product, which she sells for $300 to producer C. The tax paid by C on the $300 sale is $21, and B remits to the government $14, the difference in the amount of tax she paid and the amount she collected from C. If producer C finishes the product and sells it to the consumer for $800 (excluding tax), the consumer pays the GST of $56. C claims an input tax credit of $21 paid to B, and he therefore remits $35 to the government. The total amount of tax to the government is $56, which is paid by the consumer but has been collected by the three sellers, A, B, and C. The tax charged at each stage of production has been fully refunded at the next stage.

The total amount paid by the consumer is identical to the amount of tax that she would have paid under a 7 percent retail sales tax applied on the final sale. It is argued, however, that the multistage GST is superior to the retail sales tax because the latter may not completely avoid the taxation of productive inputs, which could lead to double taxation, higher production costs, and higher prices.

The GST applies to all business transactions throughout the production, distribution, and retailing chain, unless they are specifically excluded from the tax. Small businesses and individual traders with sales transactions of less than $30 000 annually are given the option of whether they wish to join or not join the GST system, a choice provided in recognition of the fact that very small suppliers may have limited resources to administer the tax. Those who choose to opt out of the system neither collect tax on sales nor claim input tax credits on their purchases. This arrangement can be suitable for small suppliers who sell directly to consumers, but those selling mainly to business may find it advantageous to join the GST as doing so permits the customers, as well as the supplier, to claim input tax credits.

Tax-Free and Tax-Exempt Commodities. The goods and services not subject to the tax comprise two groups: tax-free and tax-exempt sales. For tax-free sales, sometimes referred to as zero-rated sales, vendors do not collect the GST, but they are still able to claim input tax credits for any tax they have paid on purchases for production. This provision removes all tax from these goods and services. For tax-exempt sales, vendors also do not collect the GST, but they are not permitted credits on inputs purchased.

For the most part, the nontaxed items are basic consumer goods and services on which low-income groups spend a large proportion of their budgets, and their exclusion from the tax was designed to reduce the regressiveness of the GST. Tax-free items comprise basic groceries, agricultural and fish products, prescription drugs, and medical devices such as wheelchairs, contact lenses, eyeglasses, and so on, as well as exports. The list of tax-free groceries does not include soft drinks, candies, snack foods, or restaurant meals. Tax-exempt items include health and dental care, educational services, daycare services, legal aid services, residential rents, and financial services such as loans, deposits, and life and property insurance. Other exemptions include the sale of used residential homes, sales by charities, gambling and lottery winnings, sales of used goods by private individuals, trade union and mandatory professional fees, and meals and lodging provided by nonprofit organizations.

Housing and Real Property. Special provisions in the GST apply to new housing. The previous manufacturers' sales tax had excluded direct taxation of new homes, but it was applied at varying rates to building materials, such as lumber, bricks, windows, wallpaper, and so on; it was estimated that these taxes added up to the equivalent of about a 4 percent effective tax rate on new homes.[7] The GST rate of 7 percent applies to the retail price of newly constructed residential dwellings (including the value of the land component). To relieve the tax burden on new homes, however, the government provides a rebate on the purchase of new dwellings, including single-detached and semidetached houses, row houses, and condominium apartments. To qualify for the rebate, the purchaser must be a Canadian resident, and the dwelling must be the purchaser's principal residence.

The size of the rebate varies with the price of the unit. Houses priced at $350 000 or less qualify for a rebate equal to 2.5 percent of the GST. The amount of the rebate is reduced for houses priced at more than $350 000 and is removed completely for those priced in excess of $450 000.

Special provisions also apply to other real properties. In general, the GST applies to any sale or rental of real property (land and buildings) unless it is specifically exempt. For example, as mentioned earlier, long-term residential rents and sales of used residential housing are exempt. The sale or transfer of a business classified as a "going concern" is not subject to the tax. Similarly, the sale of farmland to a farmer-operator is exempt, but other sales or leases of farmland, such as a sale to a developer, are subject to the tax.

Public Sector Activities. Most public sector commercial activities, like private sector commercial activities, are subject to the GST. In recognition of the special role of the government, however, certain noncommercial public sector activities are exempt. Regulatory activities including drivers' licenses, patent fees, and construction permits, are not taxable. Most municipal-provided services financed by a direct levy, such as water supply, are also exempt. But other utilities such as telecommunications, hydroelectric power, and natural gas are taxed, as well as the services supplied by Canada Post and most other Crown corporations.

Imports and Exports. The GST applies to imports. It is payable on the duty and excise paid value of goods imported into Canada and collected at the same time as customs tariffs. Importers who have paid the tax can receive an input tax credit when they resell goods to consumers or others. The GST, however, does not apply to imports of the tax-free items already listed.

Goods made in Canada and exported are classified as tax-free items, and exporters are allowed to claim any input tax credits that may apply. This exemption from sales tax, of course, makes Canada's exports more competitive in the international market.

Sales Tax Credit. Incorporated into the GST legislation is a sales tax credit for the personal income tax that is more generous to Canadians than that provided for the manufacturers' sales tax. The GST credit is a refundable credit calculated on the basis of information from income tax returns. The amount of the credit depends on family size and income. For 1991, the GST credit for a family with income of less than $24 800 was set at $190 per adult and $100 per each dependent child. For households with net income of more than the threshold amount, the credit is reduced by $5 for every $100 of net income in excess of $24 800. The credit is based on the past year's income and family status and is paid quarterly in equal instalments. Both the credit amounts and the threshold are indexed annually by any increase in the consumer price index in excess of 3 percent.

Administration. A purchaser of a good or service is liable for payment of the GST on the day on which payment for the item is made or on the day on which the payment becomes due, whichever is earlier. The timing of payment generally corresponds to the time in which the sellers normally record the sales in their accounts.

Sellers are required to remit the tax to the government on a monthly, quarterly, or yearly basis, depending on volume of sales. Vendors with annual revenue from taxable and nontaxable items in excess of $6 million are required to file a GST return and remit the tax monthly. Vendors with sales less than $6 million remit quarterly. Those with annual revenue of $500 000 or less have the option of filing returns annually but remitting instalments quarterly. Tax returns must be filed within one month of the end of a vendor's registered reporting period. Penalties and interest are charged on late returns and on unpaid tax.

Aid For Small Business. The government has financially assisted small businesses with the costs of complying with the GST. Those with annual revenue of less than $2 million were eligible for a one-time administration payment of up to $1000.

The government also developed simplified GST accounting methods for small businesses: the quick method and two streamlined methods. The quick method is available to businesses with annual sales of $200 000 or less and to grocery and convenience stores with annual sales up to $500 000 of which at least 25 percent are basic groceries. Under this method, the vendor collects the 7 percent GST on sales (except for groceries) but does not claim specific tax credits. Instead, the amount of tax the vendor remits is calculated by multiplying total receipts (sales plus GST collected) by a specific percentage, which ranges from 5 percent for manufacturing and services establishments (repair shops, electricians, barbers, and so on) to 3 percent for retailers and wholesalers (clothing, hardware, and shoe stores) to 1 percent for grocery and convenience stores, bakeries, butcher shops, and the like whose sales consist of more than 50 percent basic groceries. This shortcut in GST calculation eliminates the need to keep track of separate input tax credits on expenses. The tax credits that normally would be claimed are accounted for by the discounted percentages applied to receipts.

The two streamlined accounting methods are available to retail merchants selling a combination of zero-rated basic groceries and other taxable goods with total sales less than $2 million. Although somewhat more complicated than the quick method, they eliminate the need to keep track of every GST transaction at the cash register. One method enables the vendor to calculate the amount of tax to be remitted by applying its own standard markup on purchases of goods for resale that are taxable. In the other method, the amount remitted is calculated by applying a prescribed markup on purchases for resale of zero-rated items. The first method is particularly useful if the vendor sells primarily basic groceries and only a few goods taxed at 7 percent; the second is most useful to vendors that primarily sell taxable items.

Inventory Credit. The replacement of the manufacturers' sales tax with the GST required some mechanism by which distributors, wholesalers, and retailers would be able to recover the tax already paid on inventories on hand on January 1, 1991, when the GST came into force. The recovery was achieved in the form of a rebate of 8.1 percent on all inventories held as of that date. The rebate was less than the 13.5 percent manufacturers' sales tax to compensate for the fact that the old tax had applied at an earlier stage of trade than the GST. The Department of Finance maintained that it would be difficult to determine the actual tax content of the goods sellers had in inventory. The 8.1 percent rate was established as an average figure.

To simplify the rebates for small grocery and convenience stores selling a mix of goods, some of which were subject to the manufacturers' sales tax and other which were tax-exempt, the government gave retailers with total inventory value of $70 000 or less the option of applying the standard 8.1 percent rebate to tax-paid goods after separating taxed from nontaxed inventory or of using a special rebate factor of 2.5 percent applied to the total value of their tax-paid and tax-exempt inventories. The government estimated the total rebate payment at approximately $2.3 billion.

Price Effects. The government expected price reductions on those goods that had been subjected to the 13.5 percent manufacturers' sales tax, but were, under the GST, taxed only at 7 percent (even though the latter applied to a higher price base). In competitive markets, competition between sellers would, in theory, ensure that the tax savings would be passed on to consumers and result in lower prices. In imperfect markets, however, prices may not be reduced. In June 1990, the government announced that a Consumer Information Office would be established to monitor the effects on prices after the replacement of the manufacturers' sales tax with the GST. The office would disseminate its findings to consumers, but it would have no legal powers to force sellers to comply with investigations or to order sellers to roll-back prices. Some large companies, such as Ford Motor Co. of Canada and General Motors of Canada had announced that the change in taxes would be fully reflected in the retail price, which for automobiles, was estimated to mean a price reduction of about 4 percent. The government intent in monitoring prices was to determine if other manufacturing sectors also passed along such savings to consumers.

Excise Taxes

In addition to the general goods and services sales tax, the Canadian commodity tax structure has a number of specific taxes that take the form of unit and *ad valorem* taxes. Unit taxes are applied to a commodity on the basis of weight, volume, or amount. *Ad valorem* taxes are expressed as a percentage of the selling price.

These excise taxes have traditionally applied to goods labelled as luxuries and to items deemed to have social costs. Recently, they have also been used as a conservation measure and as a means of raising revenue for specified purposes. The revenue from an excise tax may be earmarked; the air transportation tax, for example, is a cost-recovery measure designed to help finance airport facilities and navigation systems.

The following excise taxes were in effect during 1990.[8]

Cigarettes	$0.1069 per 5 cigarettes
Manufactured tobacco	$14.25 per kg
Cigars	40%
Jewellery, watches, etc.	10%
Lighters	$0.10 per unit
Matches	10%
Playing cards	$0.20 per pack
Coil-operated games or amusement devices	10%
Wines	
1.2 % or less alcohol	$0.0179 per ℓ
1.2 % to 7% alcohol	$0.2147 per ℓ
Other	$0.4472 per ℓ
Gasoline	
Leaded	$0.095 per ℓ
Unleaded	$0.085 per ℓ
Diesel and aviation fuel	$.04 per ℓ
Air conditioners in cars, trucks, etc.	$100 per unit
Air travel	
North America	10% to a maximum of $50
Overseas	$19
Radio and television programming services (pay TV and cable TV) (replaced by GST in 1991)	11%

A special excise tax is also applied on large automobiles as an energy conservation measure. The tax is $30 for the first 45 kilograms (100 pounds) over 2007 kilograms (4425 pounds); $40 on the next 45 kilograms; $50 on the third 45 kilograms; and $60 for each subsequent 45 kilograms.

Excise Duties

Various features distinguish excise duties from excise taxes. Excise duties are unit levies, apply to domestic goods only, are limited to liquor and tobacco products, and are imposed under the Excise Act (excise taxes are imposed under the Excise Tax Act). Furthermore, excise duties are more closely related to the supervision of production, which explains the difference in the timing of payment. They are paid at various stages of production, while excise taxes are paid at the end of the month following the sale. For example, excise duties on beer are paid at the fermenting stage, about six weeks before the beer is bottled and shipped. The excise tax on tobacco products is paid with the purchase of the excise stamp, which must be placed on the product prior to its sale. In both cases, the producer bears the burden during the period between tax imposition and sale.

The most significant excise duties and their rates as they applied in 1990 were:[9]

Distilled spirits (absolute alcohol)	$10.73 ℓ
Beer (not more than 2.5% alcohol)	9.66 hℓ
Beer (regular)	19.32 ℓ
Cigarettes	27.47 per 1000
Cigars	9.19 per 1000
Manufactured tobacco	18.33 per kg
Raw leaf tobacco	0.97 per kg

Cigarettes, cigars, and manufactured tobacco are subject to both the excise tax and excise duty.

Since 1981, the unit excise taxes and the excise duties on alcohol and tobacco have been indexed in accordance with the alcohol and tobacco subindexes in the consumer price index. The rates are thereby adjusted each September 1 as the prices of these commodities change.

Excise duties do not apply to imported goods. Instead, a customs duty is imposed on imports; the amount is equivalent to the excise duty on the domestic products.

Customs Tariffs

The customs tariff has traditionally been imposed on a wide range of goods imported into Canada and consists of both *ad valorem* and unit levies. There are four classes of tariffs: the British preferential tariff, applicable to countries of the British Commonwealth; the most favoured nation tariff, applicable to countries of the General Agreement on Tariffs and Trade (GATT) and with which Canada has trade agreements; the general preferential tariff, applicable to less-developed countries; and the general tariff.

In the early days following Confederation, the customs tariff not only protected Canada's infant industries and fostered economic development but was also the major source of federal revenue. The GATT, introduced at the end of the Second World War, served to reduce general tariffs worldwide, including the Canadian tariff structure; consequently, tariffs have become a relatively decreasing source of revenue over the years. With the phase-in of free trade between Canada and the United States beginning January 1989, tariffs were expected to continue their decline as a revenue source.

PAYROLL TAXES

Payroll taxes are levies on wages and salaries that may be imposed on the employee, on the amount paid out by the employer, or both. They are generally employed to finance social security programs.

The federal government uses payroll taxes to finance the unemployment insurance program and the Canadian Pension Plan. The unemployment insurance program is financed entirely by premiums paid by employees and employers. These premiums are adjusted annually to cover the estimated costs of the program. Prior to 1990, the federal government made special contributions to the unemployment insurance account to finance extended benefits and to cover benefits paid to fishers, but these contributions have been eliminated. In 1990, employee contributions amounted to $2.25 per $100 of weekly insurable earnings to an earning maximum of $635. Employer contributions equalled 1.4 times the amount of the employee contribution or $3.15 per $100 of weekly insurable earnings.

The Canada Pension plan is financed by equal contributions from employer and employee. In 1990, each contributed 2 percent of pensionable earnings to a maximum annual contribution of $574. In the same year, the self-employed person contributed 4.4 percent of earnings to a maximum of $1148.

TAX EXPENDITURES

The federal tax system, as already outlined, contains a number of provisions that give preferential treatment to various groups and businesses in the form of tax exemptions, deductions, reduced rates, and tax credits. Through these tax preferences, the government provides assistance and incentives and, in the process, forgoes tax revenues. Since such tax forgiveness or postponement is viewed as alternative to direct spending, it has come to be known as tax expenditure. It is equivalent to the government's first collecting the sums involved by imposing tax and then making a direct expenditure of an equal amount.

Not all exemptions, deductions, or credits are classified as tax expenditures. In determining tax expenditures, the Department of Finance has attempted to define a "benchmark" or "normal" tax structure, and only the deviations from this structure are classified as tax expenditures. The benchmark tax structure is defined as one that "provides no preferential treatment to taxpayers on the basis of demographic characteristics, sources or uses of income, geographical location, or any other special circumstances applicable only to a given taxpayer or to a particular group of taxpayers."[10]

This definition leaves some arbitrariness and ambiguity regarding which tax provisions are tax expenditures. Not considered are deductions for expenditures incurred in earning income, as these are viewed as necessary to define net income under any income tax. Most of the other exemptions and deductions found in the tax system, however, have been included in the government's tax expenditure account. In 1980, the federal government identified more than 100 provisions in the tax system that were equivalent to spending programs and estimated the erosion of the tax base resulting from tax expenditures to be $47.3 billion in 1979.

The federal government first compiled and presented a list of its tax expenditures with the December 1979 budget. In its view, tax expenditures played a very important role in government policy with significant effects on the private sector and required a full accounting in the same manner as government expenditures.

The Auditor General of Canada has raised questions, however, about the accountability of government to Parliament on the issue of tax expenditures. In 1986, the auditor noted that "nothing like the same attention that is given to direct expenditures has been given to tax expenditures," yet "tax expenditures have become one of the major ways in which the government allocates resources, delivers incentives, and influences private sector decisions." Furthermore, he concluded, the tax system is a high-risk vehicle for delivering programs because of the potential for avoidance mechanisms. Even where taxpayer avoidance mechanisms have been identified, the government has been slow to eliminate them, causing hundreds of millions of dollars of revenue losses.[11] In reply, the Department of Finance acknowledged that tax expenditures added to the complexity of the tax system and sometimes produced results other than those originally intended.[12] The department endeavoured to move more quickly on eliminating avoidance mechanism. In addition, tax reform in 1988 broadened the tax base and reduced or eliminated various tax expenditures. The government also made a commitment to providing more information on the costs of tax expenditures and the effects of these measures.

ENDNOTES

1. The main sources of information on the federal tax system are Revenue Canada's series of tax information guides and pamphlets and the tax acts contained in *Statutes of Canada*.

   Details on the most recent changes in federal taxation are presented in the Department of Finance's budget papers, supplementary information, and notices of ways and means motions on recent budgets; Canada, Department of Finance, *The White Paper: Tax Reform 1987* (Ottawa, June 18, 1987); *Tax Reform 1987: Income Tax Reform* (Ottawa, June 18, 1987); and *Tax Reform 1987: Sales Tax Reform* (Ottawa, June 18, 1987); *Goods and Services Tax: An Overview* (Ottawa, August 1989); *Goods and Services Tax Technical Paper* (Ottawa, August 1989); and GST, *Goods and Services Tax: Information for Small Business* (Ottawa, 1990). For up-to-date coverage of tax changes, the reader can also consult the Canadian Tax Foundation's annual publication *The National Finances*, and its Tax Memo series.

2. The personal exemption was established in 1973 at $1600 for a single person and $3000 for a married couple. Effective January 1, 1974, the federal government introduced a system of indexing the personal income tax by an annual inflation factor based on the consumer price index.

As a result of indexing, the basic personal exemption in 1987 was $4220. For 1988, as part of the government's tax reform objective of reducing income tax burdens on lower-income groups, the exemption was increased to $6000.

3. Canada, *Report of the Royal Commission on Taxation*, Vol. 3, Ch. 15 (Ottawa: Queen's Printer, 1966).

4. Canada, Department of Finance, *Tax Reform, 1987, Sales Tax Reform* (Ottawa, June 18, 1987), pp. 9–24.

5. Canada, House of Commons, Finance Committee, February 8, 1990.

6. Canada, Department of Finance, *Goods and Services Tax: An Overview* (Ottawa, August 1989), p. 32.

7. Ibid., p. 18.

8. Revenue Canada, Customs and Excise Branch, *Excise Bulletins* (Ottawa).

9. Ibid.

10. Canada, Department of Finance, *Government of Canada Tax Expenditure Account, December 1979* (Ottawa, 1979), p. 4. Further information on tax expenditures is presented in Canada, Department of Finance, *Analysis of Federal Tax Expenditures for Individuals* (Ottawa, 1981); and Roger S. Smith, *Tax Expenditures: An Examination of Tax Incentives and Tax Preferences in the Canadian Federal Income Tax System*, Tax Paper no. 61 (Toronto: Canadian Tax Foundation, 1979).

11. Canada, *Report of the Auditor General of Canada for the Fiscal Year Ended 31 March 1986* (Ottawa: Supply and Services Canada, 1986), paras. 4.14, 4.17.

12. Ibid., para. 4.155.

CHAPTER 6

PROVINCIAL AND MUNICIPAL FINANCE

The Constitution Act, 1867 outlined the powers of the provinces for raising revenue and limited them to direct taxation. No mention is made in the act of lower levels of government, such as municipal governments. Since they are the creation of the provincial governments, the only powers local governments have are those delegated to them by the provinces.[1]

PROVINCIAL TAXATION

Taxation at the provincial level is not uniform across Canada. In addition to the personal and corporation income taxes, which all provinces impose, there are a variety of levies, often including a retail sales tax, gasoline tax, taxes on liquor and tobacco, and taxes on specific services such as communications.

The provinces' revenue, from the various taxes they impose and from other sources, is illustrated in Table 6–1 for all provinces combined. Tax revenue accounted for almost 60 percent of total provincial revenue in 1989/90, compared to 53 percent in 1976/7. The personal income tax has been the most significant source of revenue since the 1960s, accounting for more than 24 percent of provincial revenue in 1989/90. The trend of increasing importance for the personal income tax was accompanied by a decline in the share of revenue from transfers; this change resulted mostly from the federal/provincial fiscal agreements, which gave the provinces increased tax room in the personal income taxes as a partial substitute for specific transfers, particularly for provincial health programs and postsecondary education.

The second most important tax has been the general sales tax, contributing over 13 percent of provincial revenue. Two notable trends since 1967 have been the decline in the significance of the corporation income tax and of the tax on motor fuel. Revenue from natural resources increased relative to other sources in the 1970s, reflecting high oil and gas prices and a prosperous energy sector in some western provinces, particularly Alberta, but by 1989/90, the share of natural resource revenue had declined significantly.

The relative importance of the various revenue sources varied considerably from province to province in 1989/90 as in other years. (See Table 6–2). In Newfoundland and New Brunswick, revenue from the general sales tax exceeded revenue from the personal income tax. Shares of personal income tax revenue ranged from a low of 11.5 percent of total revenue in Newfoundland to a high of 29.0 percent in Ontario, while those of corporation income tax revenue ranged from a low of 1.8 percent of total revenue in Quebec to a high of 8.6 percent in Ontario. The retail sales tax brought in more than 10 percent of total revenue in all provinces except Alberta, which does not impose a general sales tax.

Some features of the various taxes imposed by the provinces are presented in the following sections.

Personal Income Tax

Each of the provinces, and the two territories imposes a personal income tax. Except in Quebec, the tax is collected on behalf of the provincial or territorial government by the federal government, the tax rate is expressed as a percentage of the basic federal tax, and consequently the tax base used is the same as that defined by the federal government. Quebec collects its own income tax with its own set of rates.

In 1990, the rates imposed by the various provinces as a percentage of the basic federal tax (as calculated in the federal income tax return) were:

Alberta	46.5%
British Columbia	51.5%
Manitoba	52.0%
New Brunswick	60.0%
Newfoundland	62.0%
Northwest Territories	43.0%
Nova Scotia	56.5%
Ontario	53.0%
Prince Edward Island	57.0%
Saskatchewan	50.0%
Yukon	45.0%

Over the years the provinces have resorted to additional income taxes by imposing surtaxes on the basic provincial income tax payable and by levying additional taxes on taxable income. In 1990, the Alberta income tax included a surtax of 8 percent on basic Alberta income tax in excess of $3500 plus a flat rate tax of 0.5 percent of taxable income. Saskatchewan applied a flat rate tax of 2 percent of net income plus a surtax of 12 percent of the basic provincial tax payable in excess of $4000. Manitoba imposed a flat tax of 2 percent of net income plus a surtax of 2 percent of the flat tax in excess of $600. Ontario applied a surtax of 10 percent of basic Ontario tax in excess of $10 000. Prince Edward Island levied a surtax of 10 percent on provincial tax in excess of $12 500.

A number of provinces give low-income taxpayers tax relief in the form of tax credits or tax reductions. Many also offer tax relief on various investments as an incentive to promote investment and economic development in the province. In 1990, for example, British Columbia offered a renter's tax credit and a credit of one-third of any logging tax paid; it also provided a small business venture capital tax credit, which gave individuals who formed a venture capital corporation to invest in small businesses in the province a credit against provincial tax payable of 30 percent of their investment, to a maximum credit of $60 000 in a year. Alberta offered credits to renters and to investors in multiple rental units. It also established a stock savings plan whereby Albertans who invested in specified corporations (primarily Alberta companies) were eligible for a tax credit of as much as $300 per year. Similar stock savings plans have been established by Saskatchewan, Nova Scotia, and Newfoundland. In 1990, Saskatchewan provided reductions for taxpayers with net incomes of less than $10 000,

TABLE 6–1
Historical Summary of Provincial Governments' Gross Revenue

Source	1967/8	1976/7	1989/90
		(percentage of total)	
Taxes			
Personal income	17.1	19.1	24.4
Corporation income	7.0	5.7	5.0
General sales	14.7	11.9	13.3
Motor fuel	9.2	4.1	3.4
Health & social insurance levies	2.6	5.7	7.5
Other	5.1	7.0	6.0
Total tax revenue	55.7	53.5	59.6
Nontax revenue			
Natural resources	5.9	7.9	4.0
Licences, permits, etc.	5.0	2.3	2.4
Sales of goods & services	1.8	2.4	1.9
Return on investment	6.7	9.0	9.1
Other	0.2	1.0	3.9
Total nontax revenue	19.6	22.6	21.3
Total own-source revenue	75.3	76.1	80.9
Transfers			
Specific purpose	15.7	15.5	12.1
General purpose	9.1	8.4	7.0
Total	24.8	23.9	19.1
Total[a]	100.0	100.0	100.0
		($ million)	
Total amount	8 571	38 467	135 549

[a] Because of rounding, some totals are not exactly 100 percent.

Sources: Statistics Canada, *Provincial Government Finance, Revenue and Expenditures,* 1967 cat. 68–207; and CANSIM matrix 2751, July 19, 1990.

a venture capital tax credit of 30 percent of investment, a livestock investment tax credit, and a limited credit for investment in Saskatchewan corporations. Manitoba provided a property tax credit and a cost of living credit. In Ontario, no provincial income tax was payable if the tax amount was less than $150. That province provided a property tax credit for a deduction from personal income tax payable of $250 plus 10 percent of property taxes paid. It also offered a credit for provincial sales tax equal to $100 for each adult and $50 for each dependent child. The aggregate of property and sales tax credits was reduced by 2 percent of total income exceeding $4000. To assist individuals

TABLE 6–2
Share of Gross Provincial Revenue by Province, 1989/90

Source	Nfld	PEI	NS	NB	Que	Ont	Man	Sask	Alta	BC
					(percentage of total)					
Taxes										
Personal income	11.5	13.5	18.8	15.5	27.5	29.0	17.8	17.9	17.8	21.8
Corporate income	2.2	2.6	3.7	3.6	1.8	8.6	3.0	3.2	5.7	5.1
Real property	–	3.6	–	4.3	–	–	3.8	0.5	1.3	4.2
Alcohol & tobacco	1.5	3.2	2.0	2.1	1.6	1.4	1.9	2.1	1.8	2.1
General sales	16.7	12.8	16.8	16.2	11.5	19.2	10.4	10.0	–	12.6
Motor fuel	2.5	2.5	3.0	3.3	3.3	3.9	3.2	4.0	2.2	3.5
Health ins. premium	–	–	–	–	6.1	4.1	–	–	2.1	4.2
Workers' compensation	2.1	0.9	1.3	1.8	3.9	5.1	2.1	1.9	2.7	3.0
Other taxes	0.5	0.8	1.0	0.8	4.6	3.5	6.1	4.6	1.2	3.0
Total taxes	37.0	39.9	46.6	47.6	60.3	74.8	48.3	44.2	34.8	59.5
Nontax revenue										
Natural Resources	1.0	0.1	0.3	1.3	0.4	0.7	3.8	7.3	24.0	7.7
Sales of goods & services	2.0	2.9	2.8	1.7	1.7	1.8	1.9	2.6	1.5	2.2
Permits & licences	2.4	0.8	1.5	1.6	2.5	3.2	1.0	1.7	1.3	2.3
Return on investment	7.9	10.9	7.1	5.4	9.2	5.0	14.2	15.9	18.2	11.2
Liquor board profits	1.0	1.4	2.8	2.2	1.0	1.3	2.6	4.2	2.9	2.2
Universal pension plan	–	–	–	–	5.6	–	–	–	–	–
Other	0.3	0.1	0.2	0.2	1.0	0.5	0.6	0.4	0.6	0.3
Total nontax revenue	14.6	16.2	14.7	12.4	21.4	12.5	24.1	32.1	48.5	25.9
Total own-source revenue	51.6	56.1	61.3	60.0	81.7	87.3	72.4	76.3	83.3	85.4
General-purpose transfers	28.9	29.3	21.9	24.3	9.5	0.4	14.5	9.2	3.4	0.3
Specific-purpose transfers	19.2	14.7	17.0	15.8	8.8	12.3	13.2	14.5	13.2	14.4
Total[a]	100.0	100.0	100.0	100.0	100.0	100.0	100.0	100.0	100.0	100.0
					($ million)					
Total gross revenue	3 275	689	4 043	3 612	38 601	45 166	6 029	5 040	13 046	14 723

[a] Because of rounding, some totals are not exactly 100 percent.

Source: David Perry "Provincial Government Estimates, 1989–90," *Canadian Tax Journal* 37 (May/June 1989), 826, 828.

who were saving to purchase a home, the province established the Ontario Home Ownership Savings Plan to which qualifying individuals could contribute a maximum of $2000 per year and receive a tax credit of 25 percent if their income was less than $20 000; the credit declined as income increased and was reduced to zero for individuals with incomes in excess of $40 000. All the provinces except Newfoundland and Saskatchewan offered tax credits for political contributions.

The features of Quebec's personal income tax parallel fairly closely most of those found in the federal tax. These include the definition of income for tax purposes and the various reductions used to arrive at taxable income and tax payable. Personal "amounts" converted into tax credits have replaced personal exemptions and deductions, and many of these amounts are indexed. The province's April 1990 budget announced the following features of the personal income tax to take effect for 1991: a personal amount of $5300 for a single taxpayer; an equal married amount; a $2440 amount for the first child and $2110 for each subsequent child; a $2200 age amount; a $2200 physical or mental impairment amount; a retirement income amount of as much as $1000; and a $3090 tuition/education amount for dependent children in postsecondary studies. The tax credit equalled 20 percent of these amounts. For income tax reduction, a family with children could receive an additional deduction equivalent to $7570 (valued at $1514 as a tax credit). There was also a property tax refund on as much as $1150 of eligible property tax. Other income tax reductions included a dividend tax credit of 8.7 percent of taxable amount of dividends received from Canadian corporations, a research and development tax credit, and a real estate tax refund. A Quebec stock savings plan, to encourage investment in eligible corporations in Quebec, allowed deductions from gross income ranging from 50 to 100 percent depending on the nature of the corporation. The tax rate structure for 1990 began at 16 percent on taxable income of $7000 or less, 19 percent on income between $7000 and $14 000, 21 percent on income between $14 000 and $23 000, 23 percent on income between $23 000 and $50 000, and 24 percent on income of $50 000 and over.

Corporation Taxes

All the provinces impose a corporation income tax on taxable income earned within their boundaries. Some supplement this tax with other levies on corporations.

Corporation Income Tax. Seven provinces — namely, Newfoundland, Prince Edward Island, New Brunswick, Nova Scotia, Manitoba, Saskatchewan, and British Columbia — and the two territories are party to an agreement with the federal government whereby Ottawa collects their corporation income taxes, as it does their personal income taxes. These governments accept the federal government's corporation tax structure as the base for corporate taxation, including its definition of income and the various deductions applied in arriving at taxable income. The provincial tax rates are expressed as a percentage of corporate taxable income, ranging from a low of 14 percent in British Columbia to a high of 17 percent in Manitoba.

Most of these jurisdictions follow the federal system of applying lower rates to small businesses. The small business rate that is most common is 10 percent. The Yukon applies a dual rate of 2.5 percent on small business and 10 percent on large corporations. The Northwest Territories is an exception, with a single flat rate of 10 percent. Periodically, the provinces may apply special provisions, such as tax holidays for new enterprises or further reductions for very small businesses, that in effect results in three-tier rate structures. Investment incentives, such as tax credits, are also made available to corporations. For example, British Columbia offers a 100 percent credit to logging companies for logging taxes paid and a royalty tax credit for natural resource industries. Nova Scotia provides a credit of 10 percent of research and development expenditures incurred by corporations.

Ontario, Quebec, and Alberta collect their own corporation income taxes. Although doing so involves administration costs, a province that administers its own tax does have increased flexibility in taxation. It can establish its own tax base, with its own concept of income for tax purposes and its own exemptions and deductions. Ontario applies a three-tier tax rate structure (based on the federal government's classifications of business); the rate on small businesses is 10 percent, the rate for manufacturing and processing firms is 14.5 percent, and the general rate on all other corporate income is 15.5 percent. A venture capital tax incentive offers a credit of 25 percent of expenditure for equity shares in a small business development corporation. Other tax incentives and credits include provisions to encourage investment in pollution-control equipment.

Quebec employs a three-tier rate structure consisting of 3.0 percent on small business, 5.5 percent on business income from specified industries including manufacturing, processing, construction, and natural resources, and 13 percent on all other corporate income. In addition, surtaxes of 3.4 percent and 6.3 percent are applied to small and large corporations respectively. The tax incentives and credits offered cover scientific research, specified industries such as logging, and venture capital corporations.

Alberta also employs a three-tier rate structure based on the federal structure. The rates for small business, manufacturing and processing, and other corporations are 5, 9, and 15 percent respectively. The principal tax credits offered cover royalties paid and investments in venture capital corporations.

Capital Tax. Ontario, Quebec, Manitoba, and Saskatchewan impose a tax on a corporation's paid-up capital, defined as the value of issued stock, debt, and reserve funds. Tax rates differ among various types of businesses. The general rate of tax ranges from 0.3 percent to 0.5 percent of paid-up capital. Most provinces impose a tax on the paid-up capital of banks, trusts, and loan companies ranging from approximately 1.0 to 3.0 percent. The rate may vary with the financial institution taxed.

Consumption Taxes

Consumption or commodity taxes, as already noted, are generally considered to be indirect taxes imposed on one entity but expected to be passed on to another. The Constitution Act, 1867 prohibits the provinces from imposing indirect taxes. A province may, however, administer consumption or commodity taxes in a manner that qualifies them as direct taxes, which are permissible under the constitution. The provinces contend that most such taxes are consumer-purchase taxes levied on the purchaser with the seller acting as a paid collecting agent for the province. The courts have upheld this contention, thereby enabling the provinces to impose a number of sales and excise taxes, ranging from a general retail sales tax to taxes on specific items such as tobacco, fuel, and utilities. The major consumption-based taxes and the rates imposed by the various provinces are shown in Table 6–3. In terms of revenue, the retail sales tax is clearly the most important consumption tax imposed by the provinces.

Retail Sales Tax. In the nine provinces that levy a retail sales tax, the rates range from 6 percent in British Columbia to 12 percent in Newfoundland. The tax is paid by purchasers when they buy a commodity, and the seller receives a small percentage of the revenue collected as a collection fee. The seller is required to forward the tax receipts to the government each month.

Interprovincial variation in retail sales tax exemptions and rates defies neat summary. Several categories of items, including food, clothing (in some provinces), and prescription drugs, are exempted in an attempt to reduce the regressiveness of the tax. Double taxation is reduced through exempting goods used in further production, such as production equipment and materials. Similarly, farming and commercial fishing equipment is generally exempt. Some provinces provide exemptions on certain items purchased by municipalities and on building materials for the construction of schools, hospitals, and other public buildings.

Prepared meals in excess of certain amounts are taxed in all provinces except Saskatchewan and Alberta. Alcoholic beverages are taxed in all provinces except Alberta. Some commodities and services are taxed at the general rate in some provinces and at special rates in others. The list of taxed goods and services includes hotel and motel accommodations, telecommunications services, natural gas and fuel oil, laundry and dry cleaning, and repairs and maintenance to motor vehicles and household appliances.

When the federal government first outlined its plans for replacing its manufacturers' sales tax with the goods and services tax (GST), Ottawa invited the provinces to co-operate and together establish a federal-provincial national sales tax. The provinces refused, opposing a federal GST as an encroachment on the retail sales tax field. As of late 1990, however, Saskatchewan, Newfoundland, and Quebec had announced that they would harmonize their retail sales taxes with the federal GST, while British Columbia and Prince Edward Island had indicated that they were prepared to do so, reducing administrative complexities and costs.

Quebec, for example, announced that the merger of its sales tax with the GST would be completed by 1992. The provincial tax would be reduced from 9 to 7 percent but would be extended to the wider range of goods and services covered by the GST. Quebeckers would thus pay an overall, simplified consumption tax of 14 percent; it would be administered and collected by the province but Ottawa would determine the range of goods and services to be taxed. Businesses and consumers were expected to benefit from the administrative efficiencies of substituting a single tax for a two-tier system of federal and provincial taxes that required a duplication of bureaucracy.

Other Consumption Taxes. All the provinces impose taxes on cigarettes, cigars, and tobacco products. The sale of liquor is a provincial monopoly in all provinces with the province imposing a markup (or tax) on the manufacturers' price.

TABLE 6–3
Provincial Consumption-Based Taxes, 1990

	General retail	Prepared meals	Alcoholic beverages	Cigarettes	Tobacco	Gasoline	Diesel fuel	Telephone service	Hotel accommodations
	(percentage of retail price)			(cents per unit indicated)				(percentage of retail price)	
Nfld.	12	12	12	5.28/cig	3.52/g	12.2/*l*	12.3/*l*	12	12
PEI	10	10	25	4.70/cig	8.8/25 g	9.2/*l*	9.4/*l*	10	10
NS	10	10	10	4.5/cig	3.5/g	9.0/*l*	8.8/*l*	10	10
NB	11	11	11	6.7/cig	3.96/g	12.4/*l*	11.0/*l*	11	11
Que.	9	10	10	5.5/cig	2.5/g	9.6/*l*	9.6/*l*	9	–
Ont.	8	8	12	4.8/cig	4.8/g	14.3/*l*	10.9/*l*	8	8
Man.	7	7	12	6.5/cig	4.3/g	10.8/*l*	9.9/*l*	7	7
Sask.	7	–	10	6.68/cig	2.7/g	10.0/*l*	9.9/*l*	7	7
Alta.	–	–	–	4.8/cig	2.0/g	–	–	–	5
BC	6	–	10	5.0/cig	3.8/g	11.0/*l*	9.45/*l*	6	8

Sources: Millie Goodman and Deborah Ort, *1989 Tax Developments*, Tax Memo no. 76, (Toronto: Canadian Tax Foundation, 1990); provincial budgets 1989 and 1990; and information from the Canadian Tax Foundation.

Gasoline is taxed in all provinces except Alberta at a rate ranging from 9 to 14 cents per litre. Diesel fuel is generally taxed at lower rates. Fuel used for commercial and industrial purposes, in farming and fishing, and by some municipal services is either exempt or taxed at very low rates. The retail sales tax does not apply to motor fuel.

Several provinces impose special taxes on utilities, while others apply their retail sales tax to these services. Prince Edward Island, Nova Scotia, New Brunswick, Quebec, and Ontario levy special taxes, either unit or *ad valorem*, on the price of admission to amusements and entertainments. All the provinces impose a tax on pari-mutuel betting at race tracks; rates vary among provinces and also within a province depending on the number of bets — New Brunswick has a rate of 11.0 percent, Manitoba 7.5 to 12.5 percent, and Quebec 8.6 to 10.5 percent.

Health-Care Premiums and Payroll Taxes

Alberta and British Columbia levy premiums to help finance health-care programs; other provinces finance them solely from tax revenue. In British Columbia, the annual premium in 1990 was $348 for a single subscriber to the provincial health plan, $624 for a family of two, and $696 for a family of three or more.

Ontario used to use premiums for its health plan. Effective January 1990, they were discontinued and replaced with a payroll tax.

Ontario, Quebec, Manitoba and Newfoundland rely on payroll taxes for financing some part of their health services. The Employer Health Levy (EHL) in Ontario is applied to the total amount of gross wages, salaries, and other remuneration paid by an employer. The rate varies with the level of remuneration, beginning at 0.98 percent on gross remuneration of less than $200 000 and increasing to 1.95 percent on remuneration in excess of $400 000. Quebec imposes a tax on employer payrolls at a rate of 3.0 percent to finance its health services. In addition, Quebec imposes a combined employee-employer levy on payrolls at a rate of 4.1 percent of specified pensionable earnings to finance the Quebec Pension Plan. In its 1990 budget, Newfoundland levied a tax of 1.5 percent on the payrolls of corporations with annual employee earnings totalling more than $300 000. The tax includes federal corporations but excludes companies engaged in fishing, forestry, and agriculture. Manitoba imposes a 2.25 percent tax on the payrolls of companies with remuneration in excess of $100 000.

Insurance Premium Taxes

All provinces levy a tax on insurance premiums, including those for life, sickness, and fire and accident insurance. Rates generally range from less than 1.0 percent to 4.0 percent. The tax is payable by the insured.

Other Taxes

All the provinces impose a number of miscellaneous taxes. Ontario and Quebec levy taxes on the transfer of securities and bonds. New Brunswick, Ontario, Manitoba, and British Columbia levy land-transfer taxes on real estate transactions. Manitoba's tax is graduated, beginning at 0.5 percent and increasing to 1.5 percent on value of property in excess of $150 000. In New Brunswick, the rate is 0.25 percent. The British Columbia property-purchase tax equals 1.0 percent on the first $200 000 of value and 2.0 percent on any excess. In Ontario, the land-transfer tax is 1.5 percent on the value of property exceeding $250 000, and 2.0 percent on the value of residential property exceeding $400 000. Ontario also imposes a commercial concentration tax of $10.75 per square metre on all commercial properties and associated parking whose gross area exceeds 18 600 square metres.

A number of provinces impose taxes on public utilities to meet the cost of the boards and commissions that regulate them. In Prince Edward Island and New Brunswick, the provincial governments, rather than the municipal governments, impose taxes on real property. For the most part, property taxes elsewhere in Canada are reserved for the municipal governments, with the province imposing them only in unorganized or unincorporated areas.

Provincial Nontax Revenue

Nontax revenue, excluding transfers from the federal government, accounts for more than 20 percent of total provincial government revenue. The sources of this revenue include charges on natural resource industries, liquor profits, profits from provincial government enterprises, charges for incorporation and company registration fees, fines, penalties, and a variety of licences, such as those for motor vehicles, hunting, and fishing.

Transfers, which are another form of nontax revenue, make up almost another 20 percent of provincial revenue. Transfers from the federal government to the provinces are discussed in Chapters 7 and 8.

Natural Resources

Charges for natural resources take the form of levies on profits, land, and assessed value of minerals, returns from rental and leases of land, and royalties on production. The most important are levies on mining and logging and on oil and natural gas.

Revenues from natural resources increased in the 1970s but declined in recent years to constitute only 4 percent of total provincial revenue in 1989/90. These revenues, however, still account for almost 25 percent of the total revenues of Alberta and more than 7 percent of those of Saskatchewan and British Columbia.

Provincial Enterprises

In all provinces, bottled liquor is sold through government liquor stores. Beer and wine, on the other hand, are sold through both government stores and privately licensed outlets, such as brewery retail stores and, in Quebec, even grocery stores. The direct profits from sales in government-owned stores provide considerably more revenue than the sales of licences and permits to brewers, distillers, and sellers.

Provincial government enterprises other than liquor stores are found primarily in the areas of transportation, communications, and electric power. Although the gross expenditures and revenues of these enterprises may be substantial, only those revenues actually remitted to the government are considered revenues in the budget accounts, while only losses underwritten by the government are considered expenditures. The revenues remitted, plus interest and receipts from other investments, are recorded in the accounts (and shown in Tables 6–1 and 6–2) as "return on investment." The significance of this category of revenue for Alberta reflects the return on the investment of much of its earlier revenue from oil and gas.

Lotteries

Lotteries are becoming an increasingly important source of revenue at the provincial government level, although they still generate less than 2 percent of gross provincial revenue. In Ontario, for example, profits from six lotteries totalled $490 million in 1989/90, accounting for 1.1 percent of the province's revenues. Manitoba reported lottery sales of $131 million for 1988/9 with net proceeds of $47 million or about 0.8 percent of provincial government revenue.

The development of provincial lotteries has been interesting. The Canadian criminal code prohibits organizations other than governments and licensed charities from operating lotteries. During the 1970s, the federal government entered the field with a national lottery, but it withdrew in 1980 in favour of provincial operation of lotteries. In return, Ottawa received from the provinces for several years an annual payment of $24 million, which represented its share of the profits. In 1985, Ottawa and the provinces signed an agreement that the provinces would pay the federal government $100 million over three years in return for amendment of the criminal code to remove the federal government as a potential participant in lottery and gaming activities.[2]

The provinces were quick to exploit this new revenue source and established a variety of provincial and regional lotteries. Provincial lotteries are operated and administered by provincially owned lottery corporations, including the Atlantic Lottery Corporation, Loto Québec, the Ontario Lottery Corporation, the Western Lottery Foundation, and the BC Lottery Corporation. Regional and national lotteries are operated by the Interprovincial Lottery Corporation; revenues are allocated to the participating provinces in proportion to the sales in each.

Lottery profits represent approximately 30 to 35 percent of lottery sales. These profits may be placed in a province's general revenue fund or earmarked for specific purposes. Earmarked profits have been directed to areas such as sports and recreational activities, cultural activities, hospital construction, medical research, and senior citizens' housing. In Ontario, for example, lottery profits are paid into the province's Consolidated Revenue Fund and are distributed by the government to a wide variety of programs and projects; lottery profits from Ontario-only games support physical fitness, sports, culture, and recreation, while profits from interprovincial games go to health care and environmentally related health research, hospital buildings and equipment, and the support of social-service organizations such as the United Way, the Ontario Lung Association, and the Arthritis Society.[3] Manitoba established its lottery funding system to include "funding umbrellas" — organizations designated by the provincial government to distribute lottery revenue to nonprofit community groups. In addition, three provincial government departments, all of them involved in culture, tourism, recreation, and health, receive lottery revenue.

Government use of lotteries as a revenue source has sparked considerable controversy. Lotteries are attacked on the grounds that they are a form of very regressive taxation and are inequitable. Numerous studies have shown that expenditures for lottery tickets absorb a much higher percentage of the incomes of low-income groups than high-income groups, with the lowest-income group spending a share of its income two to five times greater than that of the highest-income group.[4]

Proponents of lotteries counter that lotteries are games of chance similar to various other legalized forms, including betting on horse racing and bingo. Even if lotteries are viewed as a tax, they contend, the tax is a voluntary one since no one is obligated to participate in a lottery. As a voluntary activity, the purchase of lottery tickets should not be considered a regressive tax, even though it may cause hardships in the sense that gambling does.

Critics of lotteries also oppose them on social and moral grounds. Private gambling, it is argued, is severely restricted and closely regulated by government because of perceived potential for adverse social and moral repercussions and for criminal elements to creep into the system. In operating and actively promoting lotteries through extensive media advertising, charge the critics, government is condoning and encouraging gambling. Furthermore, it is inconsistent that such activity is made permissible for governments yet is essentially barred in the private sector.

Municipal Revenues

The power of municipal governments to impose taxes is governed by provincial legislation. The only tax of significance that they levy is the property tax.[5] As shown in Table 6–4, property and related taxes account for almost three-quarters of municipalities' own-source revenues and more than one-third of their total revenues. As shown in Table 6–5, however, municipal taxes have decreased as a proportion of total municipal revenue while transfers have increased.

Property Tax

The base for the municipal property tax is real property — land and buildings — in all provinces, with the addition of machinery and equipment in some. Most provinces exempt church-, school-, and government-owned property, as well as the property of charitable organizations. The federal and provincial governments provide transfers in lieu of the taxes municipalities forgo on government property, and some provinces also provide transfers in lieu of municipal taxation of schools and hospitals.

The property tax is applied to the assessed value of the property and bears no relationship to the owner's ability to pay. The authority governing property assessment and taxation varies to some degree from province to province. In Ontario, for example, assessment is the province's responsibility, governed by the Assessment Act and administered by the Ministry of Municipal Affairs and Housing. In other provinces,

TABLE 6–4
Municipal Government Revenue, 1989

Source	Amount ($ 000)	Share of total (%)
Property and related taxes	19 915	38.2
Amusement taxes	29	0.1
Other taxes	143	0.3
Privileges, licences, permits	341	0.7
Sales of goods and services	5461	10.5
Return on investments	1331	2.6
Other revenue from own sources	1069	2.0
Total own-source revenue	28 289	54.2
General-purpose transfers		
Federal	308	0.6
Provincial	1937	3.7
Government enterprises	415	0.8
Specific purpose transfers		
Federal	162	0.3
Provincial	20 953	40.2
Government enterprises	84	0.2
Total transfers	23 859	45.8
Total gross general revenue	52 148	100.0

Source: Statistics Canada, CANSIM matrix 2764, July 19, 1990.

the responsibility is divided between the provincial government and the municipal governments, with large city governments generally authorized to undertake the assessment function.

The first step in the imposition of the property tax is to determine the assessed value of the property. Meanwhile, the municipality determines the amount of revenue it requires from property taxes. Then the latter amount is divided by the total assessed value of taxable property. The figure obtained is multiplied by 1000. The result, which is known as the mill rate, is the tax rate expressed as mills per dollar of assessed value. One mill is equal to one-tenth of one cent. Thus for example, if property is assessed at $10 000 and the tax rate is 50 mills, the tax amounts to $0.05 per dollar of assessed value for a total tax of $10 000(.05) = $500.

Most municipal governments distinguish between residential and commercial property and impose a slightly higher mill rate on commercial property. More than one authority may be involved in determining the mill rate. For instance, city council may determine one rate for general government purposes, and an additional rate may be set for education, determined by the budget presented by the school board.

Taxpayers receive a notice of assessment, which they have the right to appeal if they believe too high a value has been placed on their property. They also receive a statement

TABLE 6–5
Historical Summary of Municipal Government[a] Gross General Revenue

Source	1967	1976	1989
		(percentage of total)	
Taxes			
Real Property	41.5	32.8	38.2
Business	4.0	3.4	–
Other	4.4	2.3	0.4
Total tax revenues	49.9	38.5	38.6
Nontax revenue			
Licences and permits	1.2	0.5	0.7
Sales of goods and services	4.8	6.7	10.5
Other	4.0	6.2	4.4
Total nontax revenue	10.0	13.4	15.3
Total own-source revenue	59.9	51.9	54.2
Transfers			
Specific-purpose	34.6	42.0	40.7
General-purpose	5.5	6.1	5.1
Total transfers	40.1	48.1	45.8
Total	100.0	100.0	100.0
		($ million)	
Gross general revenue	5 346	17 055	52 148

[a] Includes Yukon and Northwest Territories.
[b] Includes grants in lieu of taxes from government and government enterprises.

Sources: Statistics Canada, *Local Government Finance*, 1967, cat. 68–204, and Statistics Canada CANSIM matrix 2764, July 19, 1990.

of tax owing. Some municipalities have adopted an instalment system by which a taxpayer may pay the tax in several parts over the year instead of in one lump-sum payment. Failure to pay the tax results in the imposition of a lien against the property; if it is not paid within a certain period of time, the property can be possessed by the government and sold at public auction.

Practices in assessment vary, but attempts are made to base it on the market value of property. (Some provinces use the term "real value" or "actual value.") The market value is generally interpreted as the price that the property could command if sold by a willing seller to a willing buyer. Since property values change over time, with some appreciating and others depreciating, and with increases from owner improvements, maintaining the equivalence between assessed and market values requires periodic reassessment of all property. Most provinces specify the time period for revaluing property. The most common practice is to reassess every three to five years, although Quebec requires revision of assessed values annually while Saskatchewan requires reassessment in rural municipalities every twelve years.

A major criticism of the property tax is its alleged regressiveness. The traditional view is that the property tax is one of the most regressive of all taxes. More recently, however, this view has been challenged by a number of economists using a different empirical approach in their study of the incidence of the property tax. The traditional approach uses income as the base for determining tax incidence and shows that lower-income families pay a larger proportion of their total income in property taxes than do wealthier families. The newer approach uses capital as the base for determining incidence and views the property tax as a tax on capital income. Since capital and capital income are highly concentrated in the hands of the relatively wealthy, this approach shows that it is they who bear most of the burden of the property tax. The two approaches are based on different assumptions that are difficult to verify empirically; therefore, the question of property tax incidence remains controversial among academics.[6]

A number of provinces have attempted to alleviate the burden of the property tax on lower-income families through schemes involving tax rebates and tax credits. In addition, some provinces have tried to prevent property taxes from escalating by assuming a greater responsibility for municipal functions, either directly or indirectly through larger grants to municipal governments.

Business Taxes

Municipal governments across Canada impose a wide variety of levies on businesses. These business taxes may take the form of a percentage of assessed value or may use as a base the business establishment's rental value, storage capacity, or square metres of floor space.

Saskatchewan uses an area base, determining the tax by multiplying total square metres of the business premise by a given rate. Storage capacity is used as a base in Alberta for the taxation of grain, petroleum, and coal establishments. A number of provinces permit municipal governments to employ the rental value of a business as the base for business taxes. The rates may be uniform for all businesses or may depend upon the type of business. Several provinces use the assessed value of real property as a base for business taxes; a given percentage is applied to this value to arrive at a business assessment, and, in turn, a tax rate is applied to the assessment. Ontario business assessments range from 30 percent of real property assessment for retailers, to 60 percent for manufacturers, to 140 percent for distillers. These percentages are established by legislation and so are uniform throughout the province.

Other Taxes and Charges

Provinces authorize municipal governments to impose user charges for certain services, such as fire protection and garbage collection, and the use of recreational facilities, such as arenas. Charges may also be imposed for area improvements, such as streets, street lighting, and sewers. In some Ontario municipalities, the charge for fire protection is a fixed fee added to the charge for utilities (hydro and water).

Some municipal governments also employ special assessments and fees for local improvements such as sidewalks, sewers, and street lighting. These assessments are made on the properties adjacent to or in the area of the improvement — the benefiting properties — with the costs assigned on the basis of frontage size.

Revenues from these miscellaneous taxes and charges for services have followed a gradual rising trend, increasing from 10 percent in 1967 to more than 15 percent by 1989.

Provincial/Municipal Fiscal Relations

The financial burden at the municipal level of government has become increasingly acute over the last few decades. Increased urbanization means increased municipal spending. Furthermore, the deterioration of the city core and the spread of suburbs have added to the strain on municipal finances. Sprawling suburbs require improved and more extensive transportation, sewage, water, recreation, sanitation facilities, new schools, new streets, and new sidewalks. Decay of the city core demands urban renewal. In addition, as people move to cities in search of employment, housing needs increase, so does the welfare roll since some are unable to find work.

One of the most important sources of revenue for the municipal governments is transfers from provincial governments. These transfers have increased since the 1960s to almost half of total municipal revenue. In addition, municipalities also receive transfers from the federal government and from government enterprises, although the amounts are relatively minor.

Provincial Transfers. Like all transfers, provincial transfers to municipalities may or may not be for a designated purpose. Specific-purpose transfers far outweigh general-purpose transfers as a share of total municipal revenue.

The bulk of provincial specific-purpose transfers received by municipal governments — in recent years, approximately two-thirds of the total — is for primary and secondary education.[7] Of the total municipal expenditure on education, approximately 70 percent is financed by these transfers. Another 15 percent of the specific-purpose transfers the municipalities receive are for health and social services. The remainder are allocated to transportation and communications, recreation and culture, the environment, housing, regional development, protection of persons and property, and general services.

The statistics are, however, averages. Transfers to municipalities vary considerably from province to province. Some provinces assume direct responsibility for certain functions that other provinces delegate to municipalities and assist in their financing with specific-purpose transfers. For example, the provincial governments of Prince Edward Island, New Brunswick, and Quebec assume direct responsibility for the administration and financing of education, and both levy and collect property taxes to help finance education. In Ontario, in contrast, education remains largely in the control of municipal governments, financed partly by specific-purpose grants from the province. Similarly, social services are a function that is primarily the responsibility of the provincial governments of Quebec, Newfoundland, Prince Edward Island, and

New Brunswick, but elsewhere is given — with financial assistance — to local authorities.

The form of general transfers also varies among provinces. The transfers may be tied to revenues collected locally, take the form of per capita grants, or be related to property assessment. In addition, most provinces pay municipal governments grants in lieu of local taxes on provincial government property.

Federal government general-purpose transfers to municipal governments consist primarily of grants in lieu of taxes on federal government property. Specific-purpose transfers are primarily for capital and community improvement projects, such as public works, sanitation, urban renewal, and winter works programs.

Borrowing. Another source of municipal government revenues is borrowing. The borrowing powers of those governments are, however, limited by provincial legislation. These limitations vary. In some provinces, a municipality may borrow only on approval of the provincial government, which must also approve the use of the funds, the type of debenture issued, and the rate of interest offered. Other provisions limit municipal borrowing to a specific percentage of total taxes collected or limit the total outstanding debt to a proportion of taxable assessment. In some cases, long-term borrowing is restricted to capital projects, upon the approval of the province.

Some provinces guarantee payment of the principal and interest of municipal debentures. The province may also purchase debentures from the municipal governments or establish loan funds from which they may borrow for specific purposes.

The Search for Solutions to Difficulties. Increasing local expenditures have led many municipalities to cry for more revenue in recent years. The property tax is the main source of municipal tax revenue, but the responsiveness of revenue to increases in this tax base (revenue elasticity[8]) is relatively low in comparison with some other taxes, such as the personal income tax. Property tax revenues increase as the property tax base increases with the construction of new homes and industrial sites, but the tax on existing structures does not respond to a growing economy as does personal income tax unless, of course, existing property is reassessed or the mill rate is changed. The low revenue elasticity of the property tax, coupled with its alleged regressive nature and increasing financial demands, has caused municipal governments to press for a share of the more elastic revenue sources. In recent years, there has been a movement toward formalized provincial/municipal tax-revenue sharing. The province of British Columbia has established a fund into which are paid the proceeds of one percentage point of the personal and corporation income taxes and 6 percent of natural resource revenue. General-purpose grants are paid from this fund. Quebec pays grants to municipal governments from an equalization fund. The province of Manitoba shares two points of its personal income tax and one point of its corporation income tax with municipal governments, distributed on a per capita basis. Saskatchewan has also established a revenue-sharing program whereby a portion of revenue from the personal and corporation income taxes and from the retail sales tax is transferred to municipalities.

Another approach is through tax system design. Given the municipal governments' heavy reliance on the property tax and their tendency to increase it to cover increasing operating expenditures, there is a real danger that low-income property owners will be overburdened. Most provinces attempt to lighten the burden on low-income owners with some form of property tax credit or rebate via the personal income tax. This has provided municipalities with added room for property tax increases.

In an attempt to reduce the revenue needs of the municipalities, some provinces have assumed responsibility for certain functions usually handled locally. For example, Prince Edward Island changed its municipal government structure in 1970 so that the provincial government assumed full responsibility for education, health, and social services. Similarly, the provincial governments of New Brunswick and Quebec have assumed full responsibility for education finance.

Despite these changes and increased provincial transfers, municipal governments continue to argue that limited revenues make it difficult for them to meet their financial obligations. There are various suggestions for easing the difficulties. It has been proposed, for example, that municipal governments begin tapping new sources of revenue, such as personal income, or that they relinquish some of their more burdensome responsibilities to the province. But the relatively small municipal jurisdictions would be confronted with numerous administrative problems in the imposition and collection of a local personal income tax or a sales tax. And although some municipal expenditure obligations could be assumed by the province, there are drawbacks in attempting to administer centrally activities of a purely local nature. It is argued that municipal governments are more attuned to the needs and desires of their own areas. Being smaller administrative units, they are unincumbered by large bureaucracies and are therefore flexible in responding to changing local conditions and corresponding needs. To the extent that this is the case, local needs can be more effectively served by maintaining the local functions at the municipal level and providing the municipal governments with sufficient revenues to carry out these functions, particularly those for which uniformity of service across local jurisdictions is not a major issue.

ENDNOTES

1. The primary sources of information for this chapter are the provincial governments' budgets; Canada, Statistics Canada, *Provincial Government Finance: Revenue and Expenditure*, cat. 68–207, annual; Statistics Canada, *Local Government Finance: Revenue and Expenditure, Assets and Liabilities* cat. 68–204, annual; Canadian Tax Foundation, *Provincial and Municipal Finances* (Toronto, biannual); and Canadian Tax Foundation, Tax Memo series (Toronto, occasional).

2. See Manitoba Lotteries Foundation, *Annual Report 1988/9* (Winnipeg, 1989), p. 29.

3. Ontario Lottery Corporation, *Annual Report*, 1988/9 (Toronto, 1989).

4. See, for example, J.R. Livernois, "The Taxing Game of Lotteries in Canada," *Canadian Public Policy* 12 (December 1986); and François Vaillancourt and Julie Gagnon, "Canadian Lotteries as Taxes: Revenues and Incidence," *Canadian Tax Journal* 36 (March/April 1988).

5. A detailed account of municipal financing is presented in Harry M. Kitchen, *Local Government Finance in Canada*, (Toronto: Canadian Tax Foundation, 1984).

6. For a more detailed discussion of property tax incidence and the approaches to analyzing it, see R.A. Musgrave, Peggy Musgrave, and R.M. Bird, *Public Finance in Theory and Practice,* Cdn. ed. (Toronto: McGraw-Hill Ryerson, 1987) ch. 21; and Harry M. Kitchen, "Property Taxation as a Tax on Wealth: Some New Evidence," *Canadian Tax Journal* 35 (July/August 1987).

7. A description of each province's specific-purpose transfers to municipal governments is contained in Canadian Tax Foundation, *Provincial and Municipal Finances 1989* (Toronto, 1990), ch. 13.

8. The revenue elasticity of a tax measures the responsiveness of revenue to a change in the tax base; it is given as $\varepsilon_R = (\Delta R/R) \div (\Delta B/B)$ where ε_R is the coefficient of revenue elasticity, R is revenue from the tax, and B is the tax base. The tax base for the property tax is the value of property; for the personal income tax, it is the level of personal income.

CHAPTER 7

FEDERAL/PROVINCIAL FISCAL RELATIONS: HISTORICAL DEVELOPMENT

Canada has a federal system of government in which powers are constitutionally divided between the federal government and provincial governments, and each is sovereign within its respective sphere of jurisdiction. This division of powers was established by the Constitution Act, 1867 at Confederation. Over time, however, changing economic and social conditions and the interpretations of the division-of-powers provisions of the act have produced a number of problems in intergovernment relations and difficulties for both levels of government.[1]

First, there is the issue of achieving a balance between expenditure responsibilities and revenue sources at the different levels of government. The federal government was given unlimited taxing powers and the provinces restricted to direct taxation, but the most expensive functions turned out to be those under the jurisdiction of the provinces. The provinces have complained of the difficulty of raising sufficient revenues to meet their large and ever-increasing expenditures. A lack of balance of expenditures and revenues between two levels of government is known as vertical fiscal imbalance.

Second, differences arise in the provinces' relative fiscal capacities, a situation known as horizontal fiscal imbalance. Because the provinces differ in economic potential and economic development, some have a good tax base while others have poor revenue sources. Ontario, for example, has a good industrial base with relatively high per capita income. It therefore has a greater capacity to obtain tax revenue to provide a wide range and high standard of services for its citizens than does a province such as Newfoundland with its relatively low per capita income. Even if Newfoundland resorts to higher levels of taxation, it has difficulty obtaining sufficient revenues to provide the same level of services as Ontario.

A third problem stems from the joint occupancy of tax fields. To a considerable degree, both levels of government levy the same taxes (income, sales), a situation that results in overlapping administration and the possibility of excessively high tax rates.

Fourth, conflicts occasionally arise from shared jurisdiction over certain responsibilities of government, such as natural resources or communications. Each level of government may have its own view regarding the direction of policy or development in the area and the extent of its jurisdiction. Examples include the disagreement between Ottawa and Newfoundland over offshore mineral rights and between Ottawa and Alberta over oil and gas pricing policies.

Finally, difficulties may arise in the implementation of fiscal policy. Unless there is close co-operation between the two levels of government, provincial expenditure and tax policies can counter federal measures introduced to achieve fiscal policy goals. For example, the federal government may reduce its income tax as part of a policy to stimulate the economy; the provinces could then conceivably take advantage of the tax room created, viewing this is an opportunity to increase their relative share of the income tax field.

Such problems have been common in Canada's history as a nation, and attempts to alleviate or solve them have been varied and numerous. This chapter and the next examine some of the basic issues and developments in federal/provincial relations in Canada. This chapter focuses on developments that led to the tax agreements between the federal government and the provincial governments and on the main features of those agreements.

HISTORICAL DEVELOPMENT OF FISCAL RELATIONS

Constitution Act, 1867

The Constitution Act, 1867, which created the Canadian nation (as the British North America Act), provided for a federal system of government. Desiring a strong central government, the founders of Confederation assigned the federal government the most costly functions of the time together with the most important revenue sources. The provinces were given what were then lesser powers, specifically enumerated in the act to include responsibility for education, hospitals, property and civil rights, licensing of business, administration of justice within the province, and matters of a local nature. At the same time, the provinces were assigned the less significant revenue sources then in existence, and each was limited to direct taxation within its own borders. Direct taxes, such as the personal income tax, were unpopular in the mid-nineteenth century and were not considered to have much potential as sources of revenue.

The residual powers of government—those not specifically assigned to the provinces — were granted to the federal government in the all-embracing section 91 of the act, which stipulates that the federal government is to "make Laws for the Peace, Order and Good Government of Canada in relation to all matters not coming within the Classes of Subjects by this Act assigned exclusively to the Legislatures of the Province."

To clarify federal responsibility, section 91 enumerates 32 specific federal powers. Included in this list is the power to raise revenue "by any mode of taxation." The most important sources of revenue in 1867 were customs and excise duties, which were classified as indirect taxes and assumed by the federal government. The provinces were left with the property tax and revenues from charges and licences. Since these revenue sources were somewhat meagre — they had accounted for only one-fifth of total revenues of the provinces of Canada in 1866 — the federal government agreed to supplement them by giving the provinces annual payments, which were specified in the act. They consisted of per capita subsidies and flat annual grants in support of government. In addition, special annual grants were arranged for Nova Scotia and New Brunswick for a ten-year interim period to give them time to develop their own taxes.[2] Grants and subsidies accounted for approximately 80 percent of the total revenues of these two provinces in the early post-Confederation period.

The arrangements just described achieved a reasonable balance between revenue needs and expenditure responsibilities in 1867. The federal government had been assigned the most costly functions and had been given the main revenue sources. The less costly functions assigned to the provinces were not expected to become financially significant, and provincial revenue needs were considered to be well below federal needs.

Any semblance of balance achieved in 1867 was shattered shortly thereafter, however, and continued to erode over time. As Canada developed following Confederation, the demands on both levels of government increased.[3] In 1879, the federal government introduced the National Policy as part of its plan for the economic development of the country. High tariffs were imposed to promote industrialization, immigration was encouraged, and transportation facilities — above all, the Canadian Pacific Railway — were constructed. The tariffs and higher excises on liquor and tobacco brought increased revenues to the federal government to finance its policy.

At the same time, despite increased federal subsidies, the provinces were finding it difficult to meet their increasing obligations in the developing economy. They began to look for and tap new sources of tax revenue. The first personal income tax was introduced by the province of British Columbia in 1876; it was followed by Prince Edward Island in 1894. In 1884, Quebec levied a flat-rate tax on corporations. The first succession duties were levied by Ontario in 1892, and by 1896 all provinces had imposed such a tax.[4] As the provinces developed and expanded their tax structures, federal subsidies became increasingly less significant relative to total provincial revenues.

The First World War marked the beginning of direct taxation by the federal government, with substantial consequences for future federal/provincial fiscal relations. Ottawa introduced a tax on corporate profits in 1916 and followed it with a personal income tax in 1917. At the same time, in an attempt to obtain increased revenues to finance the war effort, the federal government extended its participation in indirect taxes. Existing tariffs and excises were increased, and excise taxes were imposed on a large number of other items, such as luxuries, railway tickets, telegrams, and drugs. In 1920, a general sales tax at the manufacturers' level was introduced.[5]

Despite the imposition of direct taxes, the relative importance of indirect taxes to the federal government was maintained. More than 93 percent of total federal revenue was obtained from indirect taxes in 1913, and the share had dropped only to 90 percent in 1921.[6]

The Post-War Period and the Depression

The 1920s were a decade of relative prosperity for Canada. A rapidly growing economy and the spread of urbanization during the period brought a need for transportation facilities, public utilities, education, and welfare services. Many of these new and increased demands on the public sector came within provincial jurisdiction, producing a trend opposite to that expected by the founders of Confederation. The functions assigned to the provinces were becoming more socially important and more financially burdensome, yet the provincial taxing powers were limited, both constitutionally and by the practical reality of the federal intrusion into direct taxation. In seeking new sources of revenue, the provinces imposed taxes on gasoline, assumed monopoly control over the sale of liquor, and sold automobile licences. By the end of the decade, provincial tax revenues had doubled and federal subsidies had declined to only 8 percent of total provincial revenue.[7] In contrast, federal tax revenue declined during the period.

The 1920s fostered two significant developments in federal/provincial fiscal relations: specific-purposes transfers, also known as conditional grants,[8] emerged as an increasingly important means of federal financial assistance to the provinces; and the federal government entered the field of social services.

Specific-purpose transfers had first appeared in Canada at the turn of the century in the area of agriculture. They proliferated following the First World War when projects in transportation, vocational training, and health were undertaken jointly by the federal and provincial governments. The federal government contributed up to half of the cost of the projects but established conditions that the provinces were required to meet if they were to qualify for the federal payment. In 1927, Ottawa, in co-operation with the provinces, introduced an old age pension plan with the federal government paying half of the cost. This was the federal government's first major experiment in the field of social services, and it proved the most expensive of the early specific-purpose transfer programs.

Although the transfers eased the problem of the provinces' shortage of revenues and provided a means by which the federal government could assist all provinces in providing essential services, the problem of unequal fiscal capacity remained. From the beginning of Confederation, the Atlantic provinces had faced a poor tax base and the inability to provide the standard of services found in other provinces. Since 1867, the federal government had attempted to alleviate this problem using special subsidies and grants to these provinces. The situation became critical in the 1920s, however, and in 1926 the federal government appointed a royal commission to investigate the problem. The commission recommended increased general-purpose — unconditional — transfers to the Atlantic provinces.[9]

Through taxation and federal subsidies, the provinces generally managed reasonably well in obtaining revenues before 1930. The Depression, however, brought major difficulties. Rapidly declining employment and incomes reduced revenues substantially, while demands increased for expenditures in areas such as social services and unemployment relief. These were areas of provincial jurisdiction, and to assist the provinces, the federal government relied heavily on specific-purpose transfers, which increased from $2.4 million in 1927 to $72.9 million in 1937, mostly for aid to farmers and the unemployed. Specific-purpose transfers were supplemented by special grants to the Atlantic and Prairie provinces, the two regions suffering the most severely from the Depression. In 1934, the White Royal Commission was appointed to study the problems in these two regions; it recommended special assistance in the form of increased transfers to the two regions.[10]

Both the federal and provincial governments attempted to prevent revenues from declining during the Depression by increasing taxes. The federal government increased its sales tax from 1 to 8 percent, doubled the personal income tax rate, and imposed new import duties. The provinces increased the gasoline tax by 50 percent and raised succession duties and flat-rate taxes on corporations. By 1940, all the provinces were taxing personal and corporate incomes, and Saskatchewan and Quebec had introduced a retail sales tax.[11] There was little or no co-operation between the federal and provincial governments in taxation as both governments scrambled for revenues, producing a chaotic tax jungle of joint occupancy, high tax rates, duplication of administrative machinery, and regressiveness in taxation that contributed to the severity of the Depression by undermining business confidence and incentives. Moreover, the lack of co-operation made it difficult to implement effective anti-Depression fiscal policy late in the 1930s when other countries were beginning to adopt the Keynesian remedy.

The Royal Commission on Dominion-Provincial Relations

The Depression clearly highlighted the problems that can arise in a federal system when the two levels of government compete for revenues from a shrinking pool to meet increasing social and economic demands and when regions have major disparities in fiscal capacities. In 1937, the crisis gave rise to the appointment of the Royal Commission on Dominion-Provincial Relations, known as the Rowell-Sirois Commission after its chairmen. Its general purpose was to reassess the entire Canadian federal structure. More specifically, it was charged with investigating the distribution of powers between the federal and provincial governments, the increasing responsibilities of the provinces, their capacity for meeting these responsibilities, and the overlap and duplication of services and taxes at the federal and provincial levels of government. After an exhaustive investigation, the commission reported its findings and presented its recommendations in May 1940. Among its major recommendations were:

- The federal government should assume the sole responsibility for imposing personal and corporation income taxes and succession duties. This would bring simplicity and efficiency to the tax structure and avoid overlapping taxation.
- The federal government should assume responsibility for the unemployed. This would ensure a national standard of service and greater efficiency in administration.
- The federal government should assume provincial debts to permit the provinces to make a new start. They had incurred considerable debts during the Depression and the interest charges were absorbing a significant portion of their revenues.
- Canada should introduce a system of national adjustment grants — general grants to the poorer provinces based on the amount necessary to permit them to provide levels of services equal to the national average. Such a system would enable the poor provinces to provide adequate services without having to resort to heavy taxation and, being unconditional, the grants would not interfere with provincial autonomy.
- The federal government should introduce a program of emergency grants to provinces suffering from adverse economic conditions. It was recommended that grants be paid immediately to Saskatchewan, which was suffering from severe drought and crop failures.[12]

A federal/provincial conference was called in January 1941 to discuss the recommendations of the commission. The recommendations were rejected. The provinces in general felt that the proposals for the transfer of powers to the federal government involved a greater degree of centralization of power than they were prepared to accept.

There was also conflict among provinces, with Ontario, Alberta, and British Columbia refusing to shoulder the burden of adjustment grants to the poorer provinces.

By this time Canada had become involved in the Second World War, and it was recognized that the hostilities would place a heavy financial burden on the federal government. Although the provinces rejected the Rowell-Sirois proposals, they indicated that in the national interest they would be prepared to co-operate with the federal government in financial matters for the period of the war. The result was a series of federal/provincial fiscal agreements, which have been renegotiated every five years since the war.[13]

Federal/Provincial Fiscal Arrangements: 1941–1992

Tax Rental Agreements: 1941–1957

The financial burden of the Second World War prompted the federal government to seek exclusive rights over the major tax sources. It proposed to "rent" the personal and corporation taxing powers of the provincial governments for the duration of the war, and the provinces agreed. In 1941, the first tax rental agreement was negotiated. It ended in 1947 and was followed by a series of five-year tax rental agreements, which continued until 1962. For a summary of these federal/provincial arrangements, see Table 7-1.

Under the terms of the early agreements, the provinces withdrew from the personal and corporation income tax fields in return for annual rental payments. They were offered a variety of formulas and bases for calculating the rental payments, including revenues collected in earlier years from the vacated tax fields and per capita payments. For example, one option offered in 1947 was $12.75 per capita, based on the 1942 population of the province, plus 50 percent of the revenue received by the province from personal and corporation income taxes in the 1940/1 fiscal year.

Considerable emphasis was placed on the temporary nature of these arrangements, with Ottawa assuring the provinces that it was not attempting to take away their taxing powers permanently.

In 1947, special arrangements were offered to provinces not wishing to enter the agreements. The federal government provided room for them to levy their own taxes by withdrawing from the personal and corporation income tax by 5 percent of the federal tax and by 50 percent of succession duties. Ontario and Quebec refused to sign the agreement. Instead, they imposed a 7 percent tax on corporate income and continued to levy succession duties. Ontario also enacted a tax on personal income equal to 5 percent of the federal tax; it did not put it into effect, however, because it lacked administrative machinery, and Ottawa refused to collect the tax for the province.[14]

All provinces signed the 1952 agreement except Quebec, which imposed a 7 percent corporation income tax and received a 7 percent abatement from Ottawa. In 1954, Quebec introduced a tax on personal income equal to 15 percent of the federal tax, to which Ottawa responded with a 10 percent abatement.

TABLE 7–1
Summary of Federal-Provincial Tax Agreements

	Major provisions
1941	First tax rental agreements made: provinces "rent" to the federal government their personal and corporate tax fields plus succession duties.
1957	Equalization payments to provinces are formally adopted. Equalization base consists of personal and corporation income taxes and succession duties.
1962	Federal government returns the three rented tax fields to the provinces and provides tax room through abatements of the federal tax.
1965	Opting-out arrangements made: federal government offers provinces increased tax points in lieu of conditional grants for shared-cost programs. Only Quebec chooses this option.
1967	Conditional grants for postsecondary education are replaced by additional tax abatement points. Equalization base is increased to 16 provincial revenue sources.
1977	Established programs financing (EPF) adopted. Conditional grants for hospital insurance, medicare, and postsecondary education are replaced with 13.5 points of personal income tax and one point of corporation income tax, plus cash payments. Equalization base increased to 29 provincial resource sources.
1982	Equalization base increased to 33 provincial and municipal revenue sources.
1987	Limits placed on EPF cash transfers to provinces. Equalization base becomes 32 provincial taxes (since no province now levies estate duties).
1990	Cash transfers to province under EPF are frozen for a two-year period.

As the 1952 agreement neared an end, the federal and provincial governments met to discuss the possibility of establishing a more permanent taxation arrangement between the two levels of government. The provinces were experiencing rapidly escalating expenditures in the 1950s, and although most were prepared to continue to rent their tax fields, they demanded substantially increased compensation. The concept of tax-sharing emerged from the discussions and formed the basis of the 1957 agreement.

Tax-Sharing Agreement: 1957–1962

In essence, the tax-sharing agreement of 1957 was a continuation of the tax rentals. The provinces agreed to refrain from imposing personal and corporation income taxes and succession duties and in return received the following compensation:

- Rental Payments. The rental payments consisted of a share of the three standard taxes:
  - 10 percent of the personal income tax collected in the province (excluding the old age security tax).
  - 9 percent of corporation profits.
  - 50 percent of federal succession duties (later to become the estate tax), based on a three-year average.
- Equalization payment. The federal government agreed to pay to each province, in the form of an unconditional transfer, an amount that would bring the level of per capita yield from the three standard taxes in each province up to the average yield in the two wealthiest provinces, Ontario and British Columbia. Thus, the 1957 agreement marked the beginning of explicit equalization payments, which, in 1982, were entrenched in the Constitution Act.
- Stabilization. The federal government guaranteed that the amount of annual payment received by each province would not fall below previous payments.

For provinces wishing to impose their own taxes, the federal government offered abatements equivalent to the rental payment. Quebec chose this route, while Ontario agreed only to rent its personal income tax. The equalization and stabilization features of the agreement, however, applied to these two provinces.

The 1957 arrangements maintained the simplified feature of the earlier tax rental agreements in that only one level of government levied the taxes. In addition, certain basic principles could be readily discerned in these arrangements.

The rental payments were calculated on the basis of shares that took into account relative fiscal capacity. Equalization grants were designed to assist the poorer provinces in providing levels of service comparable to those of the richer provinces. All provinces except Ontario qualified for equalization payments. Prince Edward Island's equalization grants were approximately triple the amount it received in tax rental.[15] The stabilization guarantee permitted provinces to make long-term plans without the fear of declining revenues.

The arrangements also respected provincial autonomy in taxation. A province was free to impose its own taxes without being placed at a financial disadvantage relative to other provinces. Aside from acting out the principle of provincial autonomy, however, a province had little to gain from not renting its taxing powers. In fact, renting was politically attractive for provinces since it allowed them to enjoy the revenues from unpopular taxes yet not be responsible for imposing them.

Even though the provinces entered the agreement, they were not completely satisfied with its financial terms and continued to press for larger payments. After a new Conservative government was formed in 1957, a federal/provincial conference was called to consider the provinces' demands. The result was an increase in the provincial share of the personal income tax, from 10 to 13 percent. In addition, to further alleviate the problem of unequal fiscal capacities and regional disparities, Ottawa offered the four Atlantic provinces special grants, labelled Atlantic Adjustment Grants, totalling

$25 million annually. In 1959, Newfoundland was given a further grant, amounting to $8 million annually for a five-year period. Another adjustment in the arrangements was made in 1960 as a special concession to Quebec; the corporation income tax abatement was increased to 10 percent for a province not wishing to accept federal specific-purpose transfers in support of universities.

During this period, specific-purpose transfers were increased substantially with the introduction of a public health plan under the Hospital Insurance and Diagnostic Services Act. For this major shared-cost program, the federal government contributed to each province 25 percent of the national average per capita cost of the program plus 25 percent of the actual per capita cost of services within the province.

Tax rentals and tax-sharing expired with the end of the 1957– 62 arrangements. In a series of conferences beginning in 1960, the provinces voiced their dissatisfaction with the share of revenue they were receiving and demanded substantial increases. The federal government, however, was having second thoughts about tax rental and tax-sharing. Provincial demands could be met only through increased federal taxes. Since tax increases are never popular with the electorate, Ottawa was beginning to look at the tax-sharing system with more and more political disfavour. The federal view was that if the provinces required revenue, they should take the political responsibility for increasing taxes. Consequently, Ottawa proposed to return the taxing powers to the provinces, claiming federal recognition of provincial autonomy and provincial need in the sense that provinces could impose their own taxes at rates necessary to meet their needs. (Actually, this idea, was not novel; the provinces had had a similar option open to them in 1957, although only Quebec had exercised it.)

The provinces were generally not pleased with the federal proposal. It did not represent any financial improvement for them; furthermore, they would be forced to assume partial responsibility for personal and corporation income taxes. Nevertheless, the federal government stood firm, and in 1962 a new five-year arrangement was adopted on federal terms.

The arrangements were extended along similar lines every five years thereafter. In the following section, the essence of each five-year tax agreement is outlined along with developments that occurred while it was in force.

Tax Agreements: 1962–1967

Tax Arrangements. Beginning in 1962, the provinces were to resume their personal and corporation taxing powers with the federal government granting abatements to make room for the provincial taxes. Ottawa agreed to abate its "basic" personal income tax payable by 16 percent in 1962 and by one additional percentage point each year thereafter until the abatement reached 20 percent of basic personal income tax in 1966. This abatement schedule was increased in 1964 to 21 percent for 1965 and 22 percent for 1966 and then was increased again in 1965 to 24 percent for 1966. The corporation income tax abatement was fixed at 9 percent of corporation taxable income. In addition, Ottawa agreed to return 50 percent of the federal estate tax collections within a province to that province if it refrained from imposing succession duties. Provinces that levied their own succession duties were granted a 50 percent tax credit. In 1964, the provincial return and tax credit was increased to 75 percent.

To avoid unnecessary administrative duplication, the federal government offered to collect the taxes for any province, provided it adopted the personal and corporate income tax bases defined in the Federal Income Tax Act. This provision would restrict the provinces' taxing powers in that participants would have to accept Ottawa's definition of income and permit its same exemptions and deductions. This tax collection arrangement would, however, not only spare the provinces the expense of collecting the taxes involved but also reduce the compliance costs of taxpayer's who would need to file only one tax return. All the provinces except Quebec signed the collection agreement, although Ontario agreed to permit the federal government to collect only the personal income tax. Quebec, refusing to accept any direction from Ottawa, preferred to levy and collect its own taxes.

In determining their tax rates for 1962, seven provinces set their personal income tax rates at the same level as the federal abatement of 16 percent. Manitoba and Saskatchewan adopted a rate of 22 percent and in subsequent years were followed by other provinces. In 1962, Manitoba and Saskatchewan also adopted a corporation income tax rate higher than the federal abatement. They levied a tax of 10 percent, while Ontario imposed a tax of 11 percent and Quebec 12 percent.[16]

Equalization. The formula for calculating equalization payments was changed from the average per capita yield of the two wealthiest provinces to the national per capita yield. The reduction in payments that this change would have produced was partially countered by extending the formula base to include one-half of the revenues from provincial taxes on natural resources, as well as the three standard taxes. This revised formula did, however, reduce payments to provinces with an above-average natural resource tax base, most notably Alberta. In 1964 the formula was again changed to the average per capita yield of the two richest provinces.

The federal government continued the stabilization concept of earlier agreements by guaranteeing that the revenue of any province from the three standard taxes and equalization would not be permitted to drop below 95 percent of the average that it had received in the previous two years.

The special grants to the Atlantic provinces introduced in 1958 were increased from $25 million to $35 million annually, and the special $8 million grant to Newfoundland was continued. The provinces also continued to receive the statutory subsidies provided at Confederation.

The 1962 arrangements appeared to hold certain advantages for the federal government. They indicated Ottawa's respect for the provinces' autonomy by returning their constitutional taxing rights. They also appeared politically advantageous in that the federal government would no longer be under pressure to raise taxes to meet provincial demands for increased payments. If the provinces required more revenue, they could increase taxes themselves. Provincial demands for larger payments were, however, soon to be replaced by demands for larger abatements and more room for provincial taxes. Moreover, one obvious disadvantage for the federal government was its reduced ability to implement discretionary fiscal policy as it no longer had complete control over the major tax fields.

The provinces were generally dissatisfied with the arrangements. The poorer provinces stood to gain little from the revised equalization formula, and some provinces would actually lose. All provinces maintained that the level of federal abatements was inadequate. In fact, shortly after the agreements were concluded, a number turned to other taxes for increased revenues.[17]

Opting-Out Arrangements: 1965

The early 1960s brought an escalation in the federal government's use of specific-purpose transfers. Several provinces were not particularly pleased with this trend and criticized their use during the 1960 and 1961 federal/provincial conferences; the most vocal was the province of Quebec. It had refused to accept specific-purpose transfers in the past, primarily on constitutional grounds, and in the early 1960s pressured Ottawa to replace these transfers with general-purpose transfers or increased tax abatements. It was primarily as a concession to Quebec that in 1965 an opting-out provision was introduced into the federal/provincial arrangements by which certain specific-purpose transfers were replaced by additional tax abatement points for any province that preferred federal assistance in the latter form.

Under these arrangements, certain programs were designated eligible for opting-out on the basis of equalized abatement points of the personal income tax. Five major programs were designated, for which a total of 20 abatement points were offered as follows:

Program	**Equalized abatement points**
Hospital insurance	14
Old age assistance, blind and disabled persons allowances	2
Welfare portion of unemployment assistance	2
Health grants	1
Vocational training	1
Total	20

(In 1966, the programs of old age assistance, blind and disabled persons allowances, and unemployment assistance were incorporated into the Canada Assistance Plan, and four abatement points were assigned to the plan.)

To qualify for receipt of these abatements, a province choosing to opt out was required to continue the obligations and conditions of the programs as they existed for an interim or transitional period. More permanent arrangements were to be negotiated for implementation following the interim period.

Provinces were given until October 1965 to determine whether they wished to opt out, but only Quebec chose to do so. Opting out of the programs, together with the Youth Allowances Program, entitled Quebec to 23 additional abatement points of the personal income tax. The additional points did not, however, give Quebec any more revenue than it would have received had it accepted the specific-purpose transfers.

Arrangements were also made to permit opting out of federally initiated programs in areas of joint federal/provincial responsibility. The first major program involved was the Canada Pension Plan, introduced by the federal government effective January 1966. Each province was given the option of either permitting Ottawa to occupy the public pension field through federal introduction and administration of the program or introducing and administering a program of its own that adhered to certain general principles. Again, Quebec alone chose the latter alternative.

The short-run effect of the opting-out provision was negligible, since a province choosing to opt out of a shared-cost program was obligated to continue it with no changes during the interim period. It was in the long run that repercussions were expected. In those programs expected to continue following the interim period, an opted-out province would be free to vary its services as it saw fit and still receive the abatement points. The result could be erosion of national standards. It was also argued that the opting-out clause would tend to weaken federation through greater decentralization of power. On the other hand, it could strengthen federation as Quebec would be pacified and be more content to remain part of the Canadian nation.

The sequel to the opting-out arrangement of 1965 appeared in the federal/provincial conference in 1966. In negotiating a new five-year fiscal agreement with the provinces to become effective in 1967, the federal government proposed that they assume full responsibility for shared-cost programs in health and social services in return for 17 additional abatement points in the personal income tax. Ottawa furthermore proposed that abatements replace specific-purpose transfers for higher education and offered four points in the personal income tax and one point in the corporation income tax for this purpose. The provinces rejected the federal proposals, fearing that with the soaring costs of education, health, and social services the abatements offered would produce less revenue in the future than specific-purpose cash transfers. A compromise was finally reached, and a new five-year agreement was signed to become effective in 1967.

Tax Agreement: 1967–1972

Tax Arrangements. In the new agreements, the provinces were granted four additional abatement points in the personal income tax and one point in the corporation income tax as a partial substitute for specific-purpose transfers in support of postsecondary education. This change increased the abatement in the personal income tax from 24 to 28 percent and in the corporation income tax from 9 to 10 percent. In addition, each province was granted an adjustment payment calculated either to bring the revenue from education abatements up to 50 percent of the operating costs of its postsecondary educational institutions or to equal an amount that started at $15 per capita and would be adjusted annually in accordance with the rate of increase in postsecondary education operating expenditures. Newfoundland, Prince Edward Island, and New Brunswick opted for the latter form of adjustment payment, which brought the federal contribution in these three provinces to more than 50 percent of their total operating costs for postsecondary education.

Equalization. A new formula was established for determining equalization payments. The base for the calculation was extended to sixteen provincial taxes, including the three standard taxes, revenues from natural resources, the retail sales tax, gasoline tax, excises on alcohol, and motor vehicle licence fees. The payment was designed to bring the average per capita yield from these taxes in the poorer provinces up to the national average.

Stabilization was also continued under a revised formula in which the federal government guaranteed the provinces that their total net general revenues would not be allowed to fall below 95 percent of their previous year's revenues.

Opting-Out. The opting-out arrangements of 1965 remained primarily intact, except that the one abatement point granted for the vocational training program was allowed to expire in March 1967 as scheduled. Instead, the federal government assumed full responsibility for adult retraining. Abatements in the personal income tax under the 1967 arrangements were:

Program	Equalized abatement points
General	28
Hospital insurance	14
Canada Assistance Plan	4
Youth allowances	3
Health grant program	1
Total	50

Tax Agreement: 1972–1977

At the federal/provincial conference of November 1971, held to renegotiate another five-year fiscal agreement, Ontario and Alberta demanded the right to opt out of shared-cost programs as Quebec had in 1965. The federal government refused — an action termed "contradictory and illogical" by Premier Bill Davis of Ontario. The richer provinces also requested a revision of the equalization formula. British Columbia was particularly critical of the formula in force, under which large equalization payments were made to Quebec. Ottawa's response was to propose only minor changes in the equalization formula. Other changes that were introduced stemmed from the federal tax reform of 1972. The result was a new five-year fiscal arrangement.

Tax Arrangements. The tax arrangements were adjusted to conform to the changes that were introduced with tax reform in January 1972. The general abatement system in personal income taxation was abandoned except for the extra abatement points Quebec received under the opting-out agreement. Under the new system, federal tax rates no longer included the provincial abatement. They were reduced by 30.5 percent of the basic federal tax (equivalent to the former 28 percent abatement). Included in this amount were the tax points in lieu of specific-purpose transfers for education arranged in 1967. (The four points for this purpose became 4.357 points.) The provinces that had signed tax collection agreements with Ottawa were free to impose whatever tax rate they desired. It was expressed as a percentage of basic federal tax and could be more or less than 30.5 percent.

The stabilization clause was continued under an amended formula in which the federal government guaranteed each province that its total revenue would not fall below that of the previous year, unless it had changed its taxes.

In addition, the federal government introduced the income tax Revenue Guarantee

Program vis-à-vis its significant tax reform of 1972. It guaranteed for a five-year period that the provinces would not suffer a loss of revenues as a result of adopting personal and corporation income tax structures corresponding to the new federal structures. This guarantee program cost the federal government more than $1.5 billion over the period of the agreement.

The abatement system that had previously applied to the corporation income tax was retained under the 1972 agreement at 10 percent of corporate taxable income. The opting-out arrangements with Quebec were also continued but with an upward adjustment from 22 to 24 points, reflecting the new federal tax base following tax reform.

Another change was prompted by the termination of the federal estate and gift taxes. Ottawa had previously returned 75 percent of the revenues from these taxes to the provinces. A number of provinces now decided to follow the practice of Quebec, Ontario, and British Columbia and impose their own succession duties and gift taxes. It was arranged that Ottawa would collect the two taxes for these provinces for a period of three years.

Equalization. Under the 1972 equalization formula, three taxes were added to the base, bringing the total number of revenue sources in it to nineteen. These additions were race track taxes, health insurance premiums, and the provincial share of taxes on power utilities. In 1973, municipal taxes for school purposes were added to the list. In 1975, revenue from oil and natural gas was redefined, and one-third of the revenue accrued as a result of increased prices of oil and gas was brought into the equalization formula.

As the 1972 fiscal agreement neared its termination, federal proposals for the next agreement included new formulas for financing the major shared-cost programs, the establishment of ceilings on annual increases in equalization payments, and the termination of the revenue guarantee program. The federal proposals for financing shared-cost programs contained various options, all of which included limits to the federal contribution. Ottawa's objective was to transform payments to the provinces from an uncontrollable item in the federal budget to a controllable or at least predictable item.

The provinces with a good tax base favoured larger provincial tax shares as a replacement for specific-purpose transfers but insisted that the taxes in which larger shares were granted be relatively elastic ones, such as the personal income tax. The poorer provinces, on the other hand, preferred to continue with some type of cost-sharing for fear that they would lose revenue in the long run. They also opposed limits on equalization payments. All provinces vigorously opposed the proposal for terminating or changing the terms of the tax revenue guarantee. A compromise was reached, and the next five-year agreement was effected beginning April 1977.

Tax Agreement: 1977–1982

Established Programs Financing. The 1977–1982 federal/provincial agreement centred on a new formula for financing the three major established shared-cost programs: hospital insurance, medicare, and postsecondary education.[18] Federal assistance for these programs was changed from specific-purpose transfers directly related to provincial expenditures to a combination of increased tax room and cash payments — the latter related to the growth of the economy. Under what became known as established programs financing (EPF), the federal government transferred to the provinces 13.5 points of personal income tax and one point of corporation income tax plus the approximate value of these tax points in a cash payment. Since the tax point transfer included the 4.357 points of personal income tax and the one point of corporation income tax that the provinces had been given in 1967 for postsecondary education, the new tax room provided actually was 9.143 points of personal income tax. Moreover, the tax transfer and cash package included one point of personal income tax and its cash equivalent as partial compensation for the termination of the 1972 Revenue Guarantee Program, which was replaced by a limited revenue guarantee. This limited guarantee applied only to the personal income tax and was designed to cover losses in revenue suffered by the provinces as a result of federal tax change, but only if the loss exceeded 1 percent of the basic federal income tax in the province. Furthermore, the guarantee applied only to the first year after any federal tax change.

The tax points were equalized to the per capita national average yield with the cash payment to rise with the growth of the economy. Specifically, the basic cash payment to each province was determined by multiplying half of the national average per capita federal payments for the established programs in the base year (1975/6) by the population of the province. This amount was then escalated by a moving average of growth rates for per capita gross national product.

Since the value of tax room made available varied among provinces because of differences in their fiscal capacity, a transitional adjustment payment was provided to ensure that the value of the equalized tax transfer was at least equal to the value of the basic cash contributions.

An additional change involved assistance for extended health-care services, such as nursing-home care, some of which had been included in the Canada Assistance Plan. Under the new agreement, the federal government contributed $20 per capita (to grow in the same fashion as the other cash payment) toward supplementary health-related services.

Since part of the change in the financing of shared-cost programs involved the transfer of tax points, it was also necessary to change the abatement points granted Quebec under the opting-out arrangement. Under the new agreement, Quebec's abatement points were 8.5 points for health insurance, 5 points for the welfare program, and 3 points for the youth allowance, for a total of 16.5 points — a reduction from 24 points. (In 1974, the youth allowances program had been replaced with an extended family allowance plan so that the opting-out provision no longer applied. To avoid disrupting Quebec's tax structure, the 3 percent abatement was continued, but the amount was fully deducted from the cash payments to the province.)

Equalization. In order to reflect more adequately the provincial tax systems and tax potential, the equalization formula was updated by increasing the total number of revenue sources in the equalization base to 29, including half of all revenues from nonrenewable natural resources such as oil and gas. A partial ceiling was built into the formula, however, in that the amount of equalization payable in relation to revenue derived from natural resources could not exceed one-third of the total equalization payments. This provision would apply only if there were large increases in provincial revenue from oil and gas.

Stabilization. A revenue stabilization clause provided that if a province's total revenue for a particular year was less than its revenue for the previous year, it would receive a payment equal to the difference between the two amounts. A provision protected the federal government, however, from having to make large stabilization payments to resource-rich provinces should their revenues fall as a result of a decline in resource production or prices.

Tax Agreement: 1982–1987

Throughout the 1970s, the federal government continued to view with concern the increasing amounts of federal revenues transferred to the provinces and the effect of these transfers on Ottawa's budget deficit. In an attempt to control its growing debt, the federal government proposed restraint across the range of federal expenditures, including intergovernment transfers when the fiscal arrangements came under review. The "fiscal imbalance" that the provinces had claimed to suffer in earlier years was now, in Ottawa's view, to the disadvantage of the federal government, not the provinces. As evidence, the finance minister cited the persistent and growing federal deficits compared with the surplus of the provinces in total.

In February 1981, the federal government established a parliamentary task force to review major components of the EPF arrangements. The task force made public its report, *Fiscal Federalism in Canada*, in August 1981.[19] The Minister of Finance analyzed the task force recommendations, the provincial positions, and the federal position in a white paper. There was general agreement among the task force, the provincial governments, and the federal government that the principle of equalization was a key element to any successful federal structure. The disagreements concerned what taxes should be included in the base — oil and gas revenues, then very high in Alberta, were particularly controversial — and which province or provinces should be used as the standard.

Equalization. After considerable discussion, the federal/provincial agreement for 1982–87 was signed. It extended the equalization base from 29 revenue sources to 33, the most significant additions being municipal government property taxes and the full amount of revenues from natural resources. The standard of equalization was changed from the national average per capita yield, which had been used since 1967/8, to a representative provincial average consisting of the average per capita yield from the revenues of five provinces: British Columbia, Saskatchewan, Manitoba, Ontario, and Quebec. (Alberta was excluded because of its high natural resource revenues, while the Atlantic provinces were omitted as not representative because of their relatively low per capita revenues.) A national average tax rate was determined for each revenue source included in the equalization formula. A province's per capita yield for each source was determined by applying this tax rate to the province's tax base and dividing by the province's population. The difference between the province's per capita yield and the standardized yield from the revenue sources determined the equalization payment.

Although the extension of the revenue source list in the equalization formula made it a more comprehensive measure of the provinces' fiscal capacity, the exclusion of Alberta from the standard tended to diminish the equalization that accrued from the inclusion of full natural resources revenues. Quebec Minister of Finance Jacques Parizeau estimated that the changes in the equalization program, when applied to the 1977–82 period, would reduce equalization payments to the provinces by more than $700 million or 4.4 percent, with the big losers being Quebec, Manitoba, and Saskatchewan.[21]

It should also be mentioned that during this year the Constitution Act, 1982 received royal proclamation. It included a section committing Ottawa to the principle of equalization payments to the provinces, thereby entrenching the principle in the constitution.

Established Program Financing. The federal/provincial agreement for 1982–87 brought some changes in the EPF formula. Total per capita EPF compensation was made equal for all provinces by multiplying 100 percent of the national average per capita contributions for the three programs in 1975/6 by provincial population and increasing this amount annually in accordance with the 1977 GNP escalator.[22] In the new agreement, the cash transfer for each province was determined by deducting from the total compensation the equalized value of the 13.5 points of personal income tax and the one point of the corporation income tax. The cash transfers to provinces with above-average tax yields would be reduced by the excess yield.

The limited personal income tax revenue guarantee introduced in 1977 was extended to 1987. The reference to the one percentage point of the personal income tax as compensation for terminating the earlier (1972) income tax revenue guarantee, which had been included in the EPF package, was discarded, but the percentage point was retained in the EPF formula. The personal income tax component in EPF remained at 13.5 percent.

Stabilization. As in the previous fiscal agreements, the stabilization provision was maintained and, in fact, made permanent. This program protects each province against a year-to-year decline in revenues caused by adverse economic conditions (but not from lowered tax rates). Although no payments have been made under this program (because provincial revenues have been rising steadily each year), it is potentially valuable to the provinces.

Tax Agreement: 1987–1992

The Agreement. The 1987 federal/provincial fiscal agreement reflected the federal government's continued concern over its growing expenditures and its difficulty in reducing the large federal budgetary deficits. Most of the provisions of the previous agreement were maintained, but the growth in EPF cash transfers was limited by a reduction in the annual GNP escalator by 2 percent. Provision was made, however, for a special adjustment payment if the growth in EPF transfers proved less than the rate of inflation in any year.

Equalization was retained with very little change from the earlier agreement. Since all provinces had abolished succession duties and gift taxes, they were removed from the list for the equalization formula, reducing the base to 32 revenue sources. Minor technical changes were also made to the stabilization provisions.

Freezes. In 1989 and 1990, however, as budgetary deficits continued, the federal government announced further restrictions on the growth of EPF payments. In his budget speech of April 27, 1989, Minister of Finance Michael Wilson announced that the GNP escalator would be reduced by an additional percentage point to 3 percent, for an estimated additional saving in EPF payments of $200 million. In his 1990 budget, Mr. Wilson went further and proposed freezing the per capita EPF cash transfer for 1990/1 and 1991/2 at the 1989/90 level, with growth limited to the population increase of each province, or about 1 percent nationally. This freeze was extended in the February 1991 budget to the fiscal year 1994/5. In 1994/95, growth in EPF entitlements would be constrained to a rate of growth of GNP less 3 percentage points. Ottawa estimated that the freeze imposed on EPF payments would reduce federal cash transfers by approximately $870 million in 1990/1 and $1.5 billion in 1991/2.[23]

Ottawa's moves to reduce the EPF payments brought strong reactions from the provincial governments. They accused the federal government of trying to deal with its deficit problems by passing them on to the provinces, which had financial problems of their own. Ontario estimated that it would lose about $480 million annually and British Columbia claimed it would lose more than $100 million as a result of the restrictions on EPF transfers.[24] The poorer provinces argued that they would suffer the most because their relatively poorer revenue bases made it more difficult for them to absorb the losses. The loss of revenues, all the provinces argued, would force them to increase taxes or borrow to maintain levels of services or, alternatively, to reduce their spending on health, welfare, education, or other services.

Some of the provinces questioned the legality of Ottawa's move. They contended that the federal/provincial agreement of 1987 was binding on both parties for a five-year period and could not be changed unilaterally by the federal government. The provinces threatened court action. In response, federal Minister of Finance Wilson agreed to meet with the provincial ministers to discuss the issue of transfer payments, but he offered little encouragement that he was prepared to change Ottawa's position.

SUMMARY

In summary, taxation issues have been a significant component of federal/provincial relations in Canada since Confederation. The difficulties of achieving a balance between expenditure responsibilities and revenue sources and problems arising from differences in the relative fiscal capacities of the provinces have frequently placed strains on Confederation. Solutions to these problems for the most part have been the product of evolution and negotiation.

Before 1940, each level of government sought additional tax sources as revenue needs increased, with frequent overlapping and complication in tax administration. The tax agreements which began in 1941, were attempts to establish some order in taxation and to cope with the financial problems. The agreements simplified tax administration, reduced the possibility of tax inequities that could arise from joint occupancy of tax fields, established a degree of uniformity in certain taxes, and introduced a degree of tax harmony between the federal government and provincial governments. This was certainly true of the tax rental and tax-sharing agreements of 1941 to 1962. Subsequent tax agreements saw the federal government granting an increasing amount of tax room to the provinces to enable them to increase their taxes without placing excessive burdens on their taxpayers. At the same time, greater use was made of specific-purpose transfers to assist the provinces to meet their financial obligations until, in 1977, such transfers for major shared-cost programs were replaced by a combination of tax and cash transfers under the EPF arrangement. EPF cash transfers were escalated until the late 1980s when the federal government sought to place a freeze on these transfers. A significant development in federal/provincial relations was the development of equalization which was gradually entrenched as a response to the sharp differences in the fiscal capacities of the provinces.

The issue of federal transfers to the provinces is discussed further in the next chapter.

ENDNOTES

1. The problems found in Canada are generally characteristic of a federal structure of government. See, for example, Bernard P. Herber, *Modern Public Finance: The Study of Public Sector Economics*, 5th ed. (Homeworth, Ill.: Richard D. Irwin, 1983), ch. 18.
2. R. MacGregor Dawson, *The Government of Canada*, 4th ed., rev. by Norman Ward (Toronto: University of Toronto Press, 1963), ch. 6.
3. The early development of Canada and its impact on government, together with government policy, are outlined in Government of Canada, *Report of the Royal Commission on Dominion-Provincial Relations* (Ottawa: King's Printer, 1940), book 1.
4. J. Harvey Perry, *Taxation in Canada*, 3rd ed. (Toronto: University of Toronto Press, 1961), pp. 13–17.
5. Ibid., pp. 17–23.
6. *Report of the Royal Commission on Dominion-Provincial Relations*, p. 107.
7. Ibid., p. 130.
8. The terms "specific-purpose transfers," "specific-purpose grants," and "conditional grants" have frequently been used interchangeably. In Canadian federal/provincial relations in the past, the term most commonly used to describe transfers that had certain conditions attached to them was "conditional grants." Currently, however, the term most commonly used in government and other publications is "specific-purpose transfers," and this is the term most commonly used in this book. The programs that are financed jointly by the provinces and the federal government are referred to as "shared-cost programs."
9. A. Milton Moore, J. Harvey Perry, and Donald I. Beach, *The Financing of Canadian Federation*, tax paper no. 43, p. 8. (Toronto: Canadian Tax Foundation, 1966).
10. *Ibid.*, p. 11.

11. Perry, *Taxation in Canada*, pp. 23–25.

12. Moore, Perry, and Beach, *The Financing of Canadian Federation*, pp. 10–14; and *Report of the Royal Commission on Dominion-Provincial Relations*, book 2, pp. 269–76.

13. A detailed description of the early federal/provincial fiscal agreements, and events leading to them, is contained in Moore, Perry, and Beach, *The Financing of Canadian Federation*; and R.M. Burns, *The Acceptable Mean: The Tax Rental Agreements 1941–62* (Toronto: Canadian Tax Foundation, 1980). Summary information on the agreements is contained in House of Commons, Parliamentary Task Force on Federal-Provincial Fiscal Arrangements, *Fiscal Federalism in Canada* (Ottawa; 1981) and Economic Council of Canada, *Financing Confederation: Today and Tomorrow* (Ottawa, 1982). For an outline of the agreements, see Canadian Tax Foundation, *The National Finances* (Toronto: CTF, various years); Government of Canada, *Statutes of Canada* (Ottawa, various years); and David B. Perry, "The Federal-Provincial Fiscal Arrangements for 1982–87," *Canadian Tax Journal* 31 (January/February 1983). These sources serve as a partial bibliography for this chapter on the federal/provincial fiscal agreements.

    Some other sources on the taxation aspects of federal/provincial relations include: Robin Broadway and F. Flatters, *Equalization in a Federal State* (Ottawa: Economic Council of Canada, 1982); Ontario Economic Council, *Intergovernmental Relations: Issues and Alternatives — 1977* (Toronto: OEC, 1979); T. Courchene et al., *Confederation at the Crossroads* (Vancouver: The Fraser Institute, 1978); Economic Council of Canada and the Institute of Intergovernmental Relations, Queen's University, *Proceedings of the Workshop on the Political Economy of Confederation* (Ottawa, 1979); R.M. Bird, ed., *Fiscal Dimensions of Canadian Federalism* (Toronto: Canadian Tax Foundation, 1980); and George E. Carter, "Established Program Financing: A Critical Review of the Record," *Canadian Tax Journal* 36 (September/October, 1988).

14. Moore, Perry, and Beach, *The Financing of Canadian Federation*, p. 32.

15. Canadian Tax Foundation, *The National Finances, 1960–1961* (Toronto, 1960), p. 114.

16. Canadian Tax Foundation, *The National Finance 1962–1963* (Toronto, 1962), pp. 25–31.

17. Moore, Perry, and Beach, *The Financing of Canadian Federation*, pp. 73–74.

18. For a statement and discussion of the Federal-Provincial Fiscal Agreement of 1977, see Canada, House of Commons, *Minutes of Proceedings and Evidence of the Standing Committee on Finance, Trade and Economic Affairs*, no. 22, March 7, 1977 (Ottawa).

19. Canada, House of Commons, Task Force on Federal-Provincial Fiscal Arrangements, *Fiscal Federalism in Canada* (Ottawa, 1981).

20. Canada, Department of Finance, *Fiscal Arrangements in the Eighties — Proposals of the Government of Canada* (Ottawa, 1981).

21. David B. Perry, "The Federal-Provincial Fiscal Arrangements for 1982–1987," *Canadian Tax Journal* 31 (January-February 1983).

22. In the 1977 agreement, only the cash payments were made equal in per capita terms. The cash payment to each province was determined by multiplying 50 percent of the

national average per capita payments for the three EPF programs in 1975/6 by the population of each province and then applying the escalator factor. See Perry, "The Federal-Provincial Fiscal Arrangements for 1982–1987."

23. Canada, Department of Finance, *Budget*, February 20, 1990, (Ottawa) pp. 77–78.

24. *The Globe and Mail*, February 21, 1990, p. A11.

CHAPTER 8

FEDERAL/PROVINCIAL RELATIONS: SELECTED ISSUES

Chapter 7 traced the sequence of taxation arrangements between the federal government and the provincial governments and the evolution and entrenchment of equalization as an integral part of these arrangements. A number of other issues relating to federal/provincial fiscal relations are equally significant, and some, such as the use of specific-purpose transfers, are directly related to the tax agreements. This chapter examine some issues in federal/provincial financial relations that were particularly prominent in the last three decades. They include federal government transfers to the provinces and provincial dissatisfaction; constitutional change as it has affected government spending and taxing powers and shared-cost programs; confrontation over the jurisdiction and taxation of natural resources; and the co-ordination of federal and provincial economic policies.

Federal Transfers to Provinces

Federal government transfer payments to the provinces may take a variety of forms. They may be direct transfers of cash in the form of general- or specific-purpose grants, or they may take the indirect form of tax transfers — increased tax room for the provinces. The transfer of tax points was discussed in Chapter 7. The discussion here focuses on general- and specific-purpose transfers which, for the fiscal year 1990/1 are shown in Table 8–1.

General-Purpose Transfers: Equalization

General-purpose transfers are made with no conditions attached, and the recipient governments may use the funds for any purpose they wish.

Equalization. In 1990/1, approximately 90 percent of the federal general-purpose transfers to the provinces consisted of equalization payments. These payments are important sources of revenue for the poorer provinces, as illustrated in the last column of Table 8-2, where equalization payments are shown as a percentage of each province's gross general revenue (own-source revenue plus federal transfer payments).

Equalization grants are designed to bring the per capita revenue of the poorer provinces closer to that of the richer provinces. Equalization was introduced to enable the poorer provinces to provide a level of government services reasonably comparable to those available in the other provinces. All provinces are not equally endowed with resources, and they do not have similar industrial bases. Consequently, the well-endowed provinces have a higher per capita gross domestic product and therefore a

TABLE 8–1
Estimated Federal Transfers to Provinces, Territories, and Municipalities for 1990/1

	Amount ($ million)	Share (% of total)
General-purpose transfers		
Fiscal equalization[a]	7 184	20.2
Territorial financing	921	2.6
Grants in lieu of property taxes	323	0 .9
Other	622	1.8
Total	9 050	25.5
Established program financing (EPF)[b]		
Cash transfers		
Health	6 249	17.6
Postsecondary education	1 967	5.5
Tax transfers		
Health	7 012	19.8
Postsecondary education	3 318	9.3
Associated equalization[c]		
Health	665	1.9
Postsecondary education	314	0.9
Total	19 525	55.0
Specific-purpose transfers		
Cash transfers		
Canada Assistance Plan (CAP)	5 223	14.7
Official languages in education	225	0.6
Crop insurance	233	0.7
Young offenders	161	0.5
Miscellaneous health and welfare	161	0.5
Other	269	0.8
Total	6 272	17.7
Tax transfers		
Tax points to Quebec for CAP	618	1.9
Total	6 890	19.6
Total transfers[e]	35 500	100.0[d]
Cash[d]	24 183	69.1
Tax	11 317	31.9

[a] Does not include equalization associated with the tax transfer under EPF.

[b] The division of transfer payments between health and postsecondary education is from the perspective of the federal government. Tax transfers are essentially unconditional and can be used for any purpose a province desires. Some provinces view the cash transfers in a similar manner, with the split between health and postsecondary education to be determined by the province.

[c] The tax points tranferred to the provinces are equalized tax points under the equalization formula. In the government accounts these amounts appear as actually paid under the fiscal equalization program.

[d] Because of rounding, does not equal exactly 100 percent.

[e] The cash total includes $35 million in cash transfers that are not allocated by province and do not appear elsewhere in the table.

Source: Canada, Treasury Board, *News Release*, February 22, 1990 (Ottawa).

greater revenue base from which to finance government-provided goods and services than the less-endowed provinces. Table 8–3 shows the trend in GDP per capita by province as a percentage of the Canadian average. The Atlantic provinces, Quebec, Manitoba, and Saskatchewan have lagged behind Ontario, Alberta, and British Columbia. The greatest disparity is between the Atlantic provinces and the three richest provinces, and although the gap has narrowed since 1961, GDP per capita in the Atlantic region is still only about two-thirds of the national average. Given these interprovincial disparities, the governments of the poorer provinces would be forced to resort to much higher levels of taxation than do the richer provinces in order to provide a similar level of services from own-source revenue. The result would be an imbalance between tax burdens and expenditure benefits for residents of the poorer provinces relative to residents of the richer provinces. Not only are such imbalances unjust, but they may also affect factor and industry location choices.[1] Therefore, the federal government engages in fiscal redistribution through an equalization program.

This problem of fiscal imbalance was acknowledged in the early years of Confederation, but it was not until 1957 that the concept of equalization was officially recognized and accepted as a component of federal/provincial fiscal relations. It was later entrenched in the Constitution Act, 1982.

The methods of computing the equalization payments have varied. Equalization payments have been made to bring per capita revenues first up to the level of the two richest provinces, then to the national average, and since 1982 to the average of five representative provinces (Alberta, by virtue of its large natural resource revenues, and the four Atlantic provinces, which have the lowest fiscal capacity in the country, are excluded from the calculations of the average). Since the beginning of equalization transfers, the base for computing entitlements has been increased from three taxes to the current thirty-two, which include almost all provincial and municipal revenue sources. The present formula involves establishing a tax base (that is, what a tax is levied upon) for each revenue source and then calculating how much revenue each province would derive per capita, from each base if it levied a national average tax rate. Any province whose calculated total per capita revenue is less than the average of the five standard provinces (Ontario, Quebec, Manitoba, Saskatchewan, and British Columbia) receives a payment equal to the per capita shortfall multiplied by its population.

There are currently restrictions on the annual increases in equalization entitlements. They cannot increase above the total 1987/8 amount by more than the growth in GNP over the 1987 fiscal year. The equalization agreement does, however, provide for minimum entitlements ranging from 85 to 95 percent of the previous year's payments depending upon the province's revenue-raising capacity.

Methods of computation and the revenue sources to be included in the equalization formula have long been an issue of dispute among the provinces. The poorer provinces have suggested alternatives that would increase equalization payments. The wealthier provinces resist such formulas, arguing that equalization should be tied to provincial need and that slower developing areas with fewer urban centres have less need for some government facilities and services.[2] New sources of provincial revenue have also posed problems. For example, during the period of large and rapid increases in the prices of oil and gas, the oil- and gas-producing provinces of Alberta and Saskatchewan were reaping massive revenues from these resources. Including the full amount of natural resource revenue in the equalization formula would have dramatically raised payments to the poorer provinces; in fact, even Ontario would have qualified for equalization payments in some years. A compromise limited the amount of oil and gas revenues that would be included in the equalization base.

Equalization is currently one of the most significant means of intergovernment redistribution of revenues in Canada. It has become an integral component of federal/provincial fiscal relations and has been referred to as "the 'glue' that holds the country together."[3]

Other General-Purpose Transfers. Other general-purpose payments from the federal government include: cash payments to the governments of the Yukon and Northwest Territories designed to assist those jurisdictions in financing public services; grants to local and provincial governments in lieu of property taxes on federal property, including libraries, historic sites, national parklands, and buildings; a public utilities income tax transfer consisting of payment of 95 percent of the federal income tax collected from investor-owned public utilities engaged in the distribution (or generation for distribution) of electric energy, gas and steam to the public; and statutory subsidies provided in the Constitution Act, 1867.

Specific-Purpose Transfers

Specific-purpose transfers, also called conditional grants, must be spent by the recipient government on a specified area of expenditure. The donor government may attach a variety of other conditions to them. For example, a federal matching grant requires provincial governments to spend an amount on the program equal to the federal transfer. Moreover, to be eligible for the federal contribution, the program, although administered by the provincial government, may be required to meet federal standards governing quality of service, accessibility, and so on.

The federal government began to use specific-purpose grants in the early 1900s to encourage spending in areas of provincial jurisdiction in which there was perceived to be a strong national interest. By the 1920s, numerous projects in the areas of vocational training, transportation, health care, and social services were being financed through such grants. These were shared-cost programs, whereby the federal government contributed up to half the total program costs; it also established various conditions that the provinces had to meet in order to qualify for the federal payment.

TABLE 8–2
Fiscal Equalization Transfers to Provinces, 1989/90

	Equalization	Gross general revenue	Equalization as share of gross general revenue
	($ million)		(%)
Newfoundland	899	3 275	27.5
PEI	188	688	27.3
Nova Scotia	844	4 043	20.9
New Brunswick	809	3 612	22.4
Quebec	3 412	38 601	8.8
Ontario	–	45 166	–
Manitoba	797	6 029	13.2
Saskatchewan	345	5 040	6.8
Alberta	–	13 046	–
British Columbia	–	14 724	–

Source: Canada, Statistics Canada, *Provincial Economic Accounts*, annual estimates, cat. 13–213; and Canadian Tax Foundation, *Provincial and Municipal Finances*, 1989 (Toronto, 1990), p. 13:3.

TABLE 8–3
Gross Domestic Product per Capita by Province for Selected Years 1961–89

	1961	1965	1970	1975	1980	1985	1989
			(percentage of Canadian average)				
Newfoundland	50.2	51.4	56.1	53.8	56.2	58.7	59.5
PEI	49.4	50.8	52.8	52.2	53.5	55.2	57.8
Nova Scotia	65.3	62.4	68.4	63.0	57.8	72.2	72.6
New Brunswick	60.2	61.3	64.0	62.0	56.0	66.9	70.4
Quebec	90.6	90.5	90.1	87.8	87.8	87.4	92.5
Ontario	120.2	118.3	118.5	110.5	104.2	107.5	113.6
Manitoba	90.1	88.8	90.4	90.4	84.7	87.5	85.5
Saskatchewan	78.0	91.6	77.9	100.9	100.3	91.2	80.1
Alberta	108.7	105.1	107.3	138.6	156.5	146.7	112.3
BC	111.4	111.8	105.5	106.1	111.4	100.1	98.9
Yukon & NWT	107.6	119.1	126.8	126.1	143.6	155.6	146.9
				(dollars per capita)			
All-Canada GDP	2225	2908	4149	7547	12 881	18 967	24 822

Source: Canada, Department of Finance, *Quarterly Economic Review: Annual Reference Tables*, June 1990 (Ottawa).

Specific-purpose transfers grew more important in the late 1950s, when the federal government launched some major programs involving large expenditures. More programs were introduced in the 1960s, and existing programs were expanded. Federal expenditure on shared-cost programs expanded tremendously. It soared from \$76 million in the fiscal year 1953/4 to \$9249 million in 1977/8 to \$26 416 million in 1990/1 (including tax transfers).

During these years of growth, the functions to which specific-purpose transfers were directed also changed, as reflected in Table 8–4. In 1990/1, grants for health, social services, and postsecondary education accounted for approximately 97 percent of total specific-purpose transfers, compared to only 75 percent in 1953/4. An important reason was the introduction of government-supported hospital insurance (1958) and medicare (1968). Between 1953/4 and 1965/6, grants in support of health services increased from about 38 to 50 percent of total grants; since then, the percentage has remained near this level. Transfers for postsecondary education increased from about 6 percent of total transfers in 1953/4 to more than 20 percent by the 1970s. The share for social services dropped from 30 to about 22 percent and has since remained relatively constant.

An indication of trends in the significance of specific-purpose transfers relative to provincial government expenditures by function is presented in Table 8-5. Transfers increased rapidly as a percentage of provincial expenditures during the late 1950s and early 1960s, when the proportion rose from 5 to 17 percent. Further increases were recorded during the 1970s, but by 1989/90 the ratio had declined to approximately 18 percent. Variations by function are also evident in the statistics for this three-and-a-half decade period. Large increases were recorded in both health care and the social services; by 1977/8 the federal government was contributing 41 percent of gross provincial expenditure for health care and almost 29 percent for social services. Specific-purpose transfers for postsecondary education were also increasing rapidly during the 1960s until 1967, when the federal government assistance to postsecondary education took the form of a tax transfer and a cash adjustment payment. This was followed in 1977 with a package of tax and cash transfers under established programs financing EPF for postsecondary education, hospital insurance, and medicare programs.

The new arrangement reduced the significance of the traditional form of specific-purpose transfer as a form of federal assistance to the provinces. Cash transfers under the new formula may continue to be considered a form of specific-purpose transfer because the provinces are still required to adhere to certain general conditions established by Ottawa for the health-care programs in return for the receipt of these payments. As long as these conditions are adhered to, however, the provinces can presumably split the EPF payments as they desire, like tax transfer, which is unconditional and can be used for any purpose a province desires. This view has certainly been the view of the province of British Columbia, which has refused to allow any strings to be attached to its acceptance of the EPF transfers and does not consider the funds to be tied directly to health care or postsecondary education.

Of the remaining shared-cost programs, the Canada Assistance Plan (CAP) is the most costly. It provides federal sharing of costs incurred by the provinces and municipalities in providing social assistance and welfare services to persons in need and

TABLE 8–4
Historical Trend of Federal Transfer Payments by Function

Function	1953/4		1965/6		1977/8		1990/1	
	Amount	Share	Amount	Share	Amount	Share	Amount	Share
	($ million)	(%)	($ million)	(%)	($ million)	(%)	($ million)	(%)
Postsecondary education	5	6.6	170	15.3	2 081[a]	22.5	5 600[c]	21.9
Health	29	38.2	555	50.0	4 384[a]	47.4	13 926[c]	52.7
Social Services	23	30.3	239	21.5	1 837[b]	19.9	6 002[c]	22.7
Transportation & communication	14	18.4	86	7.7	110	1.2	72	0.3
Other	5	6.6	60	5.4	837	9.0	816	2.4
Total[d]	76	100.0	1 110	100.0	9 249	100.0	26 416	100.0

[a] Includes tax transfers and associated equalization amounting to $3315 million, of which $2254 million is allocated to health (medicare and hospital insurance)and $1061 million to postsecondary education. Also includes abatement to Quebec, amounting to $350 million, under the opting-out arrangements.

[b] Includes abatement to Quebec for Canada Assistance Plan amounting to five points of the personal income tax valued at $240 million.

[c] Includes tax transfers and associated equalization as shown in Table 7–1.

[d] Because of rounding, total of shares in some years is not exactly 100 percent.

Sources: Statistics Canada, *Financial Statistics of Provincial Governments, 1953*, cat. 68–207; *Provincial Government Finance, 1965*, cat. 68–207; Canada, Treasury Board, *How Your Tax Dollar is Spent, 1977–78*, (Ottawa,1978); and Canada, Treasury Board, *News Release*, February 22, 1990 (Ottawa).

TABLE 8–5
Historical Trend of Federal Transfers by Function, Selected Years 1954/5–1990/1

Function	1953/4	1965/6	1977/8	199/1
		(percentage of gross provincial expenditure)		
Education[a]	1.8	10.8	20.3	21.6
Health[ab]	11.3	36.2	41.4	38.7
Social services[b]	18.1	29.1	28.8	21.9
Transportation and communications	3.8	7.7	3.3	1.1
Other	0.3	1.0	6.4	2.2
		(percentage of provincial expenditure)		
Total transfers	5.4	17.5	21.2	17.7

[a] Includes tax transfers and associated equalization.
[b] Includes additional abatement to Quebec as part of the contracting-out arrangements.

Sources: Statistics Canada, *Financial Statistics of Provincial Governments, 1953*, cat. 68–207; *Provincial Government Finance, Revenue and Expenditure*, cat. 68–207; and Canadian Tax Foundation, *Provincial and Municipal Finances*, 1989, (Toronto, 1990), pp. 13:3–13:4.

in undertaking work activity projects, such as job retraining. The CAP is an open-ended program, and Ottawa is committed to reimbursing each province and territory for 50 percent of eligible costs related to activities in the program.

There are many specific-purpose transfer programs in other areas of government activity, although their total dollar value is relatively small. A large number of them are found in agriculture, where the most costly is the crop insurance program. In it, costs are shared on a federal-provincial-farmer basis; the provinces administer the programs, and the federal government contributes 50 percent of the total premiums. In other areas of agriculture in 1988/9 the federal government provided assistance to more than 20 shared-cost programs and activities. The basis of the federal contribution varied. For some programs, it took the form of a percentage of costs, ranging up to 80 percent, but for the majority of programs, it was a fixed dollar amount.

Shared-cost programs similar in nature to those existing in agriculture are found in communications, transportation, energy, the environment, justice, arts and culture, forestry, regional development, scientific and technological development, and Northern affairs. An inventory for 1988/9 of federal specific-purpose transfers listed approximately 175 shared-cost programs and activities.[4]

Provincial Dissatisfaction

The provinces have a history of dissatisfaction with shared-cost programs and the use of specific purpose transfers and, on various occasions, they have become very vocal and adamant in their objections to the system.[5]

Planning and Priorities. Some provinces, notably Quebec, have opposed specific-purpose transfers on purely constitutional grounds, but the major complaint has been that using them enables the federal government to move into areas of provincial jurisdiction and interfere with provincial planning of expenditure priorities. Provinces complain that they have been hampered in the planning of their budgets and the development of programs they judged to be of priority. When the federal government initiates a program and offers to bear the burden of half the cost, the provinces are forced to participate or to forgo the payment. Few provinces have found it politically or economically practical not to participate since the residents of all the provinces would be financing the program in the form of federal taxes. In 1969, Ontario Premier John Robarts expressed the view of his province:

> Massive spending initiatives by the Federal Government, such as medicare, not only rob provincial budgets of any flexibility, but also undermine any real progress toward overall control of expenditures by all governments and fail utterly to recognize provincial priorities. . .We are being pushed into medicare, which from the point of view of this government is not necessary in the province at this time and is not one of our top priorities, by a level of government that is taxing us for it before we get it.[6]

During the 1960s and 1970s, a period of rapidly increasing government spending, federal priorities were primarily in the areas of health and social services — as is evidenced by the trends in expenditure — whereas a number of provinces wanted to place greater emphasis on economic development. Economic development and diversification were particularly emphasized in the poorer provinces, which, without an adequate economic base, continued to lag in prosperity. They charged that the federal government paid insufficient attention to their needs and that its priorities tended to follow the lines of a more advanced economy in which attention shifted from economic matters (for example, transportation and communications, resource and industrial development, and trade agreements designed to benefit regional industries) to social matters (for example, health, social services, and culture). And the poorer provinces claimed that they could not afford the latter without having established the former.

Many provinces were also very critical of what they claimed was the federal government's apparent eagerness to initiate shared-cost programs without adequate planning or estimation of costs. Ottawa was accused of initiating programs in which provincial studies showed that costs had been grossly underestimated.

A further complaint from the provinces concerned the termination of shared-cost programs. They pointed to a number of programs that they claimed were terminated or reduced unilaterally by the federal government.[7] If the program was well-established at the time of termination, the participating provinces might find it difficult to discontinue, or might not desire to do so. They were consequently left to carry the federal share of the program in addition to their own. The provinces argued that they were forced to seek new funds every time the federal government introduced a shared-cost program and to find additional funds whenever it withdrew from a program they wished to continue.

The federal government offered a number of counterarguments, based on economic, social, and constitutional factors, in support of specific-purpose transfers. First, through these transfers, the federal government was able to support public projects and services that had spillover effects or external economies and that were in the national interest, such as education, health, and social services. Second, the transfers enabled provinces to provide services that they would be unable to provide through reliance on their own resources. Third, through the transfers, the federal government could ensure national priorities and, to a large degree, a uniform standard of service to all Canadians. Finally, the federal government argued, no province was constitutionally required to participate in shared-cost programs.

Throughout this period, numerous suggestions for alternatives to specific-purpose transfers were brought forward at federal/provincial fiscal conferences. It was suggested that the provinces be given larger shares of the taxes imposed jointly by the two levels of government or that greater separation of tax sources be arranged, providing the provinces with more of the available tax sources. Another suggested alternative was the replacement of specific-purpose transfers by general transfers with no strings attached. This proposal was, however, unacceptable to the federal government because it viewed its primary responsibility as being to the Canadian public as a whole; it said that it had an obligation to provide all Canadians with an opportunity for an acceptable level of services and national standards. Yet another alternative was to allow provinces to opt out of shared-cost programs in return for the fiscal equivalent — a sum equal to the federal share of the program in a province but a sum it could use in any way it desired. This proposal also met with opposition from the federal government because it would then lose complete control over its payments to the provinces.

Costs and Control. Developments in shared-cost arrangements in 1975 and 1976 renewed provincial dissatisfaction with specific-purpose transfers. These developments stemmed from the rapid escalation of the costs of shared-cost programs, particularly in health and education. Although concern over rising costs had been voiced in the early 1970s, little progress had been made in reducing the rate at which they were increasing. In 1975 and 1976, some provinces made a serious effort to control costs by closing hospitals and cutting back on other facilities.

For its part, the federal government was concerned about the open-ended nature of the shared-cost programs, which committed Ottawa to pay its share regardless of the amount of the increase. The uncertainty of future costs and the amount of its contribution caused the federal government to seek to place ceilings on its contributions to shared-cost programs, particularly in the areas of health and education. In 1972, Ottawa had limited the increase in its contributions to postsecondary education to 15 percent per year. Another step in this direction was taken in 1976, when the federal government limited the increase in its payments for the medicare program to 13 percent for 1976/7 and 10.5 percent for 1977/8 and established authority to fix limits for subsequent years. The provinces responded that federal ceilings on its contributions effectively destroyed the principle on which shared-cost programs were based and, in turn, requested that they be permitted to opt out of these programs in return for a larger share of the tax fields.

In a logical next step, Ottawa proposed, in 1977, to replace cost-sharing for major established programs with the system of tax transfers and cash payments described in Chapter 7. This arrangement had both positive and negative aspects for the federal and provincial governments, although the provinces' views varied. On the positive side at the federal level, the move, by severing the link between program costs and the federal contribution, gave Ottawa control over its payments to three major shared-cost programs. On the negative side, it reduced the control that the federal government could exercise over these programs to ensure that they conformed to national standards. The compensation to the provinces represented by tax points goes into provincial revenue to be spent as the provinces choose. There remained, however, some degree of federal surveillance because the cash compensation, for the health-care program continued to be conditional upon the provinces' maintaining the basic conditions.[8]

How the federal government could exercise some control became evident in 1983. Some of the provinces began to charge nominal user fees for hospital care in an attempt to hold down the escalating costs of health care. The federal government contended that such action was counter to the spirit and intention of the medicare program — to make health services readily available to all Canadian residents. User fees, argued the federal Minister of Health and Welfare Monique Begin, discriminated against lower-income groups including the elderly. In response to the provinces' actions, the federal government passed the Canada Health Act, in April 1984, reaffirming the earlier established conditions and criteria for federal contributions to health-care services and giving the federal government specific authority to reduce the EPF cash payment to any province that resorted to extra-billing or user charges. The reduction would be $1 for every $1 a province charged patients for health care.[9] The provinces were given three years to comply with the Act.

Established Programs Financing. The 1977 EPF arrangement for the provinces was advantageous in that it gave them greater flexibility in defining and administering their programs and freed them of detailed federal auditing of provincial expenditures, which had been necessary under the 50 percent cost-sharing formula. They ran the risk, however, that slow economic growth would reduce tax yields and the value of the tax transfer, thereby producing less revenue for the established programs than would have been provided by the previous cost-sharing formula.[10]

Furthermore, the EPF arrangements did not completely alleviate the earlier provincial concern over the possibility of Ottawa's reducing or limiting its contributions to the established programs. The open-ended feature of specific-purpose transfers had been effectively terminated in the 1970s once the federal government began to place ceilings on the rate of increase of its contributions to postsecondary education and medical care. The provinces had vigorously complained that such limits forced them either to seek alternative sources of revenue to maintain the same level of services or to curtail education and medical and other services. As the 1980s drew to a close, this problem reappeared; as outlined in Chapter 7, the federal government sought to limit the annual increase in the EPF cash payments and for 1990 to 1992 froze them at their 1989/90 level. In addition, payments to Ontario, Alberta, and British Columbia under CAP were to be held to a 5 percent increase. Ottawa's action brought back to the provinces memories of similar federal practices in the 1960s under the earlier shared-cost arrangements and heightened their awareness of continued vulnerability to potential restrictions on federal financial contributions. The British Columbia government, backed by Alberta and Ontario, initiated legal action against Ottawa for its limitation of payments under CAP, and in June 1990, the BC Court of Appeal ruled that the federal government could not seek to change the terms of its agreement with the provinces without their consent. The federal government was expected to appeal this decision to the Supreme Court of Canada. It appeared that Ottawa's main concern was the ruling's implications for the principle of flexibility to control its spending, although in the CAP case, the original agreement did include a provision that permitted the federal government to terminate the agreement unilaterally on one year's notice.

Constitutional Discussions. The general issue of shared-cost programs and the federal government's use of specific-purpose grants in areas of provincial jurisdiction was addressed in the discussions leading to the proposals for changes in the Canadian constitution in what came to be called the Meech Lake Accord of 1987.[11] The accord proposed to amend the Constitution Act, 1867 with a clause giving provinces the right to opt out of national shared-cost programs initiated by the federal government in areas of exclusive provincial jurisdiction. Provinces choosing to opt out would receive "reasonable compensation" from the federal government provided they introduced their own programs "compatible with the national objectives." This highly ambiguous clause did not define "reasonable compensation," or "compatible," or "national objectives," and some interpreted it as an entrenchment of federal spending power to launch new programs in areas of provincial jurisdiction. Controversy over the clause ranged from one extreme position to the other. Some predicted increased federal initiatives in shared-cost programs leading to greater centralization of power, while others predicted the exact opposite. For example, Premier Clyde Wells of Newfoundland contended that the provision would discourage Ottawa from initiating shared-cost programs because opting-out would reduce the federal government's influence in such programs. This, he claimed, would be detrimental to the poorer provinces, which relied heavily of federal financial aid to provide their residents with programs comparable in quality to those provided by the wealthier provinces. Discussion of this and other issues contained in the accord continued during 1990. (The story of the Meech Lake Accord and its failure is told later in this chapter.)

CONSTITUTIONAL REFORM AND FEDERAL/PROVINCIAL FISCAL ISSUES

In March 1982, the British parliament passed the Canada Act, 1982, which was proclaimed by the monarch on April 17, 1982, thus ending a half-century, contentious struggle to bring Canada's constitution home.[12] The patriated constitution of Canada contains the old British North America (BNA) Act with amendments, an amending formula, a charter of rights and freedoms, a commitment by the government of Canada to the principle of equalization payments to the provinces, and new resource guarantees.

Early Developments

Serious attempts to sever the Canadian constitution from Britain began in the 1920s when numerous federal/provincial conferences were held to try to resolve the issue. Britain was generally willing, but the federal government and the provinces could not agree on issues of provincial rights, on language, or on an amending formula. Some of the provinces, particularly Quebec, feared any formula that could potentially enable the federal government to change the constitution and encroach on provincial rights without provincial consent. The failure to reach an agreement on an amending formula in the 1920s and early 1930s continued Britain's authority over the BNA Act.

Concerns about the constitution were disrupted by the Depression and by the Second World War and its aftermath, and although some attempt was made in the 1950s and early 1960s to resolve the issue, it was not until 1967 that constitutional patriation and reform again came to the fore in federal/provincial relations. Beginning in February 1968, a series of federal/provincial conferences examined patriation of the constitution, the problem of bilingualism, and the question of the distribution of tax and expenditure powers.[13] These sessions were not confined to constitutional issues. They included discussions on a wide variety of economic and social matters: the poorer provinces complained about regional disparities; others expressed concern over federal intrusion into provincial areas of jurisdiction through Ottawa's initiation of shared-cost programs; and all provinces demanded more tax room through increased federal abatements. The fundamental issue, however, remained the constitutional problem of patriation of the BNA Act. Both the federal and provincial governments were anxious to prescribe a formula for amending the act without having to suffer the embarrassment of approaching the British parliament whenever a change was needed.

In 1971, tentative agreement was reached, producing a constitutional charter.[14] It included an amending formula providing for change with the consent of the federal government and of six provinces, that had to include Ontario and Quebec, two Atlantic provinces, and two Western provinces representing at least 50 percent of the population of the Western region. It also granted the provinces supremacy in all areas of social services except unemployment insurance; they would have the right to legislate in these areas along with the federal government, with any conflict in legislation or programs resolved in their favour. (This provision gave Quebec a part of the expanded jurisdiction it sought in the field of social services.) In addition, the charter included proposals to guarantee the equality of the French and English languages, gave provinces a voice in appointments to the Supreme Court of Canada, terminated the federal government's power of disallowing provincial legislation, and changed the title of the British North America Act, 1867 to the Constitution Act, 1867. (The charter itself was to become the Constitution Act, 1982.)

This charter was approved by all the provinces except Quebec. Its rejection was based primarily on the fact that, although the document gave the provinces the legislative supremacy in social services that Quebec demanded, there was no corresponding allocation of revenue sources to finance programs in this area. Control over expenditure functions without the necessary sources to finance them produced, in the words of Quebec Premier Robert Bourassa, "the existence of an uncertainty" rather than the complete sovereignty it wanted. Moreover, Quebec was not prepared to accept the continuation of the federal government's power to legislate and use specific-purpose transfers for social services.

The Quebec Issue

Quebec's 1971 concerns were not new (although they may have been heightened by a growing tide of nationalism in the province at that time). It had, from the beginning, opposed what it perceived as federal encroachment on provincial autonomy in both taxation and expenditures. The crisis of the Second World War did prompt Quebec to sign the 1941 tax rental agreement, but it refused to be party to any further rental agreements. The province feared that the temporary nature of tax rentals would become more permanent over time, and it opposed such centralization of power in Ottawa. Maurice Duplessis, Premier from 1944 to 1959, argued that provincial autonomy in expenditures was meaningless if the province had to depend on the federal government for the necessary funds — a sentiment echoed by successive Quebec premiers to the present day. When Ottawa began to use specific-purpose transfers, Quebec refused to accept them, arguing that through this form of assistance the federal government was interfering with provincial sovereignty in expenditures. In the late 1950s and early 1960s, Quebec did begin to accept these transfers, but only reluctantly, and in the meantime it pressed Ottawa to replace conditional grants with increased tax abatements or general-purpose transfers.

The first step in this direction was taken in 1960 when Quebec was granted an additional 1 percentage point abatement of the corporation income tax in lieu of a specific transfer to universities. When the Liberal party took office in Ottawa in 1963, the federal government began to bend toward Quebec's point of view. In 1964, it was offered a further abatement of three percentage points of the personal income tax for the Youth Allowance Program, a shared-cost program introduced by the federal government to provide allowances for sixteen- and seventeen-year-olds who remained in school. Quebec had earlier instituted its own similar program and wished to continue it. Ottawa agreed to allow the province to receive the federal contribution in the form of additional abatement points rather than as a specific transfer.

These concessions to Quebec were the prelude to the major change in 1965, when the opting-out provision was introduced into the shared-cost arrangements. As outlined in the previous chapter, Quebec was the only province to choose this option.

The specific arrangements were not enough, however. Quebec premiers since the early 1960s have echoed the demand for increased powers for their province through a changed agreement on the sharing of powers and resources. They argue that the division of powers under the constitution was rendered obsolete by the emergence of the francophone nation and urge a special status for Quebec. This "two-nations" concept of Canada was rejected by the federal government, which under Prime Minister Pierre Trudeau pressed for increased constitutional rights for the French language throughout Canada and the patriation of the BNA Act. Quebec opposed patriation and an amending formula unless they were accompanied by a substantial transfer of powers to the provinces.

Although the roots of Quebec's discontent with federalism can be traced to pre-Confederation times, not until 1976 did its political separation from the rest of Canada seem a real possibility. That year saw the election in Quebec of the Parti Québécois, a political party committed to separation. Under the PQ's proposed system, Quebec would become an independent country but retain close economic association with the rest of Canada. The Parti Québécois committed itself to a referendum to decide the issue of separation; when it was held in 1980, the PQ lost the referendum with 60 percent of the electorate voting no. Although this loss weakened the separatist movement, it did not eliminate it, and Quebec, under Premier Lévesque, fought long and hard against the constitutional changes finally adopted in the patriated constitution and the Charter of Rights and Freedoms. Moreover, the dream of independence would emerge stronger than ever in 1990.

Constitution Act, 1982

In early 1976, Prime Minister Trudeau reopened the constitutional issue by tabling in Parliament proposals for patriating the constitution and indicating that the federal government was prepared to act unilaterally if the provinces failed to reach an agreement. The provinces objected strenuously to the suggestion of unilateral federal action. They feared that a precedent would be set for further unilateral constitutional changes by the federal government, placing the safeguard of provincial rights in jeopardy.

Ottawa made another attempt at patriation and change in 1978 and 1979. This time its proposal included added resource rights for the provinces and limitations on federal powers; still, the provinces failed to agree. In 1980, following the defeat of the sovereignty referendum in Quebec, the Prime Minister proposed dividing the constitutional question into two packages: one involving the division of powers, and the other patriation and a charter of rights. This time the federal government was adamant that constitutional change must include a charter of rights and minority-language guarantees.

Federal/provincial conferences and communications on these issues continued throughout 1980 and 1981. The exchanges were frequently bitter, but Ottawa now made a firm public commitment to resolving the issues — by unilateral federal action if necessary. Six provinces filed a court challenge to the federal proposal to act unilaterally, and there was political opposition in Parliament. Following lengthy proceedings, the Supreme Court of Canada ruled in the late summer of 1981 that the federal initiative to patriate the BNA Act was legal in the strict sense but offended convention and the spirit of federalism, which included provincial agreement to constitutional change.

The lack of a clear court victory by either side forced the federal government and the provinces into compromise. A conference in November 1981 considered a variety of proposals, including a federal offer to settle the matter by a national referendum. A last-minute compromise worked out by the provinces formed an agreement that was finally adopted, although Premier Lévesque of Quebec bitterly opposed the arrangement and refused to sign it. Lévesque demanded a veto on constitutional change for Quebec, and when it was refused, he warned of serious consequences for Quebec/Canada relations.

The agreement of Ottawa and nine provinces received parliamentary approval in December 1981 and was forwarded to London for the final amendment to the BNA Act by the British parliament.

The amending formula of the Constitution Act, 1982 is twofold. Some matters require the unanimous consent of the federal Parliament and of the legislative assembly of every province; once the proposal is ratified by one of these governments, the other ten must agree to it within three years. Amending other matters is less stringent; the requirement is the consent of the federal parliament and the legislative assemblies of at least two-thirds of the provinces that have, in the aggregate and according the latest census, at least 50 percent of the country's population of all provinces. (Given the current ten provinces and their relative populations, such a matter would have to have the consent of seven provinces including either Quebec or Ontario.)

The Charter of Rights and Freedoms guarantees the fundamental freedoms of conscience and religion, of the press and other media, of peaceful assembly, and of association. It also guarantees basic legal rights, equality rights, and rights to minority language and education. And it establishes English and French as the official languages of Canada.

The Constitution Act, 1982 also addresses the issue of equalization and regional disparities. Under the act, both Ottawa and the provinces are committed to further economic development to reduce disparity in opportunities and to provide essential public services of reasonable quality to all Canadians. The Federal Government is to make equalization payments "to ensure that provincial governments have sufficient revenues to provide reasonably comparative levels of public services at reasonably comparative levels of taxation" (subsection 36(2)).

One change from the BNA Act relates to nonrenewable natural resources, forestry resources, and electrical energy. Section 92A of the Constitution Act, 1982 grants the provinces exclusive powers to make laws relating to the exploration, development, and management of nonrenewable natural resources and forestry resources within their jurisdiction, and to raise money by any mode or system of taxation in respect to nonrenewable natural resources, forestry resources, and the generation of electrical energy. In relation to the export from one province to another of the production of nonrenewable natural resources, forestry resources, and electrical energy, the federal and provincial legislatures were given concurrent powers with the proviso that should federal and provincial laws conflict, federal law would prevail. Furthermore, in exporting these products to another part of Canada, a province cannot apply any discrimination in prices. This section added considerably to the provinces' flexibility in the taxation of natural resources. It removed the restriction limiting their taxing power over natural resources to direct taxation within the province, a clause that had been a major source of federal/provincial conflict (as discussed later in this chapter).

The Meech Lake Accord

The Quebec government had not agreed to the Constitution Act, 1982. Desiring to bring Quebec into the constitutional agreement and to clarify certain federal/provincial issues, Prime Minister Brian Mulroney and the ten provincial premiers held lengthy discussions during April 1987 at a retreat at Meech Lake, Quebec. The resulting proposals for revisions and additions to the Constitution Act, which came to be known as the Meech Lake Accord,[15] were signed by the Prime Minister and all ten premiers in June 1987. Since the changes were far-reaching, they were judged matters requiring unanimous consent. Thus, the federal and provincial legislatures had to ratify the accord within three years to incorporate it into the Canadian constitution. When Quebec's National Assembly gave assent to the agreement, the deadline became June 23, 1990.

The Meech Lake Accord is examined in some detail in this section because it illustrates Quebec's demands for constitutional change, which are likely to continue into the future, as well as some of the other provinces' positions on constitutional issues.

The Accord. The Meech Lake Accord was designed to meet the minimum basic conditions that Quebec Premier Bourassa argued were necessary to make his province a party to the Constitution Act of 1982. The accord had significance for the distribution of powers and responsibilities of the federal and provincial governments. The key proposals focussed on the following issues:

- The position of Quebec. Recognition of the right of Quebec to "preserve and promote" its character as a "distinct society".
- The Supreme Court of Canada. Provision for the provinces to provide lists of new Supreme Court nominees, from which the Prime Minister would make the final selection; as in the BNA Act, three positions on the court reserved for Quebec.
- Senate appointments. Provision for the provinces to submit lists of new Senate nominees, from which the Prime Minister would make the final selection.
- Immigration. New powers for the provinces allowing them to set their own policies within overall targets set by the federal government.
- National shared-cost programs. Requirement of "reasonable compensation" to be paid to a province not wishing to participate in a national shared-cost program established by the federal government in an area of "exclusive provincial jurisdiction, if the province carries on a program or initiative that is compatible with the national objectives."
- Amending formula. Expansion of the types of constitutional changes requiring unanimous consent of the provinces to include Senate reform and the creation of new provinces.

The federal parliament and the legislatures of all provinces except Manitoba and New Brunswick were quick to ratify the Accord. Opposition in the two dissenting provinces focussed on the need for further changes and guarantees, particularly with respect to the rights of minorities, including women and Canada's native people.

As debate on the accord continued, opposition widened and stiffened, led by three newly elected provincial premiers, Gary Filmon of Manitoba, Frank McKenna of New Brunswick, and Clyde Wells of Newfoundland. In Newfoundland, Premier Wells led the legislature to rescind its earlier approval of the accord.

In addition to the issue of minority rights, critics argued that the "distinct society" clause implicitly gave Quebec special status within Confederation, with powers that would not be available to the other provinces. The Western provinces desired Senate reform — primarily an elected Senate with increased representation from the smaller provinces — and fears were expressed that the larger provinces of Ontario and Quebec would use the provision of unanimous consent for Senate change to block such changes. Newfoundland, in particular, harboured major concerns about the opting-out feature. Premier Wells argued that it would discourage the federal government from initiating new shared-cost programs, since opting out reduced Ottawa's influence over programs, and this situation would be detrimental to poorer provinces, such as Newfoundland, which relied heavily on federal financial aid. It was also argued that the wording of this clause, which spoke of "national objectives" not "national standards," eroded Ottawa's ability to establish such standards and therefore any degree of uniformity of shared-cost services across Canada.

The Death of Meech Lake. Despite numerous attempts to save the Meech Lake Accord, the June 23, 1990 deadline approached without the required unanimous consent of the provinces. Premier Bourassa, fully supported by the Mulroney government, maintained that the accord met minimum demands and that revisions or additional provisions and issues would be considered only after the agreement was ratified by all provinces. Supporters of the accord argued that to reject it was to reject Quebec as a full partner in Confederation and would serve to strengthen that province's separatist movement. The dissenting provinces and other opponents argued just as strenuously that once the accord was passed, the unanimous consent provision would make it extremely difficult if not impossible to institute Senate reforms and other changes requiring unanimity.

In a last-ditch effort to save the accord, a federal/provincial conference of first ministers was finally called on June 3, 1990, three weeks before the deadline. In a week of intense negotiations, amid threats of the break-up of the Canadian federation and much acrimony, the group hammered out a tentative agreement in which the accord remained virtually intact.

The Meech Lake Accord still required passage by three provincial legislatures, however. New Brunswick was quick to approve, but Manitoba legislature regulations required public hearings. The introduction of the legislation to the Manitoba Legislature was, however, stalled by Elijah Harper, an aboriginal member of the legislative Assembly, who argued that the accord did not address native issues. Consequently, Manitoba ran out of time to hold its required public hearings and to obtain legislative approval by the deadline. In Newfoundland, Premier Clyde Wells, rejecting what he termed last-minute "manipulations" and pressure from Ottawa and pointing to the situation in Manitoba, refused on the final day to have the legislature vote as scheduled on the accord. The June 23 deadline passed, and the Meech Lake Accord was declared dead.

Further Consideration. In essence, the controversy over the Meech Lake Accord stemmed mainly from its ambiguity and the uncertainty it created on matters such as Senate reform, minority rights, the status of shared-cost programs and specific-purpose transfers, and the precise meaning of the power granted Quebec to "preserve and promote" its "distinct society." Many opponents viewed the accord as a dilution of federal powers to pursue national goals and as a vehicle for increased fragmentation of the Canadian nation. Some also feared it was just the beginning of more and more demands by the province of Quebec for increased powers to enable it to pursue its particular destiny.

Quebec Premier Bourassa reacted to the failure of the Meech Accord by publicly stating that he would attend no more constitutional conferences but would deal directly with Ottawa to attempt to obtain bilateral agreements between his province and the federal government on issues considered important to Quebec nationalism, such as immigration and communications. The leader of the Parti Québécois, Jacques Parizeau, went much further and charged that the rejection of the Meech Accord was a rejection of Quebec, and he re-emphasized his party's position calling for Quebec's independence from the rest of Canada. Premier Bourassa announced plans for appointment of a commission to hold public hearings on the direction of future Quebec relations with Ottawa and on Quebec's position vis-à-vis the Canadian political structure. The status quo was rejected. Possibilities for change included complete independence, sovereignty inside an economic union with the rest of Canada, and to a loosening of the confederated structure with greater provincial powers. Other provinces indicated that they would also seek greater independence modelled on whatever Quebec achieved.

Confrontation over Natural Resources

The Constitution Act, 1867 divided the responsibility for natural resources, giving the federal government jurisdiction over native peoples' lands and national parks and the provinces jurisdiction over forests, minerals, oil, and natural gas and providing shared jurisdiction over agriculture, fisheries, and water resources. In addition, Ottawa claimed certain kinds of jurisdiction as stemming from its constitutional power to regulate trade and commerce and imports and exports and, in times of emergency, from the "peace, order, and good government" provision. Jurisdictional conflicts between the two levels of government have simmered and occasionally flared, as in the 1970s and 1980s when major confrontations developed over the issue of energy.[16]

The Two-Price System. To assist the development of Canada's petroleum industry in the 1950s, a national policy was instituted by which western Canadian crude oil was supplied as far east as the Ottawa Valley. The part of the country east of this line was supplied with imported oil, which could then be obtained at a lower price. This policy established a domestic market for approximately half of the Canadian oil produced; the remainder was exported to the United States.

In October 1973, the Arab-Israeli conflict and the formation of the Organization of Petroleum Exporting Countries (OPEC) resulted in a reduction in Arab oil exports and a drastic increase in the international price of oil. The price of oil imported into eastern Canada jumped from \$3.75 to \$10.50 per barrel. The Canadian government, desiring a uniform price for oil across the country and wishing both to protect consumers from large price increases and to control the export of oil, temporarily froze the price of domestic oil (at $4.10 per barrel) and imposed an export tax on oil exported to the United States. One-half of the proceeds of this tax was paid to the producing provinces, and the other half was used, under the Oil Import Compensation Program, to subsidize refiners processing imported oil in eastern Canada so as to reduce their costs to the level of refiners using domestic oil. In turn, Alberta, which produced 85 percent of Canada's oil, and Saskatchewan increased royalty charges on oil and gas. Ottawa responded by making royalty payments a nondeductible business expense for income tax purposes.

Alberta and Saskatchewan vigorously protested the various federal actions, contending that Ottawa was intruding into provincial jurisdiction over natural resources and demanding the full benefits of rising oil prices. The Eastern provinces, in turn, complained that the federal subsidy was insufficient because it left their consumers with oil and gasoline prices higher than those of their Western counterparts. In addition, the provinces receiving equalization payments demanded that the new natural resource revenues be included in the equalization formula.

After much discussion and debate, a series of federal/provincial agreements on oil and gas pricing were negotiated in the middle and late 1970s. The price of domestic oil and gas was to rise gradually, but it was to remain substantially below the international prices. As the price of domestic oil increased, the oil export charge was changed correspondingly to reflect the difference between domestic and international prices.

The National Energy Program. It was in this environment that the federal government introduced its National Energy Program (NEP) in late 1980.[17] The NEP was a long-term plan for managing Canada's energy resources. It had three primary objectives: (1) to achieve security of supply and independence from the world oil market by the end of the decade; (2) to offer Canadians an opportunity for increased participation in the development of the industry and to achieve 50 percent Canadian ownership of oil and gas production by 1990 (compared to 27 percent in 1980); and (3) to ensure fairness in petroleum pricing and revenue distribution among producers, consumers, and the levels of government.

The NEP included various tax incentives and grants for oil and gas exploration and the development of energy alternatives. It also specified additional taxes, such as an oil and gas revenue tax of 8 percent of the income related to the production of oil and gas; a tax on natural gas and gas liquids, including gas for export; and an oil compensation charge. In addition, it continued the oil export charge.

The vehicle for increasing Canadian ownership and participation in petroleum development was to be Petro-Canada, a Crown corporation, created in 1976 for the purpose of undertaking oil and gas exploration and of ensuring security of supply. It had become involved in the tar sands development as well as in Arctic and Atlantic offshore exploration; it had also began to purchase interests in other petroleum companies. (For example, it had earlier purchased Atlantic Richfields Canada Ltd. and Pacific Petroleum Ltd., and in 1981, it had paid approximately $1.5 billion to acquire Petro-Fina, a large foreign-owned oil company involved in both exploration and retail distribution.) Under the NEP, Petro-Canada was to play a major role in Canadianizing the petroleum industry through the purchase of foreign-controlled petroleum companies.

In essence, the NEP considerably extended the federal government's authority and participation in natural resource development. Consequently, it was bitterly opposed by the oil- and gas-producing provinces as an intrusion on provincial ownership rights and a resource "revenue grab" by Ottawa. Alberta, Saskatchewan, and British Columbia objected to Ottawa's unilateral fixing of prices and to the new taxes. The petroleum industry also reacted negatively, arguing that the revenue left to its firms after they deducted royalties, charges, and taxes was insufficient to finance new investment and exploration.

Premier Peter Lougheed of Alberta announced that, until provincial concerns were resolved, his province would reduce oil production by 15 percent in stages and withhold approval of two huge tar sands projects, as well as initiate a legal challenge to the proposed federal excise tax on natural gas. The confrontation between Ottawa and Alberta was in essence, a struggle for the control of Canada's natural resource policy, including issues of resource ownership, pricing, the distribution of revenues from oil and gas, and the overall direction of development.

The impasse continued for almost a year. In September 1981, after intensive negotiations, the two governments signed the Canada–Alberta Energy Pricing and Taxation Agreement, which was to continue until 1986. Similar agreements followed with the governments of British Columbia and Saskatchewan. These agreements, together with the provisions relating to the jurisdiction and taxation of natural resources introduced in the Constitution Act, 1982 (discussed earlier in this chapter), effectively put an end to the political conflict between Ottawa and the Western provinces. The agreements left the central thrust of the NEP intact but significantly changed the pricing and tax proposals it contained to meet provincial concerns.

Under the new agreements, the price of oil and gas was to continue to be regulated and increased. But this schedule was soon disrupted. The international prices of petroleum began to fall, depressing the energy sector. The petroleum-producing provinces were forced to change their royalty structures and Ottawa postponed and reduced certain resource taxes.

The Western Accord. The weakening of the OPEC cartel, increased oil production, falling prices at the international level, and the election of a Conservative government in 1984 prompted the dismantling of the National Energy Program and restructuring of federal energy policy during the mid-1980s. In 1985, the federal government and the three oil- and gas-producing provinces of Alberta, British Columbia, and Saskatchewan signed the Western Accord, an agreement to replace the NEP. It removed many of the special federal taxes that had been imposed on oil and gas under the NEP and left prices to be determined by the marketplace.

At the same time, Petro-Canada was mandated to operate as a commercial corporation in a competitive environment. Then, in the February 1990 federal budget, Finance Minister Wilson announced plans to privatize Petro-Canada by selling shares in the company to the public. The minister rationalized that the role of Petro-Canada as an instrument of public policy was becoming increasingly limited because of changes in the nature of the industry and the international energy environment. Ottawa had, by 1990, invested more than $4 billion in the company, but it still needed large capital resources for its frontier exploration and development program. A privatized Petro-Canada, the minister argued, would have access to the full range of financing opportunities available to shareholder-owned corporations in the private sector.

The sale of Petro-Canada was part of the Conservative's government's continuing program of privatizing Crown corporations. As well, it appealed to a government anxious to control its expenditures and in need of revenues to reduce huge annual deficits. The minister made no claims that Petro-Canada had achieved the government's objectives. It had by no means attained a dominant position in the Canadian petroleum industry. By 1988, its asset base had accounted for about 5.5 percent of Canadian domestic oil production and 6 percent of natural gas production, and its refining activities used about 22 percent of Canada's refining capacity.

The Offshore. The struggle over natural resources was not confined to Ottawa and the Western provinces. Offshore resource rights became a heated issue in the Atlantic region. Although an agreement was reached between the federal government and Nova Scotia in March 1982, a prolonged, bitter dispute continued between Ottawa and Newfoundland.

Newfoundland claimed jurisdiction and ownership of offshore minerals by virtue of having been an entity with its own territory before joining Canada in 1949 and of not having surrendered its extraterritorial powers to the federal government when it became a province. Various attempts at negotiation and compromise ended in failure, and early in 1983 the governments sought a constitutional ruling from the Supreme Court of Canada. In March 1984, the Supreme Court ruled that offshore mineral rights came under the jurisdiction of the federal government. Newfoundland Premier Brian Peckford responded that he would continue the fight for significant provincial control of offshore oil development.

The legal matter of ownership was settled, but there remained questions of how much the province would control the offshore resources and what share of revenues from these resources it would draw. Intensive negotiations culminated in the signing of the Canada–Newfoundland Atlantic accord in 1985. The terms of the Accord gave the province the power to control the method and pace of offshore oil and gas development and the right to impose royalties and taxes on the resources as if they were on land. In a further spirit of co-operation, the two governments entered an agreement in 1988 on the development of the Hibernia oil field off the coast of Newfoundland. The terms of the agreement provided that from 1989 to 1995 the federal government would contribute 25 percent of specified preproduction capital costs of the project to a maximum of $1.04 billion and would guarantee loans for 40 percent of the capital costs to a maximum guarantee of $1.66 billion.[18]

Co-ordination of Economic and Social Policies

The general trend in Canada during the last 25 years has been a gradual decentralization of power in terms of the relative shares of federal and provincial expenditure constituting the public sector. Along with such decentralization comes an increasing need for co-operation between the two levels of government and for co-ordination of policies. Without co-operation, fiscal policy becomes difficult to implement, taxation may produce inequities and adverse economic effects, waste and inefficiency may creep into overlaping government expenditure functions, and uncertainty may characterize areas under jurisdictional dispute. The term "co-operative federalism" has been frequently used to describe the situation in Canada, and numerous formal, informal, and ad hoc avenues for co-operation have been employed.

The most publicized method of bringing together the federal and provincial governments to discuss problems and co-ordinate policies has been the federal/provincial conference of premiers and the Prime Minister. These conferences are generally reserved for discussion of relatively general principles and issues, and because the meetings draw extensive media coverage, they frequently tend to serve as a political forum. The interests and opinions of the participants have been as varied as the regions of Canada themselves, with much controversy and conflict and only occasional consensus.

Regular discussions are also held among federal and provincial ministers of the various departments of government, such as the meetings of the federal minister of finance and provincial treasurers to discuss fiscal policies and tax and expenditure issues. In addition, liaison between the two levels of government is provided by numerous ad hoc committees at the public service level, supplemented by day-to-day contacts in the ordinary process of administering government affairs.

In 1975 the federal government established the Federal-Provincial Relations Office (FPRO), replacing a previous federal/provincial unit within the Privy Council Office. In 1986, a Minister of State for Federal-Provincial Relations was established. The FPRO serves this minister and provides assistance to other federal ministers, departments, and agencies in the conduct of their relations with provincial governments. It consists of five secretariats: one responsible for liaison with the provinces, a second responsible for policy development, a third dealing with economic policy and programs, a fourth dealing with social policy and programs, and finally one handling constitutional affairs.

Offices counterpart to the FPRO exist at the provincial level. Examples are Ontario's Ministry of Intergovernmental Affairs and Manitoba's Federal-Provincial Relations and Research Division of the Finance Department.

In addition, the Canada Intergovernmental Conference Secretariat, created, funded, and staffed by both the federal and the provincial governments, serves federal/provincial and interprovincial meetings of first ministers and ministers and officials of departments. It provides secretarial, translation, and printing services along with various assistance in arranging conferences.

A number of intergovernmental agencies have been established between the federal government and the provinces, between the federal government and certain provinces, and between provinces.[19] Their functions vary from co-ordinating government activities to providing services directly to the public. The Canadian Council of Resource and Environment Ministers, for example, consists of federal and provincial ministers and provides a forum for exchange of information and planning policies on resource development and environmental management. The Intergovernmental Committee on Urban and Regional Research, with representatives from the federal, provincial, and territorial governments, offers an avenue for information exchange on a variety of regional and local issues including housing, urban and regional development, and municipal management. The Council of Ministers of Education provides for the regular meetings of these provincial ministers and for meetings of committees of senior ministry officials to exchange information and co-operate in education projects. The Atlantic Province Special Education Authority is an interprovincial agency of the four Atlantic provinces that provides education services for persons under 21 years of age who suffer from hearing and visual disabilities. The Federal-Provincial Advisory Committee on Environmental and Occupational Health advises ministers and deputy ministers of health on environmental and health-related issues including food contamination, waste disposal, new chemicals, and workplace conditions, subcommittees carry out such activities as developing guidelines for water quality, noise exposure, and hazardous chemicals.

Various economic development agreements between the federal and provincial governments provide for consultation and co-operation as well as financial assistance. In 1984, the ten-year Economic and Regional Development Agreements (ERDAs) were signed between Ottawa and each province. The ERDA is a mechanism to facilitate consultation on and co-ordination of economic and regional development policies, programs, and activities of the two levels of government; the Department of Regional Industrial Expansion is the primary federal agency involved.

Despite this extensive co-operation between the two levels of government on economic and social policies, disagreements, conflicts, and confrontations are common. The confrontations over shared-cost programs, medicare, oil and gas pricing, and offshore mineral rights were discussed earlier. Other recent areas of dispute concern the regulation of telecommunications and the federal imposition of the goods and services tax (GST). A decision of the Supreme Court of Canada in 1989 determined that the activities of the provincially owned telephone companies in Alberta, Saskatchewan, and Manitoba were interprovincial and therefore subject to federal, rather than provincial, regulation. Those three provinces petitioned that regulatory jurisdiction be legislated back to the provinces, but the federal government refused, arguing that jurisdiction over all telephone service would enable Ottawa to establish a national telecommunications policy.

When the federal government first introduced its proposal for a goods and services tax in 1987, the Minister of Finance outlined, as an option, a joint federal-provincial sales tax. The arrangements suggested were similar to those in place for the personal and corporate tax system; the tax would be legislated separately by the federal government and the provinces with flexibility for the latter to determine their own rates. Ottawa contended that a joint tax would simplify administration and compliance and avoid a complex, double layer of sales tax. The provinces, however, were not prepared to co-operate and negotiations aimed at a joint tax failed. Indeed, the provinces were highly critical of the federal decision to impose the GST. The retail sales tax, levied by all provinces except Alberta, had been a major source of provincial revenue for years, and they viewed the federal GST as an intrusion into provincial tax territory. The provinces also refused to help Ottawa collect its tax, a course that would have avoided some duplication in administration and reduced collection costs. The federal Minister of Finance, however, left the door open for provinces to join to GST after it came into effect in January, 1991. As of late 1990, the provinces of Newfoundland, Quebec, and Saskatchewan had announced that they would harmonize their retail sales taxes with the GST. (For further details see, Chapter 6.)

ENDNOTES

1. R.A. Musgrave, P. Musgrave, and R.M. Bird, *Public Finance in Theory and Practice*, Cdn. ed. (Toronto: McGraw-Hill Ryerson, 1987), pp. 480–81.
2. Economic Council of Canada, *Financing Confederation: Today and Tomorrow* (Ottawa, ECC, 1982), p. 11.
3. A.M. Moore, J.H. Perry, and D. Beach, *The Financing of Canadian Federation* (Toronto: Canadian Tax Foundation, 1966), p. 108.
4. Canada, Federal-Provincial Relations Office, *Federal-Provincial Programs and Activities: A Descriptive Inventory, 1988–89*, (Ottawa, June 1989).
5. For a more detailed analysis of conditional grants in Canada and provincial government dissatisfaction, see J.C. Strick, "Conditional Grants and Provincial Budgeting," *Canadian Public Administration* 14, no. 2 (Summer 1971). See also George E. Carter, *Canadian Conditional Grants since World War II*, Canadian Tax Foundation, tax paper no. 54 (Toronto: CTF, 1971); and R.W. Boadway, *Intergovernmental Transfers in Canada* (Toronto: Canadian Tax Foundation, 1980).
6. Ontario, *Responsible Taxation: The Ontario Approach* (Toronto, 1969), pp. 7, 11.
7. The shared-cost programs frequently mentioned in this connection included the Winter Works Program, Road to Resources, forestry agreements, resource developments programs, and manpower programs. Federal grants for projects in these areas totalled $150.2 million in 1967/8 and $136.3 million in 1969/70.
8. Canada, *Federal-Provincial Programs and Activities . . . 1988–89*, p. 15–2.
9. Ibid.
10. A critical analysis of the EPF arrangements is presented in George E. Carter, "Established Programs Financing: A Critical Review of the Record," *Canadian Tax Journal* 36 (September/October 1988).
11. For an outline and discussion of some of the views of the clause on shared-cost programs contained in the Meech Lake Accord, see K.G. Banting, "Federalism, Social Reform and the Spending Power," *Canadian Public Policy* 4, supplement (September 1988).
12. For a detailed presentation of the developments leading to the patriated constitution, see Edward McWhinney, *Canada and the Constitution 1979–1982* (Toronto: University of Toronto Press, 1982); and J.M. Beck and I. Bernier, eds., *Canada and the New Constitution* (Toronto: Institute for Research on Public Policy, 1983), vol. 1 and 2.
13. Canada, *Proceedings of the Constitutional Conferences 1968, 1969, 1970*, and *1971* (Ottawa: Queen's Printer, 1968, 1969, 1970, and 1971).
14. Canada, *Proceedings of the Constitutional Conference*, Victoria, June 14–16, 1971.

15. For a discussion of various aspects of the Meech Lake Accord, see, "The Meech Lake Accord," *Canadian Public Policy* 14, supplement (September 1988).

16. A discussion of this conflict can be found in J. Harvey Perry, *Background of Current Fiscal Problems*, Tax Paper no. 8 (Toronto: Canadian Tax Foundation, 1982) ch. 7 and 8; and E.A. Carmichael and J.K. Stewart, *Lessons from the National Energy Program* (Toronto: C.D. Howe Institute, 1983).

17. Canada, Ministry of Mines and Resources, *The National Energy Program* (Ottawa, 1980).

18. Canada, *Federal-Provincial Programs and Activities*, p. 10–9.

19. Ibid.

CHAPTER 9

THE BUDGET AS AN INSTRUMENT OF FISCAL POLICY

The objectives of fiscal policy are generally identified as full employment, stable prices, and economic growth. Traditional fiscal policy concentrates on government management of aggregate demand through discretionary application of tax and expenditure measures, which are primarily introduced through the budget. A period of economic decline and unemployment calls for tax and/or expenditure changes, producing a budget deficit. In a period of excessive aggregate demand and inflation, a budget surplus would be the appropriate discretionary policy.

Fiscal policy first came to prominence with the Depression of the 1930s and the publication of the *General Theory of Employment, Interest and Money* by J.M. Keynes in 1936.[1] Keynes argued that the key to ending the Depression and maintaining high levels of economic growth and full employment was a high level of aggregate demand. If private demand was insufficient to achieve this, then government should step in with expansionary tax and expenditure policies. In the Keynesian theory, aggregate demand in a closed economy (one without imports and exports) consists of the demand of consumers, business, and government. The sum of consumption (C), investment (I), and government expenditure (G) constitutes gross national expenditure (Y), or $C + I + G = Y$.[2] In an open economy, exports (EX) and imports (IM) are introduced into this identity to produce $Y = C + I + G + \text{EX} - \text{IM}$. A change in any of the components will affect aggregate demand.

According to traditional Keynesian theory, an increase in aggregate demand in a period of unemployment should raise production and employment, assuming the supply of goods and services expands to meet the demand. Consequently, if the government budget is balanced to begin with, an increase in government expenditure with taxes held constant will produce a budget deficit but will also raise aggregate demand and provide a stimulus to economic activity and employment. Similarly, a reduction in taxes for consumers and business will provide increased incomes for expenditure on consumption and investment. A tax reduction with government expenditure held constant will also produce a budget deficit. A budget surplus, on the other hand, will have a contractionary effect on aggregate demand and economic activity. The impact on the economy from a budget surplus or deficit will exceed the size of the surplus or deficits by a multiple amount, through the multiplier process.[3]

More recent developments in macroeconomics and in fiscal theory focus on the management of aggregate supply as well as demand. In fact, the term "supply-side economics" was used to describe this approach to fiscal policy during the 1980s. This theory emphasizes the effects of tax changes on incentives, such as the incentive to work and to invest. Positive incentives for work or investment will increase the supply of labour and capital and may have a positive impact on productivity and economic growth. An increase in aggregate supply may moderate inflation in a period of rising prices caused by large increases in demand.[4]

The budget as a tool for implementing and analyzing fiscal policy, together with the objectives of fiscal policy, are examined in this chapter. This will provide a framework for the analysis of Canadian fiscal policy that is presented Chapter 10.

FISCAL IMPULSE MEASURES

The actual budget balance is generally viewed as a summary indicator of the government's financial position, but it may give a misleading impression of the government's fiscal policy stance. In any analysis of fiscal policy, it must be recognized that the budget can affect the economy and that the economy can affect the budget. Variations in government revenues and expenditures, and therefore in the budget balance may result from discretionary changes in tax and expenditure policies or from changes in economic conditions. The actual budgetary surplus or deficit, therefore, can be viewed as consisting of two components: a structural component produced by discretionary policy changes, and a cyclical component produced by a fluctuating economy.

The structural budget balance is defined as the balance that would occur, given the existing structure of taxes, tax rates, and expenditure programs, if the economy were operating at an average level of activity. It is based on estimates of revenues that would be generated at this level of activity and of the amounts that government would be spending on its existing programs. Changes in the structural budget balance may be viewed as indicating the direction of discretionary fiscal actions.

The cyclical budget balance shows surpluses and deficits that are produced by the state of the economy. They result from the operation of the stabilizers built into the government budget. Built-in stabilizers respond automatically to changing economic conditions or cyclical fluctuations in the economy. Assume the starting point is a balanced budget. In a period of rapid economic growth, stabilizers will increase revenues and reduce expenditures, producing a budget surplus; the fiscal restraint will help to combat inflation. In a period of economic decline, stabilizers will cause revenues to fall and expenditures to rise, producing a budget deficit that will stimulate a declining economy. Automatic stabilizers are found on both the tax and expenditure sides of the budget. Within a given tax structure, revenues from personal and corporation taxes and from sales taxes depend on income, profit, and sales levels and will change as these variables change. Similarly, certain expenditures, such as unemployment insurance payments and the unemployment component of welfare payments, vary automatically with the state of health of the economy, increasing in a recession and decreasing in periods of rapid growth and falling unemployment.

The removal of the cyclical component from the actual budget balance leaves the structural budget balance, which is also referred to as the "cyclically adjusted budget balance." Since the structural balance is calculated for an average level of economic activity over the business cycle, the cyclical component of the deficit should sum to zero over the business cycle.

Changes in the structural balance are often used to measure discretionary changes in fiscal policy, but some qualifications and notes of caution are required for so employing them.[5] The structural balance does contain some nondiscretionary elements. Changes in agricultural prices, for example, will change the amount of agriculture subsidies paid and affect the structural balance although they are clearly nondiscretionary. Similarly, interest rate changes produce nondiscretionary changes in public debt charges and affect the structural balance. The federal Department of Finance, therefore, views the structural balance excluding public debt charges — which is called the primary structural budget balance — as a more appropriate measure of the component of the budget over which the government exerts discretionary influence, particularly in the short run.

In order to estimate the structural budget balance, one must first estimate output levels in the economy in the absence of cyclical fluctuations. The methodology used by the Department of Finance for this purpose consists of determining the national output level consistent with an average rate of labour utilization and trend labour productivity.[6] The result does not necessarily represent output at full capacity or full employment but rather an approximation of the output level that could be sustained on average over the business cycle.

The Department of Finance's concept of the structural budget balance is comparable to that of the full-employment budget balance often used in US budget documents (described in detail in public finance literature).[7] The full employment budget balance is the surplus or deficit that would accrue under an existing budget revenue and expenditure structure if the economy were operating at full employment. (The concept is used in the United States in an attempt to illustrate that actual deficits in a period of unemployment have represented responsible financial management because if the economy were operating at full employment, the built-in stabilizers would produce a balanced budget.) However, the methodologies of calculating the two balances — and hence the results — differ somewhat between the two countries. The Americans use a rate of labour utilization estimated as compatible with a nonaccelerating rate of inflation, while the Canadian Department of Finance uses of an average rate of labour utilization.

The structural (or full employment) budget has certain limitations for measuring the budget balance at full employment and for analyzing discretionary fiscal changes. First, there are problems in measuring gross national product and government revenues at a high rate of capacity utilization. As the economy approaches this level, pressures on prices are likely to be greater than they are at less than full employment. Increased prices affect government revenues and spending (because of increased costs). Projecting GDP for the economy at near full capacity utilization using the same prices that prevail with a relatively high level of unemployment leads to underestimation of revenues in the structural budget balance. Furthermore, tax revenues are not independent of the mix of the elements comprising GDP (consumption and investment). As GDP changes, the mix may change, causing a change in tax revenues. Projecting GDP for a high rate of capacity utilization on the assumption that the mix does not change may lead to an overestimation or underestimation of revenues for the structural budget balance.

Another limitation of the structural budget balance methodology is its failure to recognize the different strengths of taxes and government expenditures. If one begins with a structural budget that is balanced, an increase in expenditures that is matched by a tax increase leaves that balance, indicating no discretionary macroeconomic impact. But because the multiplier of a balanced budget equals one, there is an impact on the economy equivalent to the expenditure change.

Moreover, alternative combinations of tax and expenditure changes that have the same effect on the budget balance and on the size of the surplus or deficit may not have the same impact on the economy. For example, an across-the-board reduction in the personal income tax is designed to increase consumption. Selective tax changes, such as accelerated depreciation, investment tax credits, tax holidays for certain industries, and favourable treatment of capital gains, are designed to stimulate investment and are likely to have long-term effects on economic activity and economic growth. Thus, although both of these discretionary tax measures may reduce revenues and produce a budgetary deficit of an equal amount, their fiscal impact will not be the same. It is therefore important, in the analysis of the impact of fiscal policy, to examine the mix of discretionary fiscal measures.

The Budget Accounts

The federal government presents its budget on three different accounting bases. In effect, it presents three budgets, each with a different balance. The three budgets are the administrative budget, the consolidated cash budget, and the national income and expenditure accounts budget. The first two are based on the public accounts, an accounting system designed to facilitate parliamentary control over expenditures; the third is based on the national accounts.[8] Each serves a different purpose, and the three are not equally appropriate for the analysis of fiscal policy.

Administrative Budget. The administrative budget reflects government department and agency operations, incorporating their estimates of expenditure for the fiscal year with estimates of tax proceeds and certain other revenues. The financial transactions in this budget are called budgetary transactions.

This document is commonly referred to as "The Budget," and its transactions and balance are the focus of the annual budget speech by the Minister of Finance. Its balance is the one highlighted by government and by the news media as the indicator of the state of government budgetary affairs and the extent to which the government is operating in the red or the black. The accumulated deficits in this budget since Confederation form the total net government debt, which consists of gross government debt minus the value of recorded government assets.

The administrative budget serves the administrative and financial control purposes described in Chapter 3.

Consolidated Cash Budget. The consolidated cash budget includes all government financial transactions — the administrative budget and all other payments and receipts— and is a comprehensive measure of cash flows. It is broken into three main categories of financial transactions: budgetary transactions, nonbudgetary transactions, and foreign exchange transactions. Nonbudgetary transactions consist of loans, investments, and advances; transactions related to specified-purpose accounts; and other transactions. The distinguishing feature between budgetary and nonbudgetary transactions is that the former change the net indebtness of the government, while the latter do not since they involve the creation of offsetting financial assets or liabilities.

Nonbudgetary transactions have in the past provided a net source of funds to the government and consequently have reduced the extent to which the government has had to borrow on financial markets. Loans and advances are primarily those made to Crown corporations; a loan by the government increases its financial assets since the recipient incurs an obligation to repay. The specified purpose accounts in nonbudgetary transactions include the Canada Pension Plan and the superannuation accounts (federal government employees' pension accounts), accounts that are held in trust for third parties and are self-financing. For many years, the nonbudgetary accounts included three other major funds: the Unemployment Insurance Fund, the Foreign Exchange Fund Account, and the Grain Stabilization Account.[9] In 1985, on the recommendation of the Auditor General of Canada, these three funds, along with loans to developing countries, were reclassified from nonbudgetary to budgetary transactions.[10]

Foreign exchange transactions record the purchase and sale of foreign currencies, used to stabilize the Canadian dollar in international money markets, and include a reserve of borrowed funds to provide for flexibility.

The consolidated cash budget is the most comprehensive of the three budgets and is useful for internal cash management purposes. It shows the net amount of borrowing on the financial markets the federal government requires for a fiscal year. For example, in 1988/9, the administrative budget deficit was estimated at $28.9 billion. Nonbudgetary transactions were a surplus of $6.9 billion, while the deficit in foreign exchange transactions totalled $5.8 billion. Thus, the total borrowing required amounted to approximately $28 billion. This budget, therefore, has relevance to the analysis of the effect of government on the economy in terms of its impact on the money or capital market and on interest rates.

National Accounts Budget. First presented in 1964, the national accounts budget employs the national income and expenditure accounting system developed by Statistics Canada to measure current economic activity and serves, among other things, to measure the interaction between the public sector and other sectors of the economy. The national accounts concepts are similar to those used internationally and permit comparisons from one nation to another.

The national accounts budget serves economic analysis. It is more comprehensive than the administrative budget but excludes some items found in the consolidated cash budget. Government pension and social security transactions are included, but government borrowing and lending operations are excluded, as are transactions of a purely bookkeeping nature that have no impact on the economy. The national accounts budget concentrates on income-creating and resource-absorbing transactions and therefore includes only those operations that have a direct effect on the flow of incomes in the economy. Furthermore, it is based on the accrual method of accounting in which revenues are accounted when earned rather than received and expenditures are recorded when liabilities are incurred rather than when actually paid; therefore, it measures the timing of the impact of government operations of the economy.

The system of national income and expenditure accounts employed by Statistics Canada, on which the government's national accounts budget is based, defines output as currently produced goods and services; consequently, it excludes both transactions on used goods and financial transactions that do not involve the production of new goods and services. Thus, government loan transactions are omitted, an exclusion that does limit the usefulness of this budget for analyzing the impact of the government on the economy. Some government loans have significant economic effects, and if they were incorporated into the budget, it would present a more complete picture. For example, a government loan to an industry that uses the proceeds to purchase domestically produced machinery and equipment affects economic activity and output. Although the expenditure of the loan by the recipient is reflected in the national accounts, the fact that it came from the government is not.

The difference between the administrative budget balance and the national accounts budget balance can be substantial. Usually, a large part of this difference results from the manner in which the two budgets treat transactions in the government employees' pension accounts. National accounts revenues include employer and employee contributions, as well as interest earnings, and expenditures include all benefits and interest payments. The budgetary transactions, in contrast, exclude all revenues recorded by these pension accounts and include as expenditures only the government's contribution as an employer and interest paid on surplus funds (included as interest on the public debt). Thus, the national accounts deficit is usually lower than the budgetary deficit. For example, in 1988/9, the annual surplus of the superannuation accounts, estimated to be $6.4 billion, accounted for almost the entire difference between the two deficit measures for the fiscal year (estimated budgetary deficit of $28.9 billion compared to estimated national accounts deficit of $22.0 billion for the fiscal year).[11] Despite the frequent substantial differences between the two deficit measures, it should be noted that they have tended, for the most part, to move symmetrically.

Conclusion. Although the budget based on the national income and expenditure accounts has some limitations, it is generally considered the most appropriate of the three budgets for analyzing fiscal policy and is used in the next chapter for the analysis of Canadian policy. Some reference is also made there to the balances on the administrative budget and the consolidated cash budget — the former because it affects the net national debt and the latter because it presents the government's borrowing requirements in the financial market and may affect this market and interest rates.

Goals of Fiscal Policy

The general objective of fiscal policy is to manage supply and demand in the economy, using discretionary tax and expenditure measures, to prevent or to reduce the severity of fluctuations producing periods of economic decline and unemployment and periods of excessive demand and inflation. Fiscal policy tends to focus on three main indicators of the state of health of the economy: unemployment, inflation, and economic growth. The goals of fiscal policy are usually given as a high rate of employment, reasonably stable prices, and an adequate rate of economic growth. In an open economy, fiscal policy may also be directed toward achieving a viable balance of international trade and payments.

The commitment of the Canadian government to the achievement of these goals is evident from various statements found in budget speeches and position papers throughout the aftermath of the Second World War and the following decades. Attempts were made to determine the economy's potential for full employment, price stability, and economic growth and to establish specific levels for these goals. Such an attempt was made by the Economic Council of Canada in 1964 in its first annual review, entitled *First Annual Review Economic Goals for Canada to 1970*.[12] The council determined that on the basis of the Canadian economy's potential, reasonable fiscal goals for the rest of the decade included an unemployment rate of 3 percent of the labour force, an increase in consumer price index of less than 2 percent, and an average annual increase in real GNP of 5 to 6 percent.

Over the years, actual unemployment, price, and economic growth levels have fluctuated widely and have deviated significantly from the levels established earlier by the Economic Council of Canada. There has been considerable debate on the issue of achievable rates of employment and economic growth and degrees of price stability, and the expectations of feasible goals have tended to change over time as factors affecting the economy changed. For example, the Economic Council of Canada determined in 1989 that reasonable fiscal targets for the 1989–93 period were an unemployment rate of 5 to 7 percent, an inflation rate of 4 percent, and an increase in real gross domestic product of 3 to 4 percent.[13]

Employment

Full employment was an early goal of fiscal policy, spurred by the very high unemployment rates generated by the Depression of the 1930s. In fact, the aggregate unemployment rate came to be viewed as the leading indicator of economic conditions and the measure of the hardship inflicted upon society by a depressed economy.

Unemployment has two primary adverse impacts: a production effect and a welfare impact. Their severity depends not only on the number of the unemployed but also on who they are. An increase in the unemployment of part-time and occasional workers will not have as severe an effect on either production and welfare as an increase in the unemployment of full-time workers. The welfare impact is also affected by the duration of unemployment, the number of wage-earners in the household, and their eligibility for unemployment insurance and other public welfare benefits; for instance, the unemployment of a worker in a multiearner household will likely not be as drastic for household maintenance as the unemployment of the sole wage-earner in a family. In addition, unemployment may place serious social and psychological stress on the unemployed workers and their families. For all these reasons, high or increasing rates of unemployment continue to be of major concern, winning headlines in the news media and inspiring calls for government action.

Is the Unemployment Rate an Economic Barometer? Over the last two decades, however, a growing number of economists have been questioning whether the aggregate unemployment rate is a sensitive barometer of the state of the economy and of the economic stress of society. Reservations have also been expressed over using the unemployment rate as a measure of the degree of unused labour capacity. These questions and reservations have their foundations in a variety of factors and developments, ranging from the dynamics of technology and demography to the methods of measuring the labour force and unemployment.

Since the Second World War, each decade has witnessed a higher actual average unemployment rate than the one before. The average unemployment rate was 4.2 percent during the 1950–59 decade; 5.0 percent for 1960–69; 6.7 percent for 1970–79, and 9.3 percent for 1980–89. The unemployment rate reached levels of 11.0 and 11.8 percent in 1982 and 1983 respectively and has not dropped below 7.0 percent since 1975. These figures seem to indicate a long-term upward drift in Canada's unemployment rate, part of which may be explained by institutional and demographic factors. Analysts argue that it is increasingly difficult for the economy to absorb the labour force and achieve a low unemployment rate because of several developments: rapid expansion of the labour force brought about by population growth and increasing participation rates; the changing composition of the work force with an increasing proportion of the female population and more part-time and occasional workers entering the labour market; and capital-intensive production.

The dynamics of the labour force, it has been argued, have reduced the significance traditionally placed on the aggregate unemployment rate as an economic indicator. A high unemployment rate does not necessarily signal job loss from economic decline. It may also reflect, in part, an increase in voluntary unemployment or a rapid influx of full-time or part-time workers stemming from population growth, an increase in the participation rate, or both. On the other hand, a decline in the unemployment rate does not necessarily indicate economic improvement. During periods of prolonged recession, some workers give up looking for work. This "discouraged worker" phenomenon is reflected in a reduction in the participation rate and tempers the unemployment rate as an indicator of unused labour capacity. In addition, some workers may work part-time only because they cannot find full-time jobs, so their numbers may really represent disguised unemployment. Some analysts contend that the unemployment rate remains relatively high even when the economy recovers from a slump and enters a period of prosperity because although workers who are only marginally attached to the labour force (part-time and occasional workers) are slow to leave it when economic conditions deteriorate, they are quick to join when the economy begins to improve. Therefore, as the business cycle swings upward, job creation is required not only to absorb those who could not find work during the recession but also to take up new labour force entrants and the marginally attached who reenter the labour market.

Another consideration in using the unemployment rate as an economic barometer is that regional unemployment is a serious problem in Canada, as illustrated in Table 9–1. In 1988 and 1989 when the unemployment rate in Ontario fell to 5 percent,

TABLE 9–1
Unemployment in Canada for Selected Years 1958–1989

	Atlantic region	Quebec	Ontario	Prairie region	British Columbia	Canada
	(percentage of local labour force)					
1958	12.5	8.8	5.4	4.1	8.6	7.0
1966	4.9	4.1	2.6	2.3	4.6	3.4
1974	8.0	6.6	4.4	3.4	6.2	5.3
1980	11.1	9.8	6.8	4.3	6.8	7.5
1984	15.2	12.8	9.0	9.8	14.7	11.2
1988	12.4	9.4	5.0	7.9	10.3	7.8
1989	12.4	9.3	5.1	7.3	9.1	7.5

Source: Canada, Department of Finance, *Quarterly Economic Review* (Ottawa), various issues; and *Quarterly Economic Review, Annual Reference Tables*, June 1990 (Ottawa).

indicating a relatively strong provincial economy, the same rate exceeded 16 percent in Newfoundland and was more than 12 percent for the whole Atlantic region. Thus, a high national unemployment rate does not necessarily suggest that the entire economy is in a slump and is in need of national or across-the-board expansionary fiscal policies. When unemployment is mainly regional, it is more appropriate to direct fiscal measures to those areas experiencing the highest rates of unemployment.

An Unemployment/Inflation Tradeoff? Yet another issue is the feasibility of achieving low rates of unemployment without aggravating inflation. Considerable attention has been devoted in the economic literature to the issue of a possible unemployment/inflation tradeoff. The Phillips curve, developed by the economist A.W. Phillips, illustrates this tradeoff as an inverse relationship between changes in unemployment and changes in prices. Phillips and his followers contended that when economic activity declines, producing an increase in unemployment, the rate of increase in prices falls as pressure on prices is reduced. A rapidly expanding economy with declining unemployment, on the other hand, builds inflationary pressures and prices spiral upward.

The experience of the 1970s and early 1980s, however, cast doubts on the existence of such a tradeoff as unemployment and inflation jointly moved to unprecedented high levels. In recent years, analysts have theorized about the existence of some critical limit to the unemployment rate that might stabilize the price level and about possible changes in this limit over time. According to the "accelerationalist theory," attempts to use expansionary fiscal policy to reduce unemployment below some minimum rate can succeed only in producing an accelerating rise in prices. Some estimates in the early 1980s placed the "nonaccelerating inflation rate of unemployment" or "natural rate of unemployment" for Canada in the range of 6.5 to 7.0 percent.[14] The actual data for the period 1984 to 1990 shows a decline in the unemployment rate from a peak level of 11.8 percent in 1983 to near 7.0 percent. During this decline, the inflation rate stabilized at an annual rate of between 4 and 5 percent, but resisted further decline despite the relatively large reduction in the unemployment rate, casting continued doubt on the existence of the Phillips tradeoff.

Conclusion. Given these various developments, it is becoming increasingly difficult to define some aggregate rate of unemployment as a numerical goal for fiscal policy over the longer term. Changing technology, institutional and demographic factors, and the dynamics of the labour market suggest that no single magic number exists for guiding fiscal policy.

Thus, in addition to the official unemployment rate, Statistics Canada calculates and publishes a number of supplemental unemployment rates and other measures of unemployment.[15] These include unemployment rates by province, age, gender, industry, and occupation. Other statistics show unemployment by duration, by type of work sought, by job-search methods, and by reason for leaving the last job. Such data can be helpful for designing strategies and developing programs to increase employment. In addition, an official employment rate, which measures the percentage of the population 15 years and over who actually have jobs is also calculated. The Department of Finance, in its analysis of the labour market as an indicator of economic conditions, examines these variables along with the unemployment rate, with particular emphasis on employment growth and the rate of increase in employment.[16]

Prices

Inflation is defined as an increase in the general level of prices of goods and services. Price increases may be small, moderate, or severe; they may be abrupt or develop slowly; they may be short term or prolonged. A small annual increase in the general price level is usually acceptable, as it is extremely difficult in a dynamic, complex, and open economy to have stable prices in the sense of a fixed general price level. The changing structures of supply and demand, along with inflexibility and imperfection in the market, contribute to fluctuations and a general upward movement in prices. Traditionally, economists interpreted the fiscal policy objective of reasonably stable prices to mean an annual increase in the general price level of less than 2 percent. But, as in the case of full employment, recent years have witnessed price increases or inflationary rates considerably in excess of the traditional goal.

Rising prices become a concern when there is a break in the accepted trend and the general price level rises abruptly or price increases begin to accelerate and become persistent. There are various kinds of inflation. Demand-pull inflation is caused by excessive demand relative to supply. Cost-push inflation originates on the supply side and occurs when production cost increments, in excess of productivity growth, are passed on to consumers. Inflation may be structural in nature, caused by shortages of particular factors of production or materials in particular sectors of the economy or by increased market concentration and power of particular industries. It may also be imported, if the prices of imported goods are rising. Or inflation may result from a combination of several or all of these factors.

The Consumer Price Index. Statistics Canada compiles several measures of price changes; some relate to specific categories of items, while others are more comprehensive. They include the industrial product price index, the raw materials price index, the farm input price index, the construction price index, the gross domestic product deflator, and the consumer price index. Although none of these measures purports to be a cost of living index, the one most commonly used as a general indicator of inflation and implicitly as a measure of changes in the purchasing of power of a dollar is the consumer price index (CPI).[17]

The CPI serves a variety of purposes. It is applied in the adjustment of various forms of income such as Old Age Security Pensions, for which the objective is to maintain real income levels of purchasing power in periods of inflation. It is used as an escalator in collective agreements to adjust wages and salaries for rises in the cost of living. Of particular significance here, it is used as a general indicator of inflation and economic performance, serving as a major element in the design of fiscal policy and the evaluation of its success.

The Fear of Inflation. Although some members and groups of society may benefit from inflation, there is a general public fear of it for the costs it is perceived to inflict upon individuals, society, and the economy. A high rate of inflation may have serious and inequitable effects on the distribution of income and wealth. People with fixed income and assets suffer more than those whose income and asset values increase along with prices. Inflation benefits debtors at the expense of creditors, discourages saving, and affects contracts and investments. It contributes to stress and confrontation in industrial relations as workers seek wage increases in order to maintain their real income levels. It may have adverse consequences on a country's trade and balance of payments and the international value of its currency. Rising prices may influence expectations, producing speculative behaviour that leads to a further acceleration of prices — galloping inflation — threatening a country's social and economic stability.[18]

Concern over inflation goes back many centuries, and history attests to the devastating effects of hyperinflation on national economies. Until recently, industrialized countries, such as Canada and the United States, experienced relative price stability. Direct wage and price regulation provided price stability during the Second World War, and fiscal policies of increased taxes tended to dampen the inflation that might otherwise have arisen with the outbreak of the Korean War in the early 1950s. Between 1952 and 1965, the annual average increase in the Canadian CPI was 1.4 percent, and in only four years during that period did it exceed 2 percent. Beginning in the late 1960s, however, the annual increase in the inflation rate began to accelerate, and it reached double digit levels in 1974, 1975, 1980, 1981, and 1982. The average annual increase in the CPI for 1960 to 1969 was 2.5 percent; for 1970 to 1979 it was 7.4 percent; and for 1980 to 1989 it was 6.5 percent. The inflation rate peaked at 12.5 percent in 1981, and from 1984 to 1989 it remained relatively stable between 4 and 5 percent. Thus, evidence has shown the traditional goal of an inflation rate of less than 2 percent to be elusive. The goal of price stability like that of no unemployment, has been subject to reexamination and redefinition in recent years. It has been suggested that an acceptable rate of inflation be determined in relation to price performance in other countries. Such an inflation goal would be based on a relative standard, comparing price changes in Canada with those in other industrial countries, particularly its major trading partners. An acceptable rate of inflation would be a rate comparable with that of those partners. The federal government in its budget and accompanying papers frequently compares inflation rates in Canada with those in other countries.

Inflation-Fighting. Many economists and policy-makers contend that inflation is acceptable if it is maintained at a low or moderate rate. A notable exception is John Crow, the Governor of the Bank of Canada. In 1988, Mr. Crow announced that the goal of the Bank's monetary policy was price stability defined as a zero rate of inflation. Mr. Crow argued that accepting a specified level of inflation only entrenches inflation and that any increase beyond a set target requires considerably more effort and cost to pull back than would be the case if zero inflation, or true price stability, was the target. In his words, "a commitment to a steady inflation rate is ultimately not credible."[19] Throughout 1989 and 1990, Mr. Crow consistently voiced this view and continued to maintain high interest rates in the face of severe criticism that his policies would drive the economy into recession. But despite Crow's pronouncements and corresponding anti-inflationary monetary policy, the rate of inflation began to increase in 1989 and 1990, indicating that a goal of zero inflation was somewhat ambitious and likely unattainable. Furthermore, it is difficult to understand Crow's insistence on a zero inflation target in a period when federal taxes on goods were themselves causing prices to increase. For example, in 1989 the government increased excises on alcohol, tobacco, and gasoline and raised the manufacturers' sales tax from 12.0 to 13.5 percent. These taxes are all reflected in the CPI.

The high inflation rate in the 1970s and early 1980s in Canada, as well as in other countries, arose partly from traditional inflation-producing factors, such as low productivity and rising production costs, but even more from new influences, such as shortages of energy and minerals.[20] The creation of international cartels for the sale of energy and basic materials produced rapidly escalating costs and prices in spite of depressed economic conditions. A realistic goal in this situation was to prevent an already high rate of inflation from rising further and gradually to reduce it from the double-digit level that had been reached. This goal was achieved, in part by a monetary policy of very high interest rates and in part by the easing of international causes of inflation. The annual increase in the CPI declined to 4.4 percent in 1984 and remained in the 4 percent range for the next four years, suggesting that a 4 percent inflation target is a realistic target for Canada for the early 1990s. (Indeed, that is the figure set by the Economic Council of Canada.)[21]

Economic Growth

One of the features in the evolution of fiscal policy was the turn from preoccupation with short-run fluctuations — cycles — in economic activity to long-run economic growth. It was expected that the maintenance of economic growth at a relatively stable rate would preclude wide cyclical fluctuations.

The general measure of economic growth is the annual rate of growth in real gross domestic product (GDP). The traditional goal of fiscal policy was to maintain a balance between the actual rate of economic growth and the potential rate of growth. Potential economic growth is described as the increase in the capacity of the economy to produce goods and services and is the maximum production of goods and services the economy can sustain. The potential growth rate or supply capacity is determined by a number of factors, including the rate of technological development, the rate of capital formation, and the quantity and quality of the labour force and natural resources. Actual growth can exceed potential, but only temporarily. When demand and production persistently exceed the economy's potential, pressures leading to inflation are created in the goods and services market and the labour market.

The method of balancing actual with potential growth is to maintain a level of aggregate demand that matches supply capacity. A balance ensures full utilization of resources. Excess demand generates inflationary pressures, while insufficient demand results in unemployment and idle capacity. In addition to matching actual and potential growth, it is equally important to attempt to promote and expand potential growth, without which the economy would be stagnant with depressed levels of per capita output and income. Policies designed to stimulate research and development, technological innovation, capital formation, and education and training of the labour force contribute to the expansion of the growth potential of the economy.

The actual calculation of an adequate potential rate of growth depends on a number of predetermined parameters. One of the most significant is the establishment of a level of unemployment that can be interpreted as full utilization of the labour force. The Economic Council of Canada has established and interpreted this level as the noninflationary rate of unemployment.

In the early 1960s, the Economic Council of Canada — based on its projections of the determinants of economic growth and given 3.0 percent unemployment as a goal — estimated Canada's potential annual growth rate for the decade to be between 5.0 and 6.0 percent increase in real GDP. During the 1970s, the potential growth rate was established at 4.0 to and 5.0 percent. For the period 1981 to 1990, the council estimated annual potential growth from 2.7 percent (low potential estimate) to 3.0 percent (high potential estimate) with a noninflationary rate of unemployment of 4.0 to 5.5 percent.[22] The decline in the projection for the 1980s compared to that of the previous decade was attributed to an expected slow growth in population, productivity, and investment. The Canadian economy, however, exceeded the projections for growth during the latter part of the 1980s and the gap between the potential and actual figures disappeared. The average annual increase in real GDP from 1983 to 1988 was 4.5 percent. This rise produced a decline in the unemployment rate, from 11.8 to 7.8 percent, and a relatively constant rate of inflation of between 4 and 5 percent. In his February1990 budget speech, Finance Minister Michael Wilson projected the potential growth of the economy for 1990–95 period to average 3.4 percent per year, aided by the Canada–US Free Trade Agreement, by deregulation of the economy, and by tax reform, all of which he expected to create increased investment opportunities in Canada.[23]

ENDNOTES

1. J.M. Keynes, *General Theory of Employment, Interest and Money* (1936; reprint, London: Macmillan and Co. 1960).

2. The fundamentals of macroeconomic theory can be found in introductory macroeconomics textbooks. A more advanced analysis of macroeconomics and various developments in the theory, including supply-side economics and rational expectations theory, is presented in most intermediate macroeconomics texts. See for example, W.M. Scarth, *Macroeconomics: An Introduction to Advanced Methods* (Toronto: Harcourt Brace Jovanovich, Canada, 1988); F.R. Glahe, *Macroeconomics: Theory and Policy*, 3rd ed. (San Diego: Harcourt Brace Jovanovich, Publishers, 1985); D.A. Wilton and D.M. Prescott, *Macroeconomics Theory and Policy in Canada*, 2nd ed. (Don Mills: Addison-Wesley, 1987); R.E. Hall, J.B. Taylor, and J. Rudin, *Macroeconomics: The Canadian Economy* (New York: W.W. Norton, 1990); and R. Dornbusch, S. Fischer, and G. Sparks, *Macroeconomics* 3rd Cdn. ed. (Toronto: McGraw-Hill Ryerson, 1989).

3. The multiplier is given as $1/(1-b)$ where b is the marginal propensity to consume (defined as the change in consumption from an additional dollar of disposable income). For any given change in government expenditures, the change in total expenditures will be $1/(1-b)$ times the change in expenditure. The tax multiplier is smaller and is shown as $b/(1-b)$. For a change in government expenditures matched by a change in taxes, the multiplier equals one. This is known as the balanced budget theorem. A discussion of various multipliers is contained in most macroeconomics texts.

4. For a discussion of supply-side economics, see E. Raboy, ed., *Essays in Supply-Side Economics* (Washington, DC: Institute for Research on the Economics of Taxation, 1982); M. Evans, *Truth about Supply-Side Economics*, (New York: Basic Books, 1983); and P.C. Roberts, *The Supply-Side Revolution*, (Cambridge: Harvard University Press, 1984).

5. An explanation of the methodology employed by the Department of Finance to calculate structural balances is contained in Canada, Department of Finance, *The Federal Deficit in Perspective*, (Ottawa, April 1983); and Canada, Department of Finance, *The Fiscal Plan*, April 27, 1989 (Ottawa), pp. 107–9.

6. The federal Department of Finance advises caution in using the estimates of the structural balance it provided: "Due to the uncertainty associated with any estimates of adjusted output level and the static nature of the adjustments to revenues and expenditures, any calculated level of the cyclically-adjusted balance must be treated with considerable caution." *The Federal Deficit in Perspective*, pp. 57–58.

7. For a detailed description and analysis of the full employment budget balance concept, see A.S. Blinder and R.M. Solow, "Analytical Foundations of Fiscal Policy," in A.S. Blinder et al., *The Economics of Public Finance* (Washington, DC: The Brookings Insititute, 1974). See also J. Lotz, "Techniques of Measuring the Effects of Fiscal Policy," in *Economic Outlook, Occasional Studies* (Paris: Organisations for Economic Co-operation and Development, 1971).

8. For an explanation of the difference between the budget on a public accounts basis and the national accounts budget, see Canada, *The Fiscal Plan*, pp. 65–72.

9. The Unemployment Insurance Account is financed by employer and employee contributions, and benefits are paid to eligible unemployed workers; until 1990, deficits in this account were financed by government contributions. The Grain Stabilization Program, which is designed to stabilize grain prices, is financed by a combination of producer levies and government contributions. The Foreign Exchange Fund records investment earnings from Canada's foreign exchange holdings; although these earnings are reported as budgetary revenues, they remain in the fund and are not available to finance ongoing operations of government.

10. An explanation of the changes in the budgetary and nonbudgetary accounts is given in Canada, Department of Finance, *The Fiscal Plan*, February 1986 (Ottawa), pp. 73–78.

11. Canada, *The Fiscal Plan*, p. 67.

12. Economic Council of Canada, *First Annual Review, Economic Goals for Canada to 1970* (Ottawa, 1964). For other early discussions of fiscal policy goals, see T.N. Brewis, et al. *Canadian Economic Policy* (Toronto: MacMillan of Canada, 1961); Canada, The Royal Commission on Canada's Economic Prospects, *Final Report* (Ottawa, 1957); and John J. Deutsch, et al. *The Canadian Economy: Selected Readings* (Toronto: MacMillan of Canada, 1962).

13. Economic Council of Canada, *Legacies, Twenty-Sixth Annual Review 1989* (Ottawa: Supply and Services, 1989), p. 67.

14. Economic Council of Canada, *Lean Times, Policies and Constraints, Nineteenth Annual Review 1982* (Ottawa: Supply and Services, 1982), pp. 11–13.

15. For a description of labour market concepts and of the labour force survey, see Statistics Canada, *The Labour Force* (cat. 71–001, monthly).

16. Department of Finance, *Quarterly Economic Review 1990* (Ottawa, 1990), quarterly.

17. For a description of the Canadian consumer price index, see Statistics Canada, *The Consumer Price Index Reference Paper*, cat. 62–553 (Ottawa, 1989); and *The Consumer Price Index* (cat. 62–001, monthly).

18. A review of the issues concerning inflation is presented in J. Selody, *The Goal of Price Stability*, Bank of Canada Technical Report no. 54 (Ottawa, 1990).

19. John Crow, *The Work of Canadian Monetary Policy*, Eric J. Hanson Memorial Lecture University of Alberta, January 18, 1988.

20. See Canada, Department of Finance, *The Budget*, 1979 through 1983.

21. Economic Council of Canada, *Legacies, Twenty-Sixth Annual Review 1989* (Ottawa: Supply and Services, 1989), p. 67.

22. Economic Council of Canada, *Seventeenth Annual Review* (Ottawa, 1980), pp. 49–55.

23. Canada, Department of Finance, *The Budget*, February 20, 1990 (Ottawa) pp. 51–55.

CHAPTER 10

APPLICATION OF FISCAL POLICY IN CANADA

The Keynesian approach to economic stabilization was formally accepted by Canada in 1945 with the issue of a policy paper committing the government to the maintenance of high levels of employment and income in the economy. This chapter examines the federal government's application of discretionary fiscal policy for economic stabilization. The examination is from both a macroeconomic and a microeconomic perspective.

The macroeconomic indicator of fiscal policy is the budget balance on a national accounts basis, employing the three budget balance concepts discussed in the previous chapter.

- The actual budget balance.
- The structural budget balance, also called the cyclically adjusted budget balance, which is the actual budget balance with the cyclical component removed; in other words, it is the balance that would occur, given the existing structure of taxes, tax rates, and expenditure programs, if the economy were operating at an average level of activity.
- The primary structural budget balance, which is the structural balance minus public debt charges.

Actual, structural, and primary structural balances are presented in dollar amounts and as percentages of gross domestic product. The actual budget balance as a percentage of GDP provides an indication of the impact of the fiscal system on the economy. The differences between the actual budget balance and the structural budget balance suggests the effects of automatic stabilizers. The direction of discretionary fiscal policy is signified by the change in the primary structural balance between adjacent years. The primary structural balance as a percentage of GDP provides a gauge of the relative strength of the impact on the economy of discretionary fiscal policy. Movement toward a higher surplus or lower deficit implies a contractionary or restraining impact on the economy, while movement toward a lower surplus or higher deficit means an expansionary stance in discretionary policy. (Keep in mind, however, the qualifications regarding structural balances discussed in Chapter 9. Thus, they are used only as rough indicators of the shifts in the government's fiscal stance.)

The microeconomic approach to fiscal policy analysis involves an examination of specific fiscal measures, such as the introduction of new taxes, changes in existing taxes, and changes in expenditure programs. This approach is used to supplement the macroeconomic indicators in the analysis of fiscal policy in recognition of the fact that fiscal impact is not independent of the mix of discretionary tax and expenditure changes.

Four periods are identified for purposes of analysis — namely, the period following the Second World War to 1963, the 1963–74 period, the 1974–84 period, and the 1984–90 period. Economic conditions prevailing in each period are highlighted using the primary economic indicators of real changes in GDP, the unemployment rate, the employment growth rate, and the consumer price index (CPI). The budget balances and changes therein are examined, and specific discretionary tax and expenditure measures are highlighted. Particular attention is given to the more recent periods.

BACKGROUND

Before 1930, the doctrine of annually balanced budgets was firmly entrenched in Canadian economic thought. Taxes were regarded as a means of financing expenditure, and as expenditure changed, they were adjusted to balance the budget. There was no recognition of the possibility of the discretionary use of government expenditure and taxation to stabilize the economy. From the period 1935 to 1939, however, under the influence of the leading economists of the time, Canadian governments began to experiment with policies to stimulate economic activity and employment to end the Depression.

Thus, at the beginning of the Depression government policy was to attempt to maintain a balanced budget.[2] Despite tax increases, government revenues fell as income and production declined. Accordingly, attempts were made to hold down expenditures. Federal, provincial, and municipal governments reduced their spending between 1930 and 1933, and this move, coupled with high taxes, served to aggravate the economic decline. Even after the emergence of fiscal policy theory in the latter part of the decade, there appeared to be some reluctance on the part of the Canadian federal government to pursue expansionary fiscal measures actively.

At the outbreak of the Second World War in 1939, Canada was still experiencing a relatively high unemployment rate (12 percent). But the problems of unemployment and idle productive facilities disappeared in the war economy. As productive factors and materials were diverted to the war effort, the shortage of consumer goods and services began to place pressure on prices. The CPI increased by 18 percent between 1939 and late 1941. The Canadian government's answer to the rising prices was a wage and price freeze, which succeeded in containing inflation.[3]

Concern about the problems of the wartime economy did not, however, reduce concern about the problems that had plagued prewar Canada. It was anticipated that when the hostilities ended, the difficulties of the Depression would return and added to them would be dislocations the war had created in the economy. In 1945, in a policy white paper entitled *Employment and Income*, the Canadian government officially accepted "a high and stable level of employment and income, and thereby higher standards of living, as a major aim of government policy."[4] The white paper implicitly embraced Keynesian philosophy, proposed the use of the budget for purposes of fiscal policy, and subscribed to planned budgetary surpluses and deficits.

The difficulties of the postwar reconstruction period did not arise with the severity that had been envisaged. Reconversion took place rapidly, and the demand for consumer and durable goods that had been repressed during the war period not only kept productive facilities operating at capacity but provided for rapid expansion.[5]

Thus, immediately after the war, the objectives that had been declared to be of primary importance were achieved mostly through the market mechanism. But if anyone believed that economic instability belonged to the past and that the market mechanism alone was capable of achieving and sustaining the objectives stated in 1945, this illusion was to be shattered in subsequent years. Since 1946, the Canadian economy has experienced periods of rapid economic growth and prosperity, recession and unemployment, inflation, and a combination of inflation and unemployment.

Postwar Years: 1947–1963

Table 10–1 illustrates the trends in the major economic indicators during this period.[1] The primary concern in the immediate postwar period was inflation as consumer demand that had been pent up during the war was released and tended to outstrip supply.

TABLE 10–1
Canada: Primary Economic Indicators for 1947–1963

	Change in real GDP[a]	Unemployment rate	Employment growth rate[b]	Change in CPI
		(percent)		
1947	1.8	2.2		9.4
1948	1.5	2.3		14.5
1949	4.5	2.8		3.1
1950	7.8	3.6		2.8
1951	4.5	2.4		10.6
1952	8.3	2.9		2.5
1953	5.0	3.0		−0.9
1954	−1.1	4.6	1.2	0.6
1955	9.5	4.4	5.7	0.2
1956	8.6	3.4	5.8	1.4
1957	2.5	4.6	4.1	3.2
1958	2.2	7.0	−1.6	2.7
1959	3.9	6.0	4.0	1.1
1960	2.9	7.0	−1.0	1.2
1961	3.1	7.1	2.1	0.9
1962	7.1	5.9	4.6	1.3
1963	5.2	5.5	3.6	1.9

[a] In constant 1986 dollars.

[b] Statistics Canada series on employment growth rates start in the mid-1950s.

Source: Canada, Department of Finance, *Economic Review*, 1974 (Ottawa); and *Quarterly Economic Review, Annual Reference Tables*, 1990 (Ottawa).

The government's response to these inflationary pressures was to remove wartime price controls only gradually. Taxes were reduced during this period. Although tax reduction during a period of inflation may appear contrary to accepted fiscal policy doctrine, taxes during the war had been exceedingly high relative to prewar levels and there was considerable public pressure to have them reduced once hostilities had ended. Government policy was to gradually reduce those taxes considered to be impeding work and production but otherwise to maintain taxes as high as reasonably practical in attempts to dampen aggregate demand. Combined with large reductions in defence spending, this policy produced large budgetary surpluses. Given the economic conditions during this period of reconstruction and adjustment, the government's fiscal policy can be considered appropriate.

The beginning of the Korean War brought rapidly rising prices. The CPI jumped 10.6 percent during 1951, partly because of the increase in government defence spending and partly because of public fear of wartime shortages, which brought a large increase in demand for consumer durables. The government responded with a policy of retrenchment in nondefence expenditure and substantial tax increases to finance the defence build-up. The tax changes included extension of the excise tax to a large number of commodities and an increase in existing excises; a 20 percent defence surcharge on corporate and personal income taxes; an increase in the manufacturers' sales tax from 8 to 10 percent; and deferrence of depreciation on capital expenditures. In addition, the government attempted to restrain the buying public with a policy restricting consumer credit. These measures can be viewed as textbook fiscal policy to combat demand-pull inflationary pressures. These discretionary measures combined with the automatic stabilizers to produce budget surpluses and a contractionary fiscal tone, contributing to bringing inflation under control.

After the Korean War, following a short period of adjustment, the Canadian economy prospered. As shown in Figure 10–1, large actual surpluses were recorded, but they were primarily cyclical, produced by a rapidly growing economy.

The government's first major challenge in antirecessionary fiscal policy occurred with the recession that began in 1957 and was to continue into the early 1960s. Numerous factors combined to produce this recession. The period of prosperity in the mid-1950s had fostered major increases in capital investment and the accumulation of inventories. Heavy investment in plant construction and industrial machinery had produced considerable excess capacity, with the result that during 1958 and 1959 investment declined by 33 percent from its 1957 level. The manufacturing index had increased at an average annual rate of 8.1 percent during the 1954–57 period. With the accumulation of inventories, it declined by 8.4 percent in 1958. Furthermore, massive investment projects in the resource industries and in transportation, such as the building of the Trans-Canada Highway and the St. Lawrence Seaway, were completed at almost the same time, and few projects replaced them. There was also a huge increase in the labour force, partly a result of a record level of immigration in 1957 and partly through an expanded participation rate. This rapid growth in the labour force, coming at a time when the economy was slowing down and fewer new jobs were being created, contributed to a rate of unemployment of 7.0 percent in 1958, a comparatively high rate for the period.

FIGURE 10–1
Actual and Structural Budget Balance, 1953–1963
Percentage of GNP[a]

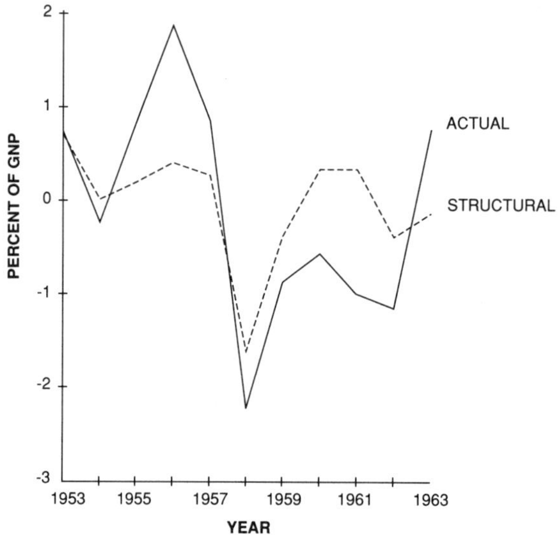

[a] Actual balances are shown as a percentage of actual GNP. Structural budget balances are calculated as a percentage of cyclically adjusted GNP.

Source: Canada, Department of Finance, *Economic Review*, April 1980 (Ottawa), p. 226.

Fiscal policy fluctuated during this recession, partly because of a misreading of economic conditions. The structural balance (as a percentage of GNP) tended to exert an expansionary effect, then a contractionary one, and then another expansionary influence (see Figure 10–1). This tone of fiscal policy can also be observed in the specific measures that were introduced. In 1958, discretionary measures consisted mostly of expenditure increases for social security, economic development, housing and community works, and a winter works employment program. Restrictive fiscal measures were introduced in 1959 with an increase in government spending of only 4.3 percent and an increase in personal and corporation taxes of 2.0 percent. It was clearly the wrong policy for a relatively stagnant economy with an unemployment rate of 7.0 percent. The return to expansionary measures in 1960 included a reduction in the corporate income tax, a repeal of the 4.0 percent surtax on investment income and of the 7.5 percent excise tax on automobiles, a policy of double depreciation for new industry locating in areas of chronic unemployment, and incentives for scientific research and productivity improvement. It should be noted that toward the end of this period, rather than relying primarily on expenditure policies in its fiscal policy mix, the government began to place greater stress on taxation, particularly in the form of tax incentives to industry.

ECONOMIC GROWTH: 1963–1974

As Table 10–2 illustrates, most of this period was characterized by a relatively high rate of economic growth. Only in 1967, 1970, and 1974 was the annual increase in real GDP less than 5 percent. The years of strong GDP growth were generally accompanied by relatively high rates of employment growth. High inflation rates threatened in the late 1960s but did not become a problem until the end of the period. The unemployment rate fell during the early period and then fluctuated, reaching 6.2 percent in 1971 and 1972 before again declining.

In each year of this period, the primary structural budget recorded a surplus, as shown in Table 10–3. The direction of the changes in this surplus indicate that discretionary policy was expansionary in the 1964 to 1966 period and in 1969 to 1972, and restrictive in the years 1966 to 1969 and 1972 to 1974 (see Figure 10–2). Given the inflationary tendencies during the latter two spans, the restrictive policy appears to have been appropriate. The expansionary policy between 1969 and 1972 also appears to have been appropriate, given a rising unemployment rate and relatively low employment growth. Not so obvious, however, was the need for expansionary measures between 1964 and 1966, a time of strong economic growth, rising employment growth, and falling unemployment. Inflation began to build during this period with an increase in the CPI of 3.5 percent by 1966.

TABLE 10–2
Canada: Primary Economic Indicators for 1963–1974

	Change in real GDP[a]	Unemployment rate	Employment growth rate	Change in CPI
		(percent)		
1963	5.2	5.5	2.4	1.9
1964	6.7	4.7	3.7	1.8
1965	6.6	3.9	3.8	2.4
1966	6.8	3.4	4.2	3.5
1967	2.9	3.8	2.9	3.7
1968	5.4	4.5	1.9	4.1
1969	5.4	4.4	3.1	4.5
1970	2.6	5.7	1.1	3.3
1971	5.8	6.2	2.3	2.9
1972	5.7	6.2	3.0	4.7
1973	7.7	5.5	5.0	7.7
1974	4.4	5.3	4.2	10.9

[a] In constant 1986 dollars

Source: See Table 10–1.

FIGURE 10–2
Actual, Structural, and Primary Structural Budget Balance, 1963–1974
Percentage of GDP[a]

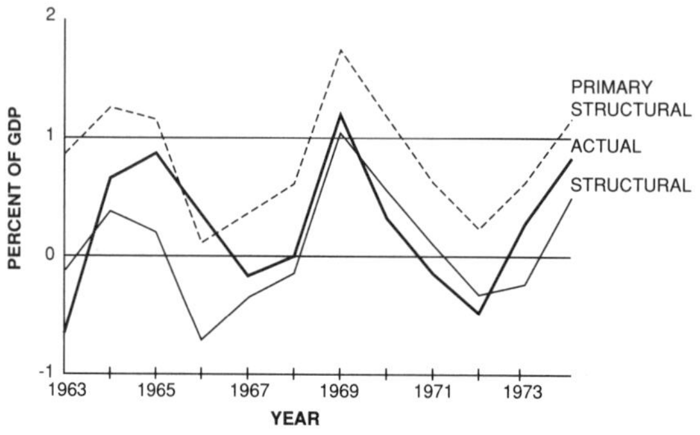

[a] Actual balances are shown as a percentage of actual GDP. Structural and primary structural balances are shown as a percentage of cyclically adjusted GDP.

Source: Canada, Department of Finance, *Quarterly Economic Review, Annual Reference Tables*, 1990 (Ottawa), p. 107

An examination of tax and expenditures changes from 1964 through 1966 shows numerous expansionary measures. Expenditure measures included a municipal winter works incentive program to combat seasonal unemployment; a $400 million fund from which municipalities could borrow for approved projects with a high employment content; a winter housing bonus program providing a grant of $500 to the first purchaser of a home constructed between the months of December and March; and a system of grants to encourage industrial development in depressed areas. A number of programs were introduced to improve labour mobility and reduce bottlenecks in the labour market, including a program for retraining older workers, a relocation fund to help cover workers' moving expenses, and financial assistance to industry to help defray the cost of research into the effect of technological change on employment and personnel utilization. Expansionary tax measures included accelerated depreciation and a three-year tax holiday for new manufacturing and processing firms locating in designated areas; reduction of the corporation income tax on income from increased sales (by 50 percent on the first $50 000 and by 25 percent on the remainder); a deduction of 150 percent of expenditures on scientific research for industrial purposes; accelerated depreciation, permitting new investment in machines and equipment to be written off in two years, to encourage firms to modernize; and an across-the-board personal income tax cut of 10 percent of the basic tax.

The threat of inflation in 1967 caused the government to rescind some of its earlier tax reductions and to impose new taxes to dampen aggregate demand. They included a 3 percent surtax on the personal income tax, a social development tax of 2 percent on taxable income, increased excises on tobacco and liquor, and accelerated corporation income tax payments. The effects of these discretionary tax increases were reflected in a substantial increase in the primary structural surplus from $231 million in 1967 to

$1382 million in 1969 — a 1 percent increase when measured as a percentage of GDP. By 1970, with the assistance of a voluntary wage-price control program, prices had stabilized. The government had achieved its goal of stabilizing prices, but not without cost. The unemployment rate had risen from 3.8 percent in 1967 to 5.7 percent in 1970, and the increase in real GDP had dropped to 2.6 percent.

In his budget speeches, the Minister of Finance placed priority on the problem of unemployment from 1970 to 1972. The introduction of a number of further expansionary measures reduced the primary structural surplus. They included removal of the 3 percent surtax on the personal and corporate income taxes; further reduction of the personal income tax by 3 percent and the corporate income tax by 7 percent for 1972; removal of the 15 percent excise tax on radios, television sets, and stereos; and elimination of the income tax on persons with taxable incomes of $500 or less. Expenditure programs that were expanded included personnel training, housing, grants and loans to provincial and municipal governments to finance job-creating public works programs, and grants and incentives to industry to locate in depressed areas to alleviate regional unemployment problems. By 1973, the employment growth rate had reached 5 percent and unemployment had begun to fall, but serious inflation loomed on the horizon and the government turned to restrictive anti-inflationary measures.

The inflationary surge that began in 1973 pushed the CPI up by 10.9 percent in 1974. Inflation, which was practically worldwide, was rooted in international developments including rapid increases in aggregate demand for many primary products, shortages caused by supply disruptions in agricultural markets, and the decision of the international oil cartel to raise prices substantially.[6] As the effects of these developments began to be reflected in rising consumer prices, inflationary expectations strengthened. Workers expecting persistent price increases were demanding higher and higher wages and salaries in attempts to protect their real incomes. Contributing to the inflationary pressures of this period was a massive increase in the money supply (see Figure 10–3) and a decrease in productivity.

The government's announced policy in 1973 was to attempt to combat both unemployment and inflation. Emphasis was placed on tax reductions designed to stimulate output and employment and, at the same time, to ease the pressures on prices. Personal exemptions were increased, the personal income tax was reduced by 5 percent, the manufacturers' sales tax on childrens' clothing and footwear was abolished, and tariffs on a wide range of imports were reduced by an average of 5 percent. The Minister of Finance expressed the hope that the tax reductions would be taken into account as representing increases in disposable income during negotiations on wage settlements.

Despite the announced tax reductions in 1973, the actual and structural budgets showed increased surpluses by the end of 1973 and 1974. They were partly the result of the tax reform introduced in 1972. It had broadened the income tax base (including a tax on capital gains), and certain tax increases did not come into effect until 1973 and 1974. The expenditure structure was also changing, producing a reduction in the rate of increase in federal spending. In this period of inflationary pressures, the aggregate restrictive stance of discretionary policy was in the right direction and was supplemented by the fiscal drag exerted by the automatic stabilizers.

FIGURE 10–3
Financial Developments, 1971–1989
Money Supply Changes and Interest Rate Levels

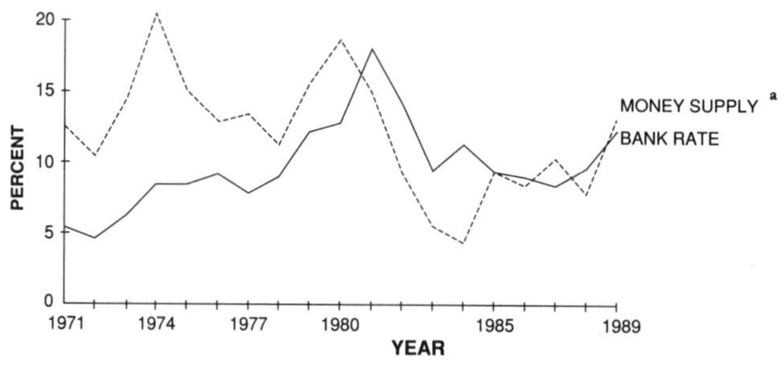

[a] Percentage change in Money Supply (designated as M2 by the Bank of Canada) consisting of currency plus all chequable, notice, and term deposits.

Source: Canada, Department of Finance, *Quarterly Economic Review, Annual Reference Tables*, June, 1990 (Ottawa), p. 107.

Overall, the Canadian government's application of fiscal policy during 1947 to 1972 followed the Keynesian remedy and can be viewed as reasonably appropriate, given the economic conditions that prevailed. In terms of achieving stated fiscal goals, the economy's overall performance for this period proved much better than the record for the years following 1974, albeit the problems of the later period were considerably more complex. It could be contended that the economy of 1947 to 1974 more closely resembled the tradeoff pattern illustrated by the Phillips curve, characterized by periods of unemployment *or* inflationary pressures and periods of reasonably low unemployment coupled with reasonably stable prices. Traditional fiscal policy is more readily applicable in such a pattern as compared to the economic conditions that prevailed during the later 1970s and the early 1980s. Indeed, although the actual federal budget balance fluctuated between surpluses and deficits during the 1947–72 period, the net balance was close to zero over the period as a whole. This pattern was to change after 1974 when the government incurred continuous and substantial budgetary deficits as recorded by the actual and structural budget balances and with two exemptions, on the primary budget balance as well.

Fiscal Dilemma: 1974–1984

The economic period from 1974 through the early 1980s produced a major dilemma for fiscal policy in most Western countries, including Canada, as inflationary surges combined with unemployment rates higher than any experienced since the Depression. The developments shook many economists' and governments' confidence in the traditional fiscal policy of aggregate demand management. Alternative methods to combat the problems were attempted on a wide scale; they included wage and price regulation, supply-side management, and increased emphasis on monetary policy. When prices finally stabilized in 1983 and unemployment began to fall, the federal government was left with the problem of very high annual budgetary deficits as illustrated in Table 10–3.

TABLE 10–3
Federal government Actual, Structural, and Primary Structural Budget Balances for 1963–1989

	Actual	Structural[a]	Primary structural[b]
		($ million)	
1963	–303	–119	366
1964	330	188	676
1965	517	140	665
1966	201	–450	84
1967	–108	–289	231
1968	–36	–152	448
1969	994	885	1 382
1970	247	439	1 042
1971	–139	72	608
1972	–530	–415	176
1973	434	–392	695
1974	1 268	629	1 902
1975	–3 823	–3 212	–1 532
1976	–3 337	–3 421	–1 277
1977	–7 343	–7 354	–4 946
1978	–10 854	–11 024	–7 738
1979	–9 383	–10 070	–5 353
1980	–10 663	–10 303	–4 173
1981	–7 315	–7 454	1 780
1982	–20 281	–13 260	–1 585
1983	–24 993	–17 778	–5 761
1984	–30 024	–25 756	–10 581
1985	–31 424	–29 453	–10 999
1986	–23 617	–22 670	–3 077
1987	–21 613	–22 670	–1 688
1988	–20 862	–24 932	–754
1989	–23 082	–27 232	2 026

[a] The structural balance is an estimate of the budget balance adjusted for cyclical influences.
[b] The primary structural budget balance is the structural balance exclusive of net interest payments.

Source: Canada, Department of Finance, *Quarterly Economic Review, Annual Reference Tables*, June 1990 (Ottawa), p. 106.

The years 1974 to 1982 were characterized by erratic economic growth, high rates of unemployment, and high rates of inflation as shown in Table 10–4. Discretionary fiscal policy was largely expansionary from 1974 through 1978. As shown in Figure 10–4, the primary structural balance changed from a surplus of about 1.1 percent of GDP to a deficit of 3.2 percent of GDP. Discretionary policy then turned restrictive, and the primary structural balance returned to a surplus position by 1981. It is noteworthy that during the 1974–82 period, the actual and the structural budget balances were practically identical, implying that the budget balance was essentially structural – that very little of the deficit was attributable to automatic stabilizers.

A development that tended to reduce the degree of built-in stability in the budget was the policy, begun in 1974, of indexing elements of the personal income tax by the full amount of inflation. Indexation tended to reduce the automatic stabilizing influence inherent in the structure of the tax. In a period of inflation, indexation of the tax has the same effect as a discretionary tax reduction.

TABLE 10–4
Canada: Primary Economic Indicators for 1974–1991

	Change in real GDP[a]	Unemployment rate	Employment growth rate	Change in CPI
		(percent)		
1974	4.4	5.3	4.2	10.9
1975	2.6	6.9	1.7	10.8
1976	6.2	7.1	2.1	7.5
1977	3.6	8.1	1.8	7.9
1978	4.6	8.3	3.5	8.8
1979	3.9	7.4	4.1	9.2
1980	1.5	7.5	3.0	10.2
1981	3.7	7.5	2.7	12.5
1982	–3.2	11.0	–3.5	10.8
1983	3.2	11.8	0.5	5.8
1984	6.3	11.2	2.4	4.4
1985	4.8	10.5	2.6	4.0
1986	3.3	9.5	2.8	4.1
1987	4.0	8.8	2.9	4.4
1988	4.4	7.8	3.2	4.1
1989	3.0	7.5	2.0	5.0
1990[b]	1.3	8.5	0.8	4.7
1991[b]	3.0	8.5	1.2	5.1

[a] In constant 1986 dollars.
[b] Projections by the Department of Finance.

Source: Canada, Department of Finance, *Quarterly Economic Review, Annual Reference Tables*, June 1990, (Ottawa); and *Budget*, February 20, 1990 (Ottawa).

Inflation Concern: 1975–1978

The year 1975 witnessed a stagnant economy with an increase in real GDP of only 2.6 percent and an unemployment rate of 6.9 percent, coupled with price increases of 10.8 percent. The Minister of Finance analyzed the inflation as being of the cost-push variety, arising from escalating domestic costs of production in an underemployed economy. Low productivity gains combined with relatively high labour compensation (see Table 10-5) tended to put pressure on prices. The government tried but failed to obtain a consensus from business and labour on a framework for voluntary wage and price restraints.

The focus of discretionary fiscal policy was on supply and featured tax incentives to stimulate output and employment. They included an investment tax credit against the corporation income tax equal to 5 percent of investment in new buildings, machinery, and equipment (increased to 7.5 percent and 10 percent in designated areas of chronically high unemployment); a 3 percent deduction on inventories held at the beginning of a corporation's fiscal year for profit calculation; and a reduction in the manufacturers' sales tax from 12 to 9 percent. The substantial drop in the primary structural balance, from a surplus to a deficit position between 1974 and 1978, was partly attributable to these discretionary tax reductions and partly to major increases in government program spending, which averaged 12.4 percent annually. (Recall that only program spending appears in the primary structural budget.)

FIGURE 10–4
Actual, Structural, and Primary Structural Budget Balance, 1973–1990
Percentage of GDP[a]

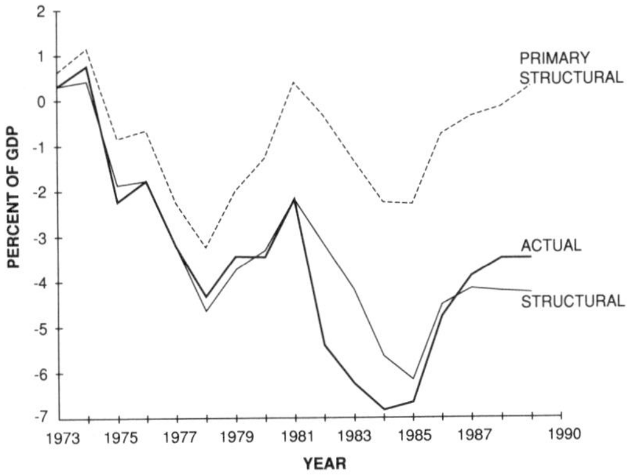

[a] Actual balances are shown as a percentage of actual GDP. Structural and primary structual balances are shown as a percentage of cyclically adjusted GDP.

Source: Canada, Department of Finance, *Quarterly Economic Review, Annual Reference Tables*, June 1990 (Ottawa), p. 107.

During 1975, the rise in prices continued unabated, and in October, the government finally adopted a program of mandatory wage and price regulation to bring inflation under control. The government expected that its continued efforts to stimulate output, combined with an improving world economy, would gradually reduce unemployment, while its wage and price regulations, which it announced would continue for three years, would bring inflation under control. From 1975 to 1976, inflation was reduced from 10.8 to approximately 7.5 percent. Despite this reduction, the government maintained that strong inflationary pressures were still present. It therefore continued the wage-price control program and resisted pressures to introduce massive temporary expenditure programs to combat unemployment, which reached a post–Second World War high of 8.3 percent in 1978.

Stagflation: 1979–1983

In the spring of 1979, the Liberal government was defeated and a minority Conservative government elected. The new government announced a "new approach" to Canada's economic problems. As explained by the Minister of Finance John Crosbie, the general policy was to "focus more . . . on the medium- and long-term potential opportunities of the country and less upon fine-tuning in the short-run."[7] Concern was expressed about the high unemployment and inflation rates, the country's poor productivity record (see Table 10-5), the rapid rise in government expenditure, and the sizeable government deficits. The announced objective of fiscal policy was to reduce the budget deficits gradually and bring down the rate of inflation.

The Conservative government never had an opportunity to implement its programs, however, because it was defeated in a vote on the budget, and the ensuing election returned a majority Liberal government.

Faced with slow economic growth, high unemployment, and double-digit inflation — a combination called stagflation — the new government announced a fiscal policy of balancing restraint to combat inflation with measures to promote economic growth to reduce unemployment. Successive budget speeches also hammered at the need to bring government expenditure growth under control and to reduce the size of the deficit. Revenue-raising measures included a corporate income surtax and a tax on petroleum, natural gas, and gas liquids. The latter tax was to yield almost $3 billion in annual revenues and contributed to the substantial reduction recorded in the primary structural deficit by 1981.

Nevertheless, the government's fiscal position worsened sharply during 1982. The change was largely attributed to the decline in GDP by 3.2 percent, a fall that had not been expected. The effects of the automatic budgetary stabilizers, together with discretionary policy changes, caused federal revenues to increase by only $1 billion while expenditures rose by $14 billion in that year, and the actual deficit jumped from $7 billion to more than $20 billion. On the tax side, the government had been forced to reduce its taxes on petroleum as international oil prices began to fall. At the same time, government expenditure rose, driven by such factors as the increased costs of servicing the public debt as interest rates soared, increased unemployment insurance payments, and increased discretionary expenditures for job creation. In an attempt to restrain

TABLE 10–5
Canada: Productivity and Costs 1974–1989

	Service industries		Manufacturing industries	
	Output per person employed	Labour compensation per person employed	Output per person employed	Labour compensation per person employed
	(percentage change)			
1974	–1.0	12.3	0.9	14.3
1975	1.0	11.7	–4.5	13.2
1976	3.5	13.0	6.8	14.3
1977	–1.2	6.8	5.9	11.0
1978	0.8	5.2	1.3	7.8
1979	1.2	8.9	0.2	9.3
1980	0.6	10.2	–4.2	10.3
1981	–0.3	9.3	3.6	13.8
1982	–2.6	9.4	–5.6	9.4
1983	2.0	3.7	8.7	7.4
1984	3.2	6.0	9.6	5.9
1985	0.1	3.6	2.9	5.1
1986	2.9	5.1	–1.2	3.8
1987	2.8	7.3	2.7	6.1
1988	2.5	6.0	3.2	6.5
1989	0.9	7.4	1.0	7.2

Source: Canada, Department of Finance, *Quarterly Economic Review, Annual Reference Tables,* June 1990 (Ottawa) pp. 69, 71.

government spending, a pay restraint was imposed on the federal public sector. Increases in public servants' wages were limited to 6 percent in 1983 and 5 percent in 1984. (Many provincial governments followed suit.) This "6 and 5" pay restraint was expected not only to save the federal government about $500 million, but also to lead the private sector to restrain wage demands voluntarily and help control cost-push inflation pressures. The "6 and 5" policy was applied to other areas as well. Ceilings of 6 percent for 1983 and 5 percent for 1984 were placed on the indexing factors applicable to the personal income tax, family allowances and old age security payments, public servants' pensions, and postsecondary education transfers to provinces under the established programs financing (EPF) agreement. These measures were estimated to produce annual savings of $3 billion. They were offset, however, by announced expenditure initiatives and tax reductions to stimulate employment. A special recovery program planned over four years offered $2.2 billion for capital projects and $2.4 billion of special incentives for private investment. Other discretionary measures included more attractive depletion provisions for the mining industry; lower energy taxes; additional funds to spur housing construction; an additional $710 million over two years for new and expanded employment initiatives, including retraining programs and student summer employment; and increased support for research and development. These expansionary measures increased the primary structural deficit to more than $10.5 billion or 2.3 percent of GDP by 1984 and, combined with rising public debt charges and automatic stabilizers, increased the actual budget deficit to more than $30 billion.

Inflation, a problem since the early 1970s that was international in scope, finally showed signs of moderating in late 1982. By early 1984, it had been reduced to 4.5 percent. Although the decline resulted from numerous factors, including falling energy prices and a moderation in international inflation, the government of Canada like that of the United States, had relied primarily on monetary policy in combating inflation. Unprecedented high interest rates between 1979 and 1982 (see Figure 10–3) were a major factor in dampening inflationary pressures, even though they contributed to the seriousness of the recession both countries experienced during this period.

Economic Stability and Rising Public Debt: 1984–1990

By 1984, the economy was on the road to recovery from the recession of the early years of the decade. Economic growth produced a steady increase in job creation, and employment began to grow more than 2 percent per year. The economy continued to expand at a reasonably healthy pace, with moderate inflation, through the remainder of the 1980s, and unemployment was gradually reduced to 7.5 percent by 1989.

The main problem the government faced in its budgets during this period was the continuation of large budget deficits. Despite the strong economy, discretionary tax increases almost annually and attempts at expenditure restraint, the government was unable to bring its actual budget deficit to less than $20 billion or its structural deficit to less than $22 billion. The tone of discretionary fiscal policy was contractionary. Discretionary measures featured tax increases and reductions in the rate of increase in program spending, which gradually reduced the primary structural deficit until a surplus was recorded in 1989. The size of the structural and actual deficits remained very similar from 1985 through 1987; after that year, the structural deficit exceeded the actual. In this latter period, both the automatic stabilizers and discretionary measures acted to reduce the deficit but were offset by the large increases in the interest on the public debt. (It is worth noting that the 1986 reduction of the indexation factor applicable to the personal income tax — to the amount that inflation exceeded 3 percent – tended to enhance the automatic stabilizing influence inherent in the tax.)

The general election of September 1984 brought to power a Conservative government with a huge majority, and fiscal policy came under the direction of Minister of Finance Michael Wilson for the remainder of the decade. The new government immediately embarked on a program of "economic renewal" highlighted by three major objectives: control the national debt, manage government more effectively, and invest in productive activities to promote economic growth and job creation. The focus of budgetary policy was "to control the dangerous trend of rising debt,"[8] but the Finance Minister cautioned that this goal had to be balanced with the other fiscal goals of maintaining economic growth and reducing unemployment.

Federal budgets from 1985 through 1990 contained numerous measures designed to achieve the stated fiscal goals. Government announcements kept reasserting the need for reduction in the growth of government spending, coupled with selective tax changes to stimulate sectors of the economy and numerous tax increases designed to raise additional revenues for deficit reduction. Table 10–6 outlines the tax changes made during this period. Only in his February 1990 budget did Finance Minister Wilson proudly announce that "there will be no new taxes in this budget,"[9] undoubtedly much to the relief of most tax-paying Canadians.

TABLE 10–6
Federal Tax Changes, 1985–1989

	Change
1985	A lifetime capital gains exemption of $500 000
	A 1 percent increase in the manufacturers' sales tax to 11 percent
	Increases in excises on cigarettes, tobacco, alcohol, and gasoline
	A tax on the capital of banks and trust companies
	A surtax on higher income individuals
	A surtax on larger corporations
1986	Replacement of the 1985 surtaxes with a 3 percent surtax on federal personal income taxes and on corporation income taxes
	An increase in the manufacturers' sales tax to 12 percent
	Reductions in the general corporation income tax rate from 36 to 33 percent
	A reduction in the investment tax credit from one-half to one-third of the cash dividends received from Canadian companies
	A 4 percent increase in excises on alcohol
	A 6 percent increase in excises on tobacco
	Reduction in indexation of the personal income tax: tax brackets and exemption to be increased only by the amount that inflation exceeds 3 percent
1987	Increases in the excises on gasoline, cigarettes, and tobacco products
	Extension of the manufacturers' sales tax to cover snack foods
1988	Reform of the personal income tax, estimated to reduce revenues from it by $2.4 billion by 1992
	Reform of the corporation income tax, estimated to increase revenues from it by $1.5 billion by 1992
1989	Increase in the personal income surtax from 3 to 5 percent with an additional 3 percent new surtax for high-income individuals
	Increases in the excise on alcohol, tobacco, and gasoline
	An increase in the manufacturers' sales tax to 13.5 percent
	Imposition of a large corporations tax
	Imposition of the "clawback tax" on family allowances and Old Age Security payments received by higher-income individuals

TABLE 10–7
Budgetary Program Expenditures and Public Debt Charges, 1984–1990
(public accounts basis)

	1974–84[a]	1984–85	1985–86	1986–87	1987–88	1988–89	1989–90	1990–91[b]
				(percentage change)				
Program expenditures	12.0	10.5	-1.1	4.6	7.6	3.1	4.0	3.0
Public debt charges[c]	21.4	24.2	13.3	4.8	8.9	14.3	18.7	4.4
Total budgetary expenditures	13.4	13.0	1.8	4.6	7.9	5.7	7.7	3.4

[a] Average annual change.
[b] Estimated by the Department of Finance. Estimate of public debt charges is based on a forecast decline in interest rates. By spring 1990, however, the bank rate had risen to more than 14 percent.
[c] Changes in public debt reflect changes both in the size of the debt and in interest rate levels. The trend in interest rates in the economy, as reflected by the average bank rate, were11.3 percent in 1984, 9.6 percent in 1985; 9.2 percent in 1986; 8.4 percent in 1987; 9.7 percent in 1988; 12.5 percent in 1989.

Source: Canada, Department of Finance, *The Fiscal Plan*, (Ottawa), various issues.

As part of its expenditure control program and its pledge to manage government more effectively, the government in late 1984 appointed the Ministerial Task Force on Program Review to undertake a detailed examination of government expenditure programs with the purpose of eliminating unnecessary and obsolete programs, increasing the efficiency of the remainder, and reducing the size of the public service. Regulations that hampered business efficiency were to be streamlined or eliminated if possible. Crown corporations with no public policy purpose were to be sold in a program of privatization of government enterprise. Subsidies to agriculture, transportation, and other business were also to be reduced.

The government was reasonably successful in reducing the growth of its program expenditures (defined as total expenditures less public debt charges). As shown in Table 10–7, the average annual increase in program expenditures had been 12.0 percent during the 1974–84 period. This figure was reduced to 4.8 percent for the 1984–89 period.

The reduction in the growth rate of program spending was achieved on a variety of fronts. Savings were realized through cuts in subsidies for energy, transportation, and direct business activity; greater efficiency in government operations, including a reduction of 10 000 in authorized person-years; reductions in unemployment insurance payments as unemployment fell; reduced subsidies to Crown corporations, including Canada Post, which was made self-sufficient; and limitations to the indexation of family allowance payments and EPF transfers to provinces. At the same time, the privatization program was continued with the sale of Crown corporations, including Canadair, de Havilland, Canadian Arsenals, Fishery Products International, Air Canada, and Teleglobe. Privatization, the government maintained, would bring "increased vitality and efficiency to both the corporation and the economy."[10] It also reduced the need for government subsidies to these corporations whenever they incurred financial difficulties.

In his February 1990 budget, Finance Minister Wilson announced further action to reduce the deficit, including a number of expenditure reductions. A slowdown in the economy was forecast, along with rising unemployment. Inflationary pressures, however, had begun to build during 1989, and the minister emphasized the importance of controlling inflation to maintain Canada's competitiveness in international markets and to achieve long-term stability and economic growth. He maintained that reduction of the deficit would have a contractionary fiscal impact on the economy that would complement restrictive monetary policy and help to control inflation.

In a major attack on government expenditure increases, the government announced the introduction of a two-year expenditure control program. It eliminated some government programs, identified others (mostly basic social programs) as not to be subject to cuts, and specified restraints for most of the others. The government claimed that the fiscal impact of these expenditure control measures would amount to more than \$3 billion in 1990/91 and a savings of \$19.4 billion over a five-year period.

The expenditure restraints that stirred up the most controversy were those placed on federal transfer payments to the provinces. Transfers under the Canada Assistance Plan (CAP), which had been based on 50:50 cost-sharing of eligible provincial spending, were limited to a 5 percent increase per year in the three wealthiest provinces —

Ontario, British Columbia, and Alberta. Transfers under EPF were frozen to the 1989/90 per capita amount for a two-year period. These constraints were expected to save the federal government approximately $2 billion in 1999/2.

The announcement of restrictions on transfers to the provinces was a federal attempt to gain some control over these statutory expenditures, which had been increasing at an annual average rate of 4.5 percent since 1984/85 — faster than the 3.6 percent annual average growth rate in total program spending. The Finance Minister justified his actions by saying that the deficit was a national problem demanding a national solution and "provincial governments must do their part."[11]

Predictably, the provincial governments expressed outrage at what they viewed as the transfer to them of the burden of federal deficit reduction, and they claimed that Ottawa's actions could force them to increase their taxes, reduce expenditures for the programs concerned, or both. British Columbia, supported by Manitoba, launched legal action against Ottawa for what it said was a unilateral federal action contrary to the legal terms of the federal/provincial agreement governing CAP payments. In June 1990, the British Columbia Court of Appeal rendered a decision in favour of the provinces. It ruled unanimously that the federal government did not have the power to limit its obligation to contribute 50 percent of CAP payments and by a majority of four to one that the provinces had a legitimate expectation that Ottawa would seek their consent before changing the terms of its obligation.

By early 1991, the Canadian economy was experiencing a major recession. Partly fueled by the introduction of the GST, the annual rate of inflation jumped from 5 percent in December 1990 to 6.8 percent in January 1991. At the same time, real GDP contracted by 1.2 percent in the last half of 1990 and unemployment increased to 9.7 percent by January 1991. In this economic environment, Finance Minister Wilson introduced his 1991/2 fiscal year budget on February 26, 1991.[12] Predicting that the recession would end by the middle of 1991, Wilson reiterated his long-standing position on the need for reducing the federal deficit, which precluded any major increases in government spending to combat the recession. Nevertheless, program spending was expected to increase by 6.9 percent for 1991/2, partly caused by rising unemployment insurance payments and farm-support payments to counter the effects of depressed markets. Revenue-raising measures, expected to increase revenues by $3.4 billion, consisted of an increase in tobacco taxes and a 24 percent increase in unemployment insurance premiums. In addition, it was announced that public service wage increases would be held to 3 percent a year for the next three years, and the earlier introduced restrictions on transfer payments to the provinces were extended for 3 additional years. The government pinned its hopes for an end to the recession on declining interest rates, which were expected to fall from an average of 13.0 percent in 1990 to 9.5 percent during 1991. Inflation was also expected to stabilize at between 4 and 5 percent during 1991, and an inflation target of 3.0 percent was set for the end of 1992.

The Minister of Finance proposed two major initiatives for deficit reduction. He announced plans to legislate mandatory spending limits that would restrict program spending increases to an average of 3 percent annually for a five year period. Plans were also announced for the establishment of a Debt-Servicing and Reduction-Fund to be used to pay the interest on the national debt. The fund was expected to be financed with revenue from the goods and services tax as well as revenue raised from the sale of Crown corporations.

The Deficit Dilemma

Deficits were recorded in the federal government budget every year from 1975 to 1991. The actual deficits in the earlier part of this period resulted from a combination of automatic stabilizers and deliberate expansionary fiscal policy measures. Beginning in 1984, however, the government committed itself to a policy of deficit reduction. Yet the primary structural deficit was not eliminated until 1989, and there was only modest success in reducing the actual budgetary deficit.

Why is the deficit so difficult to eradicate? The question takes on more urgency when one realizes that the government made some serious attempts to balance revenue and expenditure with significant tax increases and cuts in various expenditure programs. Total federal revenues increased by an average of 9.5 percent annually over the 1984–90 period. The rate of spending increases was down (see Table 10–7). For the five-year period from 1985/6 to 1989/90 the average annual increase in program expenditures registered 3.6 percent — less than the annual inflation rate so that the real growth of program expenditures actually declined by an estimated 0.7 percent. Further reductions would be difficult, the Department of Finance explained, because "about 60 percent of program expenditures ... consists of a number of large statutory programs which, for the most part, are either formula-funded or indexed to inflation."[13] These programs included Old Age Security benefits, unemployment insurance, the Canada Assistance Plan, family allowances, veterans' allowances, and transfers to the provinces. Nevertheless, as the government pointed out, between 1984/5 and 1989/90, the actual budget operating balance — the difference between program expenditures and budgetary revenues — reversed from a deficit of almost $16 billion to a surplus of almost $9 billion.

The source of the deficit problem is implicit in the definition of "actual budget operating balance," which can be rephrased as the budgetary deficit *excluding* public debt charges. In 1989/90, those charges rose an estimated $6.4 billion from the previous year, absorbing approximately 80 percent of the forecast $8 billion increase in budgetary revenues.[14] The cumulative deficits correspondingly increased the total public debt, absorbing an increasing proportion of total budgetary revenues. Finance Minister Wilson pointed out that in 1969, just 12 cents of the taxpayer's dollar went to interest payments on the public debt, but by 1989, it took more than 35 cents of each tax dollar to finance a net public debt of $352 billion.[15]

Thus, deficit reduction was hampered by the drain of financing the deficits themselves. Each year that a deficit was incurred meant a substantial increase in the revenue required just to cover interest charges. For example, an average interest rate of 10.5 percent on the $30 billion budgetary deficit in 1984 added $3.2 billion to the government's revenue requirements for that fiscal year alone.

Moreover, approximately 60 percent of the government's total outstanding debt (primarily Treasury bills and Canada Savings Bonds) has to be refinanced or repriced each year.[16] If a year is characterized by rising interest rates, revenue requirements are raised further because part of the public debt issued earlier at lower interest rates matures and has to be refinanced at the new, higher rates. In 1990/1, with unmatured debt at about the $300 billion level, refinancing 60 percent of it with a 1 percent increase in interest rates would require an additional $1.8 billion.

Summary

In summary, deficit reduction was the central theme in every federal budget from 1985 to 1990. At the beginning of the period, the government announced that its attack on the deficit had to be tempered by other fiscal objectives. The economy was still recovering from the recession and inflation suffered early in the decade, and the government was anxious to maintain this recovery and promote economic and employment growth. The government's balancing act, in the words of Finance Minister Wilson, was to "control and reduce deficits in a balanced and careful way that will not tip the economy off its current course of growth."[17]

The minister's objective was reflected in various changes to the tax structure designed to stimulate private initiative and business activity, accompanied by expenditure restraint and numerous tax increases to raise revenue for deficit reduction. But the government failed to make major inroads in reducing the actual budgetary deficit in absolute terms. Success was recorded in the sense of reducing the deficit measured as a percentage of GDP; from a high of 6.8 percent in 1984, it declined steadily to 3.5 percent in 1989. The size of the deficit relative to total federal spending was also reduced after 1984 (see Figure 10–5), so an increasing portion of expenditures was financed from tax revenue and other levies, rather than by borrowing.

FIGURE 10–5
Federal Government Budget Balance, 1960–1990
Percentage of GDP and Percentage of Federal Government Spending

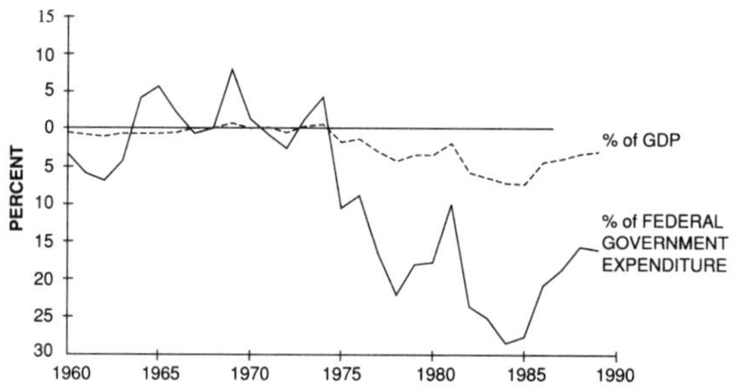

Source: Canada, Department of Finanace, *Quarterly Economic Review, Annual Reference Tables*, June, 1990 (Ottawa).

Nevertheless, Finance Minister Wilson's goal of reducing the growth of the national debt to less than that of the economy by the end of the decade was not achieved. The federal gross debt increased from 45 percent of GDP in 1984 to 56 percent in 1989, and the net debt increased from 36 to 49 percent of GDP over the same period and was expected to peak at 56 percent in 1992.

The significance of the government's failure to make substantial inroads on the size of the deficit is magnified by the fact that the economy enjoyed relative prosperity during most of the period. From 1984 to 1988, the average annual real GDP growth was 4.7 percent, prices stabilized at roughly a 4 percent annual increase, employment grew, and unemployment fell from 11.2 to 7.8 percent (see Table 10–4).

The failure to reduce the deficit during the period of relative prosperity in the 1980s placed the government in a difficult position when the economy went into a recession in the latter part of 1990 and early 1991. The government was severely restrained in its ability to apply expansionary fiscal measures to counter the recession and was not prepared to permit the existing large budget deficit to grow substantially larger through tax reductions and/or major expenditure increases.

ENDNOTES

1. Analysis of the 1947–63 period can use some but not all of the methodology described at the beginning of the chapter. Information on the structural budget balance is available beginning only in 1953, and information on the primary structural balance is unavailable. Indications of the direction of fiscal policy are obtained from examining the actual and structural balances and from the specific measures that were introduced.

   The major sources of information and the data on economic conditions and federal government fiscal policy from 1947 to the present are the budget speeches of the Minister of Finance, the various accompanying budget papers and reports prepared by the Department of Finance, publications of Statistics Canada, and Department of Finance, *Quarterly Economic Review*, various issues.

2. For an account of the attitude of the government of Canada toward fiscal policy prior to 1940, see Irving Brecher, *Monetary and Fiscal Thought in Policy in Canada, 1919–1937* (Toronto: University of Toronto Press, 1957).

3. Price and wage controls in Canada during the Second World War are described in K.W. Taylor, "Canadian War-Time Price Controls, 1914–1946," *Canadian Journal of Economics and Political Science* XIII, No. 1. (1947).

4. Government of Canada, Department of Reconstruction, *Employment and Income* (Ottawa: King's Printer, 1945). The federal government had earlier enacted statutes, such as the Unemployment Insurance Act, 1940, and the Family Allowance Act, 1944, which, it was believed, would partly meet future problems of declining incomes.

5. Of the plants that faced a reconversion problem following the termination of the war, more than half had completed the reconversion process by March 1946. Of the remainder, 75 percent completed the process before the end of the year. Approximately 45 percent of the plants had completed or were undertaking modernization or expansion programs, and a large number of new establishments were coming into

operation to produce for the peacetime market. Of the 1 000 000 people who gave up their wartime occupations in the fall of 1945, close to 800 000 had found employment by March 1946. See the statement by C.D. Howe in Government of Canada, *House of Commons Debates, 1946* (Ottawa: King's Printer, 1946), pp. 112–120.

6. For an analysis of inflation in Canada during the 1970s, see Canada, Department of Finance, *Canada's Recent Inflation Experience*, November 1978, (Ottawa).

7. Canada, Department of Finance, *Budget Speech*, December 11, 1979 (Ottawa), p. 2.

8. Canada, Department of Finance, *Budget Speech*, May 23, 1985, (Ottawa), p. 5.

9. Canada, Department of Finance, *Budget Speech*, February 20, 1990 (Ottawa), pp. 134–35.

10. Canada, Department of Finance, *The Agenda for Economic Renewal: Principles and Progress*, February 18, 1987 (Ottawa), p. 11.

11. *Budget Speech*, 1990, p. 12.

12. Canada, Department of Finance, *The Budget*, February 26, 1991 (Ottawa).

13. Canada, Department of Finance, *Budget Papers*, February 18, 1987, (Ottawa) p. 13.

14. Canada, Department of Finance, *The Fiscal Plan, Controlling the Public Debt*, April 27, 1989, (Ottawa), p. 52.

15. Canada, Department of Finance, *The Budget Speech*, April 27, 1989 (Ottawa), p. 1.

16. *The Fiscal Plan*, p. 52.

17. Canada, Department of Finance, *Budget Speech*, May 23, 1985, p. 21.

APPENDIX TO CHAPTER 10

WAGE AND PRICE REGULATIONS

Traditional fiscal policy to combat inflation in Canada has several times been supplemented by experiments with wage and price controls. The first application of controls occurred during the Second World War, and they almost certainly contributed to relative price stability in that period. This appendix briefly describes the three following attempts: the Prices and Incomes Commission of 1969 and 1970; the wage and price controls of 1975 through 1978; and the "6 and 5" restraint program of 1983 and 1984.

Prices and Incomes Commission

Canada's first postwar experiment with wage and price controls began in 1969 with a program of voluntary guidelines administered by a Prices and Incomes Commission. The guideline for annual wage increases was 6 percent; the guideline for prices was that increases were to be less than the amount needed to cover all increases in costs.

In February 1970, the commission succeeded in bringing together approximately 250 business and professional representatives at a conference on price restraints and obtained from them a commitment to follow the price guidelines it recommended. Organized labour, however, refused to attend the conference or to co-operate with the commission. The Canadian Labour Congress said that it was not in a position to make commitments for its member unions. Labour in general argued that a wage ceiling would hold the status quo on income distribution, a situation that would be inequitable as labour had considerable catching up to do on profits and other forms of income. Labour also refused to accept wage controls on the grounds that other forms of income, such as rents, profits, and interest, were not subject to restraints.

During the early months of 1970, the Prices and Incomes Commission did manage to persuade various industries to agree to a moratorium on price increases, and between January and March a number of announced and intended price increases were postponed. Without the co-operation of labour, however, the commission's task was extremely difficult, for it was apparent that business was not prepared to maintain price freezes for any length of time if costs continued to rise. By late 1970, business declared that it no longer could co-operate with the commission, and in December, the government announced that it was abandoning its program of voluntary price restraints. The commission would continue to function but only as a research agency to study the causes and processes of inflation and to promote public understanding of the problem.

How successful was the commission in controlling inflation? The rate of inflation decreased during the latter months of 1970 — the consumer price index (CPI) increased from 127.9 in December 1969 to 130.5 in July 1970 and then stabilized, falling slightly to 129.8 by December 1970. But it is difficult to determine to what extent the work of the commission contributed to this moderation. The rate of economic growth declined in 1970, and aggregate demand levelled off; both factors could be expected to have some moderating influence. Moreover, in October, a price war broke out among the major grocery chains, resulting in a three-point decline in the food price index (food is a major component of the basket of goods used to determine price changes). One can only speculate on what the degree of price increases would have been in 1970 if aggregate demand had not become depressed or if food prices had not declined.

Mandatory Controls

Canada's second experiment in wage and price regulation began in 1975. The Liberal government had rejected mandatory controls in the autumn of 1974 and even waged an election campaign denouncing the wage and price control proposals of the Conservative party. When in power, the Liberal government at first argued that controls had been attempted and abandoned by most Western nations over the past decade and cited the various traditional arguments against controls, such as difficulties of administration and distortions caused in the allocation of resources.[1]

By October 1975, however, with prices increasing at an annual rate of approximately 11 percent, wage settlements exceeding 14 percent per year, and productivity stagnant, the government reversed its position and introduced an anti-inflation program of wage and price controls.[2] Wages were controlled directly. Prices were controlled by a complex system of monitoring corporation profit margins. In addition, a list was established of some 500 companies that were required to give advance notice of planned price increases. The controls also covered dividends, the incomes of professionals, and the federal public service, and under agreements with eight provinces, the regulations also applied to their employees.

It was announced that the program would continue for three years. Inflation rate targets were set at 8, 6, and 4 percent for the first, second, and third years respectively. Wage guidelines were based on the inflation target factor plus a productivity and experience adjustment factor, with a maximum annual increase of $2400. For 1976, the guideline could vary between 8 and 12 percent; it would decline for each of the subsequent years, although provisions were included to permit additional flexibility if necessary to maintain historic relationships between income groups.

The government established three administrative bodies to administer the program: the Anti-Inflation Board to establish guidelines, to review wage settlements and income increases, and to monitor prices and profits; an administrator to investigate contraventions of the guidelines and to enforce compliance where necessary; and the Anti-Inflation Appeal Tribunal to consider appeals on the rulings of the administrator.

During the first program year (October 14, 1975 to October 13, 1976), compensation plans covering approximately 3 million employees in the public and private sectors were submitted to the Anti-Inflation Board. Plans covering over one-third of these employees contained increases beyond the guidelines and required a decision by the board. Some compensation increases approved early in the program exceeded the guidelines, primarily to maintain historical relationships. As the program continued, compensation plans showed a continued deceleration in the rate of wage increases being sought and being approved (see Table A10–1). During the second program year, for example, approximately 70 percent of employees sought increases within or below the guidelines, while the remaining 30 percent sought increases averaging 1.8 percent above the guidelines. The effective rate of increase in the average of settlements was reduced steadily in each year of the program. It is estimated that the average wage rollback by the Anti-Inflation Board was 2.0 percent in the first year and 1.2 percent in the second year. The increase in the first-year wage settlements of large bargaining units was reduced from 21.1 percent in 1975 to 8.0 percent in 1977, and by the end of the second quarter of 1978, the first-year wage settlement in collective agreements of bargaining units of 500 or more employees had fallen to 6.6 percent.[3]

The wage and price controls were gradually phased out during 1978 and expired at the end of the year. During the regulation period, the increase in the CPI moderated from 10.9 percent in 1974 to 7.5 percent in 1976, but it then began to move upward gradually, reaching 8.9 percent by 1978. Although the country beat the inflation rate target set for 1976 (8 percent), the targets for the second and third years were not achieved.

Wage and price regulation is extremely difficult to evaluate for its effectiveness in controlling inflation because one does not know what would have occurred in its absence. As in 1970, part of the improvement in the rate of change in the Canadian CPI reflected factors beyond the direct control of the program. During the first year of the experiment, unemployment increased and international inflation abated to a degree, which may have had a moderating impact on the rate of inflation in Canada. Then there were variables, such as food prices, which increased by only 2.7 percent in 1976 compared to an increase of 12.9 percent a year earlier; this falloff helped to moderate the increase in the CPI, yet food at the producer level was exempt from the controls of the anti-inflation program. Moreover, the food component of the shopping basket became a factor contributing to inflation in 1977 and 1978 when rising food prices refuelled inflation.

Fear was expressed that, with aggregate inflation again on the rise, inflationary expectations would also be raised and lead in the postcontrol period to higher wage and salary demands and to a renewed wage and price spiral. This did indeed occur. The average negotiated wage settlement, which had declined considerably between 1975 and 1978, began to increase in 1979 and, with consumer prices, continued to rise into 1982.

The "6 and 5" Program

Fearing a renewed surge in the wage and price spiral, the government again turned to wage restraints in June 1982. In his budget of that month, Finance Minister Allan MacEachen introduced a pay restraint policy for the federal public sector and expressed hope that the other levels of government and the private sector would follow Ottawa's example. Under this program, increases in the public employees' wages were limited to 6 percent in 1983 and 5 percent in 1984. The same limits were applied to the indexation factor for a number of federal transfer payments. Some provinces had

TABLE A10–1
Anti-Inflation Board and Wages:
Summary of Effective Rates of Increase in Compensation and Relationship to Wage Guidelines by Program Years

	No. of employees	Average effective increase[a]	Average guideline
	(000s)	(%)	(%)
Immediate preprogram	183	12.5	10.6
First program year (1975/6)[b]	3019	9.3	9.7
Second program year (1976/7[b])	3406	7.3	7.6
Third program year (1977/8[c])	471	5.2	5.6
All program years	7079	8.2	8.4

[a] Weighted average of settlements within guidelines and after board decisions.
[b] October of one year to October of the following year.
[c] October 1977 to February 1978. Employee groups began to be freed from the guidelines in early 1978.

Source: Department of Finance, *Economic Review*, April 1978 (Ottawa), p. 36.

already announced measures to limit the pay increases of some categories of their employees, and others were quick to introduce restraints similar to the federal program.

The momentum of rising wage settlements and earnings began to break in 1982 and continued to decline into 1983. Combining with the "6 and 5" program to contribute to the decline were numerous factors, including a high rate of unemployment, a serious recession, and a moderation in international inflationary forces.

ENDNOTES

1. For a summary of various arguments against wage and price controls, see R.G. Lipsey, "Wage-Price Controls: How To Do a Lot of Harm by Trying To Do a Little Good," *Canadian Public Policy* 3 (Winter 1977).
2. A detailed description of the wage and price control program and the decisions of the Anti-Inflation Board is presented in the board's technical bulletins and reports.
3. For one analysis of the effectiveness of the Anti-Inflation Board in Restraining wages, see D.A.L. Auld et al., "The Impact of the Anti-Inflation Board on Negotiated Wage Settlements," *Canadian Journal of Economics* XII, no. 2 (May 1979).

CHAPTER 11

PROVINCIAL BUDGET POSITIONS

In recent decades, as the provincial governments' revenues and expenditures increased in significance, they have become increasingly active in attempting to apply fiscal policies to influence their respective economies. As explained in Chapter 2, expenditure responsibilities have slowly become more decentralized in Canada, so the provinces currently administer a larger proportion of total government activities than does Ottawa. Provincial tax and revenue shares have increased correspondingly.

Before the early 1960s, the provincial governments had little expenditure or tax room for manoeuvrability for fiscal policy on their own initiative. Nevertheless, they did participate in fiscal policy in such federally initiated shared-cost programs as winter works and labour-retraining. Following the termination of the tax rental agreements and the return of provincial taxing powers, the provinces gradually came to enjoy greater tax flexibility. This situation was furthered by the federal/provincial agreements, which substituted increased tax room for specific-purpose transfers from Ottawa to the provinces. This trend culminated in the established program financing (EPF) arrangements that began in 1978. These arrangements considerably raised the provinces' share of the personal income tax and increased their potential for flexibility in expenditure and taxation. In addition, the provinces generally continued to participate in short-term expenditure programs initiated by the federal government to combat seasonal and regional unemployment.

Fiscal influence can now be exerted by all the provinces with relatively large economies — Ontario, Quebec, and, to a lesser extent, Alberta and British Columbia. (In 1988, these four provinces together accounted for about 87 percent of Canada's GDP; the relative shares were: Ontario, 41.4 percent; Quebec, 24.0 percent; British Columbia, 11.2 percent; and Alberta, 10.5 percent.)

Unfortunately, it is not possible here to analyze provincial fiscal policy on the basis of structural and primary structural budget balances. The data are not readily available.[1] An analysis of provincial discretionary fiscal policy and whether the net effect of tax and expenditure changes was expansionary or contractionary would therefore be difficult and is not attempted here. Instead, the actual budget balance is presented in the aggregate and as a percentage of GDP for the provinces combined, as shown in Table 11–1. Changes in these levels may be viewed as a macro indicator of the tone of the fiscal system — the effects of discretionary changes and automatic stabilizers combined. This macro measure is supplemented with brief descriptions of some of the discretionary measures introduced in recent years by each of the provinces.[2]

As the federal government was struggling to bring its budgetary deficit under control during the past several years, many of the provinces were experiencing similar deficit problems. In the process of analyzing the provinces' fiscal policies, the text briefly examines their actions and degree of success in controlling their deficits. Table 11–2

TABLE 11–1
Provincial Government Revenues, Expenditures, and Budget Balances (national accounts basis)

	Revenue	Expenditures	Balance	Balance as percentage of GDP
	($ million)			(%)
1970	13 890	14 146	–256	–0.3
1971	16 023	16 510	–487	–0.5
1972	17 718	18 440	–722	–0.7
1973	20 605	20 719	–144	–0.1
1974	26 142	25 431	711	0.5
1975	29 869	31 569	–1700	–1.0
1976	34 391	35 844	–1453	–0.7
1977	40 984	41 557	–573	–0.3
1978	46 574	45 556	1018	0.4
1979	52 543	52 549	–6	–
1980	59 254	59 806	–552	–0.2
1981	68 520	69 596	–1076	–0.3
1982	76 094	81 765	–5671	–1.5
1983	83 806	90 070	–6264	–1.5
1984	92 614	94 382	–1768	–0.4
1985	98 626	102 635	–4009	–0.8
1986	101 763	109 714	–7951	–1.6
1987	112 352	115 943	–3571	–0.7
1988	124 524	123 410	1114	0.2
1989	130 987	131 739	–752	–0.1

Source: Canada, Department of Finance, *Quarterly Economic Review: Annual Reference Tables*, June 1990 (Ottawa) pp. 11, 94, 95.

highlights the budgetary position of each provincial government during the recession of the early 1980s and during subsequent, more prosperous years.

Throughout most of the 1975–83 period, as the economy performed erratically and unemployment remained high, most of the provinces incurred budget deficits. (The exceptions were the three resource-rich Western provinces of British Columbia, Alberta, and Saskatchewan, which enjoyed surpluses, thanks to high oil and gas prices and royalties.) Where deficits were incurred, the fiscal system would have an expansionary impact on the provincial economy. From 1976 to 1980, the provincial budgets taken together show a small deficit in relation to GDP; it increased to 1.5 percent in the high recession years of 1982 and 1983. In all years after 1983 except 1986, the aggregate deficit fell to less than 1 percent of GDP, partly a result of provincial efforts at deficit reduction.

Budgetary Policies: 1980–1983

Atlantic Region

The Atlantic provinces have traditionally suffered greater unemployment than other parts of Canada, and the late 1970s and early 1980s were no exception. By 1982, the unemployment rate had risen to 14.4 percent, 3.4 percentage points more than the national average. The four provinces participated in joint job-creation programs with the federal government and announced increased expenditures on public works, resource development, and labour training programs.

As pressure was mounting for increased spending to combat unemployment, these provinces were experiencing a slowdown in revenue growth caused by the economic recession of the early 1980s. Expressing concern over the deteriorating financial position as deficits began to rise, they sought additional revenues from taxation. Between 1981 and 1983, all four raised a variety of taxes. Newfoundland increased its taxes on gasoline and tobacco products; Prince Edward Island increased its retail sales tax from 9 to 10 percent and raised taxes on liquor and tobacco; New Brunswick increased its personal income tax rate from 55.5 to 58.0 percent, its corporation income tax rate from 12 to 14 percent, and its retail sales tax from 8 to 10 percent and raised taxes on tobacco products, gasoline, and property. Nova Scotia increased its personal income tax from 52.5 to 56.5 percent, its corporation income tax from 13 to 15 percent, and its retail sales tax from 8 to 10 percent. Despite these tax increases, the budgetary deficits of all the Atlantic provinces except Prince Edward Island increased substantially from 1980 to 1984 in both dollars and as a percentage of budgetary expenditures.

Central Canada

Quebec's policy to promote growth and employment in the early 1980s included a reduction in the personal income tax, increased funds for housing and public works, job-creation programs in the tourist and forestry industries, and assistance to firms. The last involved a number of tax changes, such as increased tax credits for business losses, a 100 percent capital cost allowance for film production, a tax credit for business expenditures on research and development, and a policy of earned depletion for the mining industry similar to that of the federal government.

In late 1983, Premier René Lévesque announced an ambitious economic plan designed to aid economic recovery and reduce the province's 13.5 percent unemployment rate, which stood two percentage points higher than the national average of 11.5 percent. The program included matching grants to firms for funds they spent on training programs, work programs for female workers, retraining programs for workers in declining industries, improvements in student loans, a fivefold increase in the province's reforestation program, reduced hydroelectric rates for industry that settled in Quebec, and increased funds for the construction of public works. During this period, the budgetary deficit remained relatively constant at slightly more than $0.5 billion.

Ontario introduced a number of selective tax cuts in its 1983 budget. Designed to stimulate economic activity in specified sectors, they included a temporary sales tax

TABLE 11–2
Provincial Government Budget Balances for 1980–1990
(public accounts basis)

	1979/80		1983/4		1986/7		1989/90[a]	
	Amount	% of expenditure[b]	Amount	% of expenditure[b]	Amount	% of expenditure[b]	Amount	% of expenditure[b]
	($ million)	(%)	($ million)	(%)	($ million)	(%)	($ million)	(%)
Newfoundland	–139	–9.3	–285	–12.8	–131	–5.0	6	0.2
PEI	–12	–4.0	7	1.6	–18	–3.3	22	3.3
Nova Scotia	–67	–3.8	–344	–11.7	–385	–11.2	–242	–5.6
New Brunswick	40	2.7	–242	–9.6	–219	–7.1	–106	–2.9
Quebec	–513	–3.1	–795	–2.9	–155	–0.5	–955	–2.4
Ontario	–685	–4.1	–2422	–9.3	–1072	–3.2	35	–
Manitoba	–22	–1.0	–525	–13.0	–481	–10.0	43	0.7
Saskatchewan	81	3.5	–242	–6.3	–470	–9.9	–173	–3.3
Alberta	1780	26.2	1121	9.1	–2871	–20.0	–1653	–11.2
British Columbia	593	10.5	–930	–8.8	–875	–7.5	65	0.4
All provinces	1056	1.9	–4657	–5.1	–6677	–5.9	–2958	–2.1

[a] Estimates

[b] Budget balance as a percentage of relevant provincial budgetary expenditure.

Source: Statistics Canada, *Provincial Government Finance, Revenue and Expenditure, 1980, 1984,* cat. no. 68–207, various issues; Canadian Tax Foundation, *Provincial and Municipal Finances, 1989* (Toronto: CTF 1990), p. 3:13; and provincial government budgets 1990/1.

exemption on new furniture and appliances, a sales tax exemption for production machinery and equipment, and the extension of the 1982 tax holiday for small business. Any business income reinvested in a firm was excluded from provincial tax. The expenditure side of the budget included an amount of $242 million for a number of private sector expansion and job-creating programs. In the 1984 budget, the provincial government announced a $450 million, three-year Ontario Youth Opportunities Fund to provide a wide range of programs aimed at assisting young people in the labour market. Ontario also adopted the federal "6 and 5" pay restraint program for its public sector for 1983 and 1984, in an attempt to restrain government expenditures and set an example for private sector wage settlements.

The Ontario government also expressed concern over the province's rising budget deficit, which exceeded $2 billion or almost 10 percent of its expenditure in 1983. To raise revenue, the government increased several taxes. A temporary surtax was imposed at a rate of 2.5 percent of provincial income tax for 1983 and 5 percent for 1984; the corporation income tax rate was raised from 14 to 15 percent; and taxes on tobacco and alcohol and the health insurance premium were all raised.

The West

Manitoba, faced with a high unemployment rate and a stagnant economy, introduced in its 1983 budget a job fund of $200 million. Job-creation projects were to be financed in a wide range of areas, including transportation, forestry, housing, and recreation. At the same time, an attempt was made to control the size of the budget deficit by increasing a number of taxes, including the corporation income tax from 15 to 16 percent, the retail sales tax from 5 to 6 percent, and the taxes on liquor, beer, tobacco, and gasoline.

During the first part of the 1980s, Alberta, British Columbia, and, to a lesser extent, Saskatchewan, with their wealth in resources, were in a more enviable fiscal position than their counterparts. They were also concerned, however, with unemployment and inflation and followed selective policies similar to those of other provinces. Saskatchewan increased technical training facilities, extended grants to purchasers of new homes, offered grants to municipal governments to construct recreational facilities, and offered tax concessions to small businesses that hired new employees. It financed these programs with revenue from its heritage fund (established with revenues from natural resources). At the same time it increased the taxes on gasoline and tobacco products and raised the corporation income tax from 14 to 16 percent.

Alberta enjoyed a budgetary surplus equal to 26 percent of its expenditure in 1980. But the reduction in international petroleum prices and a glut in the oil market began to depress the province's economy severely, prompting an expansionary policy. A major economic stimulation program, costing more than $1 billion, was announced in 1982. The Alberta Heritage Fund financed much of the expansionary program. However, the government, fearing the decline of budget revenues and a deterioration of its fiscal position, also increased taxes on tobacco products and increased health insurance premiums and stated that budget expenditure would not be increased by more than 8 percent in 1983/4. In late 1983, an increase in personal income taxes was announced to take effect in 1984, providing the province with additional revenues to meet its rising expenditures. Alberta tightened its expenditure restraint policy for 1984/5. The budget of March 1984 reduced total government expenditure by 1.7 percent, or approximately $170 million, and eliminated 1100 provincial civil service positions. Nevertheless, with unemployment in the province hovering around 11 percent, the government proposed to provide and maintain employment with a major capital works program costing more than $3 billion. No tax changes were introduced but for the third year in a row, the government planned to tap the $14 billion heritage fund to finance part of the budget expenditures.

Policies in British Columbia fluctuated with changes in the province's economy and in its government. From 1977 to 1981, it had enjoyed a relatively healthy economy with unemployment a percentage point below the national average. A severe economic decline followed; unemployment jumped from 6.7 percent in 1981 to 12.1 percent in 1982, projected budget revenues were gravely reduced, and the budget deficit stood at almost $1 billion. In 1983, declining revenues and concern over the deficit prompted the Social Credit government to introduce a program of expenditure restraint, including reduction of employment in the public sector. The restraint program included scaling down some regional offices, closing or reducing various agencies, and discontinuing or curtailing specified expenditure programs, such as grants to first-home buyers and tax credits to renters. The government provided increased funds for job creation, including $245 million from an employment development account to finance capital works, such as highway and hospital construction, and to subsidize new jobs in the private sector. Seeking additional revenues to reduce the deficit, the government raised the retail sales tax from 6 to 7 percent and increased taxes on tobacco, gasoline, and property. The objective of the 1983 program was retrenchment in government expenditure, a retreat in government involvement in a variety of social and economic activities, and increased reliance on the private sector to provide economic recovery and growth.

The government continued this restraint policy in its 1984/5 budget, despite an unemployment rate of 15.2 percent in early 1984. Little direct relief was offered the unemployed. Government spending was reduced 6.2 percent, and there were increases in taxes, including a personal income surtax of 4.0 percent, producing a small reduction in the deficit between 1983/4 and 1984/5. Social services continued to be cut back; at the same time, tax concessions and subsidies were planned for business to stimulate investment, production, and technological developments in keeping with the government's objective to stimulate the private sector and to make the private sector more responsible for providing for the needs of society.

Summary

In general during the early 1980s, the provinces were faced with problems of weak economies and deterioration of their budget balances. Most sought to stimulate weak sectors of the economy with selective tax and expenditure measures and to reduce unemployment with specific job-creation programs. These selective measures served to augment the expansionary measures introduced by the federal government during this period. At the same time, the provinces sought to increase revenues to avoid massive budget deficits. Provincial treasurers' statements and budgets speeches from this time give an impression of great concern about incurring larger deficits, particularly over an extended period.

Balancing Provincial Budgets: 1984–1991

As the Canadian economy recovered from the recession in 1983 and 1984 and began a period of relative prosperity, economic growth and prosperity were far from uniform among the various regions. While unemployment dropped from 10 to 5 percent in Ontario between 1983 and 1988, it remained more than 12 percent in the Atlantic region and more than 10 percent in British Columbia.

Most provinces had incurred budgetary deficits in the early 1980s during the recession. As the economy recovered and continued to grow, there was a movement toward deficit reduction. In general, provincial policies aimed to restrain government spending and to increase revenues, although at the same time providing incentives to sustain investment and economic growth and reduce unemployment.

Atlantic Region

In the latter 1980s, Newfoundland, plagued with chronic unemployment that exceeded 21 percent in 1985, emphasized the need to promote economic growth and provided stimuli for industry, worker training, and small business. This program was accompanied by revenue-raising measures, which helped to reduce the budgetary deficit gradually. A small surplus was forecast for 1989/90.

Nova Scotia, concerned about a large deficit of almost 12 percent of expenditure over the period 1984 to 1986, introduced a three-year plan for gradual deficit reduction in 1987. It called for increased expenditures on employment-creating capital programs, projects such as highway construction and municipal water and sewer projects, but decreased spending on other government services. No major tax measures were introduced from 1986 to 1988. By 1990, however, with the deficit at approximately $240 million, the government introduced a number of tax changes, including an increase in the personal income tax from 56.5 to 59.5 percent of the basic federal tax, a personal income surtax, an increase in the corporate tax rate from 15.0 to 16.0 percent, an increase in the capital tax on financial institutions from 1.5 to 3.0 percent, and higher levies on tobacco and gasoline. Together with expenditure restraint, the program was expected to push down the deficit by about $100 million.

New Brunswick, in 1984, announced a plan to reduce its budgetary deficit drastically by 1987, primarily through expenditure restraint. With some tax increases, including a rise in the retail sales tax from 10 to 11 percent, the budgetary deficit declined slightly by 1986/7, and it continued to fall until it stood at just over $100 million in 1989/90.

Central Canada

Quebec experienced a healthy rate of economic growth, averaging 4 percent per year during the mid-1980s, although unemployment remained more than 10 percent. In 1983/4, gradual reduction of the provincial deficit became a priority. It was expected to be reduced from almost $800 million to $94 million by 1985/6 through tax increases and expenditure restraint. Actual expenditures, however, were higher than forecast so that year the deficit in fact jumped to almost $1.2 billion. In an attempt to reduce it, a 7.25 percent surtax was levied on corporation income tax payable in 1986. Although the budget deficit did decline in 1986/7, it was estimated to reach $1 billion for 1989/90. The 1990/1 budget announced further tax increases, including a rise in the corporation surtax to 15 percent, but at the same time public works spending was increased to stimulate the economy.

The Ontario budgetary deficit stood at about $2.5 billion from 1982 to 1984. The government's plan in subsequent years was to restrain expenditure growth and, given some tax increases and increased revenues resulting from a rate of economic growth above the national average, to balance the budget by the end of the decade. In 1986, the personal income tax rate was increased by 2 percentage points to 50 percent of basic federal tax and then increased again to 51 percent in 1988, 52 percent in 1989, and 53 percent in 1990. A personal income surtax of 3 percent in 1986, raised to 10 percent in 1988, was levied on individuals with provincial tax in excess of $10 000. Other revenue-raising measures included rises in gasoline, alcohol, and tobacco taxes and an increase in the retail sales tax from 7 to 8 percent in 1988. Despite the government's emphasis on expenditure control, budgetary expenditure increases averaged 8.8 percent per year from 1984/5 to 1989/90. A growing economy, together with discretionary tax increases, brought an announced budget surplus of $35 million for 1989/90. A surplus of $30 million was projected for 1990/1, but deteriorating economic conditions over the last half of 1990 and a change in government and, subsequently, policies produced a projected $2.5 billion deficit.

The West

Both Manitoba and Saskatchewan recorded deficits of more than $0.5 billion in 1985/6 and focussed on deficit reduction in subsequent years. Gasoline, alcohol, and tobacco taxes were increased over this period. In 1987, Manitoba imposed a flat tax of 2 percent on individual net income and raised the retail sales tax from 6 to 7 percent. Saskatchewan, experiencing a drop in oil revenues as international petroleum prices dropped, increased its retail sales tax from 5 to 7 percent in 1987 and imposed a 1 percent flat rate tax on individual net income, which rose to 2 percent by 1988, together with a 2 percent surtax on large resource corporations. By 1989/90, Manitoba was able to record a small budgetary surplus, and Saskatchewan had reduced its deficit by more than one-half.

Buoyed by high oil and gas prices, Alberta had recorded large budgetary surpluses in the early 1980s. Falling prices in subsequent years, however, drastically reduced revenues so that by 1986/7, it had a budgetary deficit of $2.8 billion. In eight years, Alberta had gone from a surplus equal to 28 percent of provincial budgetary expenditures to a deficit equal to 20 percent of expenditures. An announced plan called for the reduction of the budgetary deficit by 40 percent in 1987/8, and a balanced budget by 1990/1, to be achieved through a combination of expenditure restraint and tax increases. In 1987, the personal income tax was increased from 43.5 to 46.5 percent of the basic federal tax, and an 8 percent surtax was imposed on tax exceeding $3500. Taxes on gasoline, tobacco, and alcohol were increased, along with health insurance premiums and the corporation income tax. Further increases in tobacco and gasoline taxes and health premiums were imposed in subsequent years, plus an increase in the tax on small business and a 2 percent tax on the capital of financial institutions. By 1989/90, Alberta still registered a deficit of more than $1.6 billion, the largest of any province, but the government announced that major expenditure cuts, plus increased revenues would reduce it to $0.6 billion in 1990/1.

British Columbia, after running a healthy surplus in 1980/1, had registered record budget deficits in the early 1980s; by 1982/3, the deficit exceeded $1 billion or almost 10 percent of provincial expenditures. Even as most of the country began to recover from the recession, falling prices for the province's principal exports hurt British Columbia's economy and revenues, so the large deficits continued into the mid-1980s. As early as 1983, the government had emphasized the need to reduce the deficit, but this objective was tempered by the desire to stimulate the sluggish economy. Taxes were increased in 1984 but not again until 1987, when the income tax rate was raised from 44 to 51.5 percent of the basic federal tax, the corporation tax on small business was increased from 8 to 11 percent, and taxes on gasoline, tobacco, and alcohol were increased. These increases were combined with a reduction in the retail sales tax from 7 to 6 percent. Subsequent years witnessed further increases in tobacco and gasoline taxes and an increase in health insurance premiums. By 1988/9, the province recorded a budgetary surplus of $618 million before special fund transactions. (British Columbia has established a budget stabilization fund into which are placed budget surpluses in prosperous years, to be used to cover deficits in years when revenues fall short of expenditures. In 1990/1, for example, a projected budgetary deficit of $522 million was expected to be covered by funds from the budget stabilization fund to attain a balanced budget.)

Summary

From 1984 to 1991 a common objective of provincial budgetary policy was to reverse the trend of continuous annual deficits. They were partially the outcome of discretionary fiscal policy during the recession of the earlier period but appeared to have become permanent even after the economy had recovered and entered a period of relative prosperity. Most provinces followed the federal strategy of expenditure restraint coupled with measures to increase revenues. Provinces such as Ontario and British Columbia, which enjoyed rates of economic growth above the national average, were generally more successful at deficit reduction than were those provinces that suffered from chronic high unemployment and relatively slow economic growth.

Overall an examination of budget speeches and government economic statements reveals that the provinces were very much concerned with economic growth, inflation, and unemployment during the 1970s and particularly with the stagflation all regions suffered in the early 1980s. They co-operated with the federal government in job-creation programs and initiated programs of their own. Various tax incentives were introduced to encourage investment and productive activity. Most provinces incurred deficits during the economic decline of 1980 to 1983, and those provinces that had a budget surplus in 1980 saw a decline in their surplus. As the economy recovered and economic growth accelerated after 1984, the provinces attempted to balance the objective of encouraging continued growth to reduce unemployment with the objective of reducing or eliminating their budget deficits. By the late 1980s, the objective of deficit reduction appeared to assume priority in most provinces.

ENDNOTES

1. Data on structural balances are available for the provincial and municipal levels of government combined.

2. The primary sources of information on provincial government revenues, expenditures, budget balances, and fiscal measures are Statistics Canada, *Provincial Government Finance, Revenue, and Expenditure*, cat. 68–207, various issues; and the provinces' annual budgets. Also useful are various publications of the Canadian Tax Foundation, including *Provincial and Municipal Finances*, various issues; the *Tax Memo* series; and articles by Foundation staff on provincial budgets — for example, David Perry et al. "Provincial Budget Roundup 1989," *Canadian Tax Journal* 37 (March/April 1989).

CHAPTER 12

GOVERNMENT BORROWING AND THE PUBLIC DEBT

BORROWING

Borrowing is an alternative to taxation as a means of raising revenue to finance government operations. But rather than being compulsory, like taxation, borrowing is a voluntary transfer of funds from the public to government. In the process, the government sells securities and pays interest for the use of the borrowed funds.

Governments can borrow from a number of sources, including individuals, the chartered banks, financial institutions other than banks, and the central bank (only the federal government can borrow from the central bank). The economic effects of borrowing vary with the source, as will be described later.

All three levels of government in Canada have resorted to borrowing to supplement tax and nontax revenue. Before the development and acceptance of discretionary fiscal policy, borrowing was generally reserved for emergencies or abnormal situations; for example, much of the federal government's debt in 1946 was the result of having borrowed to finance the Second World War. With the emergence of discretionary fiscal policy and the consequent acceptance of deficit financing to stimulate the economy, governments have tended to rely more heavily on borrowing as a means of finance. Nor have they reserved it for covering government deficits in periods of unemployment and economic decline. During the 1970s and 1980s, the federal and many provincial governments began to employ borrowing to finance general expenditure when revenue fell short and they were reluctant to raise taxes. The federal government has not recorded a balanced budget or a surplus since 1974, and the aggregate budget balance for the provinces combined also recorded deficits throughout most of the period.

At the municipal level of government, borrowing is commonly used to finance large capital or nonrecurring expenditures, which, if financed by taxation, could result in a heavy tax burden during the period the expenditures are made. Borrowing permits the government to spread the burden over a number of years, an approach particularly appropriate for major capital projects, such as the construction of highways, schools and hospitals, sewage plants, and hydroelectric plants, that yield benefits to society over many years or decades.

There are no constitutional limits to federal and provincial borrowing powers, and they may borrow from both within and outside the country. Traditionally, the provinces have been less reluctant than the federal government to borrow by floating bond issues in other countries, and as a result, a greater proportion of their debt is held externally. With recent huge deficits and consequent heavy financial requirements, however, the federal government has come to rely increasingly on foreign sources of borrowed funds. The main places outside Canada where both federal and provincial bonds are sold are the United States, the United Kingdom, Western Europe, and Japan.

Features of Securities

The two basic types of securities commonly used to obtain financing are debt securities and ownership securities. Debt securities are generally called bonds, debentures, or notes; their purchasers do in fact lend their money to the issuer. Ownership securities take the form of stocks, shares, or equities: the purchasers of these securities become part owners of the entity issuing the security. Governments issue debt securities, although some government-owned (Crown) corporations issue ownership securities (in which case, they become jointly owned by the government and the private sector investors). The holder of a debt security is paid a stipulated amount of interest on specified dates during its term, usually annually.

The backing or security behind government bonds and other debt issues is the government's authority to impose taxes on the country's citizens, residents, and businesses. In addition, the federal government possesses the power to print money, which it could use to meet interest payments and to redeem maturing securities.

Governments can issue a number of different types of debt securities. Two primary features differentiating them are their term and their marketability. Term is the security's lifespan; it may be short term (generally less than three years), medium term (three to ten years) or long term (more than ten and as much as or more than twenty-five years). At the end of its term, the security is said to mature and is redeemed. That is, on the maturity date, the issuer repays the full principal or amount borrowed, which is known as the face or par value of the security.

Securities that are marketable are bought and sold (before maturity) in the bond or money market. Their prices fluctuate as interest rates fluctuate. The prices of outstanding — "old" — bonds move in the direction opposite to the movement of interest rate levels in the economy. As interest rate levels rise, say from 8 to 10 percent, the holders of old bonds wishing to sell them are forced to offer them on the bond market at a discount from their face since potential investors are unwilling to purchase old 8 percent bonds when newly issued securities are now yielding 10 percent. The price of the old 8 percent bond will therefore fall to the level at which the yield — return to the investor — is 10 percent.

Nonmarketable securities are not transferable by the holder so they do not trade in the money market. The only nonmarketable bond issued by Canadian governments is the Canada Savings Bond (CSB). A unique feature of CSBs is that although they have a specific maturity date, they can be redeemed at full face value at any time before maturity.

Securities may also have callable and extendable features. A callable bond is one that may be redeemed, — "called in" — by the issuer before its maturity date. This feature is not commonly used by government because it tends to diminish the attractiveness of a bond. An extendable bond has a specified maturity date, but the purchaser has the option of continuing to hold it for a specific number of additional years. Some medium-term bonds issued by the federal government can be exchanged on maturity date for new bonds bearing the same interest rate.

Federal Securities

The Canadian government issues several types of securities, including Treasury bills, marketable bonds, Canada Savings Bonds, as well as interest rate swaps plus notes and loans payable in foreign currencies. To raise funds in the Canadian domestic market, the government relies primarily on the first three debt instruments. These borrowing transactions, domestic and foreign, comprise Canada's unmatured debt. The amounts as of March 31, 1989 are shown in Table 12–1.

Rates of interest on government securities vary depending on their specific features and the current interest rates in the market. Traditionally, interest rates on long-term securities have been higher than those on short-term securities as an incentive for lenders to part with liquidity for the longer period. This was not the case during the early and late 1980s, however, when short-term interest rates, reflecting economic conditions and expectations, temporarily surged ahead of long-term interest rates.

TABLE 12–1
Composition of Federal Government Debt as at March 31, 1989

	Amount	Percentage of gross debt
	($ millions)	(%)
Unmatured Debt[a]		
Payable in Canadian currency		
Marketable bonds	115 748	31.8
Canada Savings Bonds	47 756	13.1
Treasury bills	102 700	28.2
Payable in foreign currencies	8 415	2.3
Less: Government holdings of its own debt	1 262	0.3
Total unmatured debt	273 357	75.1
Other liabilities		
Superannuation accounts	57 913	15.9
Interest and debt accounts	7 123	2.0
Other[b]	25 462	7.0
Gross public debt	363 855	100.0
Less: Net recorded assets	42 937	
Net public debt	320 918	

[a] Does not include unmatured debt of Crown corporations, which in 1988/9 totalled $13.3 billion.
[b] Includes loan guarantees by the federal government which amounted to $8.9 billion in 1988/9.

Source: Canada, Supply and Services, *Public Accounts of Canada*, 1989, vol. 1, cat. P51-1 (Ottawa). Reproduced with the permission of the Minister of Supply and Services Canada, 1991.

Treasury Bills. A Treasury bill is a short-term certificate of indebtedness issued by the government of Canada to pay a sum of money on a given date. The most common terms are 91, 182, and 364 days, and bills for all three terms are issued weekly. Treasury bills are sold at a discount of their face value; the difference between the price paid and their face value is the yield expressed as an interest rate per annum. For example, suppose a 91-day Treasury bill of $100 is bought at a price of $96.750; then $100 is paid at the end of 91 days (Treasury bill prices are quoted from a $100 maturity value to three decimal points). The $3.250 earned over those 91 days is equivalent to about 13.4 percent yield on an annual basis.

Treasury bills are offered in denominations ranging from $1000 to $1 million. The Bank of Canada acts as the federal government's fiscal agent. It auctions new Treasury bills each Thursday to a group of chartered banks and investment dealers (the primary distributors) through a competitive process of sealed tenders. The size of the weekly offering of bills depends on the amount of funds the government requires to finance its operations and for redeeming maturing bills. Successful bidders are determined in descending order with the tenders of the highest bidders (lowest discount rate) filled first. The Bank of Canada places a reserve bid to prevent the sale of bills at less than a minimum price, and there is generally a very small spread between high and low bidders. For example, in an auction of $3.65 billion of 91-day Treasury bills on June 8, 1990, the low accepted bid was $96.746 for a yield of 13.49 percent and the high accepted bid was $96.765 for a yield of 13.41 percent.

The primary distributors of Treasury bills resell them in secondary markets, which are dominated by large institutional buyers. In this active secondary market—the money market—Treasury bills are bought and sold in the same manner as shares in the stock market. Maturing bills are redeemed at face value to the holder by the Bank of Canada.

The weekly auction of Treasury bills determines the bank rate (the rate of interest the Bank of Canada charges the chartered banks and a number of investment dealers on funds they borrow from the Bank). It is set at 0.25 percentage points higher than the average yield on each week's sale of 91-day Treasury bills. For example, in the June 8, 1990 auction, the average yield for the 91-day bills was 13.47 percent, so the bank rate was set at 13.72 percent. Through this process, the bank rate is closely tied to short-term interest rates, and it can be viewed as the primary indicator of the trend in interest rates in the economy.

When Canada first issued Treasury bills in1934, they were held primarily by financial institutions and their total amount was relatively small. They have become much better known and more widely held over the past decade. As shown in Table 12–1, they now account for almost one-half of the federal government's total marketable bonds. During the late 1980s, as large government deficits persisted and the public debt increased correspondingly, large transactions of Treasury bills were recorded. In 1988/9 the average size of the regular weekly Treasury bill offering, to cover refinancing and net new funds, was $4.3 billion with several offerings of $5 billion or more.

The late 1980s also witnessed the increased use of cash management bills by the federal government. These are very short-term Treasury bills with terms to maturity of 7 to 45 days. They are auctioned in the same manner as regular Treasury bills but on different days. The government uses them to increase the efficiency of cash management as they can be issued at any time and enable it to avoid longer-term borrowing to meet short-term fluctuations in cash balances. Since these bills have the shortest term of any offered, they carry the lowest interest rate and help to minimize the cost of borrowing to the government.[1]

Marketable Bonds. Government of Canada marketable bonds are interest-bearing certificates that are bought and sold in the open market and have fixed dates of maturity. They may be expressed in Canadian or in a foreign currency. The Bank of Canada, acting as the government's distributing agent, sells the bonds to a group of primary distributors (chartered banks and investment dealers). Traditionally, the bonds were offered to these dealers at retail price less a discount, but more recently the government has placed greater emphasis on selling by auction. In 1988/9, eighteen auctions accounted for 60 percent of all the marketable bonds issued. The primary distributors resell the bonds to the public through an active secondary market. The term on these government bonds ranges from one to twenty-five years. Interest is payable in either coupon or registered form. In the former case, the bonds have attached coupons, one for each date on which interest is due and the coupon can be cashed. A registered bond shows the owner's name, and interest payments are sent directly to that person by the Bank of Canada on the date specified on the bond. At maturity, the bonds are redeemed by the Bank at their face value.

Canada Savings Bonds. Canada Savings Bonds (CSBs) have long been one of the most familiar and popular securities issued by the Canadian government. Starting as the Victory Bonds of the Second World War, they were continued after the war as Canada Savings Bonds.

The CSBs which are issued in denominations from $100 to $10 000 are nonmarketable, interest-bearing certificates issued only to Canadian residents only once each year (in early November). Available through chartered banks or by payroll deductions, CSBs are very popular with the small investor because they offer an attractive yield and are highly liquid — they are redeemable on demand by the holder with accrued interest calculated to the end of the previous month.

Canada Savings Bonds are usually issued with a maturity date of seven years or more and are not subject to call before maturity. During periods of rising interest rates, the government has often increased the rates on outstanding CSBs or offered cash bonuses payable at maturity, both actions being inducements for individuals to hold the bonds to maturity and thereby reduce the degree of refunding required. For example, the November 1981 issue offered 19.5 percent for a one-year period, and the rate on all outstanding CSBs was increased for the year to the same level. Similarly, in early 1990, with interest rates rising and people dumping CSBs for higher-yielding investments, the federal government increased the rate on all those outstanding from 10.5 to 11.5 percent for a period of six months.

In recent years, CSBs have been losing ground to Treasury bills as the latter have become better known.

Other Securities. The federal government borrows from the accumulation in the Canada Pension Plan by issuing to the fund special nonmarketable bonds. They are non-negotiable and nontransferable. The provincial governments also borrow from this fund.

In addition, the Canadian government borrows from other countries through notes and loans payable in foreign currencies. Most foreign borrowing is from the United States, Switzerland, Germany, and Japan.

Provincial and Municipal Securities

The provincial governments issue debt securities similar to those issued by the federal government; Treasury bills are auctioned through competitive tender to fiscal agents consisting of banks and investment dealers. New issues of marketable bonds are also sold to fiscal agents, who in turn distribute them to other investors. Both types of securities are actively traded in the secondary market.

Municipal borrowing is governed by provincial regulations. In most cases, specific borrowing must be authorized by the province. The exception is short-term or interim borrowing to meet current expenditures; in this case, however, limitations are placed on the amount that may be borrowed. Municipal debentures are issued through arrangement with the province or, for large cities, through a fiscal agent.

Possible Economic Effects of Government Borrowing

The economic effects of government borrowing depend on the amount and source of borrowed funds and the state of the economy when the borrowing occurs.[2] Some potential effects include crowding-out, inflation, and the transfer of burdens to future generations.

Crowding-Out. To the extent that individuals, chartered banks, and financial institutions switch funds into government securities from alternative investment opportunities in the capital market, government borrowing may crowd out private borrowing. In other words, the competition for available loanable funds may contribute to an increase in interest rates, making capital more expensive for the private sector and possibly retarding private investment, business expansion, and operations. Whether crowding out does indeed occur has been a topic of considerable debate, partly fuelled by the enormous budget deficits of the federal governments of Canada and the United States in the 1980s. Much depends on the overall supply of and demand for loanable funds. Some analysts have argued that crowding-out did not occur in the early 1980s despite the deficits because the recession during this period was not conducive to investment and expansion by private industry, and consequently the demand for borrowed funds by the private sector was relatively small. In addition, the savings rate in Canada was exceptionally high, providing an adequate supply of funds. There has been concern, however, that in an expanding and prosperous economy, such huge government budget deficits could lead to crowding-out and consequent upward pressure on interest rates.[3] During the latter part of the 1980s, when the economy did prosper and large government deficits continued, some of the pressure in Canadian capital markets from public borrowing was eased by greater government reliance on foreign sources for funding. Only about 2.6 percent of the outstanding federal debt was held by foreigners in 1975, but this proportion had increased to almost 20 percent by 1988. This pronounced increase raises serious concerns about the debt burden. Large principal and interest payments to foreigners represent a transfer of real resources out of the country.

Inflation. Large-scale borrowing from the Bank of Canada can produce inflationary pressures through expansion of the money supply. When the government sells securities to the Bank, the amounts borrowed are credited to the government's account and drawn upon to finance its expenditures. The chain reaction through the banking deposit process creates an increase in the money supply and increased consumer and business spending; to the extent that excess aggregate demand is created, there is upward pressures on prices which is inflation.

Transfer of Burden. Economists have a long-standing and lively debate about whether borrowing to finance current expenditure programs shifts the burden of paying for these programs to future generations when the debt is repaid. Two opposing views have been put forward.

The traditional theory considers burden in real terms (the use of resources) and holds that the real burden of current borrowing can rarely be shifted. It falls on the present generation in the form of reduced consumption when current resources are transferred from the private to the public sector and are used by government as it spends the borrowed funds. Only if the present generation reduces its rate of savings can the burden be shifted to future generations. Reduced savings lower investment. The result is that future generations have a smaller quantity of productive capital to inherit and consequently a smaller amount of production of goods and services — and therefore less income and consumption for the future. Before concluding that the future generations of society will experience such a burden, however, one must consider the application of the borrowed funds. Losses from reduced investment and capital accumulation in the private sector may be balanced by potential gains from public investment. The government's present use of borrowed funds for public goods and public investment may provide benefits that extend to future generations.

The alternative view interprets the concept of burden mainly in financial terms, rather than real terms. These analysts maintain that the present generation bears no burden when purchasing government securities since they are bought voluntarily. Buyers exchange savings or postpone consumption for government securities and do not consider that they are making a sacrifice. There is no reduction in their assets, only a change in their asset mix. The sacrifice (or burden) rests with future generations, who suffer reduced consumption when they pay the higher taxes needed to finance the debt or to redeem the debt.[4]

Although proponents of both views recognize that there is a burden involved in financing government by borrowing, they disagree about the time that the burden is realized. The traditional view, despite detractors, remains widely held in public finance theory.

The real burden of borrowing may also be shifted forward to future generations by borrowing abroad. In this case, borrowing does not cause any reduction in current domestic consumption. Future consumption suffers, however, when taxes are imposed to service and redeem the external debt.

PUBLIC DEBT IN CANADA

Public debt results from government borrowing and the accumulation of deficits. Features of the public debt at all three levels of Canadian governments are illustrated in the tables in this chapter. Before discussing these tables, however, it is useful to define some of the terms found in them.[5]

Gross debt represents the total liabilities of the government; it includes unmatured debt and other liabilities. Unmatured debt represents the government's financial obligations resulting from bonds, Treasury bills, and other certificates that mature or are redeemable in the future. Unmatured debt is net of the government's holdings of its own debt. "Other" liabilities include accounts, such as pension accounts, accounts payable, insurance and trust accounts, and loan guarantees. Government liabilities are partly offset by various assets, such as cash, investments, sinking funds, securities held in trust, and loans to other levels of government, Crown corporations, and international governments and agencies. These items are called net recorded assets (notice that they do not include real assets, such as buildings). Subtracting these net recorded assets from gross debt produces net debt. In effect, net debt represents the accumulated budget deficits.

Features of Public Debt

Tables 12–1, 12–2, and 12–3 illustrate the liabilities of the federal, provincial, and municipal governments. Liabilities include bonded debt, Treasury bills, specific-purpose accounts (for example, government employees' pension plans), and various advances and payables. The provincial data shown in Table 12–2 include the guaranteed debt of the provinces, which consists primarily of guarantees as to principal and interest of loans and securities of government enterprises.

Tables 12–4 and 12–5 show the distribution of debt for the federal and provincial governments. Roughly 14 percent of the 1988 federal debt was held by the Bank of Canada and the chartered banks. Canada Savings Bonds, held by individuals, constituted 19 percent of the debt. For the provinces, one of the main sources of borrowed funds has been the Canada Pension Plan; as of 1987, almost 29 percent of their borrowed funds came from it, with another 11 percent coming from provincial pension plans. The Quebec government has the Quebec Pension Plan available as a source of borrowed funds. Sources of borrowing at the municipal level in 1986 consisted of the general public (46 percent), provincial governments (32 percent), and foreign sources (10 percent)

One of the significant features of the distribution of the provincial debt is the proportion held externally, which has long been considerable and is increasing. In 1981, approximately 19 percent of provincial borrowed funds came from external

TABLE 12–2
Composition of Provincial Government[a] Liabilities and Guarantees as at March 31, 1988

	Amount	Percentage of total
	($ million)	(%)
Direct liabilities		
Bonds, debentures, and other securities	120 701	49.6
Treasury bills	5 240	2.2
Accounts and other payables	15 215	6.3
Deposits and other liabilities	27 836	11.4
Total	168 992	69.5
Guaranteed debt[b]		
Guaranteed bonds and debentures	59 006	24.3
Guaranteed bank loans	3 509	1.4
Other guarantees	11 649	4.8
Total	74 164	30.5
Total liabilities and guaranteed debt	243 156	100.0

[a] Includes the Yukon and Northwest Territories.
[b] Primarily the debt issued by provincial government enterprises.

Source: Statistics Canada, CANSIM matrix 3201, July 19, 1990.

sources; by 1987, 29 percent of bond issues, mainly marketable issues, was held externally (see Table 12–5). A similar trend found at the federal level was noted earlier, although the percentage is smaller (see Table 12–4). Having large amounts of external borrowing and reliance on foreign exchange affects the foreign exchange rate and Canada's balance of payments. As already mentioned, an externally held debt also imposes a burden on the country when interest is paid to foreigners and when the debt is redeemed.

Debt Management

In addition to issuing securities to finance the current deficit, governments continually engage in refinancing or refunding debt by redeeming maturing securities. To obtain the funds to do so, they issue new securities. The principal objective of debt management is to raise the funds required at minimum cost over the long run. This involves judgements about the types of debt securities to issue, their terms and maturities, and the level of cash balances to retain. The refunding of a high volume at any one time could strain the money market, pushing up interest rates and thus increasing the cost of refunding; such sharp rises in interest rates could also produce adverse effects on the economy. Furthermore, major refunding at a time when interest rates are high increases the cost of servicing the debt.

TABLE 12–3
Composition of Municipal Government Liabilities 1988

	Amount	Percentage of total
	($ million)	(%)
Bonds and debentures	29 994	75.7
Short-term borrowings or advances	3 920	9.9
Accounts and other payables	2 824	7.1
Other liabilities	2 890	7.3
Total liabilities	39 628	100.0

Source: Statistics Canada, *Financial Flow and National Balance Sheet Accounts*, 1988, cat. 13–214 (Ottawa, 1989).

In the view of the Department of Finance, one of the most important elements of debt management is the appropriate mix of fixed and floating rates for the debt.[6] The federal government's fixed-rate securities are its marketable bonds that have fixed coupons; most are medium or long term. Its floating-rate securities are Treasury bills and CSBs. In the long run, savings in interest charges can be realized by maintaining a substantial proportion of outstanding debt in floating-rate form because generally it is cheaper to borrow short term than long term. In a period of high interest rates, borrowing short term allows for opportunities for savings once interest rates decline, whereas issuing long-term bonds locks in the high rates. Savings can be achieved by issuing short-term securities even when short-term rates are higher than long-term rates, since such a situation is likely to be temporary. Issuing fixed-rate securities offers savings, however, if rising interest rates are anticipated and expected to last for some time. Decisions on the mix of the debt, therefore, "must assess these cost and risk factors and take account of the fact that if the debt is concentrated too much in one form it can affect interest rates adversely, thus reducing or eliminating potential cost savings."[7] For example, a large concentration of short-term debt may place pressure on short-term rates when the securities are issued and again when they mature and have to be refunded within a concentrated time span.

Table 12–6 illustrates the maturity schedule of federal government unmatured debt. Approximately 50 percent of this debt is of the floating-rate form (CSBs and Treasury bills) and therefore must be refunded or refinanced every year. The government claims that by maintaining a large proportion of its debt in short-term floating instruments, particularly Treasury bills, it has benefited from the generally lower short-term rates. This benefit was particularly evident during the period 1981 to 1987, when the trend in interest rates was downward (the bank rate declined from 17.9 percent to 8.4 percent).

TABLE 12–4
Distribution of Federal Government Debt (Direct and Guaranteed Securities) by Type of Holder, 1988

Holder	Amount	Percentage of Total
	($ million)	(%)
Bank of Canada	20 653	7.5
Chartered banks	17 669	6.4
Government of Canada accounts	4 632	1.7
Trust companies	4 715	1.7
Mortgage loan companies	3 844	1.4
Investment dealers and funds	8 458	3.1
Credit unions and caisses populaires	2 686	1.0
Life insurance companies	11 062	4.0
Other insurance companies	6 757	2.5
Trusteed pension funds	23 198	8.4
Nonfinancial corporations	7 685	2.8
Provincial governments	13 343	4.9
Municipal governments	1 242	0.5
Other holdings of market issues by Canadian residents	42 128	15.4
Canada Savings Bonds	53 318	19.5
Residents of Canada, total holdings	221 390	80.8
Nonresidents , holdings	52 466	19.2
Total	273 856	100.0

Source: Bank of Canada, *Review*, April 1990, (Ottawa), pp. S96-S97.

In addition to holding a large part of the debt in floating form, the government also changed the maturity structure of its marketable bonds during this period. As interest rates went down, the proportion of marketable bonds with maturities of three years or less declined from 36 percent of the total in 1981 to about 18 percent in 1987, while bonds with maturities of three to ten years increased from approximately 22 to 46 percent of the total, and long-term bonds decreased from 42 to 36 percent of the total. In essence, the government's debt management strategy with respect to marketable bonds during 1981 to 1987, when interest rates were falling but long-term rates exceeded short- and medium-term rates, was to lock an increasing proportion of its marketable bond debt into medium-term maturities, thereby avoiding both the higher long-term rates and the potential costs of unexpected increases in short-term rates. As interest rates started to rise in 1988, the government began to switch more of its maturing long-term marketable bonds into maturities of three years or less.

TABLE 12–5
Market and Nonmarket Bond Issues Outstanding of Provincial and Territorial Governments, as at March 31, 1987

	Amount	Percentage of total
	($ million)	(%)
Market issues		
Domestic	16 136	15.9
Foreign	29 433	29.0
Total	45 569	44.9
Nonmarket issues		
To provincial governments	4 085	4.0
To provincial government enterprises	7 757	7.7
To provincial pension plans	11 667	11.5
To Canada Pension Plan Investment Fund	29 302	28.9
To other	2 988	2.9
Total	55 799	55.1
Total issues	101 368	100.0

Source: Statistics Canada, *Provincial Government Finance, Assets, Liabilities, Source and Application of Funds for the Fiscal Year Ending March 31, 1987*, cat. 68–209.

The Debt Treadmill

Tables 12–7 and 12–8 illustrate the growth of debt of the federal government and the provincial governments as a percentage of gross domestic product. While the aggregate provincial debt, (shown as direct liabilities) increased from 11 percent of aggregate GDP in 1966 to 18 percent in 1975 and then rose to about 31 percent by 1986, the federal net debt fell from 32 percent of GDP in 1965 to about 17 percent in 1975 and then jumped to 45 percent in 1985 and 53 percent by 1989.

Much of the federal government's debt before 1960 consisted of the debt that had been incurred to finance Canada's involvement in the Second World War. In 1947, the net public debt measured 106.6 percent of GDP, but as the economy grew in subsequent years and budget deficits, when incurred, were relatively small, the size of the debt relative to GDP continued to decline until it reached a postwar low of 16.8 percent in 1975. Beginning in that year, the federal government began to accumulate a string of consecutive budgetary deficits that not only increased the dollar amount of the debt from approximately $25 billion in 1975 to $320 billion in 1989, but also increased the debt/GDP ratio.

TABLE 12–6
Federal Government Debt: Maturity and Average Interest Rate

	Marketable bonds		Canada Savings Bonds		Total unmatured debt	
Maturity	Amount	Average interest rate	Amount	Average interest rate	Amount	Average interest rate
	($ million)	(%)	($ million)	(%)	($ million)	(%)
1990	10 687	10.8	4 423	10.5[a]	119 961[b]	11.2
1991	11 139	10.1	4 598	10.5	15 880	10.2
1992	9 905	10.5	5 203	10.5	15 108	10.5
1993	10 829	10.7	6 637	10.5	17 495	10.6
1994	11 773	10.5	4 308	10.5	16 800	10.3
1995–99	31 851	10.2	22 586	10.5	54 437	10.3
2000–04	15 437	11.3			15 437	11.3
2005–09	12 400	11.8			12 400	11.8
2010–14	7 100	8.5			7 100	8.5
Total maturing 1990–2014	121 121	10.6	47 755	10.5	274 618	10.5

[a] Increased to 11.5 percent in May 1990 until November 1990.
[b] Includes $102 700 million in Treasury bills for 1990.

Source: Supply and Services Canada, *Public Accounts of Canada*, 1989, vol. 1, cat. P51-1 (Ottawa, 1989). Reproduced with the permission of the Minister of Supply and Services, Canada, 1991.

The growth of the federal public debt has stemmed partly from deficits incurred from financing program expenditures but increasingly from deficits for paying interest on the public debt. Each year deficit-financed interest payments were added to the public debt, so in each subsequent year, interest was paid on the accumulated interest (compound interest). Money invested at a compound rate of 10 percent approximately doubles in seven years and grows to almost eight times its original size in twenty-one years. Minister of Finance Michael Wilson estimated the net public debt for 1989/90 to be about $350 billion, an increase of about $150 billion over a five year period. Of this increase, the minister estimated that more than 80 percent consisted of the compounding of interest on the $200 billion debt of 1984/5. As these statistics illustrate, the public debt is self-perpetuating; it feeds on itself. In the words of Finance Minister Wilson, the government was on a "treadmill of borrowing money to pay interest on the past debt ... [and this] ... helps to explain why the deficit is still at $30 billion in spite of the reduction in spending and increased tax revenues over the past five years."[8] As long as the interest rate exceeds the growth rate of GDP and public debt charges are financed wholly by deficits, the public debt will grow not only in dollar terms but also as a percentage of GDP. Wilson emphasized in his 1990 budget speech that the government was determined to reduce the growth of the public debt absolutely and relative to GDP. This reduction would be achieved through the accumulation of larger and larger annual surpluses in the government's operations budget (budgetary revenues and expenditures excluding interest payments) so the deficit would gradually become increasingly less than the interest on the debt. As the deficit declined, the rate of increase of the public debt would eventually fall below the rate of increase in GDP and the public debt/GDP ratio would decline. Eventually tax revenue would cover the deficit, the budget would be in balance, the public debt would stabilize in absolute dollars, and it would continue to decline as a percentage of a growing GDP. The Finance Minister projected in February 1990 that the net public debt as a percentage of GDP would peak at approximately 56 percent in 1991/2 and then begin to decline.

Issues and Concerns

The public debt draws much general interest, and it has always stirred controversies. Its recent, rapid growth has fuelled these controversies and heightened existing concerns. People frequently allege that a large public debt undermines domestic and foreign confidence in the economy with consequent adverse effects on investment and expansion of productive capacity; that it places heavy strains on the economy in the form of interest charges; and that it may even produce national bankruptcy in the sense of the government's being unable to meet its interest and security redemption obligations. Some view a growing public debt as poor financial management on the part of the government. Others object to the taxes necessary to meet the high interest payments, arguing that the revenue could be used for more productive purposes and needed social programs. Moreover, on the assumption that the debt is held by wealthy individuals and corporate institutions, some analysts allege that the tax and transfer process involved in financing the debt leads to a redistribution of income to the wealthy, contrary to accepted standards of equity.

Economists generally believe that borrowing and therefore increasing the public debt in a period of economic prosperity is inappropriate and unsound fiscal policy, especially if inflationary forces are building. In this regard, the Canadian government receives failing grades for its huge deficits and the massive growth of the public debt during most of the 1980s.

Whether the existence of the public debt and consequent service charges contributes to an inequitable distribution of income and wealth depends primarily upon the tax structure and the distribution of debt holdings. The recent reduction in the number of tax brackets and progressiveness of marginal rates in the personal income tax will likely combine with the introduction of the goods and services tax to reduce the degree of progression in the federal tax structure. This change, combined with the fact that the bulk of the public debt is held by institutions and higher-income groups, may have some adverse redistribution effects. Those effects may, however, be reduced by the extent that the debt-holders who receive the interest payments are, in turn, taxed on these payments.

The issue of the strain on the economy must be viewed in terms of the size of the debt and of the proportion of it held externally. There is general agreement that the

TABLE 12–7
Federal Public Debt and Gross Domestic Product for Selected Years as at March 31

	Gross public debt	Net recorded assets	GDP	Net public debt: Amount	Net public debt: Percentage of GDP
		($ million)			(%)
1927	2 726	378	5 145	2 348	45.6
1937	3 452	458	4 643	3 084	66.6
1947	16 849	4 180	11 855	12 669	106.6
1957	16 491	5 045	32 058	11 446	35.7
1965	26 204	9 291	52 191	16 913	32.4
1970	33 260	15 684	83 026	17 576	21.2
1975	52 866	27 285	152 111	25 581	16.8
1980	104 862	32 703	276 096	72 159	26.1
1985	237 112	38 020	444 735	199 092	44.8
1989	363 855	42 937	601 508	320 918	53.4

Source: Canada, Department of Finance, *The Budget*, February 20, 1990, (Ottawa), p. 148.

significance of the public debt is not its absolute amount but its size in relation to GDP. The larger a country's GDP — its productive capacity — the greater its ability to carry debt. If this debt is held internally — that is, by Canadian residents — payment of interest on the debt from tax proceeds simply involves a transfer from the taxed party to the parties holding the debt and involves no loss of resources to society. It is then said of the debt, we owe it to ourselves. The potential problem of redistribution remains, however.

The consensus among economists is that the existence of a public debt normally poses little threat of national bankruptcy or major adverse effects on the economy if it is declining relative to GDP and the government enjoys a sound credit position domestically and abroad. A government in such a position should have little difficulty in meeting its obligations. A problem may arise, however, if the size of the debt begins to rise relative to GDP. The debt/GDP ratio could conceivably become so large as to require relatively high levels of taxation to finance the debt charges, providing disincentives for investment and retarding economic growth. In Canada, the federal net public debt declined after the Second World War from 106.6 percent in 1947 to 16.8 percent in 1975, and then it rose to reach more than 50 percent in the late 1980s (see Table 12–7). Public debt charges, which had remained relatively constant at 10 to 12 percent of federal budgetary expenditures between 1955 and 1975, rose to 26.6 percent of that amount by 1989 (Table 12–9). The rise contributed to tax increases, as outlined in Chapter 10, resulted in lessening of the proportion of the budget allocated to social and economic programs. By 1990, 35 cents of every dollar Ottawa collected in taxes went to pay the interest on the public debt, and that money represented funds unavailable to address

TABLE 12–8
Provincial Debt and Provincial Gross Domestic Product for Selected Years[a]

	1966			1975			1987		
	GDP	Debt[b] Amount	% of GDP	GDP	Debt[b] Amount	% of GDP	GDP	Debt[b] Amount	% of GDP
	($ million)		(%)	($ million)		(%)	($ million)		(%)
Nfld.	829	322	38.8	2 228	1 582	71.0	6 754	5 010	74.2
PEI	178	84	47.2	461	205	44.5	1 491	667	44.7
NS	1 513	444	29.3	3 894	1 606	41.2	12 949	6 410	49.5
NB	1 222	359	29.4	3 112	1 077	34.6	9 990	5 236	52.4
Que.	16 641	1 937	11.6	40 944	7 420	18.1	117 219	49 206	42.0
Ont.	26 182	3 035	11.6	68 164	13 551	19.9	201 228	46 587	23.2
Man.	2 669	371	13.9	6 915	1 644	23.8	18 442	11 854	64.3
Sask.	2 965	572	19.3	6 907	1 156	16.7	17 144	10 794	63.0
Alta.	5 016	44	0.9	18 598	2 135	11.5	58 087	15 561	26.8
BC	6 538	52	0.8	19 486	1 471	7.5	57 050	17 443	30.6
Total	63 753	7 219	11.3	170 709	31 847	18.7	500 354	168 768	33.7

[a] Calendar year for GDP. Debt as at March 31, 1967, 1976, and 1988.
[b] Debt is defined as direct liabilities as outlined in Table 12-2.

Source: Statistics Canada, *Provincial Government Finance,* Debt 1965, cat. 68–209; and CANSIM matrix 3202–3211, July 19, 1990; and Canada Department of Finance, *Quarterly Economic Review, Annual Reference Tables,* June 1990 (Ottawa).

urgent social and economic needs such as environmental protection, health care and education, and research and development. The debt, growing faster than the economy and consequently faster than the nation's ability to pay, caused growing alarm among Canadians. To business and financial communities especially, the public debt seemed to be growing out of control, portending dire financial and economic consequences.

Real per capita debt provides another measure of the magnitude of the public debt and trends in the debt. Calculated in constant 1981 dollars, the federal net debt fell from $2538 in 1965 to $1926 per capita in 1975. It then began to increase and by 1988 stood at $8643 per man, woman, and child in 1981 dollars — and at $12 385 in 1988 dollars.

As suggested earlier in this chapter, various problems may arise if a substantial proportion of a large public debt is held externally. Large principal and interest payments to foreigners represent a transfer of real resources out of the country and are, therefore, a drain on the economy. Furthermore, the value of the domestic currency may decline as foreign investors convert it into their own currency; the decline causes import prices to rise, which may fuel inflation. Moreover, there is always the danger that domestic economic or political problems may cause foreign debtholders to lose confidence in the government and begin dumping its securities, forcing it either to offer higher interest rates as an incentive to foreign investors, or to increase taxes to meet its redemption obligations. Both options have potentially serious effects for the national economy.

TABLE 12–9
Public Debt Charges and Government Expenditures for Selected Years 1950–1989

	Interest Charges as Percentage of Expenditures[a]		
	Federal	Provincial	Local
1950	18.0	6.9	4.6
1955	10.1	5.1	5.0
1960	11.2	4.0	7.0
1965	12.3	4.3	7.5
1970	12.2	5.4	7.5
1975	10.4	5.8	6.5
1980	16.1	8.1	7.9
1985	21.5	11.8	8.6
1988	24.3	12.7	7.4
1989	26.6	12.7	7.1

[a] National income and expenditure accounts basis.

Source: Canada, Department of Finance, *Quarterly Economic Review, Annual Reference Tables*, June 1990 (Ottawa).

TABLE 12–10
International Comparison of Government Net Debt[a]
in Selected Years 1980–1990

	Canada	US	UK	France	Germany	Italy	Japan
	(net debt as percentage of GDP or GNP)						
1980	12.3	19.7	47.5	14.3	14.3	53.6	17.3
1982	16.5	22.3	45.9	17.8	19.8	63.4	23.2
1984	26.2	25.8	47.6	21.7	21.6	74.2	26.9
1986	36.7	29.9	45.9	25.3	22.1	85.6	26.6
1988	37.6	30.3	39.1	26.6	23.8	92.0	24.6
1990[b]	40.2	28.6	31.6	27.5	24.7	98.1	11.6

[a] Net debt of general government (all levels of government).
[b] Estimate.

Source: Canada, Department of Finance, *The Fiscal Plan*, April 27, 1989, (Ottawa), p. 99.

Traditionally, the Canadian government avoided large foreign debt: until the late 1970s, less than 5 percent of the federal debt was held by nonresidents. But the financial requirements resulting from the continuing large deficits of the last decade forced the federal government, as well as provincial governments, to rely more heavily on foreign markets for funds. As noted earlier, by 1988 almost 20 percent of the federal debt was held by nonresidents while 29 percent of provincial securities was held externally.

Similar problems may arise at the provincial and municipal government levels. An individual province or municipal government, given its limited revenue sources and inability to print currency, could be faced with default if it exceeds its ability to service or manage debt. Although Canadian provincial and municipal governments have so far been able to manage their debts without major difficulty, some US city governments were on the verge of defaulting on their public debt interest payments in the early 1980s.

In general, the Canadian provinces have been better able to control the size of their budgetary deficits and debts than has the federal government (see Tables 12–8 and 12–9). They are not, however, free from problems. Historically, the Atlantic provinces have usually had a higher debt/GDP ratio than the other provinces, but during the late 1980s the ratios in Manitoba and Saskatchewan surpassed those in all provinces except Newfoundland. The trend since 1966 for most provinces and for all provinces combined has generally been upward, but the increase in total provincial debt as a percentage of aggregate GDP since 1975 has been much smaller than the corresponding increase in the federal debt. Some of the largest relative increases in the debt/GDP ratio have occurred in the West, particularly in Alberta and British Columbia, two provinces that were virtually debt-free in 1966.

In an attempt to give some perspective on Canada's deficits and growing debt, in 1989 the federal Department of Finance presented a comparison of the trends in Canada and other countries, particularly its major trading partners. Data on total government net debt relative to GDP are presented in Table 12–10. No country in the table experienced as rapid a growth of the debt/GDP ratio as Canada in the 1980s. Whereas the ratio increased by almost half in the United States, remained relatively constant in Japan, and declined significantly in the United Kingdom, it increased more than threefold in Canada.

Canada is not, of course, alone in struggling with a huge public debt and large federal deficits. The United States too has had difficulty. During the 1980s, the United States like Canada, was plagued by large deficits, but as a percentage of GDP and a percentage of federal expenditures, the US deficit was much lower than the Canadian. Moreover, concern about the continuous deficits led the US Congress, in 1985, to pass the Balanced Budget and Emergency Deficit Control Act, which specified annual deficit reductions until a balanced budget was achieved. Canadians are not comforted by the fact that their federal government, despite announced commitments to bring the deficit under control, has continued to incur large deficits and a mounting public debt.

ENDNOTES

1. The federal government also makes use of interest rate swaps, which were introduced in 1988 as a cost-effective substitute for Treasury bills. In this process, bonds are issued by the government and swapped into a floating rate form. Under the swap agreements, the government receives interest payments at a fixed rate from swap counterparties, generally Canadian financial institutions, and applies these payments to the interest cost on its outstanding fixed-rate bonds. In exchange, it makes floating-rate payments on equivalent principal amounts to the counterparties, based on three-month bankers' acceptance rates. Even a small spread between the latter rates and three-month Treasury bill rates produces a savings for the government. Such spreads occurred in 1988 and 1989. It was estimated, for example, that the $0.4 billion in swaps completed in 1988 and ranging in terms from two to fourteen years would produce future cost savings of about $11 million per year. A more detailed explanation of interest rate swaps is presented in Canada, Department of Finance, *The Fiscal Plan*, April 27, 1989 (Ottawa), p. 119; and Bank of Canada, *Annual Report, 1989* (Ottawa, 1990), p. 38.

2. A general discussion and analysis of various aspects of borrowing and the public debt are contained in most standard textbooks in public sector economies. See, for example, R.A. Musgrave, Peggy Musgrave, and R.M. Bird, *Public Finance In Theory and Practice*, Cdn. ed (Toronto: McGraw-Hill Ryerson, 1987) ch. 31; and Harvey S. Rosen, *Public Finance* (Homewood, Ill.: Richard D. Irwin, 1988), pp. 266–72. See also Robert Heilbronner and Peter Bernstein, *The Debt and the Deficit*, (New York: W.W. Norton, 1989); and Ontario Economic Council, *Deficits: How Big and How Bad* (Toronto: OEC 1983).

3. See Canada, Department of Finance, *The Federal Deficit in Perspective*, (Ottawa, April 1983).

4. See J.M. Buchanan, *Public Principles of Public Debt*, (Homewood, Ill. Richard D. Irwin, 1958).

5. These terms are presented as defined by the Department of Finance and Statistics Canada.

6. Canada, Department of Finance, *The Fiscal Plan*, April 27, 1989 (Ottawa, 1989), pp. 115–19.

7. Canada, Department of Finance, *The Fiscal Plan*, p. 115.

8. Canada, Department of Finance, *The Budget*, February 20, 1990 (Ottawa: 1990), p. 9.

APPENDIX A

SUGGESTIONS FOR FURTHER READING

Chapter 1

Brander, James A. *Government Policy toward Business.* Toronto: Butterworths, 1988. Ch. 3, 14.
Hyman, David N. *Public Finance: A Contemporary Application of Theory to Policy.* 3rd ed. Toronto: Dryden Press, 1990. Ch. 2–4.
Musgrave, Richard A., Peggy Musgrave, and Richard M. Bird, *Public Finance in Theory and Practice.* Cdn. ed. Toronto: McGraw-Hill Ryerson, 1987. Ch. 1, 3, 4, 5.
Rosen, Harvey S. *Public Finance.* 2nd ed. Homewood Ill. Richard D. Irwin, 1988. Ch. 5–8.
Ruggeri, G.C., ed. *The Canadian Economy, Problems and Policies.* 3rd ed. Toronto: Gage, 1986. Ch. 4, 11, 13.
Stiglitz, Joseph E. *Economics of the Public Sector.* 2nd ed. New York: W.W. Norton, 1988. Ch. 3–8.
Strick, John C. *The Economics of Government Regulation: Theory and Canadian Practice.* Toronto: Thompson Educational Publishing, 1990. Ch. 1, 2, 3, 5.

Chapter 2

Bird, Richard M. *The Growth of Government Spending in Canada.* Tax Paper no. 51. Toronto: Canadian Tax Foundation, 1970.
———*Federal Finance in Comparative Perspective,* Toronto: Canadian Tax Foundation, 1986.
Brander, James A. *Government Policy toward Business.* Toronto: Butterworths, 1988. Ch. 4, 13.
Borcherding, T.E., ed. *Budgets and Bureaucrats: The Sources of Government Growth.* Durham, NC: Duke University Press, 1977.
Breton, Albert. "The Growth of Competitive Governments." *Canadian Journal of Economics* XXII, no. 4 (November 1989).
Canadian Tax Foundation. *The National Finances, 1988–89.* Toronto: CTF, 1990.
———*Provincial and Municipal Finances, 1989.* Toronto: CTF 1990.
Perry, J. Harvey, *A Fiscal History of Canada — The Postwar Years.* Tax Paper no. 85. Toronto: Canadian Tax Foundation, 1989. Ch. 17, 18.
Savoie, Donald J. *The Politics of Public Spending in Canada.* Toronto: University of Toronto Press, 1990.
Steinberg, Norman, "A Policy Framework For Privatization." *Optimum* 20–3 (1989–90).

Chapter 3

Brown-John, C. Lloyd, et al. *Public Financial Management.* Scarborough, Ont.: Nelson Canada, 1988. Ch. 5, 8, 13.

Graham, K.A., ed. *How Ottawa Spends.* Ottawa: Carleton University Press, 1989. Ch. 1.

Hirsch, Z.W., and A.M. Rufolo. *Public Finance and Expenditure in a Federal System.* Toronto: Harcourt Brace Jovanovich, 1990. Ch. 15.

Perry, J. Harvey. *Taxation in Canada.* 5th ed. Tax Paper no. 89. Toronto: Canadian Tax Foundation, 1990. Ch. 19–21.

Strick, J.C. "Zero-Base Budgeting: Innovation or Rediscovery of Old Concepts?" *Canadian Tax Journal* 28, no. 1 (January/February 1980).

Simeon, James. "The Central Decision-Making Process in the Federal Government: Past, Present, and Future." *Optimum* 21–1 (1990–91).

Chapter 4

Bird, Richard M., and N.E. Slack. *Urban Public Finance in Canada.* Toronto: Butterworth, 1983. Ch. 6.

Bossons, J. "International Tax Competition: The Foreign Government Response in Canada." *National Tax Journal* XLII, no 3 (September 1988).

Canada, *Summary of 1971 Tax Reform Legislation.* Ottawa: Queen's Printer, 1971.

———Department of Finance. *The White Paper: Tax Reform 1987.* Ottawa, June 15, 1987.

Hirsch, Z.M., and A.M. Rufolo. *Public Finance and Expenditure in a Federal System.* Toronto: Harcourt Brace Jovanovich, 1990. Ch. 5, 11.

Hyman, David N. *Public Finance: A Contemporary Application of Theory to Policy.* 3rd ed. Toronto: Dryden Press, 1990. Ch. 11, 12.

Musgrave, Richard A. Peggy Musgrave, and Richard M. Bird. *Public Finance in Theory and Practice.* Cdn. ed. Toronto: McGraw-Hill Ryerson, 1987. Ch. 10–14.

Perry, J. Harvey. *Taxation in Canada.* Toronto: University of Toronto Press, 1961.

———*Taxation in Canada.* 5th ed. Tax Paper no. 89. Toronto: Canadian Tax Foundation, 1990. Ch. 1.

Sproule-Jones, M. and J. White. "The Scope and Application of User Charges in Municipal Governments." *Canadian Tax Journal* 37 (November/December 1989).

Stiglitz, Joseph E. *Economics of the Public Sector.* 2nd ed. New York: W.W. Norton, 1988. Ch. 16–20.

Whalley, John. "Recent Tax Reform in Canada: Policy Responses to Global and Domestic Pressures." In M.J. Boskin and C.E. McLure, eds., *World Tax Reform.* San Francisco: ICS Press, 1990. Ch. 5.

Chapter 5

Anderson, A. *Preparing Your Income Tax Returns 1990 Edition.* Don Mills, Ont.: CCA Canadian Ltd., 1990.

Canada, Department of Finance. *The White Paper: Tax Reform 1987.* Ottawa, June 18, 1987.
———*Tax Reform 1987: Income Tax Reform.* Ottawa, June 18, 1987.
———*Tax Reform 1987: Sales Tax Reform.* Ottawa, June 18, 1987.
———*Goods and Services Tax: Technical Paper.* Ottawa, August, 1989.
———*Goods and Services Tax: An Overview.* Ottawa, August 1989.
———*Goods and Services Tax Draft Legislation and Explanatory Notes.* Ottawa, October 1989.
Canadian Tax Foundation, "The Goods and Services Tax — An Overview." *Report of Proceedings of the Forty-First Tax Conference.* Toronto: CTF, 1990.
Due, John F. "The New Zealand Goods and Services (Value-Added) Tax — A Model For Other Countries." *Canadian Tax Journal* 36 (1988).
Dungan, P., J. Mintz, and T. Wilson. "Alternatives to the Goods and Services Tax." *Canadian Tax Journal* 38, (May/June 1990).
Grady, Patrick. "Real Effective Corporate Tax Rates in Canada and the United States after Tax Reform." *Canadian Tax Journal* 38 (May/June 1989).
Perry, J. Harvey. *Taxation In Canada.* 5th ed. Tax Paper no. 89. Toronto: Canadian Tax Foundation, 1990.
Perry, David B. "International Tax Comparisons." *Canadian Tax Journal* 38 (September/October 1989).
Rand, Clifford. *Understanding the Income Tax Act.* Toronto: Carswell, 1989.
Robinson, A.J. *The Retail Sales Tax in Canada.* Tax Paper no. 77. Toronto: Canadian Tax Foundation, 1986.
Whalley, John and Deborah Fretz. *The Economics of the Goods and Services Tax.* Tax Paper no. 88. Toronto: Canadian Tax Foundation, 1990.

CHAPTER 6

Canadian Tax Foundation. *Provincial and Municipal Finances, 1989.* Toronto: CTF, 1990.
Dean, James M. "A Note on Interprovincial Variations in the Base for the Retail Sales Tax." *Canadian Tax Journal* 37 (July/August 1989).
Goodman, Millie. *Tax Developments.* Tax Memo series, Toronto: Canadian Tax Foundation, periodic issues.
Kitchen, Harry M. *Local Government Finance in Canada.* Toronto: Canadian Tax Foundation, 1984.
Livernois, J.R. "The Taxing Game of Lotteries in Canada." *Canadian Public Policy* 12 (December 1986).
Perry, J. Harvey. *Taxation In Canada.* 5th ed. Tax Paper no. 89. Toronto: Canadian Tax Foundation, 1990. Ch. 12–18.
Vaillancourt, François, and Julie Gagnon. "Canadian Lotteries as Taxes: Revenues and Incidence." *Canadian Tax Journal* 36 (March/April 1988).

CHAPTER 7

Burns, R.M. *The Acceptable Mean: The Tax Rental Agreements, 1941–1962.* Toronto: Canadian Tax Foundation, 1980.

Canadian Tax Foundation. *The National Finances, 1989–90.* Toronto: CTF, 1990. Ch. 16.
Carter, George E. "Established Program Financing: A Critical Review of the Record." *Canadian Tax Journal* 36 (September/October 1988).
Economic Council of Canada. *Financing Confederation: Today and Tomorrow.* Ottawa ECC, 1982.
Moore, A. Milton, J. Harvey Perry, and Donald I. Beach. *The Financing of Canadian Federation: The First Hundred Years.* Tax Paper no. 43. Toronto: Canadian Tax Foundation, 1966.
Perry, J. Harvey. *A Fiscal History of Canada — The Postwar Years.* Tax Paper no. 85. Toronto: Canadian Tax Foundation, 1989. Ch. 15–17
Ruggeri, G. C., ed. *The Canadian Economy Problems and Policies.* 3rd ed. Toronto: Gage, 1987. Ch. 6, 7.

CHAPTER 8

Banting, Keith G. "Federalism, Social Reform and the Spending Power." *Canadian Public Policy* 14, supplement (September 1988).
Bird, Richard M. *Federal Finance in Comparative Perspective.* Toronto: Canadian Tax Foundation, 1986. Ch. 7, 8.
———"Federal-Provincial Fiscal Transfers in Canada: Retrospect and Prospect," *Canadian Tax Journal* 35 (January/February 1987).
———ed. *Fiscal Dimensions of Canadian Federalism.* Toronto: Canadian Tax Foundation, 1980.
Canada, Federal-Provincial Relations Office. *Federal-Provincial Programs and Activities: A Descriptive Inventory, 1988–89.* Ottawa, 1989.
Helliwell, John F., et al. *Oil and Gas in Canada: The Effects of Domestic Policies and World Events.* Tax Paper no. 83. Toronto: Canadian Tax Foundation, 1989. Ch. 3–5.
Hirsch, W.Z., and A.M. Rufolo, *Public Finance and Expenditure in a Federal System.* Toronto: Harcourt Brace Jovanovich, 1990. Ch. 13.
Hyman, David N. *Public Finance: A Contemporary Application of Theory to Policy.* 3rd ed. Toronto: Dryden Press, 1990. Ch. 19.
Simeon, Richard. "Meech Lake and Shifting Perceptions of Canadian Federalism. *Canadian Public Policy* 14, supplement (September 1988).

CHAPTER 9

Blinder, A.S., and R.M. Solow. "Analytical Foundations of Fiscal Policy." In A.S. Blinder et al., *The Economics of Public Finance.* Washington: The Brookings Institute, 1974.
Canada, Department of Finance. *The Federal Deficit in Perspective.* Ottawa, 1983.
———*The Fiscal Plan.* Annual. Ottawa.
Crow, John. "The Work of Canadian Monetary Policy." Eric J. Hanson Memorial Lecture, University of Alberta, January 18, 1988.
Keil, M.W., and J.S.V. Symons. "An Analysis of Canadian Unemployment." *Canadian Public Policy* 10 (March 1990).

Melvin, James R. "Regional Inequalities in Canada: Underlying Causes and Policy Implications." *Canadian Public Policy* 13 (September 1987).
Musgrave, Richard A., Peggy Musgrave and Richard M. Bird. *Public Finance in Theory and Practice.* Cdn. ed. Toronto: McGraw-Hill Ryerson, 1987. Ch. 25–28, 30.
Wilton, D.A. "An Evaluation of Wage and Price Controls in Canada." *Canadian Public Policy* 10 (June 1984).
Wilton, D.A., and D.M. Prescott. *Macroeconomics Theory and Policy in Canada.* 2nd ed. Don Mills, Ont.: Addison-Wesley, 1987.

CHAPTER 10

Canada, Department of Finance. *The Fiscal Plan: Controlling the Public Debt.* Ottawa, April 27, 1989.
———*Budget Speech.* Annual. Ottawa.
———*Quarterly Economic Review.* Quarterly. Ottawa.
Gillespie, W. Irwin. "Postwar Canadian Fiscal Policy Revisted." *Canadian Tax Journal* 27 (May/June 1979).
Johnson, David R. "An Evaluation of the Bank of Canada Zero Inflation Target." *Canadian Public Policy* 16 (September 1990).
Perry, J. Harvey, *A Fiscal History of Canada — The Postwar Years.* Tax Paper no. 85. Toronto: Canadian Tax Foundation, 1990.
Ruggeri, G.C., ed. *The Canadian Economy, Problems and Policies,* Toronto: Gage, 1987. Ch. 8, 14, 15, 20, 21.
Scarfe, Brian. "Economic Fluctuations and Stabilization Policy in Canada: The State of the Art." *Canadian Public Policy* 13 (March 1987).
Scarth, William. "Unemployment, Inflation and Deficits: A Review Essay." *Canadian Public Policy* 13 (June 1987).

CHAPTER 11

Amirkhalkhali, S., and B. Jamieson. "Provincial Public Finance in the Atlantic Region, 1965–1984.", *Canadian Public Policy* 14 (June 1988).
Canadian Tax Foundation. *Provincial and Municipal Finance.* Biennial. Toronto.
Perry, David, Terry Segal, and Karin Treff. "Provincial Budget Roundup, 1989 — Part I." *Canadian Tax Journal* 37 (March/April 1989).
Perry, David, Segal, Terry, and Treff, Karin, "Provincial Budget Roundup, 1989 — Part 2." *Canadian Tax Journal* 37 (May/June 1989).

CHAPTER 12

Canada, Department of Finance, *The Federal Deficit in Perspective.* Ottawa, 1983.
———*The Fiscal Plan: Controlling the Public Debt.* Ottawa, April 27, 1989.
———*Budget.* Annual. Ottawa.

——— *The Fiscal Plan.* Annual. Ottawa.

Hyman, David N. *Public Finance: A Contemporary Application of Theory to Policy.* 3rd ed. Toronto: Dryden Press, 1990. Ch. 13.

Musgrave, Richard A., Peggy Musgrave, and Richard M. Bird. *Public Finance in Theory and Practice,* Cdn. ed. Toronto: McGraw-Hill Ryerson 1987. Ch. 31.

Perry, David B. "The Increase in Debt Charges Incurred by Canadian Governments Since 1950." *Canadian Tax Journal* 36 (January/February 1988).

APPENDIX B

SOURCES OF GOVERNMENT FINANCIAL STATISTICS

Periodic Publications

Bank of Canada, *Bank of Canada Review*. Annual. Ottawa.
Canada, Department of Finance. *Budget*. Annual. Ottawa.
———*Quarterly Economic Review*. Quarterly. Ottawa.
———*Quarterly Economic Review: Annual Reference Tables*. Annual. Ottawa.
Canada, Statistics Canada. *Corporation Taxation Statistics*. Annual Cat. 61–208. Ottawa.
———*Federal Government Finance: Revenue and Expenditure, Assets and Liabilities*. Annual. Cat. 68–211. Ottawa.
———*Financial Flow and National Balance Sheet Accounts*. Annual. Cat. 13–214. Ottawa.
———*Local Government Finance: Revenue and Expenditure, Assets and Liabilities, Actual*. Annual. Cat. 68–204. Ottawa.
———*National Income and Expenditure Accounts*. Quarterly. Cat 13–001, Ottawa.
———*Provincial Government Enterprise Finance*, Income and Expenditure, Assets, Liabilities and Net Worth. Annual. Cat 61–204. Ottawa.
———*Provincial Government Finance: Revenue and Expenditure*. Annual. Cat. 68–207. Ottawa.
———*Provincial Government Finance: Assets, Liabilities, Source and Application of Funds*. Annual. Cat. 68–209. Ottawa.
Canada, Supply and Services, *Estimates for the Fiscal Year Ending March 31*. 3 vol. Annual. Cat. BT31. Ottawa.
———*Public Accounts of Canada*. 3 vol. Annual. Cat. P51. Ottawa.
Canadian Tax Foundation. *Federal Government Finances*. Annual. Toronto.
———*Provincial and Municipal Finances*. Biennial. Toronto.
Economic Council of Canada, *Annual Review*. Annual. Ottawa.

Statistics Canada's CANSIM Data

Statistics Canada makes available much of its data, current and historical, through a computerized database called CANSIM (Canadian Socio-economic Information Management System). Identification of various series is by matrix number. Publication of a number of Statistics Canada titles, including some of those listed in Appendix A, has been suspended; the data are now accessed through CANSIM.

Information about CANSIM services, including on-line access, data retrieval services, and microcomputer packages can be obtained from the Electronic Data Dissemination Division, Statistics Canada, Ottawa, Ont. K1A OT6.

The following are some of the statistics on government finance available through CANSIM.

Consolidated Government Finance: All Levels of Government Gross General Expenditure. Annual. Matrix 3160.

Consolidated Government Finance, All Levels of Government: Gross General Revenue. Annual. Matrix 3159.

Federal Government Debt. Annual. Matrix 3199.

Federal Government Finance, Gross General Expenditure. Annual. Matrix 2778.

Federal Government Finance Gross General Revenue. Annual. Matrix 2777.

Local Government Finance: Gross General Revenue and Expenditure. Annual. Matrix 2764.

Provincial Government Finance Gross General Revenue and Expenditure. Annual. Matrix 2751.

INDEX

TO THE OWNER OF THIS BOOK:

We are interested in your reaction to J.C. Strick's CANADIAN PUBLIC FINANCE, Fourth Edition. Through your feedback we may be able to improve this book in future editions.

1. What was your reason for using this book?
   - ☐ University course
   - ☐ As a supplementary text
   - ☐ Other (please specify) ______________________________

2. What was the best feature of this book? ______________________________

3. Can you suggest any improvements? ______________________________
   ____

4. Did you use this book for a course offered in an economics department, or in a business school? ______________________________

(fold)

Business
Reply Mail

No Postage Stamp
Necessary if Mailed
in Canada

Canada Post Postes Canada
43652

POSTAGE WILL BE PAID BY

Scott Duncan
Editorial Director

College Division
Holt, Rinehart and Winston of Canada, Limited
55 Horner Avenue
Toronto, Ontario
M8Z 9Z9

(tape shut)